MAKING DEMOCRACY WORK:

A Framework for Macroeconomic Policy in South Africa

MAKING DEMOCRACY WORK:

A Framework for Macroeconomic Policy in South Africa

A report to members of the Democratic Movement of South Africa

from the

MACROECONOMIC RESEARCH GROUP

1993

Centre for Development Studies
South Africa

CENTRE FOR DEVELOPMENT STUDIES
University of the Western Cape, South Africa

MAKING DEMOCRACY WORK:
A Framework for Macroeconomic
Policy in South Africa

ISBN: 1–86808–183–4

First published December 1993
© Centre for Development Studies 1993

Published by:
The Centre for Development Studies (CDS),
University of the Western Cape, Private Bag X17,
BELLVILLE 7535, South Africa.
Distributed in Europe by:
Nordiska Afrikainstitutet
(The Scandinavian Institute of African Studies),
PO Box 1703, a–751 47 UPPSALA, Sweden.
Also distributed by:
Almqvist & Wiksell International,
PO Box 4627, S–116 91 STOCKHOLM, Sweden.
Agent in the UK:
The Africa Book Centre,
38 King Street, LONDON WC2E 8JT.
Distributed elsewhere by:
Oxford University Press,
PO Box 1141, CAPE TOWN 8000, South Africa.

Designed and Set in 10 on 12 pt Palatino
by ray brink & amaal bruwer
Printed by Clyson Printers, Maitland, Cape Town

For those who strive—
to make democracy work

Contents

List of tables
(all tables appear at the end of each chapter)

List of figures
(all figures appear at the end of each chapter)

Foreword to the MERG Vision Statement and Macroeconomic Policy Framework Document

As the structures for a Transitional Executive Council and democratic government in South Africa become a reality, the new government has to respond to a whole range of inherited problems that have plunged the economy of the country into the gravest crisis in its history. Disturbing levels of unemployment, the mass of people living in absolute squalor and deprivation, the crisis in education and in the provision of other social services, aggravated more recently by a stagnation in the growth in output, are all the inevitable legacies of close to fifty years of the abhorrent apartheid system.

The removal of this regime and its replacement by a democratic government represents a necessary but by no means sufficient condition for alleviating the crisis. The new democratic government will have to create an economic system that has as its core objective, not only the rectifying of past mistakes, but also the continued and sustained provision of employment, shelter, education and training, food and health services, as well as other factors essential to an acceptable quality of life. The failure of a future government to achieve these objectives will inevitably threaten democracy itself.

In such a critical phase in the country's development, the MERG initiative to produce an economic framework to address these issues is to be enthusiastically welcomed. The Framework represents not only a crucial contribution to the democratic government's understanding of the various problems, but also offers a serious and well-reasoned economic strategy to resolve the multitude of problems. In this document a coherent and viable set of policies is presented, capable of ensuring sustainable growth and an improvement in the quality of life of the majority of the population and, at the same time, addressing the severe deprivation of those people in greatest need.

On behalf of the universities which participated in the MERG process, may I extend my congratulations to MERG, its co-ordinator, its staff and researchers and various committee members, for their unstinting efforts in producing this comprehensive framework in such a short period of time. The launching of the Framework could not be more timely.

S M E Bengu — Vice-Chancellor, University of Fort Hare

Preface

The Macroeconomic Policy Framework is a crystallisation of a large body of research work by South African economists from the democratic movement and others who have been and are associated with the MERG project. Their names are listed in the acknowledgements which follow. Particular mention needs to be made of the contributions from our 13 research teams based at the Universities of Fort Hare, Durban-Westville, the North, Western Cape and Witwatersrand. These teams produced a large number of working papers which are listed in the bibliography. As a result of the efforts of these research teams, some 45 graduates and others have developed their capacity to undertake research in a number of disciplines related to economics.

I also wish to acknowledge the excellent co-operation MERG has received from the senior officers of the five universities mentioned above. They have housed our research teams, and the Department of Economics of the University of the Witwatersrand, where MERG is located, has provided excellent facilities and a highly congenial and stimulating environment for our work.

MERG owes a considerable debt of gratitude to our donor friends. Without their support and co-operation this Framework would not have been completed. I particularly wish to mention the support we have received from the Australian International Development Assistance Bureau, the Canadian International Development Agency, the European Community, the Friedrich Ebert Stiftung, the International Development Research Centre of Canada, the Netherlands Embassy, the Overseas Development Administration of the United Kingdom, the Swedish Agency for Research and Economic Co-operation with Developing Countries, the Swedish International Development Authority and the United States Agency for International Development .

Last, but not least, I want to express the warmest thanks of MERG to the economists from abroad. In a spirit of solidarity with our anti-apartheid and liberation cause they have given of their time, their expertise, their rich experience and their labour to help develop the Framework over the past 11 months.

Vella Pillay — MERG Co-ordinator

Acknowledgements

Goolam Aboobaker (University of the Western Cape), Ismail Adams (University of the Western Cape), Alice Amsden (New School of Social Research, New York), Rafiq Bagus (University of the Western Cape), Trevor Bell (Rhodes University), Peter Brain (National Institute of Economic and Industrial Research, Australia), Raphaél (Ray) Brink (Centre for Development Studies), Fuad Cassim (University of the Witwatersrand), Cheryl Carolus (ANC), David Cooper (LAPC), Billy Cobbet (ANC), Brian Craig (University of the Western Cape), Chris Cramer (MERG), Renfrew Christie (University of the Western Cape), Merton Dagut (University of the Witwatersrand), Paul Daphne (University of Fort Hare), Rob Davies (University of the Western Cape), Helena Dolney, Diane Elson (Manchester University), Randi Erentzen (Centre for Development Studies), Alec Erwin (COSATU, NUMSA), Ahmed Essop (Centre for Education Policy Development), Lindsay Falkov (University of the Witwatersrand), Bernie Fanaroff (NUMSA), Ben Fine (SOAS, University of London), Peter Franks (University of the North), Stephen Gelb (University of Durban-Westville), Bill Gibson (University of Vermont and University of DurbanWestville), Alfie Green (MERG), Frene Ginwala (ANC), Derrick Hanekom (ANC), Laurence Harris (SOAS, University of London), Estherlene Hart (Education Policy Unit), Gerry Helleiner (University of Toronto), Alan Hirsch (University of Cape Town), Kevin Hosking (University of the Western Cape), Lesley Hudson (Education Policy Unit), Loretta Jacobus (MERG), Sadiq Jaffer (University of the Western Cape), Jaya Josie (SOAS, University of London), Paul Jourdan (ANC), Anthony Julies (University of the Western Cape), Brian Khan (University of Cape Town), Timothy Layman (University of the Western Cape), Bheki Langa (University of Durban-Westville), Dave Lewis (University of Cape Town), Lieb Loots (University of the Western Cape), John Loxley (University of Manitoba), Sandy Lowitt (University of the Witwatersrand), Mats Lundahl (Stockholm School of Economics, Sweden), Bushy Maape (University of the Western Cape), Lesley Maasdorp (University of the Witwatersrand), Manku Mahlalela (MERG), Stanley Manana (MERG), Mac Makalima (University of Fort Hare), Trevor Manuel (ANC), Shepherd Mayathula (University of Fort Hare), Tito Mboweni (ANC), Charles Meth (University of Natal), Job Mokgoro (University of the Western Cape), Terence Moll (Old Mutual), Zunaid Moola (University of the Western Cape), Mike Muller (Development Bank of Southern Africa), Jayandra Naidoo (COSATU), Jay Naidoo (COSATU), Benno Ndulu (African Economic Research Consortium, Kenya), Peter Nolan (Jesus College, Cambridge), Vishnu Padayachee (University of Durban-Westville), Vella Pillay (MERG), Max Price (Centre for Health Policy), Maria Ramos (SOAS, University of London), Peter Robbins (Twin Trading), André Roux (University of the Western Cape), Zav Rustomjee (SOAS, University of London), Cyrus Rustomjee (University of DurbanWestville), Neva Seidman-Makgetla (Wits University), John Sender (University of the Witwatersrand and SOAS, University of London), Bethuel Sethai (Development Bank of Southern Africa), Rushdy Siers (Centre for Development Studies), Max Sisulu (MERG), Ivan Stein (University of the Witwatersrand), Huda Syed (University of the Western Cape), Lance Taylor (New School of Social Research, New York), Paul Theron (University of Cape Town), Christopher Torr (UNISA), Servaas van der Berg (University of Stellenbosch), Phillip van Rynoveld (University of the Western Cape), Dirk van Serventer (Development Bank of Southern Africa), Heribert Weiland (Arnold Bergstaesser Institute, Freiberg University, Germany), Eric Wood (University of Cambridge), Gordon Young (Labour Research Service) and Harry Zarenda (University of the Witwatersrand).

CHAPTER 1
The transition to democracy

.

1.1 What can be achieved

The political transformation of South Africa will make it possible to achieve economic growth and to set realistic goals for improved living standards and economic security for all South Africans, especially the most disadvantaged. Without a new growth path to put these goals within reach, political transformation itself will be put in jeopardy.

Despite difficult conditions globally and domestically, this new economy can be achieved. Other countries have made transitions which are similar in scale, although their specific problems have differed from those of South Africa. What is required is effective state intervention, a vigorous private sector, the active involvement of women and men in all spheres of society, and a carefully-designed, implementable, and well-supported macroeconomic strategy for transition.

MERG has formulated a feasible and affordable programme to achieve major gains during the next decade. These gains correspond to the published objectives of the democratic movement.

The central goal of ANC economic policy is to create a strong, dynamic and balanced economy that will be directed towards:

- Eliminating the poverty and the extreme inequalities generated by the apartheid system;

- Democratising the economy and empowering the historically oppressed;

- Creating productive employment opportunities at a living wage for all South Africans;

- Initiating growth and development to improve the quality of life for all South Africans, but especially for the poor;

- Developing a prosperous and balanced regional economy in southern Africa based on the principles of equity and mutual benefit.

In 1992 the economic policy conference of COSATU set out a growth path which emphasised the following elements:

- An industrial policy designed to widen the income base through job creation and new economic activity, and deepen that base by developing human resources and technological capability that will increase productivity, wages and incomes and lower the cost of production;

- A strong, decisive and democratic state which intervenes strategically within the framework of the growth path in support of economic reconstruction;

- The building of workers' power;

- Mutually beneficial agreements and co-operation to secure growth and development in the southern African region.

The four pillars of the COSATU reconstruction programme are:

- Job creation;

- Human resource development to extend the skill base of the working population;

- A social wage, including the effective delivery of social services (housing, electricity, health, education and water), and security provisions (unemployment benefits, pensions);

- The empowerment of civil society, including improvement in the economic and political rights and circumstances of workers, women, rural people, etc.

MERG took these objectives of the democratic movement as its starting point. The aim of the MERG framework is to secure a rapid improvement in the quality of life of the poorest, most oppressed and disadvantaged people in South Africa. The policy recommendations stress projects to initiate job creation and training programmes for the unemployed; to improve the status of the poorest women in rural areas; to improve the availability and quality of education, health, housing and electrification; to raise the minimum level of wages of low-income earners; and to improve the skills of employed workers.

Some key data provided by the MERG macroeconomic model illustrate the way in which these objectives will be achieved over the next few years.

- The MERG growth objective is for GDP growth to rise steadily through the 1990s to reach almost 5 per cent per year in the early years of the 21st century. Such growth should create about 300 000 additional jobs a year. The total number of jobs created between 1992 and 2004 would then be 2.5 million, compared to the zero growth between 1982 and 1992. The growth projections are feasible; they involve an increase in GDP of only 1.1 per cent in 1994, rising to an average of 3.8 per cent between 1995 and the year 2000.

- In education, MERG proposes a minimum of R5 billion (in 1992 prices) in annual recurrent and teacher training expenditures and a lifting of annual education capital expenditures from the current R0.5 billion to R1 billion. This level of expenditure will provide the infrastructure (teachers, classrooms and incidentals) to offer universal access to a minimum of ten years of education.

- In adult basic education, MERG proposes a four-year programme for persons already in the work-force, at the rate of 50 000 new trainees per year; and a programme for unemployed persons who will be engaged on physical infra-structural projects, and who will receive training similar to that for employed workers, at the rate of 100 000 new programme entrants per year. The com-bined effect of the proposals for education and training will result in a radical change in the characteristics and productivity of the labour force.

- In health, MERG proposes a programme to provide 2000 clinics at a capital cost of R300 million (in 1992 prices) and a recurrent cost of R1.5 billion per year; and a basic health care and nutrition programme which will be imple-mented at a cost of R1 billion per year.

- In housing, MERG proposes that the government triples the number of hous-ing sites from the current 100 000 to 300 000 per year. The number of formal houses completed should rise, step by step, from the current levels of approxi-mately 38 000 per year to 350 000 per year by the early part of the next century.

- In rural development, MERG proposes that the state intervenes to redistribute land within a short period of time to the benefit of adult female members of landless households in the rural homelands. A policy capable of ensuring stable and affordable prices of basic foods is also recommended.

- MERG proposes the establishment of a realistic statutory minimum wage, set initially at about two-thirds of the Minimum Living Level (MLL). Such a policy will have positive macroeconomic and microeconomic consequences.

- The industrialisation and trade strategy proposed by MERG is based on increasing export revenues by extending existing natural resource advantages, but avoids the danger of getting stuck in a new rut and falling prey to fluctuating prices for primary commodities. Production of manufactured goods for both local and export markets is emphasised. Trade policy stresses institutional reform and carefully phased tariff reductions, together with newly-designed and more cost-effective export support programmes focused on the potentially most dynamic exporters of manufactures, and renegotiated trade preference arrangements. Industrial policy emphasises technological capacity-building to develop productive skills, and competition policy aimed at eliminating monopolistic inefficiencies. The competition policy advocated should improve the links between big and small firms. It would also involve setting up market-related programmes for smaller black-owned businesses. The macroeconomic policies critical for industrial growth are described; these include the maintenance of the real effective exchange rate at an appropriate level.

- The MERG proposals for other sectors of the economy support its overall economic programme. Detailed and practical proposals have been developed to restructure the banking and finance sector. Such proposals include extending facilities to the majority of the population by creating a cheap, widely available system of money transfer, and improving the availability and terms of finance for investment in targeted growth sectors. To complement these proposals, MERG recommends changes in the structure of company tax in order to widen its base and strengthen incentives for investment.

The MERG strategy contrasts sharply with the approach of the Normative Economic Model (NEM) of the government (CEAS, 1993). The NEM favours the advantaged sections of society and assumes that the trickle-down effects will distribute the benefits to the disadvantaged. The MERG approach, however, targets the disadvantaged directly.

The proposed strategies will immediately contribute to growth, but have also been designed to achieve sustained growth and macroeconomic balance. Government consumption expenditure will be contained at roughly its present level in real terms until the end of the 1990s. A moderate growth in tax revenue is to be achieved by making some changes in the composition of total tax revenue. Such changes have been designed to be sustainable. It will be shown that the MERG strategy is consistent with required macroeconomic balances. The realisation of MERG objectives will be impossible unless policy is characterised by prudent and risk-averse fiscal, monetary and balance of payments management. Sound macroeconomic policies should ensure sustainability and increased capacity to deliver social goods and will facilitate, rather than constrain, the development strategy of the democratic movement. Success will also depend upon the absence of any major deterioration in the ability to gain from trade in world markets.

1.2 What the old regime offers

The apartheid system involved the violent enforcement of white privilege through racial segregation, the denial of political and other rights, the compound labour system, bantustan policy, job discrimination, unequal property rights, unequal education and unequal access to houses, health and other social and economic services.

The recent removal of the most overt forms of legislated racial oppression will not be enough to redress the inequalities created by apartheid, and will not necessarily guarantee a more effectively functioning economy.

The Normative Economic Model offers little more than a prescription for maintaining the current features of South African society. These features include:

- Dramatic inequalities in income, wealth, employment opportunities and in the provision of social and economic infrastructure (education, housing, electrification, health, telecommunications, etc.). These inequalities are not associated simply with racial divisions, important as these are. Unacceptable levels of inequality are found in other areas as well. For example, there are stark inequalities between women and men, between people in rural and urban areas, and between the employed and the unemployed.

- Extreme fragmentation in the provision and administration of services, especially in the provision of infrastructure. As a consequence of apartheid, the public sector operates inefficiently through a multiplicity of administrative authorities.

- A central government which continues to hold the purse strings and continues to maintain the political upper hand, despite a degree of autonomy at lower administrative levels. In short, the apartheid state has managed to yield a combination of the worst forms of over-centralisation and fragmented decentralisation. The current institutional environment is incapable of handling the economic tasks that have been set and will be set.

- Gross inefficiency (segregated housing, for example, has required huge costs in terms of transport from townships to places of work); the existence of excess capacity in schooling and health (alongside a desperate need as a result of segregated facilities) and vicious circles between sectors (for example, between nutrition and health, between health and education, and between each of these and fertility, labour market access, etc.).

Attempts to address these problems have been characterised by unilateral action on the part of a discredited government, and by gross economic mismanagement. Macroeconomic mismanagement, which is quite separate from pervasive corruption in the public sector, has been a central feature of economic policy for decades, as chapter after chapter in this Framework will demonstrate. One example is the failure by the monetary authorities to ensure adequate control and monitoring of short-term debt in the 1980s. At a critical period, the Reserve Bank had no idea of the extent of foreign debt or of the nature of the maturity structure. The uncontrolled accumulation of short-term debt contributed to the severity of the debt crisis.

Macroeconomic mismanagement, rather than exogenous factors, is largely responsible for the present economic crisis: the unprecedented fiscal deficit is a result, in part, of irresponsible expenditures in 1992/3 (amounting to over R3 billion) to benefit the major grain farmers. Real gross domestic fixed investment declined by no less than 23.5 per cent from the third quarter of 1989 to the second quarter of 1993, and inventory stock holdings as a percentage of GDP have now fallen to their lowest recorded levels. The capacity of the economy to create or maintain employment has been deteriorating for many years and shows no signs of improving.

The Normative Economic Model, besides relying on faulty arithmetic and disputable macroeconomic assumptions, presents inconsistent forecasts of output and employment increases (and improvements in income distribution) which favour its policies. Its projected employment and equality improvements are far more optimistic than its own figures can support. The NEM report focuses narrowly on the alleged constraints which face the economy; the result of this focus is a policy which will lead to little or no improvement in the economic prospects for most South Africans. Its policy prescriptions differ little from the (failed) policy platforms favoured by conservative political parties in the 1980s in many industrialised countries.

The NEM suggests that the only way to improve growth is through the supply side. It advocates generating adequate saving via lower tax rates. It encourages privatisation, deregulation and competition in the hope of stimulating private sector investment, higher growth and employment. The argument is that any alternative strategy would be counter-productive since it would limit or crowd out private sector potential.

The major reason given for this 'crowding out' effect stems from the unsupported assumption that there is only limited capacity to support alternative activities. The NEM ignores the potential which exists (under present conditions of spare capacity) for a number of years of demand-led growth. It does so on the grounds of a balance of payments constraint.

The idea of a balance of payments constraint needs to be closely examined. This idea was given new impetus by foreign debt restrictions and capital flight since the mid-1980s. Two aspects of this constraint are inadequately investigated in the NEM. The first is that there is every likelihood of negotiating a favourable foreign debt repayment arrangement. The advent of a democratic government could reduce the reluctance of banks to lend to South Africa, and to roll over existing credits. The second relates to the strong possibility of new foreign capital inflows, although South Africa should not expect the same level of inflows that took place in the 1970s. Both these factors should ease the balance of payments constraint.

The NEM stance on other key macroeconomic issues is also open to criticism. In its view, inflation, by decreasing the real interest rate, affects the price of capital and labour. Its policy conclusion is to shift the relative price of capital and labour towards the former. Hence real interest rates should remain positive and high. A very low level of inflation is regarded as essential for economic growth. The problem with this argument is that investment has several effects. One is to increase capital intensity (which is not desirable, but is perhaps inevitable in some sectors); the second is to raise output through the effect on demand (which is desirable). Most importantly, investment increases total output capacity and therefore, lower investment means lower long-run growth. To maintain a high interest rate in the hope that it will bring about a desirable capital-labour ratio in the long run will certainly crush output in the short run. Employment will fall, not rise.

The NEM view that corporate saving is a constraint on business investment, which underpins the recommendation to lower corporate taxes, is also questionable. The fact is that private sector financial surpluses (in gross terms) are high and have been increasing since 1988. The solution is to improve the investment climate directly. There appears to be a wide consensus (from the World Bank to democratic movement economists) that the two major stimulants to private sector economic activity are higher levels of economic activity, and the 'crowding-in' effect of public sector investment spending, particularly on physical infrastructure.

In the post-World War II economic policy debate in South Africa, there was never any question about using public sector instruments to invest in the development of human resources, to improve the quality of rural life, and to pursue national growth objectives. However, in the areas of trade, industry, labour relations and foreign exchange policy, ideas which are very different from those which played a major part in policy design during earlier periods of extreme economic difficulty, are now being proposed by the NEM. The NEM has changed the rules of the game now that the majority has potential access to those political institutions and policy instruments to which the white minority has had privileged access.

The MERG proposals offer a different vision of the future. They have been designed to address the current imbalances, through more direct intervention, in a way which will benefit all sections of the South African population. A significant proportion of government consumption expenditure which the NEM sees as an obstacle to growth, represents investment in human resources. A careful reallocation of this expenditure will deliver the skills which will enable the overwhelming majority of the population to close the income gap between themselves and the privileged minority.

MERG is convinced that a sea change in economic policy is essential to generate growth in the next few years. Its strategy is coherent and affordable.

1.3 How it all fits together and is affordable

The equations of the MERG model and a set of the data sources needed to run it will be made available on request. The purpose of this section is to provide a brief overview of the way the recommendations have been tested for feasibility and consistency. The critical assumptions of the model are highlighted.

The projected results of adopting the full package of MERG policy recommendations are illustrated in Table 1.1, which indicates the growth performance that can be expected by the major components of demand and supply over the next decade. The growth path envisaged by MERG may be divided into two phases: the initial public-investment-led phase (between 1993 and 1999), and the sustained growth phase (between 1999 and 2004). The sustained growth phase is characterised by the private sector playing a role equal to its potential in the growth process.

Two features of Table 1.1 deserve special attention. Firstly, even with a high rate of growth of fixed investment, it is only at the end of the initial phase that fixed investment will return to the levels of the 1980s. Secondly, growth in employment is only marginally higher than the rate of growth required to absorb new entrants into the work-force. MERG projections present the minimum requirements needed to avoid a disastrous economic and political outcome. Alternative tests of the model which assume a continuation of current policy, show that the resulting macroeconomic outcome is unacceptable.

Figure 1.1 shows the year-by-year GDP and employment growth profile. It illustrates a steady acceleration in GDP growth towards the 5 per cent level. The absolute change in non-agricultural sector employment opportunities increases until the 300 000 mark is approached at the end of the ten year horizon. The high employment growth rate (compared to the GDP growth rate) in the second half of the 1990s is attributable to the MERG proposals for new labour market policies (see Chapter Five). The projected labour statistics for each of the population groups are given in Table A.1 of Appendix A.

The proposed GDP growth rate during the initial growth phase is achieved in the model because more than half of the growth in GDP (54 per cent) is accounted for by social and physical infrastructure expenditures. These expenditures cover:

- General government investment (excluding housing)
- Public and private investment in health and education

- Housing investment

- Utility investment (i.e. electricity, water and gas).

Tables A.2 and A.3 provide some details concerning the changes in expenditure required. Overall, the growth target requires that these social infrastructure expenditures increase from R14 billion (in 1985 prices) in 1992 to R26 billion by 2004. This means that the share of social infrastructure expenditures in GDP increases from 11 per cent in 1992 to 13 per cent in 2004. It also means that the share of general government (excluding public enterprises) capital expenditure rises from the current level of 1.3 per cent of GDP to 3 per cent by 2004.

The fiscal policy settings required in the model to achieve the MERG targets are discussed in Chapter Two. The critical assumptions are that:

- The real long-term interest rate is reduced to 2 per cent;

- Ordinary government revenue rises only moderately as a share of GDP;

- Non-interest government outlays grow at no more than 3.5 per cent per year on a trend basis.

In the model, the real rate of interest is brought down steadily to the target range which requires that the inflation rate should not exceed 8 per cent. It also requires that, over the entire period 1993 to 2004, the nominal aggregate wage outcome is held at an average of 10 per cent per year which, in turn, sets the real pre-tax wage increase at approximately 1 per cent per year on average over the whole period.

In the initial growth phase, the model allows only rather modest increases in real average earnings. In fact, real pre-tax average earnings are confined to 0.7 per cent per year in the period 1993 to 1999, before increasing to average 1.2 per cent per year in the second growth phase. Key components of the social wage (improvements in workers' education, health, etc.) will grow rapidly, and it will be possible during the second growth phase to improve real per capita transfer payments (on pensions, for example).

In the MERG model, the growth in capacity output generally mirrors the growth of GDP (see Appendix A, Figure A.1). This is because the rate of growth of capacity output in the South African economy is assumed to be a function of:

- The rate of growth of corporate (including parastatal) sector investment and associated capital stock;

- The rate of growth of general government capital stock;

- The desired capacity utilisation rates set by industrialists;

- The rate of growth of productivity, especially capital productivity.

The capacity utilization rates required in the model are presented in Table A.4. For these rates to be achieved, it is necessary for the corporate sector to mount merely the same investment effort relative to cash flow that it has achieved in the past. During the initial public-investment-led growth phase, the rate of growth of corporate sector capital stock relative to GDP growth is low, but it picks up during the sustained growth phase. This occurs because it is assumed that during the initial phase domestic investors will remain uncertain about long-term economic prospects. The model projects an acceleration of the rate of growth of corporate sector capital stock in the period 2000 to 2004, which is an important factor in accounting for the acceleration of GDP growth in the latter years of the projection.

An even higher rate of growth of corporate sector investment will be required if the MERG assumptions concerning the rate of improvement in capital productivity are not realised. This higher rate of growth of corporate sector investment would lead to a greater deterioration in the balance of trade than MERG is projecting, which would lead to a lower GDP growth profile.

The MERG projections for gains in capital productivity during the initial growth phase are critical for the success of the growth path envisaged and for the ability of the system to avoid capacity bottlenecks and balance of payments constraints. Figure 1.2 shows that MERG projections for changes in capital productivity are moderate — particularly for the initial growth phase up until the late 1990s. In addition, there are a number of sound economic arguments for anticipating these improvements in capital productivity over the levels recently achieved. These include movement in the structure of production away from the irrationalities of the sanctions-busting era, and improvements in the motivation and skills of the work-force as a result of implementing sound labour market policies.

In order for the MERG growth projections to be achieved, the underlying projections concerning international trade need to be fulfilled. It is not unreasonable to expect that, with appropriate policy interventions, as outlined in Chapter Seven, the outcomes required by the MERG model will in fact be achieved.

As can be seen from Table 1.2, international trade makes a negative contribution to GDP growth since import growth (on a sustained basis) is faster than export growth. However, the MERG strategy calls for only a slow decline in the trade surplus expressed as a percentage of GDP, especially during the initial phase (i.e. from about 3.5 per cent in the initial years to about 1.9 per cent in 1998 — see Figure A.2). To achieve a manageable outcome for the trade surplus as a percentage of GDP, it will be necessary for the export growth rate to be between 3 and 4 per cent per year in most years over the next decade.

The required growth rates of exports of goods and non-factor services are shown in Table A.5. There are reasonable grounds for expecting these export targets to be achieved. MERG research on the international prospects for the minerals and metal industries indicates that, on conservative assumptions, this sector is capable of achieving a rate of growth of gross export receipts that translates into a net additional contribution to foreign exchange receipts of 3 per cent per year during the remainder of the 1990s. After the turn of the century, prospects turn rather gloomy. It will therefore be necessary for other export sectors to grow by between 6 and 10 per cent per annum after the year 2000.

The model makes cautious assumptions concerning the level of activity in major trading partners; their GDP growth is assumed to average 2.5 per cent per year over the next decade, while the South African terms of trade are also assumed to improve only slowly (see Figure A.3). Moreover, it is not unreasonable to anticipate some growth in exports of services, since receipts from tourism, in particular, have been held back below their potential by the political consequences of apartheid.

Imports will have to be monitored and managed carefully if the MERG strategy is to succeed. The dangers are illustrated by the experience of 1988, when GDP rose by 4 per cent and imports by 20 per cent; if this were to occur again over the 1993 to 1996 period, the prospects for macroeconomic balance would be very bleak.

MERG research indicates that the elasticity of imports with respect to GDP growth lies between 2.0 and 2.5. The model coefficients for the elasticity of imports with respect to industry supply for the equipment industries lie between 1.8 and 2.2. For other industries the elasticities average 1.4. For the results in Table 1.1, the elasticity of imports with respect to GDP during the initial growth phase is set at 1.5.

This import elasticity assumption for the initial growth phase is realistic. Infrastructure expenditures drive the GDP growth rate in this phase, and these expenditures generate a low direct import content. Besides, the MERG analysis of capacity in the industries supporting the construction sector suggests that excess capacity is at present about 50 per cent. If general private consumption expenditure is allowed to grow too rapidly before 1999, then there is a danger that import growth could pose problems for the strategy as a whole.

Table 1.1 is also based on the assumption that during the sustained growth phase, the elasticity of imports with respect to GDP approaches 2. Given the anticipated build-up in corporate sector investment over this second phase, holding the outcome at this level will require the rapid implementation of the full range of industrial and trade policy measures recommended by MERG.

The model assumptions concerning international trade translate into a positive balance of trade surplus during the initial growth phase, as shown in Figure A.2. This allows a decline in gross foreign debt as a percentage of GDP to the end of the century (see Figure A.4). After that date, the rapid growth in corporate sector investment will push the trade balance into deficit and lead to increases in the gross foreign debt to GDP ratio.

The achievement of the projected trade balance profile illustrated in Figure A.2 is important for the success of the MERG strategy. If South Africa were to be forced to continue to maintain a trade balance surplus at current levels (for example, if the international capital market was unwilling to provide, on reasonable terms, the levels of finance required to maintain a smaller surplus), GDP growth over the decade would have to be considerably slower.

If, however, the initial growth phase is successful, the net debt to GDP ratio will be only about 8 per cent by the end of the century, compared to a level of 30 to 40 per cent for many other countries. This means that South Africa will have no difficulty in attracting the capital inflows required to finance the growth profile after the year 2000, especially if the corporate sector capital stock growth is concentrated in the tradeable sector. The policy proposals presented in Chapters Two and Eight will help to ensure that corporate sector investment is focused in these areas.

The rationale for the growth strategy proposed by MERG is reflected in Table 1.2. Here, the contribution of the major demand categories to GDP growth in each of the two phases is shown. (Tables A.5 and A.6 provide the equivalent projections for the more conventional categorisation of the demand and investment aggregates.)

During the initial phase, social and physical infrastructure expenditures are the source of about 54 per cent of GDP growth. Further contributions to growth are provided by the ending of rent and local government services boycotts (about 20 per cent), while other private sector sources of growth explain about one third of overall GDP growth. In contrast, during the sustained growth phase, private (general consumption and investment) expenditures become much more significant, contributing almost 60 per cent to the overall growth rate, while the contribution of infrastructure expenditures to growth is reduced to 20 per cent.

If the private sector is prepared to co-operate with the state in addressing some of the inefficiencies and inequalities in human resource development, the private sector will itself reap handsome rewards within a relatively short period of time.

1.4 The building blocks for our future

The eight chapters which follow provide a wealth of detailed analysis and a great many policy recommendations. It is hoped that they will constitute the first building blocks in constructing a solid future for the South African economy. The purpose of this section is to provide an overview of the document. The economic issues are complex and challenging; the policy solutions cannot be simplistic nor, unfortunately, can they be conveniently presented in the form of snappy phrases suitable for journalists.

The chapters that follow provide an analysis of past policy failure in each of the critical areas of economic management: fiscal, monetary and exchange rate policies; investment in social and physical infrastructure; the labour market; rural development and food policies; industrial, corporate and trade policies; the banking and financial system; and the management of the public sector. The purpose of providing these accounts of failure is to lay a sound basis for the formulation of new economic thinking and new policies that are capable of addressing the severe problems faced by all South Africans.

1.4.1 Fiscal policy

In Chapter Two, the starting point for the design of fiscal policy is the principle that the relative size of public sector investment needs to be increased. If the targeted rate of growth in non-interest government expenditure is to be sustained, the proposed increases in public expenditure must be directed into investment in infrastructure and human resource development, not into low productivity employment in the public sector, nor into consumption-oriented social welfare.

On the revenue side, a democratic government should commit itself to not increasing the share of personal income tax in GDP while restructuring the personal tax system within these totals. Part of the restructuring will involve the removal of features that discriminate against women and low-income taxpayers. A democratic government should not increase the nominal rate of company tax, although the structure of this tax will have to be changed, in order to widen its base and strengthen incentives for investment.

The next government should commit itself to a multiple-rate VAT system to ensure that VAT has a progressive effect, imposing lower average rates on the expenditure of the poor and higher average rates on the expenditure of the rich. There are detailed discussions of capital gains taxation, capital transfer taxation, customs and excise duties, wealth taxes and taxes on property. Advice on the design of these and other taxes will be delivered by an independent Fiscal Commission. Recommendations concerning the role and functions of such a commission are provided.

The share of government revenue in GDP is projected to rise moderately between 1993 and 2003. However, this moderate increase, given reasonable assumptions concerning the rate of growth of GDP, will make a huge difference to state revenue. Chapter Two pays attention to measures that will improve the efficiency and management of public spending. Recommendations include the introduction of a system of multi-year expenditure planning and rolling budgets, as well as institutionalised performance auditing.

1.4.2 *Macroeconomic balance, monetary policy and exchange rate policy*

Chapter Three is concerned with monetary and exchange rate policy. Because of low debt ratios, there is some scope for higher levels of foreign borrowing. Capital inflows in the years ahead should reverse the current situation of outflows of between 2 and 3 per cent of GDP. This chapter also justifies the MERG proposal that the Reserve Bank should attempt to maintain a fairly stable real effective exchange rate. The real rate should be compatible with both a decline in unemployment and increases in non-traditional exports.

It is not proposed that exchange controls on foreign investors be tightened in any way, nor that restrictions be placed on profit remittances. The focus of exchange controls will continue to be on domestic residents. Moves towards capital account liberalisation are not envisaged in the short-term, and a number of conditions are spelled out, which will have to be met before any such moves are contemplated.

It is argued that monetary policy since 1989 has been too narrowly focused on inflation, resulting in a policy stance which has been excessively tight in the face of severe recession and falling employment. While lower inflation is preferable to higher inflation, the costs of reducing a moderate level of inflation to a low level must be examined closely. The real interest-rate target recommended is positive, but low.

1.4.3 *Social and physical infrastructure*

Proposals for investment in social and physical infrastructure are set out in Chapter Four, which is divided into four sections covering housing, schooling, basic health services and electrification. The key issue in these areas is not simply the macroeconomic question of how much to spend and how to finance this spending; a series of microeconomic questions about the capacity to deliver must also be addressed. Cost and financing will not necessarily be binding constraints on infrastructural provision. If the current inequalities and inefficiencies in infrastructural provision are addressed in terms of financial constraints, an undue and simplistic emphasis will be placed on the role of user charges, access to credit, and funding.

In addition to proposals for a building programme rising to at least 350 000 units per year, the housing section contains proposals for a water supply programme and an access and feeder road construction programme. The needs of the rural population are emphasized in these programmes, which require the establishment of a unitary national housing authority with wide-ranging responsibilities and powers. It will be necessary to regulate both the housing and building supplies markets. Particular attention is paid to the need for a variety of forms of housing tenure, delivery, upgrading and products to reflect the full range of housing needs. Instead of focusing attention on the building of owner-occupied houses through indirect financial mechanisms, it makes more sense to use the finance available to the state to fund a housing programme directly, so that the poor can rent subsidised housing.

Chapter Four estimates the costs of the priority programme for ten years of universal education in terms of its annual salary component, the teacher training requirements, the school building programme and the necessary supplies of consumables to schools. Proposals are made for the training of teachers by means of distance-learning methods, and through an enhanced commitment to teacher-training by all institutions of higher learning.

Arguments for the regulation and monitoring of private-sector education are presented, and the role of user charges in the financing of education is placed in perspective, by querying the rationale for using the schooling system as a fiscal unit. The provision of extra funding to make up for missing schools, shortages of qualified teachers, and so forth, will succeed only if accompanied by programmes that provide for employment, housing, transport, and nutritional support. This is because economic and social deprivation undermine learning, and because subsequent job prospects are an important component in raising the incentive to learn, as well as in utilising what has been learned.

The main thrust of the proposed public-sector health programme is growth in the provision of primary and preventive care, capable of providing a basis for expanded public provision of higher levels of curative treatment at a later stage. Primary health services in rural areas are a priority, with emphasis on the low-cost preventative and curative measures that serve the majority of the population and which will achieve very high social rates of return. The costs of providing vaccinations, essential drugs, oral rehydration and supplements to address nutrient deficiencies are estimated. Estimates are provided for the costs of a nutrition-intervention programme covering two million infants and pre-school children. Expenditures to meet the capital and recurrent costs of constructing 2000 rural clinics are proposed.

The implementation of these proposals will require the creation of a single Department of Health. For this Department to fulfil its responsibility, it will require the resources necessary to develop and strengthen the health information system, so that valid data for policy evaluation is available.

To facilitate the major role that electrification and electricity will play in support of developmental goals, it is recommended that Eskom remains in public ownership. The institutional restructuring of electricity distribution in order to eliminate rent-seeking by local authorities, and to tap economies of scale in distribution is proposed, together with the development of an electrification programme for the southern African region.

Additional recommendations are made concerning the role of user charges and the requirements needed to meet the anticipated growth in the demand for electrical consumer durables. The scale of the programme is demonstrated by the fact that within a short period, 400 000 new connections per year will be completed.

1.4.4   Labour market policies

One of the main arguments of Chapter Five is that active labour market intervention will be required to achieve the objectives of the democratic movement. Some increase in the rate of growth of employment may be anticipated as a consequence of higher rates of output growth. However, the trickle-down effects on labour market conditions of a more favourable macroeconomic environment will not be sufficient to prevent an escalation of the social, political and human costs of labour under-utilisation and poverty wages.

The required interventions in the labour market are discussed under three headings: investment in human resources; proposals for a living wage; and proposals for labour-based infrastructural investment. Simulations indicate that the wage-earning capacity of the black labour force will rise rather rapidly, and that a shift in that proportion of the black labour force confined to the lowest education/skill categories can be achieved. The net result is that black workers' skills and wage profiles will move considerably closer to those of white workers over the period of the investment programme.

The primary aim of the national minimum wage proposed by MERG is not to achieve a rapid general rise in wages, but to improve the wages and productivity of the lowest-paid members of the work-force, say the bottom 10 per cent of earners. A conservative and cautious initial approach to setting the national minimum wage is proposed, which takes a fraction of the Minimum Living Level as its starting point. The consequences for the level of inflation, the growth of exports, and the level of employment are considered.

The infrastructural investment programme will combine the objectives of delivering physical structures to selected sectors, increasing the employment opportunities available to women and the poorest people, and ensuring that all expenditures result in genuine investments with high rates of return. A phased programme of Public Works will be implemented over the years 1994 to 2004, so that the overall share of general government capital expenditure (i.e. excluding public enterprises) rises from the current level of 1.3 per cent of GDP to 3 per cent by the end of this period. The number of new employment opportunities created will be significant.

1.4.5   Rural development and food policy

Chapter Six lists the economic arguments for granting the agricultural and agro-industrial sectors priority in the growth strategy. The main characteristics of the poor in South Africa are provided. The largest number of the poor, and the most acute forms of poverty, are to be found in rural areas amongst black females. Well over half the rural poor depend on agricultural wage employment for their survival, and the impact of rural development policy on the demand for agricultural wage labour is therefore a crucial issue.

The policy recommendations include a land-redistribution programme, which focuses on women living in landless households in the rural homelands; a programme of investment in rural social and physical infrastructure, also designed to benefit women; a range of incentives for the more dynamic capitalist farmers and agri-businesses, which will encourage them to employ a large amount of productive labour at a living wage and to make a significant contribution to export revenues. Institutional reforms, the most important of which are aimed at developing the organisational strength and political voice of landless rural females and rural wage labourers, are recommended.

It is not proposed that there should be a rapid convergence to a rigid link between world and domestic staple grain prices. The more efficient domestic producers, and all low-income consumers of staple grains, should be cushioned from world market-price fluctuations through state intervention, using variable tariffs on maize and wheat to ensure price stability. The most vulnerable households would be targeted through nutritional programmes focused on specified rural clinics and their female and infant clients. This chapter contains proposals to increase the purchasing power of the most food-insecure households by raising their incomes from employment. This will be achieved through the introduction of a national minimum wage, and through the increase in the number of rural employment opportunities available as a result of the recommended Public Works programme and the programme of support for investment on the farms of efficient employers.

1.4.6   Industrial, corporate and trade policy

Chapter Seven presents an overview of the causes and consequences of manufacturing decline, and of industrial policy since the 1930s. The skewed composition of industry and the continuing absence of a broader range of manufacturing capability is highlighted. The central features of South African industry are analysed. Mining and mineral processing are identified as the core of the South African industrial production structure. Some key strategy proposals are addressed. These relate to competition policy (including an assessment of market and ownership structures, as well as the role of small, medium and micro-enterprises); trade policy; and strategies aimed at strengthening the capacities required to revitalise manufacturing, particularly in the area of human resource development and technological capabilities.

Revenues earned from mineral exports have been considerably depressed as a result of transfer pricing and excessively high levels of commissions paid for handling these exports. MERG recommends the creation of a state mineral marketing auditors office. Further co-operation between the private-sector mining and minerals companies and the state is recommended in order to promote beneficiation more effectively, to maximise the possibility of developing efficient depletion and extraction programmes, and to deal with chronic excess capacity.

The arguments in this chapter do not support a programme of dismantling the conglomerates. However, a much more vigorous anti-trust policy is advocated, as is the strengthening of the resources and punitive powers of the existing competition authorities. Proposals are made to promote greater co-operation between firms, including the development of industrial districts. Proposals are also made to expand the role of small and medium enterprises in the South African economy.

The conclusion concerning technological capabilities is that the combination of private initiative together with an incoherent and weak state policy has resulted in highly deficient capability. Existing institutional arrangements for technology promotion are too weakly designed to complement and supplement the workings of the market. The MERG proposals include policies to strengthen incentives to firms to invest in the development of in-house technological capabilities; also proposals to restructure funding and other incentives that affect the operations of the system of statutory science councils.

The trade policy proposals are designed to lower costs to domestic industry by reforming protection without jeopardising development strategies, and to coordinate export support programmes with protection policy, while making them more cost-effective. Detailed policies for the reform of import protection and for changes in export support are recommended.

1.4.7   Banking and finance

Chapter Eight describes the crucial role that the financial system will play. It argues that the financial liberalisation policies of the past decade have not created a financial system which provides a strong base for economic transformation. These were based on the philosophy that unrestricted, competitive financial markets would facilitate an improved allocation of finance, which would underpin efficient economic growth and prompt improvements in banking and other financial intermediaries. By contrast, the policies that MERG proposes do not rely only on competition to promote improvements in the financial system. They involve direct initiatives in building institutions oriented to the needs of the new South African economy.

The initiatives proposed include a People's Bank based on the post-office network to give all South Africans access to a cheap and effective means of transferring money and receiving payments. MERG considers it is important to raise the personal savings ratio, and proposes that a savings-related housing finance institution be established, as well as an earnings-related, funded, contributory state pension scheme. In addition, it is proposed that the portfolio of the Post Office Savings Bank be widened and its saving schemes be strengthened.

To strengthen the financing of productive investment, this chapter proposes measures which increase the orientation of the capital market toward productive infrastructural ventures rather than financial speculation. These include changes in the tax structure, especially the creation of a capital gains tax and prescribed asset ratios for pension funds and life assurance companies. With the same objective, measures are proposed which would improve the relations between the banking system and corporations.

Chapter Eight proposes the strengthening of bank regulation and policies to safeguard the savings of depositors. It is also proposed that the Reserve Bank should be accountable, subordinate to the Ministry of Finance and subject to parliamentary scrutiny.

1.4.8   The state and the economy

Chapter Nine argues that the state should to provide leadership and co-ordination for widely-based economic development and must intervene directly in key areas to facilitate this development. To achieve these objectives, the state structures will need to be changed. The machinery of government, in addition to being democratic, with strong mechanisms of accountability and transparency, must serve the purposes of a developmental state. The perspective of MERG is that the developmental state should itself be efficient and should not absorb a high level of resources for its own functioning. Unlike the present South African state, it should be a slim state, disciplined by mechanisms which provide incentives for efficiency and for monitoring of performance. The structure of ministries and state agencies will have to be redesigned so plans for investment and economic development are carefully coordinated.

This chapter also proposes that the mechanisms and criteria for operating state-owned industries should be restructured to improve enterprise efficiency. A commission should be established to evaluate proposals for a change of ownership (from private to public ownership or vice versa) in selected enterprises. The investment programmes of state-owned enterprises and other state agencies should be set within overall totals which enable public sector investment to raise the rate of gross domestic investment. These programmes should be designed so that private and public sector investment are mutually reinforcing.

The final section of Chapter Nine discusses the role of the state in the southern African region. An active role for the state in the development of new regional structures is proposed.

Δ

Table 1.1   MERG macroeconomic outcomes
(annual average rate of change, per cent)

	1982-92	1993-99	1999-04
Demand Aggregates:			
Private consumption expenditure	1.6	2.5	5.4
Government consumption expenditure	3.1	2.4	3.3
Fixed investment	-4.2	9.6	8.7
Exports of goods and services	2.1	2.9	4.1
Imports of goods and services	0.6	5.3	8.0
Gross Domestic Product	0.7	3.3	4.5
Industry Supply Aggregates: *(Real value added by industry)*			
Agriculture	-0.7	1.5	3.9
Mining	-0.5	3.1	3.8
Manufacturing	-0.7	3.0	4.3
Utilities	3.0	3.4	4.4
Construction	-2.5	10.4	7.1
Trade	1.0	2.6	5.0
Transport and communication	0.9	2.7	4.6
Finance	2.1	3.0	4.0
Community services	3.0	3.5	4.7
Government	2.5	2.4	3.3
Non agricultural formal sector employment	0.0	3.8	3.8

Source: MERG simulations

Table 1.2   Sources of growth for the MERG strategy (average percentage contribution to GDP growth)

	1994-99	2000-4
1. Private general consumption expenditure (excluding private education, health and rent expenditures)	0.4	2.2
2. Social infrastructure expenditures (private and public health and education expenditures)	0.7	0.6
3. Physical infrastructure expenditures (general government investment, housing and utility industry investment)	1.1	0.4
4. Other (mainly private) fixed investment	0.7	1.7
5. Inventory investment	0.2	0.2
6. International trade	-0.8	-1.3
7. Other (e.g. rent, government administration/defence, etc.)	1.0	0.7
Total GDP	3.3	4.5

Source: MERG simulations

Figure 1.1:   Growth rate in non-agricultural employment and GDP growth rate, 1990-2004

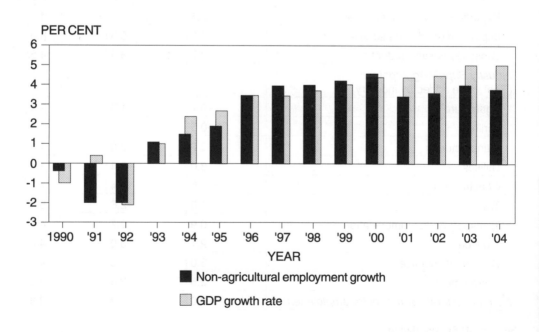

Source: MERG simulations

Figure 1.2   Capital productivity, 1978-2004

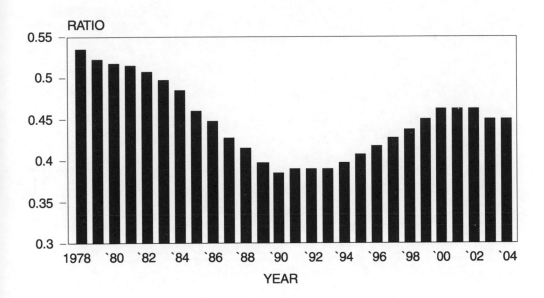

Source: MERG simulations

CHAPTER 2
Fiscal policy

2.1 The failures of recent fiscal policy

Fiscal policy, which encompasses taxation, public expenditure and government budget deficits, is the focal point of economic policy in South Africa. How the government spends its funds and finances its spending has a fundamental influence on the country.

Every aspect of fiscal policy is a focus of dispute, for economic and political interests are affected in different ways. Since different groups' perceptions of whether they will gain or lose in the transformation are shaped by tax and spending policies, fiscal policy is the focus of political conflict as well as economic dispute.

The contested nature of fiscal policy is illustrated by the problems the old regime has faced. The introduction of VAT with the rates and coverage first proposed was strongly opposed by a broad alliance led by COSATU. More generally, since the early 1980s, the state has experienced a fiscal crisis as the wealthy resisted further taxation and the majority resisted both taxation by an unrepresentative regime and expenditure cuts. The military and administrative costs of apartheid escalated, and the option of foreign borrowing was no longer available. This fiscal crisis, which was also due to financial mismanagement, was a factor in making the old regime unsustainable. Any similar crisis in the future will jeopardise the ability of the government to achieve a new economic, social, and political structure. The difficulty of constructing appropriate fiscal policies is compounded by the fact that taxes and subsidies as normally defined are only part of the picture. Resistance to taxation often includes other sources of public sector revenue, as has been shown by the boycotts of municipal rents and other charges.

The broad objectives underlying MERG recommendations are the overall goals of economic transformation, namely, the achievement of growth and redistribution. Fiscal policies are judged in terms of their effects on the living standards and opportunities of black people, their effects on the status and income of women, their impact on the rate of investment, their direction and efficiency, and their impact on trade. Equally important is the need to ensure a sustainable flow of finance for the proposed programmes of state expenditure, and to minimize the administrative difficulties and costs of tax collection. Total spending and total taxation also have to be judged in terms of the desirability of the budget surplus or deficit that results. The criteria and objectives of fiscal policy have previously been set out in the ANC 'Policy Guidelines for a Democratic South Africa'.

Past governments have not created a sound system of public finance. As well as being a reminder of the problems that any future government will face, the experiences of the past also provide a benchmark. The policies outlined here are designed to ensure that public finance is more soundly managed and contributes positively to growth and redistribution, instead of being a source of weakness. Some of the deficiencies of the past are outlined in the following paragraphs.

2.1.1 Budget management

Fiscal policy can be sound only if the civil service structures for budget management operate well. The state must have the ability to plan and forecast revenues and expenditure, and to monitor them accurately. The record on this score is bad, as is indicated by the persistent tendency to spend more than the budgeted figures and by the discrepancy between forecasted and actual levels of public sector deficits. In 1988/9, 1989/90, and 1990/1, there was a tendency to underestimate revenue and the actual deficit was much lower than anticipated. But in the 1991/2 fiscal year, because of errors in planning, the deficit moved in the opposite direction and by 1992/3, the deficit was greatly underestimated (by 50 per cent).

One reason for this poor record is the poor quality of information flows reaching the budget office, which result from the structures created by the apartheid state. For example, disbursements on health, education, and other services were channelled through the many complex state structures of apartheid (such as homeland authorities) under general budget headings or specific, but different, budget headings. Consequently, the central state and lower-level authorities lacked complete and consistent data on such expenditure. They have therefore been unable to budget properly. Other items, such as military and security spending, have been deliberately disguised, which has further distorted the information used in budget management. Problems caused by the strategy which prevented good information flows have been compounded by the failure to adopt modern budget planning methods.

A priority for a democratic government will be the construction of sound and transparent data collection methods to ensure that proper budget planning and management is possible. This is not merely a technical matter. It is a prerequisite for an accountable, democratic government which is open to scrutiny. The previous deficient information resulted from secrecy, non-accountability, and undemocratic methods. A full restructuring of the institutions involved in budget management and public finance, and their accountability, is proposed.

2.1.2 Low government investment

A second component of the fiscal crisis was the decline in public sector investment at the same time that private sector investment declined. The decline in state investment together with the rise in government borrowing has been a symptom of the fiscal crisis. The government has increasingly had to borrow to finance current rather than capital spending. (The fact that some items of current spending, such as education spending, can be regarded as an investment in human resources will be discussed later.)

While Gross Domestic Investment (by private and public entities) was over 30 per cent of GDP at the beginning of the 1980s, it had fallen to 16 per cent by 1992 and, after allowing for depreciation, Net Domestic Investment was negative in that year. Instead of giving the lead to much needed capital formation, cuts in public sector investment contributed to the decline. Gross public sector investment fell from over 14 per cent of GDP to 4.8 per cent over this period. Moreover, as the Normative Economic Model (NEM) shows, the present government is continuing to consider inappropriate policies, by putting more emphasis on reducing taxation and increasing public sector saving, than on increasing public sector infrastructural investments and ensuring the effective delivery of complementary activities. The MERG proposals seek to reverse this trend by expanding the role of public sector investment to give it an active role in development.

2.1.3 *Expenditure structure*

The fiscal crisis has also been a reflection of expenditure inequalities, which increase black people's resistance to taxation, while whites have resisted the prospect of financing reductions of those differentials. Per capita spending on whites is still approximately four times higher than on Africans. In addition to the racial inequalities in spending, apartheid has resulted in prioritising categories of spending which undermined state finances. The pattern of spending in the past decade or more did little to contribute to sustainable economic growth, and therefore to the tax base, while spending for large categories such as military spending contributed nothing to the process.

The defence budget was approximately 4.5 per cent of GDP from 1983 to 1991. This was about twice the proportion other upper-middle-income developing countries (UMIC) spent, and indicates a large drain of public resources from the total which could have been invested in growth, especially since the related item, the 'public order' budget, absorbed an increasing proportion of GDP over the period. Spending on education was a higher proportion of GDP than other UMIC countries, but the inequalities of apartheid education resulted in this amount being inadequate for generating a population with the skills needed for growth.

The ability of state spending to contribute to growth, and hence to underpin state finances, has also been reduced by the high proportion of resources consumed by a public wage bill swollen by overstaffing. This is a characteristic feature of the post-1948 state which historically, has provided protected employment for Afrikaner middle classes. Public authorities increased employment by six times as much as the private sector (36.1 per cent and 5.7 per cent respectively) between 1975 and 1992. Over the last three years, while employment in the private sector has fallen by 7 per cent, it has actually increased in the public sector. This suggests that no serious attention has been given to the rationalisation of public authorities in order to release more resources for spending on reducing the backlog in physical and social infrastructure and housing. Another indicator of the same structural problem is the ratio between the amount of state spending allocated to wages and salaries, and that allocated to other goods and services. South Africa devotes a high proportion of its budget to wages and salaries, and this trend has been upwards, as in other African countries, while Europe and the western hemisphere have reduced their wage allocation.

Opponents of significant change in South Africa have often suggested that in the future, the country will suffer the same problems as other African countries, typified by a large, wasteful state payroll. Previous governments have already followed this path. The task of a democratic government will be to restructure state employment in order to reduce the drain of resources, and concentrate resources on an efficient public service.

2.1.4   *Inefficient public expenditure*

The effect of public spending failures on the fiscal crisis, through their failure to generate the growth that would underpin public finance, is due to the inefficiency of each category of public spending, rather than the composition of the total. The total spent on public education, for example, is not low, but the system is designed and run so badly that the results are very poor. In the past, a large proportion of the public education budget has provided income and jobs for unnecessary office holders, while another part has concentrated funds on educating a privileged minority.

It is impossible to obtain a direct estimate of the extent of inefficiency in government spending, but an indirect indication can be gleaned from comparative data. Life expectancy, adult illiteracy, the infant mortality rate, and the maternal mortality rate can be taken as indicators of the efficiency of expenditure on education and health. The poor results stem not only from inefficiency in the services in an absolute sense, but from the whole structure of apartheid. The results measure the failure of public services to remedy the effects of apartheid on health, education and other conditions.

With the exception of Zimbabwe (which has in fact reduced education expenditure since 1990), and Botswana (a very special case), South Africa has spent a higher proportion of its budget on education than any other country. Moreover, as Table 2.1 shows, as a percentage of GDP, South Africa spent more than twice as much (6.4 per cent in 1990, 7.3 per cent in 1993) on education than any other upper-middle-income country (UMIC), and also much more than any high-income country. In spite of this, the South African adult illiteracy rate (about 35 per cent) was higher than that of any other UMIC, and in fact higher than most of the lower-income countries. Sri Lanka, for example, has a remarkable adult illiteracy rate of only 12 per cent, even though its GDP per capita is less than a fifth of that of South Africa, and its education expenditure, as a proportion of GDP, about a third of that of South Africa.

The health situation looks even worse. Of all the countries shown in the table, only Hungary and the UK spent a higher proportion of GDP on health than South Africa (with three per cent of GDP). The Pacific Rim countries and Sweden spent only a tenth of the proportion of GDP on health spent in South Africa. Yet, life expectancy in South Africa is lower than in virtually all the countries listed, and equal to the average of the low-income countries. Even Sri Lanka, where health expenditure was only 1.5 per cent of GDP (or $7.05 per capita compared with $88.50 per capita in South Africa), has a life expectancy higher than that of South Africa, and in fact as high as the best UMICs.

The South African infant mortality rate is by far the highest of the countries listed above and is approximately as high as the average for low-income countries. The maternal mortality rate is scandalous (at 550 per 100 000 live births) and is exceeded only by some much poorer countries where women still live under very oppressed conditions.

Another example of the inefficiency of social expenditure in South Africa, is provided in Table 2.2. Although the South African government spent as much on housing as the average UMIC (Table 2.3), and in fact spent relatively more on housing and community services combined, it has a poor housing outcome relative to most comparable countries, some of which are listed in Table 2.2 (with indicators of the housing conditions prevailing in their biggest cities). A far lower proportion of houses (73 per cent) consisted of permanent structures and a much lower proportion of houses (58 per cent) were connected to water. Over the last five years, housing conditions in and around the big cities in South Africa have worsened significantly.

Expenditure should be redirected in favour of government investment, especially in the form of infrastructural development. In a relatively short period of time, this spending should increase to at least 5 per cent of GDP. A commitment should be made to maintain the overall level of government consumption at roughly its present level in real terms. Government investment in social infrastructure and human development should be significantly increased as a proportion of GDP and optimal use should be made of borrowing for a few years. The deficit should be brought down gradually to a sustainable level, and total tax revenue should be increased moderately and to the extent necessary to ensure the required balance. An example of how this might be achieved is presented in the simulations below.

2.2 An initial quantification of the public expenditure strategy

The strategy for public expenditure needs to be planned in some detail, and quantified estimates made for each expenditure item, with adequate attention given to the standards, coverage, timing and sequencing of policies. For some key categories, this exercise has already been carried out in Chapter One, and the basis of the calculations for social and economic infrastructure expenditure is discussed in Chapter Four. In the present section, estimates of total spending by central government within an illustrative framework of alternative scenarios are presented. The starting point for the calculations is the principle that in order to overcome a major failure of policy in the recent past, the relative size of public sector investment needs to be increased.

It seems reasonable to assume a 3.75 per cent real, annual growth in non-interest government expenditure over ten years, for the purpose of this exercise. This rate of growth is not offered in any prescriptive or normative sense, but is used only as an initial estimate for exploratory purposes. It so happens, however, that it represents more or less the maximum growth in expenditure that appears feasible from a macroeconomic perspective, and it would enable a democratic government to make a substantial improvement to living conditions.

A crucial assumption in this exploratory exercise is that a democratic government succeeds in creating consensus around a coherent and comprehensive national development strategy, and that the content and implementation of this strategy succeeds in raising the growth capacity of the economy to about 5 per cent over a period of four years. If this does not happen, the expenditure strategy will have to be reviewed and revised.

If the 3.75 per cent growth in central government expenditure is fully utilised for the removal of backlogs and the provision of additional investment in social infrastructure and human development in basic education and training, primary health care, housing, electrification, urban infrastructure and labour intensive public works programmes, as well as economic restructuring, a dramatic change should be possible. The current level of real total expenditure is around R105 billion. The cumulative additional amount that can be spent over the ten year period adds up to R248 billion (in real terms). This is summarised in Table 2.4.

This first spending scenario increases government investment (defined here as including social investment), from 5.9 per cent of total government expenditure, to 31.4 per cent in 2002 (not shown in the table). As a proportion of GDP, it increases from 0.02 per cent to 11.3 per cent of GDP by 2003. Such an increase would have a dramatic effect over ten years on South African society. It may, however, be too ambitious.

It could be argued that it is not realistic to keep other non-interest spending constant, as the population is growing, and these public services ought to grow with the population. This is also provided for in Table 2.4. If it is assumed that the population grows at 2.75 per cent per year and that the sum of the other expenditures also grows at 2.75 per cent per year, R175 billion of the additional R248 billion will now be used to maintain the per capita spending (in real terms) of non-interest functions. This is shown in the table. This will still leave an estimated R73 billion for the removal of backlogs, the provision of social infrastructure, and human development. This may be enough for this purpose, as the maintenance of per capita spending in the other areas of expenditure will take care of most of the additional recurrent costs associated with the expanded social infrastructure. Moreover, if other financing instruments are used in addition to public finance, including the cross-subsidisation of urban infrastructure, and foreign financing for economic restructuring aimed at increased export performance, the R73 billion could be sufficient.

The second spending scenario, as can be seen in Table 2.4, increases social investment expenditure from 5.9 per cent of total expenditure in 1993 to 13.7 per cent in 2003. As a proportion of GDP it increases from 0.02 per cent to 2.85 per cent in 2003. While this amounts to a dramatic improvement on the current situation, there is the possibility that it will not be enough to bring about the required economic transformation within the ten year period. It may also be too conservative concerning the possibility of more effective and efficient utilisation of public resources.

It is possible that an attempt to rationalise public spending will be at least moderately successful, that existing spending can be done more effectively and efficiently, and that public services can be maintained without the need for related expenditure to grow at the population growth rate. This scenario is represented by the assumption that 55 per cent of the additional spending of R248 billion can be used for the removal of physical backlogs, the provision of social infrastructure, urban development, and economic capacity (together referred to as new investment expenditure). This amounts to R136 billion. The remainder of the R248 billion, i.e. R112 billion, can then be used for the financing of any increases in recurrent spending, whether as a result of the growth of existing services, or because of the new services prompted by the extension of the physical infrastructure. This scenario is probably more realistic than either of the first two.

This third spending scenario, which is summarised in Table 2.4, results in an increase in social investment from 5.9 per cent of total expenditure in 1993 to 20 per cent in 2003. As a proportion of GDP it increases from 0.02 per cent in 1993 to 5.13 per cent in 2003. These 2003 percentages are comparable with those of successful East Asian countries. This offers a reasonable figure for the kind of increase in social investment, and the accompanying change in the composition of public expenditure that will be required, if South Africa is to be turned into an economic success story based on human development and the expansion of productive capacity.

Table 2.4 also shows that, given the assumptions of GDP growth and growth in real interest payments on public debt, total government expenditure will initially grow as a proportion of GDP, from 38 per cent in 1993 to 40 per cent in 1996, after which it will begin to decline to 36 per cent of GDP in 2003. These changes are not offered in any prescriptive or normative sense, but simply reflect the outcome of the set of underlying illustrative assumptions made in this exercise. The initial increase in the share of the public sector in GDP results from the assumption that expenditure will increase faster than GDP. Later on, when GDP grows faster than public expenditure, the trend will be reversed. These assumptions can be changed, of course. For example, if it is assumed that public expenditure will grow as fast as GDP after 1998, then its share of GDP will remain constant at about 40 per cent of GDP. This will have implications for public debt and interest payments.

In this exercise, public debt will initially rise because of the assumption that public expenditure increases faster than tax revenue. The latter is the result of both a lower growth rate in GDP and a lower growth in the share of government revenue in GDP. Consequently, the share of interest payments on public debt will increase from 17.5 per cent of total government expenditure in 1993 to a peak of 21 per cent of total government spending in 1999. Thereafter, because of the higher GDP growth rate and the slower growth rate in government spending, interest payments will begin to decline, to reach 18 per cent of total spending in 2003. As a proportion of GDP (not shown in the table), interest payments will increase from 6.7 per cent of GDP in 1993 to 8.4 per cent in 2000. They will then begin to decline and return to their current share of 6.7 per cent of GDP by 2003.

This exercise suggests that such an expenditure plan is sustainable and fiscally responsible. The critical assumption is the GDP growth rate. The change in the composition and level of public expenditure must increase the human and social capacity for production, and offer improved prospects for profitable private sector investments. A carefully constructed national development strategy can achieve this. It will not happen, however, if increased public expenditure simply goes to higher, consumption-oriented social welfare and low productivity employment in the public sector.

2.3 Taxation for equity and efficiency

2.3.1 Redistribution and revenue raising

Weaknesses in the existing tax system have contributed to the fiscal crisis of the old regime. What changes in the tax system can be made to strengthen its role? In this section, some key issues of tax policy to be faced by a democratic government are outlined. Since their task will be to transform the economy substantially, tax policy, too, will have to be implemented with a view to transformation.

However, tax authorities are not omnipotent and there are limits to what can be achieved through taxation alone. In some circumstances tax changes can affect inequality (for example, they increased inequality in Britain during the 1980s), but it is almost impossible to attain reduction of poverty and human development objectives through the tax system alone. In effecting redistribution by bringing about greater equity through poverty reduction and human development, the expenditure side of the budget will have a predominant role, and taxation a supporting role.

Although one objective of taxation is to reduce inequality, a tax system also needs to maximise revenue over the long run, so that the redistributive programme through public expenditure (which is clearly a long-term goal) can be sustained. The role of the tax system, therefore, is to raise revenue effectively in order to finance government spending which is designed to meet its economic and social objectives in a mixed economy. The tax system also promotes these objectives through its differential impact on the private sector. A progressive tax system has an effect on inequality, and taxes on particular goods and services affect both the demand for them and their production. But these tax effects have to be seen in context. The most direct effect in reducing inequality is achieved through government expenditure programmes, especially those aimed at improving the position of the poorest; and improving the effect of taxes on demand and supply in particular sectors is part of a complex set of influences, including pricing arrangements.

2.3.2 Tax systems

A balanced system of complementary taxes

One of the implications of the need to have a tax system that is both efficient and perceived to be fair, is that a country must have a range of taxes. A balanced system of a wide range of complementary taxes is more likely to be both efficient (in terms of the cost-effective optimisation of revenue) and perceived as fair.

A range of complementary taxes will be more likely to place all citizens in the tax net in a progressive manner. For example, a self-employed person may be in position to avoid income tax, but less able to avoid consumption taxes or excise duties. In this case, having very low consumption taxes will result in the self-employed person paying very little tax overall. A balanced tax system is one that does not place excessive weight on one or a few taxes. It must be balanced in terms of both the range of complementary taxes and the relative weights of the taxes in the system.

An additional reason for ensuring that the tax system consists of a broad structure of complementary taxes, is that a broadly based system gives tax revenues greater flexibility. To avoid fiscal crises, tax revenues and their growth must have an element of stability, which is best assured by basing tax revenues on a broad range of sources so that a decline in one source may be balanced by strength in another. At the opposite extreme, a narrowly based tax system, such as the taxes of many poor countries which are dominated by export and import taxes, causes revenues to be fragile, as a cyclical or general decline in such sources (foreign trade) has a disproportionate impact on total government revenue.

Consistency and predictability

Tax policy is one of the factors that makes the economic environment more or less favourable to growth. It is important that tax rules should be consistent and predictable so that investors (and ordinary people) can make long-term investment plans. Predictability and consistency are necessary for a tax system that will not subject people to changes that appear arbitrary. It is proposed that a Fiscal Commission be established to advise a new democratic government on tax reform proposals. The government should appraise this advice and quickly commit itself to a tax reform strategy in order to shorten and minimise the period of uncertainty about the direction of tax reform. Some proposals for reforms in the major taxes are made in the following paragraphs.

The existing structure

The starting point for tax reform is the existing tax system. Its principal features are that (compared to other upper-middle-income countries) the percentage of central government revenue collected by taxes on income, and the percentage collected from taxes on goods and services, are not unusual, but taxes on income are heavily concentrated on personal income, while corporate taxation makes little contribution to government revenues. The taxes on individual income are badly structured. The absence of a tax on capital gains and the weak taxes on capital transfers (gifts and inheritances) mean that the rich can escape taxation on a large part of their income. Existing tax rules mean that income taxes are collected from a narrow base which is bad for state revenue flows, and enables companies and the rich to have a light tax burden.

The main features of the existing tax structure are illustrated in Tables 2.5 and 2.6. The significant role, in South Africa, of revenue from individual income tax is highlighted in Table 2.6. More than two-thirds of income from taxes comes from individual income tax. The table shows that this high proportion developed during the 1980s as the loss of mining income tax and the decline in company tax was made up by a rapid rise in the individual income tax burden.

Table 2.7 shows that the high reliance on individual income tax is a fairly recent phenomenon. During the 1970s direct taxes (mostly individual income tax) rose, in per capita terms, at about the same rate as individual income. This changed dramatically during the 1980s as gold revenues started falling (which reduced taxes from gold-mining), and inflation began the process of bracket creep (which pushed individuals into higher income tax brackets, even though their real income had not risen proportionately). This growing trend is continuing during the 1990s, albeit at a somewhat slower rate.

The burden of rising personal income tax has also not been equitably distributed. Table 2.8 simulates the effect of a 10 per cent increase in nominal income (for example, due to inflation) on a few income levels, with the tax brackets being kept constant. Not only does this increase in nominal income, with a constant real income, result in an increase in the average tax rate applicable to each level of income, but the tax elasticity (the multiple by which tax increases for a given increase in income) is about four times higher for the low income than for the high income (4.6 compared with 1.2). The tax burden rises much faster for the lower income categories than for the higher income categories. Given constant real incomes and rising nominal incomes as a result of inflation, the increasing income tax share has been regressive in its impact on disposable incomes. This is the inevitable outcome of an individual income tax structure that is progressive, consists of many brackets, and is not indexed.

What makes this regressive nature of the inflationary increase in individual income tax even more disconcerting, is the fact that the lower income groups consist mostly of black workers who have recently experienced real wage increases, partly as a result of trade union struggles, and who have for most of their lives suffered under the oppression of apartheid. Now, soon after they have experienced real wage increases for the first time in decades, they find their disposable incomes disproportionately eroded, since inflation pushes low income earners into higher tax brackets. Moreover, higher income earners, who are mostly professionals, self-employed business people and executives in the corporate sector, probably succeed in maintaining their disposable incomes because they are in a position to pass on the incidence of the tax. International studies have found this to be the case in other countries.

Further confirmation of this possibility, and a very rough estimate of the avoidance of personal income tax in South Africa, is provided by Table 2.9. The first three deciles of households do not receive incomes high enough for the main breadwinner to cross the tax threshold. The next three deciles make up the 'lost' share of taxable income, i.e. their share of taxable income is so much higher than their share of gross income, that they almost take the cumulative taxable income share of the first five deciles up to their cumulative share of gross income. The rest of the household deciles have almost identical shares for gross and taxable income. The total estimated household income of R177 595 million, which is not too far from the national accounts figure of R181 322 million, is about R50 000 million more than the total for taxable income. This could either reflect the extent of allowances or deductions, or tax avoidance, or both (under the assumption that tax evasion will not show up in a household survey — the source of the gross income estimates). As most allowances are supposed to decline in proportional terms (e.g. through the existence of nominal ceilings), the share of taxable income should rise with the richer deciles. The fact that it doesn't, can be taken as some indication of the existence of avoidance behaviour, which rises as income increases.

This is yet another unfortunate legacy that will be faced by a democratic government. Reform of the individual income tax system will be imperative at a time when the new government will be most under pressure to find all the resources it can. The difficult nature of this problem is illustrated by Table 2.10. The South African government has increased personal income tax to a GDP share (8.7 per cent in 1987), far outstripping all comparable middle-income developing countries. Zimbabwe is the only country in this table with a similar share, although South Africa has now overtaken Zimbabwe with a share of 11.5 per cent in 1992.

Corporate income tax was maintained at a level of about 4.3 per cent of GDP during most of the 1980s (Table 2.6). During the latter part of the 1980s, it increased a little as a result of the reduction by the government of tax expenditures. In the 1990s, its share of GDP first rose and thereafter declined to 3.6 per cent in 1992, as a result of the combined effect of a rate reduction, and (perhaps more importantly) serious economic decline leading to a shrinkage of the corporate tax base. Since the mid–1980s the government has attempted to solve its fiscal problems by raising the proportion of GDP paid as income tax by individuals, while reducing the relative amount paid as taxes on company profits. The policy has been continued up to the present, with a reduction of the rate of company tax in 1993.

2.3.3 Policies for personal income taxation

Personal or individual income tax is the mainstay of the South African tax system. As a result of inflation (bracket creep), its share of total revenue has more than doubled since 1970, when it was 18 per cent. It is now about 11 per cent of GDP, compared with less than 2 per cent in middle-income countries and about 11 per cent in industrial countries. This is too high. In view of the principle that tax revenues should be drawn from a balanced, broad system of varied tax instruments, it is undesirable for over 40 per cent of revenues to come from one source, especially income tax. Another is that the increase in income tax revenue has had an unfairly regressive burden on different groups of people.

Professionals and business executives, the really high income earners, have either been adopting tax avoidance strategies (made possible by the unequal struggle between an understaffed and overextended Department of Inland Revenue and a highly skilled tax consultant industry — not to mention the complexity of the tax system), or have been able to maintain their real after-tax earnings by passing the effective tax increases on to their customers. The consequence of this is that the major increase in the tax burden has fallen on two groups. The first group is the middle to upper-middle class salary earners, manifested by a bulge or peak of average effective rate increases around the middle. This is the same group most likely to feel a dramatic change in their fortunes over the next few years as they lose their privileged subsidies, especially in education. The second group consists of those skilled and semi-skilled workers who experienced real wage increases during the 1970s and early 1980s, and have started to buy houses and join provident funds or take out insurance policies. They now find, as a result of bracket creep, that they have to pay significantly higher income tax at the same time as they are experiencing a decline in their real wages. Any further increase in income tax rates will be felt severely by these two groups. In addition to the unfairness of those features, they are undesirable because they may reduce voluntary compliance among these groups.

A democratic government should commit itself not to increase the share of personal income tax in GDP any further, while it should restructure the system within those totals. The number of tax brackets should be reduced and the bulge of steep increases in average tax rates in the middle ranges flattened. There is a strong case for having only three tax bands, with the basic rate covering a larger majority of wage and salary earners, as long as methods can be found to reduce the marginal rate incurred by low income earners who are entering the basic tax band. The most important restructuring, however, is to reduce the allowances and tax breaks which allow the rich to avoid income taxes. One of the most important steps in that direction is the creation of a tax on capital gains. In addition, the personal income tax system has traditionally had a structure which discriminated against women. Although recent changes have begun to alter this, it is proposed that a thorough reform should be undertaken to overcome all discriminatory features.

If restructuring occurs, and if it is assumed that total revenue from personal income tax is initially kept at more-or-less its current share of GDP, i.e. 11.5 per cent, and then gradually reduced to 9 per cent of GDP as the economy moves onto a sustained growth path, then personal income tax should become a smaller proportion of total government revenue. Assuming an annual growth rate for GDP of close to 5 per cent, the share of personal income tax in total government revenue would decrease from from 48 per cent in 1993 to 28 per cent in 2003. Although this would still be high by international standards, it would be a significant movement of the tax structure in a more balanced direction. Even so, because of the assumed GDP growth in this simulation exercise, it still raises additional cumulative revenue of about R28 billion over ten years.

2.3.4   Capital gains tax

Income taxation is, at present, seriously incomplete because South Africa has no capital gains tax. There is no distinction, in principle, between capital gains and other forms of income, so the absence of such a tax enables taxpayers, especially the wealthy, to evade taxes. Not only do they escape tax on the profit they make by buying and selling shares, bonds, and other assets, they also avoid tax on their normal income by employing an army of tax advisers to transform normal income into the non-taxable form of capital gains. All OECD countries have capital gains tax in one form or another; it is a tax which is necessary to improve the fairness of the tax system. The absence of a capital gains tax distorts decision-making and reduces the income tax base.

A democratic government must commit itself to introducing capital gains tax. The rate of capital gains tax should parallel the rates of the general income tax, but some items such as capital gains on a person's home should be exempt. The government should announce such a tax without delay and legislation should be drafted as soon as possible.

In the MERG simulation, it is assumed that a capital gains tax is introduced as a separate tax and phased in over ten years. When it is fully implemented in 2003, it is assumed that it will generate revenue of R5 billion, or 1 per cent of GDP. This will constitute about 3 per cent of total revenue in 2003. The tax should be fully implemented in a much shorter time span.

2.3.5   Company income tax (profits tax)

Company taxation is a potentially powerful instrument which can be used to influence rates of saving and investment. In particular, allowances against tax are able to provide incentives for investment in physical capital or in training; differential taxes on distributed and undistributed profits influence the rate of corporate and personal saving.

There is no conclusive evidence that company tax (including mining) as a proportion of GDP (about 3.5 per cent) is too high, although it is clearly not low compared with other middle-income countries (about 3 per cent), or industrial countries (about 2 per cent). This tax rate can be very misleading, since it is the effective rate (after tax incentives, etc. have been deducted) that is important, together with the overseas tax environment. The nominal rate of 40 per cent is higher than in most countries which are in competition with South Africa. Some indication of how the effective tax rate in South Africa may differ from the nominal rate, is obtained from Table 2.11. It gives a straightforward average effective tax rate of 28 per cent in 1992, based on national accounts data. The data suggests that the effective rate has risen since the mid – 1980s. During this period, a number of incentives and allowances were removed or reduced, including initial and investment allowances, employees training allowances, LIFO accounting, accelerated depreciation, export marketing allowances, concessionary treatment of consumable stores and work in progress, hotel allowances, building investment allowances, and allowances for bursaries for staff members.

MERG recommends that the next government should not increase the nominal rate of company tax, and should change the structure of the tax in order to widen its base and strengthen incentives for investment.

Investment incentives

The new dual tax rate, or withholding tax on distributed dividends (of 15 per cent) should be maintained in order to encourage investment out of retained profits. It could be adjusted to encourage investment. Investment incentives should be expanded and focused; their principal form should be accelerated depreciation allowances for new investment in plant and machinery, with write-offs of more than 100 per cent in the first year for certain types of investment. Such allowances should be an investment incentive only for firms which are sufficiently profitable and should be complemented with carry-over tax credits to encourage investment ventures with low initial profits. Special allowances should be introduced against company tax for the costs of approved training schemes for the improvement of the skills of previously disadvantaged groups, especially black and female workers.

Tax floor and transnational corporations

The base of company taxation should be broadened to ensure that fewer companies are able to avoid it. A minimum level of company tax payable by all companies should be introduced for that purpose. Special tax provisions should be made to prevent transnational corporations from using their international operations to underpay tax on profits generated by their South African operations.

Company taxation in South Africa is complicated by the highly concentrated nature of company ownership, and by the fact that leading conglomerates are transnational corporations with extensive foreign operations carried out by companies within their groups. Tax authorities in every country face special problems in taxing transnational companies, since they are able to transfer profits across borders to countries with lower rates of company tax. The most obvious mechanism used is the

under-invoicing of exports or general manipulation of transfer pricing. These transfers have contributed to a flight of capital from South Africa, which is estimated to
have totalled between $12 billion and $55 billion between 1970 and 1988. Such large
magnitudes represent a reduction in the amount of profits on which companies pay
tax in South Africa, and tax and reporting provisions must be made to bring such
profits within the tax net.

Since the 1970s, the most prominent proposal for strengthening the taxation of
transnational corporations has been worldwide unitary taxation, which California
and other states of the USA have attempted to implement. If implemented, such
unitary taxation would imply that the amount of group profits taxed in South Africa
would be calculated as a proportion of the worldwide profits reported for the group
as a whole. The proportion should be based on a formula reflecting the country's
percentage of worldwide sales or employment. Legal, political, and administrative
difficulties have prevented such taxes from being fully implemented. Their introduction would involve great difficulties because of the administrative burden; in addition, there will be difficulties defining the composition of a transnational group,
especially since South African groups have separated their international operations
into holding companies such as Minorco and Richemont. Nevertheless, the principle
of apportionment which underlies the idea of world unitary taxation should be
incorporated.

Mineral taxation

The taxation of companies in the mineral sector presents special problems which have
to be treated in the context of production conditions and marketing arrangements.
Such issues are not considered in this chapter. However, it is recommended that
differential taxation should be used as an instrument in industrial policy. Since
mineral beneficiation industries should be promoted as a major sector, tax policy
should treat pre-tax profits from more processed minerals more favourably than
profits on minerals which have low levels of processing.

On the assumption that company taxes are kept constant at 3.75 per cent of GDP,
with GDP growth rates the same as before, an estimate of projected company taxes
can be obtained. These are summarised in Table 2.12. Corporate taxes are about R7
billion higher in 2003 than in 1993, as a result of the assumed growth in GDP.
However, the share of company taxes in total tax revenue falls to about 12 per cent
by 2003. These estimates serve as an example of how much tax revenue could be
collected under a particular set of assumptions. They do not represent an ideal that
should be aspired to, but present an illustration of how additional revenue can be
obtained in accordance with the principles discussed.

2.3.6   Value added tax

VAT is here to stay, and the exemption of basic foodstuffs is a necessary part of it. It
is proposed that a democratic government remove the current ambivalent government attitude, and commit itself to a multiple-rate VAT structure. The multiple rate
structure should be extended to ensure that the VAT system has a progressive effect,
imposing lower average rates on the expenditure of the poor and higher average rates
on the expenditure of the rich. A higher rate of VAT, or luxury tax, should be imposed

on consumption goods above a certain value, type or quality. In addition to the aspect of fairness, its purpose will be to shape the pattern of South African industry and trade. A high tax rate on large, powerful cars, for example, would be intended to shift vehicle production in South Africa towards a mass market with a demand for smaller vehicles. The merits of imposing such a tax as a special VAT rate instead of as an excise tax are investigated below.

For the purpose of this exercise, it is assumed that a higher rate of 30 per cent on luxury goods is phased in after a few years. Luxury goods make up about 12 per cent of the current VAT base. The simulation results are summarised in Table 2.13. The VAT simulation suggests that by introducing a relatively high VAT rate on luxury goods, VAT revenue can be increased to about 9 per cent of GDP (from its 1993 proportion of 7.5 per cent). In this simulation, it raises additional resources accumulated to a total of R105 billion (in real terms) over ten years.

2.3.7 Customs duties

It seems likely that trade reform over the next few years will require that South Africa reduces its reliance on trade taxes as a source of revenue, if only because of the implications of GATT membership. The SACU transfers are under review, so the effect on revenue is not yet clear. There are good reasons why South Africa should not reduce its implicit development aid to its neighbours by too much. A democratic government will have to find alternative revenue sources to replace at least a proportion of revenue from trade taxes.

This is reflected in the assumption that customs duties will gradually fall over the decade to 2003. The lost revenue is made up by tax increases elsewhere. It is also assumed that South Africa Customs Union Agreement contributions to other countries rise slightly, rather than falling. This is summarised in Table A.7.

2.3.8 Excise taxes

An obvious additional source of revenue is excise taxes (including taxes on gambling). This is one of the few revenue sources that can be increased in the short term.

An issue on which the Fiscal Commission can advise a democratic government, concerns the appropriate way in which luxury goods should be taxed. For example, an excise tax, included in the price of a commodity for VAT purposes, may be a better alternative than a higher VAT rate. In this simulation, however, luxury goods are covered in the VAT estimates, and not under excise taxes.

It is assumed that excise duties increase steadily and significantly over the decade, from 1.47 per cent of GDP in 1993, to 2.6 per cent in 1998, and 3.8 per cent in 2003. According to this simulation, excise duties collected in 2003 will be R20 billion, in real terms, compared with R5 billion in 1993.

Fuel levies are assumed to remain more or less at their current level of 2.5 per cent of GDP until 1997, out of consideration for the inflationary impact of fuel price increases, and the remarkably large share of transport costs in the budgets of the poor in South Africa. After 1997 it rises moderately to reach 3 per cent of GDP in 2003. Then it will raise about R16 billion (in real terms) compared with the R7.6 billion in 1993.

2.3.9   Capital transfer tax

South Africa does currently have estate duties and gift taxes. These are not properly co-ordinated and are exceptionally low. These taxes should be integrated into a comprehensive capital transfer tax, without loopholes. In the interim, whilst the capital transfer tax is being investigated and the legislation prepared, the present taxes should be maintained, with some intermediate measures adopted to curtail tax avoidance through trust funds and other mechanisms.

For this simulation, it is assumed that some of the loopholes are closed and the base significantly extended, and that the rate is significantly increased over a period of four years. This increases the revenue collected from this source from 0.03 per cent of GDP in 1993 to 0.15 per cent of GDP in 1996 and beyond.

2.3.10   Wealth taxes

Various forms of wealth tax have been proposed and hotly debated. South Africa already has tax on some forms of wealth in the form of a property tax, which is discussed below. A Fiscal Commission will have to give advice on the desirability and feasibility of some form of wealth tax. The proposal made here is that a democratic government commits itself not to introduce a wealth tax before the Fiscal Commission gives a strong recommendation to that effect. There are a number of reasons for this proposal.

Firstly, it is highly unlikely that South Africa has the administrative capacity and expertise at present to cope with the introduction of a wealth tax. Secondly, because of its complexity, the legislation will take a long time to prepare, a problem made worse by the massive legislative programme, including other tax legislation, that a democratic government will have to deal with. Thirdly, a wealth tax rarely raises much revenue, so it will not make much of a difference to the bridging of the fiscal gap. Fourthly, the announcement of a capital gains tax and a capital transfer tax will meet the political need for perceived fairness.

A democratic government should give a clear and irrevocable commitment to protect people's savings and wealth, to protect them from confiscatory taxes, and to ensure that any general wealth tax would affect only the wealthiest.

2.3.11   Tax on fixed property

The major tax levied by local authorities is a tax on property, or rates. This should remain a tax collected at the local level. Changes will obviously have to be made in terms of the 'one city, one tax base' principle. Metropolitan or similar sub-regional authorities will have to collect all local revenue in some single pool, from which allocations can be made to the constituent local authorities. This principle is now broadly accepted and under negotiation.

A number of changes to the property tax system from central government level, should be investigated by the Fiscal Commission. Firstly, the property tax should be a tax on the value of land (currently, improvements on the land are also taxed only in the Cape Province). Secondly, the property tax should be extended to all land in the country, including non-urban land. Thirdly, the normal rate structure must be uniform, although the tax is collected locally. Fourthly, the rate structure, in order to be based on the value per unit of land (rather than total value), should be made progressive by introducing a zero rate for land with a value below a specified amount per unit (e.g. square meter), and a higher rate for more highly valued land. Fifthly, a local authority should be able (subject to rate capping arrangements which might already be in place) to add an additional levy to the nationally determined rate structure.

Most of these proposals are self-explanatory. A property tax is a tax on wealth that is easy to measure, impossible to avoid, and for which an administrative infrastructure already exists. While valuations will have to be made consistent nationally, and be repeated annually, the skills, information, and technology required to do this already exist. It also offers a means of making the tax system more progressive without reducing efficiency or encouraging avoidance. Property taxes do not feature in the MERG simulation.

2.3.12 Other taxes

There are many other minor taxes in South Africa. These include stamp duties, securities tax, financial transactions tax, turnover tax, and employment/wage bill tax. Space does not allow for all of them to be discussed here. Some of these taxes can be viewed as proxies for a tax on financial assets, although in reality they are taxes on the transfer of financial assets. It is proposed that they be retained, and extended in some cases (see Chapter Eight), so as to tax the movement of financial assets through the financial system.

In the simulation exercise, it is assumed that these financial taxes are increased moderately from a total of about 0.7 per cent of GDP in 1993 to about 0.9 per cent of GDP in 2003. It may be possible, and even desirable, to increase these duties and levies more (and capital gains tax less) than in this simulation. This is in fact the sort of issue that a Fiscal Commission will have to investigate and advise the democratic government on.

The possibility of a reconstruction levy has been raised. The situation of Germany after the war is usually given as an example of such a tax. As with most analogies, it should not be taken too far. There are many differences between Germany in 1948 and South Africa in 1995, one of which is that South African total tax revenue as a share of GDP is significantly higher than that of Germany at the time. Nevertheless, the desirability and feasibility of a reconstruction levy must be investigated.

Two possible mechanisms for raising such a reconstruction levy without major legal and administrative costs, seem to be a levy on personal income tax, or a levy on property tax. The former is more problematic. In addition to the constraints on increasing income tax, it will also place a less effective levy on those (usually more wealthy) members of society who can avoid income tax. In fact, one of the underlying principles in this simulation exercise is that alternative means of taxing the wealthy should be found. Taxes must be found which are not easily avoidable and which do not have the same disincentive effect as income tax.

The other possibility is that a certain proportion of the property/land tax rate, which will in practice amount to an additional levy, should be transferred as a reconstruction levy to a fund administered by something like a 'Council for Reconstruction and Development'. This would offer a relatively easy and quick way of raising some kind of reconstruction tax. It would also hold an element of redress, in that it was through the Land and Group Areas Acts that most of the material losses under apartheid were incurred. The imposition of a reconstruction levy will have to be carefully investigated by the Fiscal Commission before a decision is made.

In the simulation, 'Other Revenues', which are negative in 1993 because of tax transfers to the TBVC states and self-governing territories, not only turn positive as these areas are reincorporated, but increase to 2.25 per cent of GDP in 2003. This is because of the assumption that the gradual introduction of social security contributions will begin under a democratic government.

2.3.13   Total tax revenue

All the assumptions for the simulation exercise in this chapter are brought together in Table A.7 which illustrates how an increase in tax revenue can be phased in over the next decade. It also summarises, in simulation form, a possible quantification of some of the principles that were suggested for guiding tax reform.

The overall share of government revenue in GDP is assumed to rise from 27 per cent in 1993 to 32 per cent in 2003. With the assumed growth rate in GDP, this increase makes a huge difference to state revenue.

The composition of total tax revenue undergoes some significant shifts. Largely as a result of increased taxes on capital gains and capital transfers, luxury goods and services, excise goods and services ('sin taxes'), and the reduction of the share of individual income taxes due to a lessening of the burden on middle and low-income taxpayers, the relative shares of direct and indirect taxes change significantly. For example, the share of direct taxes declines from 56 per cent of total revenue (or 15 per cent of GDP) in 1993, to 43 per cent of total revenue (or 14 per cent of GDP) in 2003. Indirect taxes concomitantly increase from 44 per cent of total revenue (or 12 per cent of GDP) in 1993, to 57 per cent of total revenue (or 18 per cent of GDP) in 2003. This reflects a move towards a more balanced tax structure and a shift to more indirect but less avoidable taxes on the wealthy.

This simulation serves only as an example of how fiscal policy could be planned. It must not be interpreted as a normative proposal. A strategy for tax reform must be the subject of a thorough investigation by the Fiscal Commission.

2.4 The sustainability of fiscal policy

The foregoing analyses and simulations can be brought together, along with the borrowing and debt servicing implications of the expenditure and tax assumptions made above, to investigate the fiscal sustainability of the programme. A number of simulations, which must not be interpreted as MERG forecasts, have been performed with the aid of a debt model. These are summarised in Tables A.8 to A.13 below.

The simulations show that growth is the factor that makes the policy feasible. Scenario 1 (in Table A.8) includes the fiscal stance assumed in the simulations above. The assumptions of the first scenario are:

- The real long-term interest rate is reduced to 2 per cent (compared with the 1993 level of at least 5 per cent) and kept there throughout the decade;

- The GDP growth rate is assumed to pick up slowly at first, and then stay at about 5 per cent;

- Total government expenditure grows at 3.75 per cent per annum;
- Ordinary government revenue rises moderately, but steadily, each year as a share of GDP (T/Y), to reach 32 per cent of GDP in 2003.

The scenario is sustainable from a fiscal perspective. The debt/GDP ratio (D/Y) does not rise above 60 per cent and, in fact, comes down again by 2003 to about the same level as in 1993 (44 per cent of GDP). Interest payments never exceed their current share of government spending (I/E), and slowly decline to about 17 per cent of total expenditure by 2003. Government spending remains at about its current level of GDP (E/Y), except for the last few years, which suggests that if the expected growth materialises, the government will have ample scope for further increasing government spending after a few years, or for reducing public debt, or bringing down the tax burden. The fiscal stance underlying this scenario seems fairly robust, with substantial cushioning potential against unforeseen developments.

Whether or not Scenario 1 as an indicative projection is sustainable from a macroeconomic point of view is an important question, since some pressure is exerted on the balance of payments. If the foreign exchange constraint can be kept at bay, and if an appropriate national development strategy can instill in workers and investors alike a vision of improved economic conditions, so that the reasonable GDP growth rates can be realised, the indicative example of a fiscal plan presented in this paper will be a realistic and sustainable one.

Scenario 2 (Table A.9) differs from Scenario 1 only in that non-interest expenditure is growing at 5 per cent per annum. Although this appears sustainable from a fiscal perspective, it is not genuinely sustainable because of the balance of payments constraint. In spite of the fact that the debt ratio rises to 65 per cent of GDP, interest payments, expressed as a proportion, change only marginally. This is because of the structure of debt. If the assumed growth rates can be realised, the 'borrow rather than tax' strategy is not only feasible, but perhaps even a misnomer as, over ten years, tax revenues will increase more than total expenditure.

In Scenario 3 (Table A.10), the real long-term interest rate is assumed to stay at 6 per cent (the NEM proposal). Its main consequence is a higher debt ratio, which rises to 82 per cent of GDP in 2003. Interest payments as a proportion of total spending are consequently also higher than in the first two scenarios, i.e. 21 per cent for much of the period. This, in turn, pushes up total government expenditure to 41 per cent of GDP in 2003, compared with 35 per cent of GDP in Scenario 1. In the macroeconomic simulation with the MERG model, this scenario was not sustainable.

Scenario 4 (Table A.11), is the status quo scenario. It assumes no economic restructuring, so that the economy cannot grow at more than 3 per cent without the monetary authorities cooling down the economy to ease the balance of payments constraint. It also assumes high real interest rates (still in line with NEM proposals), onto which is grafted high expenditure growth of a kind that does not build productive capacity. It is clearly not sustainable from either a fiscal or a macroeconomic perspective. In spite of the slightly speeded-up increase in the total tax burden, the debt ratio reaches a level of 130 per cent of GDP in 2003. Interest payments absorb the whole budget, and total expenditure gobbles up no less than 80 per cent of GDP in 2003! Long before this could happen though, the IMF would dispense a strong dose of structural adjustment medicine.

Scenario 5 (Table A.12) suggests how a somewhat orthodox response might try to restore fiscal stability if it is realised in 1997 that the economy is on the Scenario 4 disaster path. By 1998, the spiralling interest payments (24 per cent of total government spending) would have pushed up total government expenditure to 44 per cent of GDP. This prompts a cut in the growth of spending to 3 per cent per year, and a rapid increase in taxation to reach 40 per cent in 2003. This is one example of a desperate dose of medicine to a critically ill patient, suffering from a self-inflicted illness.

In Scenario 6 (Table A.13), the worst case is simulated. Succumbing to IMF ideology that not more than 3 per cent of GDP should be borrowed, the new government increases taxation rapidly along with high expenditure growth. It also accepts the high real interest rate prescription. Without a national development strategy that can instill a vision of opportunities in the minds of economic actors, and without economic restructuring resulting in new prospects for profitability, the investment strike continues, and the economy continues to stagnate. Because of increased unemployment, spending continues to grow at a high rate, but this growth is absorbed by security and consumption spending. Asset creation is minimal and the spending does not add to economic growth. The size of government grows rapidly to absorb approximately 44 per cent of GDP. Like so many other developing countries, South Africa will have failed economically because the state was seen only as an instrument for redistribution, and not also as a strong guiding force for bringing about economic restructuring towards profitability in the private sector. Ironically, the preoccupation with limiting borrowing and increasing taxation has resulted in increased borrowing and a debt situation which by 2003 is clearly beginning to get out of control, all because of the lack of growth.

When the government realises that its policies have failed, and when interest payments reach 24 per cent of total spending, it brings down the real interest rate to 2 per cent, cuts down the growth in public spending, and increases taxation rapidly to reach 40 per cent of GDP in 2003. As with the other pessimistic scenarios, the ultimate failure here is the GDP growth rate. It illustrates once more the imperative for a democratic government to design a package of economic policies that will generate high economic growth. Its key elements must be human development, investment in social infrastructure, and the creation of prospects for profitable investments that will bring about the necessary restructuring of the economy.

Scenario 1 presents a moderate growth in tax revenue. Its GDP share rises by about 0.5 per cent per year, to reach a GDP proportion of 32.5 per cent in 2003 (compared with the 26.8 per cent in 1993). In Scenario 6 a major or rapid increase in the GDP share of taxation is represented. Over the first four years it increases from 27 per cent to 39 per cent. It fails because it does not generate high economic growth. The moderate approach, as has already been indicated, will still be enough to finance even a 5 per cent growth in government spending. This is a far cry from the government proposal, which amounts to a rigidly orthodox or status quo fiscal stance, that taxation be reduced by about 5 per cent of GDP.

2.5 Reforming the fiscal institutions

2.5.1 *Independent fiscal commission*

In the discussion so far, reference has often been made to the role of a Fiscal Commission. The Fiscal Commission is envisaged as a statutory body consisting of independent fiscal experts and specialists from business, labour, civil society and government, appointed by parliament (or transitional interim authorities). Its brief should be to advise a democratic government on fiscal policy matters in order to ensure greater transparency, efficiency, consistency and predictability of fiscal policy. It should replace all existing government committees dealing with fiscal matters that function in a closed and unrepresentative manner.

By having one body to co-ordinate all the policy and implementation advice to government, South Africa can move away from the ad hoc approach of the past, especially if the terms of reference of the Commission commit it to operate within the framework of a national development strategy. Another important reason for a single Fiscal Commission is that information will more likely be made available to all interested parties and thus ensure better debate and more informed decision-making. Moreover, a new democratic government will inherit a civil service which may not be co-operative or which may, out of habit, keep information from the government or use it to promote its own interests.

A Fiscal Commission, with full statutory powers to request information, will provide government with another, perhaps more reliable, source of policy options and different perspectives on the implementation of government policies. Without it, the complexity and interrelatedness of fiscal policy issues may well result in a new government, dependent on an inherited civil service, finding that it is frustrated in its efforts to formulate and implement policies.

The constitutional and actual positions of the Fiscal Commission must not be allowed to diverge. The position agreed to in the constitutional negotiations is that an independent Fiscal Commission, with special responsibility for regional fiscal allocation, should be established with a purely advisory role. In practice, there would be a tendency for its advice to take on a mandatory character, unless adequate parliamentary mechanisms are established to scrutinise and evaluate fiscal policy. South Africa should establish specialised parliamentary committees to scrutinise tax legislation and monitor the operation of the tax system.

2.5.2 *Fiscal relations between different levels of government*

Fiscal policy will also have to deal with the fiscal relations between different levels of government. Given the fact that the powers and functions of the different levels of government must still be negotiated, policies in this regard can at this stage be concerned only with broad principles. Five of the most important principles are discussed in this section.

The need to prioritise development

The first principle that is proposed is that priority must be placed on developmental objectives. This will give a perspective on fiscal relations very different from the view which sees different levels of government as a power-sharing arrangement, or a means of distributing the spoils of state, or, as in the past, as a form of divide-and-rule. From a developmental perspective, each level of government will have a role as a developmental agency commensurate with the overall objectives of a developmental state. The fiscal relations between the different levels of government can thus be worked out in a coherent manner. The functions assigned to the different levels of government are then more likely to be integrative, rather than divisive. It is then also more likely that the different layers of the developmental state can work harmoniously to promote the goals of poverty reduction, greater equality through human development, and economic growth and employment.

The maintenance of macroeconomic stability

The second principle which should guide fiscal relations between different levels of government, is that such relations should not undermine fiscal discipline and the maintenance of macroeconomic stability. A fiscal system that is strongly pro-cyclical and likely to amplify cyclical movements, must be avoided. In Germany, for example, special measures were introduced in the post-war period to promote contra-cyclical spending behaviour by lower levels of government. Lower levels of government should be allowed to borrow only under the supervision of the central fiscal authorities and in accordance with guidelines that will ensure compliance with the macroeconomic management objectives of government. Lower levels of government should not be able to borrow at their discretion, since the central government might have to foot the bill if the country is faced with an unsustainable debt.

Tax where it can be done most efficiently

A third principle is that taxes should be levied by the jurisdiction that can do it most efficiently. For example, income taxes can be raised most efficiently by central government for at least three reasons. Firstly, incomes are often generated across domestic boundaries and to try to determine the source of income generation will not only be inefficient, but will also encourage different levels of government to compete by lowering tax rates. Secondly, highly skilled staff and integrated computerised records are needed in a sophisticated economy with complex tax laws; such resources are unlikely to be available at several levels of government. Thirdly, experience in other countries has taught that if tax jurisdiction lies with the lower levels, it is more likely that corruption and mismanagement will undermine the effective tax base. In contrast, property taxes can be collected more efficiently at the local level.

Functional responsibility to match accountability

The efficient delivery of public services is dependent on accountability. The responsibility for the various functions of government should be given to the level of government that can most effectively be held accountable for its efficient delivery. For instance, refuse removal belongs at the local level and defence at the national level. There are many functions, however, that may not at present reside with the level of government that can most effectively be held accountable for them. Primary education may be an example of a function for which a local or some other lower level of government can more effectively be held accountable than a large regional or national authority. The latter, however, could remain responsible for formulating curricula and standards. If functions are allocated according to this principle and lower authorities cannot generate enough local taxes to finance them at the prescribed standards, transfers from central government must make up the difference.

Intergovernmental transfers on the basis of formulae

To minimise regional conflict and arbitrary decisions, as many intergovernmental transfers as possible, both on the revenue and expenditure sides, should be done in accordance with objectively determined formulae. For example, if a proportion of local property taxes has to be transferred to a metropolitan authority so that it can be redistributed to poorer jurisdictions in that region, this should be done according to objectively determined formulae. Likewise, for example, transfers from central government to lower authorities to effect equal per capita spending on education and other services, should be determined by formulae. Such formulae should make use of appropriate socio-economic indicators and performance measures to ensure the fair distribution of resources across the country.

The Fiscal Commission could be responsible for developing the formulae and accompanying indicators and measures to give effect to the principles laid down in the constitution or enabling legislation. The decentralised responsibility for taxation could be governed by guiding principles, on the basis of which a Fiscal Commission should make recommendations to government. This is preferable to fixing responsibilities indefinitely in the constitution on the basis of current fiscal technology and economic structure, both of which can change quite dramatically over time.

2.5.3   Efficiency and management of public spending

Media revelations in recent years have exposed the tip of what must surely be an iceberg of mismanagement, wastage and corruption in the public sector. This may have been affordable in an undemocratic system in which the ruling oligarchy and its puppets were the main beneficiaries, but it can certainly not be afforded in a democracy where the government will be accountable to all the people. If South Africa is going to have a truly developmental state, and not a bloated civil service committed to narrow ideological or sectional interests, then a variety of measures will have to be adopted to ensure better targeting and efficiency in public spending. It is proposed that a future democratic government commit itself to at least the few critical measures listed here.

Delivery mechanisms for better targeting

The civil service will have to be transformed to become an efficient agent for development. More specifically, new and improved delivery mechanisms will have to be used, or created where they do not exist, so that the intended beneficiaries of public spending can be better targeted. There are many examples at present of broad measures and blunt instruments that are aimed at a wide target in the hope that the minority for whom they were intended are reached. This results in costly and wasteful programmes.

In some instances, better targeting itself may require more specialised institutions. In other cases, government should not provide the services itself, but rather make use of the private sector, NGOs, or development agencies to ensure effective targeting. In many such cases, the state may still have to lay down standards and guidelines, and remain responsible for the ultimate financing of those services. This may not only result in better targeting, but could also be more cost-effective. Moreover, during the first few years, when a democratic government will have to contend with major, time-consuming problems on a broad front, including the reorientation of an inherited civil service, this may be the quickest way to ensure effective delivery of the services. This will also open up the possibility of new and creative financing instruments that could allow state funding to be used for leverage.

Multi-year expenditure planning

The lack of openness and transparency in the public sector also manifests itself in the conduct of fiscal policy in South Africa, and in the drawing up of the budget. This has undermined the legitimacy and effectiveness of the government expenditure programme. The British colonial tradition of secrecy, and the rather farcical process of an annual guessing game about what surprises the Minister of Finance is going to spring upon the country, have no place in an open, democratic system of government which strives towards both efficiency and participatory democratic decision-making. In such a process, perhaps led by open deliberations of parliamentary committees, there should be ample opportunity for the public to voice their concerns or objections before legislation or the budget becomes law.

Since public spending must be restructured to remove inequalities and address basic social needs, while promoting growth and employment creation, scarce resources must be managed efficiently. The current system of annual budgets is an important contributing factor to the inefficiencies that prevail at present. The budgetary process is not only closed and overly bureaucratic, but tends to perpetuate the misallocations and inefficiencies of the past. Departmental allocations are made in aggregate terms on the basis of past shares and expected inflationary increases. Within departments, programmes are given budgetary allocations primarily on historical grounds (except for capital projects which tend to be cut if the budget is under pressure) and not on the basis of performance. The small percentage of the budget that is available for new projects each year, is usually introduced without clear objectives or a time being specified within which the projects have to be achieved. The situation is exacerbated by the annual budgetary cycle, which results in wasteful expenditure when the end of the financial year approaches. This undermines proper planning and effective implementation.

Openness and transparency, more effective expenditure planning and greater efficiency and effectiveness in spending must be promoted through a system of multi-year expenditure planning and rolling budgets. Each year the Department of Finance should publish a set of multi-year budgets (e.g. for the next and three more years) with sufficient information about programme objectives, timeframes and past performance to enable informed public debate, analytical scrutiny and open special-interest representations to be made. Mid-way through the financial year, and in response to changing circumstances and the feedback received, revised estimates should be published, with the process started all over again at the beginning of the next financial year, when the current budget of that year is legislated in all its relevant detail, and a new year is added to the forward estimates. This means that when the actual budget is presented to parliament (e.g. in March of each year), it will have gone through many incarnations and revisions. It will have been thoroughly debated and broad participation will have been achieved. It will also already have acquired a certain degree of legitimacy. Such a budgetary process is in place in some countries, and the evidence is that it has made a remarkable difference in bringing about fiscal discipline and efficiency in public spending. Australia is a good example.

A logical addition to multi-year budgeting is to introduce rolling budgets so that wasteful behaviour is not induced by rigid and artificial fiscal year boundaries. Departments must not feel pressure to spend the whole of their allocation in one fiscal year because of the fear that they will otherwise lose the money. Funds must be carried over if the implementation of the project for which they were voted can be enhanced by it. Greater managerial responsibility and discretion, but increased accountability, is a necessary corollary of this system. This is another characteristic of the Australian success story.

Measurable objectives

The goal of better targeting and efficiency will remain unrealisable as long as the objectives of publicly funded projects are not made clear. It is preferable that these objectives be stated in measurable terms whenever possible, and that the mechanisms through which they will be realised spelled out. Without such measurable objectives (which should be interpreted as including delivery mechanisms), the public debate, scrutiny and participation referred to above, will not be possible, or will be ineffective as an instrument for bringing about better targeting and efficiency. The clear statement of objectives is also necessary for the measurement of performance, discussed in the next section. The Fiscal Commission should advise a democratic government on how measurable objectives can be introduced and what such objectives might be in cases where quantification might be difficult, as in the case of policing. It should also advise on how quality of delivery, rather than just quantity, can be built into project objectives.

Institutionalised performance auditing

A logical addition to the measures for improving targeting and efficiency already mentioned, is the introduction of effective, institutionalised performance auditing. South Africa has a fairly good system of financial auditing, although it is somewhat emasculated by the legal constraints on the scrutiny of secret funds. What is seriously lacking, however, are adequate institutional arrangements and capacity to undertake effective performance (or value-for-money) auditing. The latter is concerned with how a project or agency has performed in terms of its objectives, i.e. not just whether or not the money has been spent legally, but whether or not it has been spent effectively towards the realisation of the objectives. For example, if the objective of a project was to build 10 000 houses of a certain quality, a performance audit will investigate whether 10 000 houses were in fact constructed and built, according to the standard specified.

A performance audit must also assess whether or not the service or good was delivered in the best and most cost-effective manner. In terms of the housing project example, it is possible that the required 10 000 houses were built according to the standard specified, but that this was not done in the most cost-effective manner. For example, over-budgeting could have allowed excessively high overheads, or excessive bureaucratic costs, or inadequate tendering procedures, or poor control over implementation. Performance auditing is supposed to identify such shortcomings.

A nominal commitment to performance auditing does not ensure that it is effective. The Auditor-General in South Africa is nominally committed to performance auditing, but cannot implement it in practice because of inadequate resources, constraining legislation, and the absence of most of the other ingredients of a strategy required to bring about better targeting and efficiency. It is proposed, therefore, that as an integral part of a comprehensive strategy to make the public sector more efficient, adequate funds for effective performance auditing be guaranteed, perhaps by stipulating in the constitution that a percentage of the budget be earmarked for a performance audit by an independent body (which could be part of the Auditor-General's Office) and that all civil servants or recipients of public money can be compelled to provide the performance auditor with information.

It is also proposed, as a necessary consequence of the foregoing, that all reports of the performance auditor be submitted to parliament and the public for open discussion and debate. Without adequate performance auditing and public scrutiny, a democratic government may find that its policies are circumvented by a bureaucracy that is opposed to the policies of the government. The urgent need to bring about stability by delivering social services at the grassroots level cannot be undermined by a recalcitrant section of the civil service. Effective performance auditing can make a significant contribution towards ensuring that the policies of a democratic government are effectively implemented.

In order to get the full benefit from an institutionalised system of performance auditing, it must be linked to the other elements of the overall strategy. More specifically, the performance auditor must accumulate a database of information of measures and procedures that worked, or did not work, and why; of types of corruption and mismanagement; and of inadequacies in programme design and implementation. This accumulated knowledge of how to avoid poor targeting and inefficiencies can be fed back into the system by means of the performance auditor advising departments (at the planning stage of projects) on how to ensure better targeting and delivery.

Transparency and disclosure of information

The apartheid state is characterised not only by its lack of transparency, but also by its reluctance to disclose information. Apart from the fact that access to information should be a democratic right, greater efficiency in the public sector will be more likely if the state is compelled to be transparent and to disclose information. Of particular concern here is information that relates to public policy and programme implementation. For example, it is incomprehensible that the Reserve Bank should formulate monetary policy that affects the whole of society, on the basis of a model or of information that is kept secret, even after policy has been made and implemented. This is not only contrary to the accepted practice that prevails in most democratic countries, but is also dysfunctional with regard to good policy making. Likewise, it does not make sense for the Department of Finance to keep secret the criteria for budgetary allocations, or information on income tax returns (given that such information should be made available in such a manner that individuals cannot be identified). A democratic government must commit itself to bring about, through legislative means, maximum transparency and disclosure of information.

Rationalisation of public expenditure

The package of measures aimed at better targeting and efficiency of public expenditure must be completed with a thorough programme of rationalisation. This is not rationalisation apartheid-style, but rationalisation in order to ensure that apartheid structures and procedures are eliminated or transformed in terms of the major objectives already outlined, and in order to bring about a more effective and efficient delivery of public services and goods. 'A slim, but strong state', and in fact a non-apartheid state, can only be brought about through a process of rationalisation which involves retrenchment for many existing office holders.

2.6 Conclusion

This chapter can only scratch the surface of the many complex and interrelated aspects of fiscal policy. Nevertheless, it has attempted to put forward a vision that differs from both the supply-side orthodoxy of the Normative Economic Model (NEM), and the simple credo of 'soaking the rich' in order to provide the poor with guaranteed employment and higher incomes.

The importance of macroeconomic stability, and the interrelatedness of fiscal, monetary and exchange rate policy in maintaining it, are dealt with in other chapters. It is necessary, however, to point out that the specific measures or policies mentioned above, have been considered in terms of the commitment to macroeconomic stability.

It is unfortunate that some commentators have used the term 'macroeconomic constraints' when referring to the need for macroeconomic stability, as this is misleading and incorrect. Sound macroeconomic policies should ensure sustainability and increased capacity to deliver social goods in future, and will thus facilitate, rather than constrain, the implementation of a development strategy. The reverse is also true. Policies that ignore macroeconomic stability collapse after only a few years, and usually result in the poor being worse off than before.

Given the key role of fiscal policy, along with monetary and exchange rate policies, in the macroeconomic management of the economy, the same argument about constraints applies to the fiscal balance. To argue for the maintenance of a sound fiscal balance is not constraining, but enabling. It is how that balance is managed which is important, and about which major differences exist. The Normative Economic Model, for example, argues that fiscal balance is to be achieved by reducing government consumption from about 21 per cent of GDP in 1992 to about 15 per cent of GDP by 1995, while at the same time bringing about significant reductions in tax revenue. This is not only unattainable, but also undesirable.

A more realistic and necessary approach, if social stability and a climate conducive to economic growth are to be achieved within a few years, will entail the following:

- The containment of government consumption expenditure over this period to roughly its present level in real terms;

- Significant growth in social infrastructure and human development spending in order to increase the growth capacity of the economy;

- Moderate tax increases and continued borrowing at current levels for a few years;

- The gradual reduction of the deficit, after the debt/GDP ratio has increased to about 60 per cent, to sustainable levels through positive government savings after several years of good economic growth.

Fiscal stability is essential for the major objectives of fiscal policy outlined above. That macroeconomic stability, anchored by sound fiscal management, can facilitate, rather than constrain, the implementation of a national development strategy, has been shown with the aid of the simulation exercises reported above.

There is a need for a substantial increase in government spending on human development, social infrastructure, and the expansion of productive economic capacity. Such an increase is a prerequisite for the achievement of high economic growth rates. While moderate and gradual increases in taxation will be necessary, they should not be such as to undermine the growth potential of the national development strategy. It is feasible and desirable during the first few years of the new programme, while the growth rate is still picking up, to finance increased spending with public sector borrowing, rather than with rapid increases in the tax burden.

The simulations presented in this chapter serve to illustrate that such a programme is sustainable. Independent simulations with the MERG model suggest that the proposed programme will also be macroeconomically sound, provided that the foreign exchange constraint can be avoided. The critical question is whether or not the assumed growth rates will materialise. The key role of higher economic growth in any future scenario makes it imperative that priority be given by a new democratic government to the design of a national development strategy that can help to bring this about.

Δ

Table 2.1 Indicators of the efficiency of social spending in South Africa and other economies

	GNP per $ capita	Av. annual growth 65-90	Central govt. expen. % GNP	Educ. as % of GNP	Health as % of GNP	Housing social & welfare % GNP	Life expect (years)	Infant mortality rate	Maternal mortality rate	Adult Illiteracy %
Low Income	350	2.9					62	69		40
China	370	5.8					70	29	44	27
Sri Lanka	470	2.9	28.4	2.8	1.5	4.2	71	19	90	12
Lowr Mid. Inc.	1530	1.5					65	51		25
Zimbabwe	640	0.7	40.5	9.5	3.1	1.6	61	49	150	33
Thailand	1420	4.4	4.9	1.0	0.3	0.3	66	27	270	7
Tunisia	1440	3.2	-4.5	-0.7	-0.3	-0.6	67	44	1000	35
Turkey	1630	2.6	24.6	4.7	0.9	0.9	67	60	207	19
Chile	1940	0.4	32.8	3.3	1.9	11.1	72	17	55	7
Botswana	2040	8.4	42.2	8.5	2.0	4.5	67	38	300	26
Mauritius	2250	3.2	24.2	3.5	2.1	4.1	70	20	99	
Malaysia	2320	4	31.3	0.0	0.0	0.0	70	16	59	22
Argentina	2370	-0.3	15.5	1.4	0.3	6.3	71	29	85	5
Uppr Mid. Inc.	3410	2.8					68	45		16
Mexico	2490	2.8	18.4	2.6	0.3	2.4	70	39	92	13
South Africa	2530	1.3	30.5	6.4	3.1	2.6	62	66	550	35
Brazil	2680	3.3	36	1.9	2.6	7.2	66	57	150	19
Hungary	2780		54.8	1.8	4.3	19.3	71	15	28	
Portugal	4900	3	43.3	0.0	0.0	0.0	75	12	15	15
Korea	5400	7.1	15.7	3.1	0.3	1.9	71	17	34	
High Income	19590	2.4					77	8		4
Singapore	11160	6.5	23.3	4.2	1.1	2.7	74	7	11	
Hong Kong	11490	6.2					78	7	4	
U. K.	16100	2	34.8	1.1	5.1	12.1	76	8	7	
Canada	20470	2.7	23.4	0.7	1.3	8.7	77	7	2	
U.S.A.	21790	1.7	24	0.4	3.2	6.8	76	9	9	
Sweden	23660	1.9	42.3	3.7	0.4	23.6	78	6	4	
Japan	25430	4.1	16.7				79	5	15	

Source: World Bank: World Development Reports

Table 2.2   Indicators of urban housing sector performance in South Africa and other economies

Housing outcome	Thailand	Tunisia	Turkey	Jordan	Malaysia	Brazil	S Africa	Algeria	Korea
Permanent structures (%)	96.5	95.7	100.0	96.5	85.4	99.0	72.8	96.8	97.1
Water connection (%)	76.4	86.4	94.0	97.0	94.0	95.0	58.0	94.5	99.6
Housing investment/ GDP (%)	3.9	7.4	4.5	n.a.	8.5	3.6	2.6	n.a.	4.5
Infrastructural investment/ Population ($)	102	n.a.	n.a.	457	n.a.	129	552	n.a.	455
GNP per capita ($ US)	1000	1230	1280	1500	1940	2160	2290	2360	3600

Note: Data is for the following cities: Bangkok, Tunis, Istanbul, Amman, Kuala Lumpur, Rio de Janeiro, Johannesburg (PWV), Algiers and Seoul.

Source: World Bank: Housing Indicators Programme, 1991

Table 2.3   Implications of public expenditure growth in South Africa and other economies

	Year	% of GDP	% of Total Exp.
TOTAL EXPENDITURE			
South Africa	1987	34.05	100.00
South Africa	1991	36.61	100.00
Upper Middle Income Countries	1987	34.20	100.00
EDUCATION			
South Africa	1987	6.22	18.27
South Africa	1991	7.05	19.25
Upper Middle Income Countries	1987	4.20	14.10
HEALTH			
South Africa	1987	3.28	9.64
South Africa	1991	3.43	9.37
Upper Middle Income Countries	1987	2.60	7.60
SOCIAL SECURITY & WELFARE			
South Africa	1987	2.04	6.00
South Africa	1991	2.83	7.73
Upper Middle Income Countries	1987	8.70	23.00
HOUSING			
South Africa	1987	1.92	5.63
South Africa	1991	1.56	4.25
Upper Middle Income Countries	1987	0.20	1.00
TOTAL SOCIAL PROGRAMMES			
South Africa	1987	13.98	41.06
South Africa	1991	15.38	41.99
Upper Middle Income Countries	1987	15.70	45.70
DEFENCE			
South Africa	1987	4.25	12.49
South Africa	1991	4.05	11.06
Upper Middle Income Countries	1987	2.30	8.60

Sources: IMF and South African Reserve Bank

Table 2.4 Implications of public expenditure growth (1993 to 2003) (MERG)

Year	Total exp.	Growth non-interest expend.	Non-interest payments	Increase over 1993	Growth at 2.75%	Increase over 1993	Difference (3.75-2.75)	Inv. exp. increase 55% of 3.75%	Inv. ex./ tot. exp.
	Rm	%	Rm						
1993	127 126	-	104 946	-	104 946	-	-	-	5.90
1994	132 284	3.75	108 956	4 010	107 872	2 926	1 084	2 206	7.57
1995	139 155	3.75	113 120	8 174	110 880	5 934	2 240	4 495	9.13
1996	148 355	3.75	117 442	12 496	113 971	9 025	3 471	6 873	10.60
1997	153 245	3.75	121 930	16 984	117 149	12 203	4 781	9 341	12.00
1998	159 845	3.75	126 589	21 643	120 415	15 469	6 174	11 904	13.35
1999	168 219	3.75	131 426	26 480	123 773	18 827	7 654	14 564	14.66
2000	172 220	3.75	136 448	31 502	127 224	22 278	9 225	17 326	15.96
2001	177 730	3.75	141 662	36 716	130 771	25 825	10 892	20 194	17.26
2002	182 693	' 3.75	147 075	42 129	134 417	29 471	12 659	23 171	18.58
2003	187 092	3.75	152 696	47 750	138 165	33 219	14 531	16 262	19.94
Total over ten years				247 885		175 176	72 709	136 336	

Year	Inv. ex./ GDP	Inv. exp. growth 3.75-2.75	Inv. ex./ tot. exp.	Inv. ex./ GDP	Ass. GDP (real)	Tot. exp./ GDP	Ass. GDP growth (real)	Ass. Inter. growth (real)	Int. pay. (real)	Int. pay./ tot. exp
	%	Rm	%		Rm		%		Rm	%
1993	0.02	-	5.90	0.02	331 342	38.37	-	-	22 190	17.45
1994	0.67	1 084	6.72	0.34	338 036	39.13	2	5	23 328	17.63
1995	1.31	2 240	7.51	0.67	348 330	39.95	3	11	26 035	18.71
1996	1.92	3 471	8.27	0.98	362 546	40.37	4	10	28 913	19.76
1997	2.47	4 781	9.02	1.28	381 134	40.21	5	8	31 315	20.43
1998	2.99	6 174	9.76	1.58	400 675	39.89	5	6	33 258	20.81
1999	3.48	7 654	10.50	1.84	421 218	39.46	5	5	34 793	20.93
2000	3.94	9 225	11.26	2.11	442 815	38.89	5	3	35 771	20.77
2001	4.36	10 892	12.03	2.36	465 518	38.18	5	1	36 068	20.29
2002	4.76	12 659	12.83	2.61	489 386	37.33	5	-1	35 617	19.50
2003	5.13	14 531	13.67	2.85	514 447	36.37	5	-3	34 397	18.39

Source: MERG estimates

Table 2.5 **Comparison of main sources of central government revenue, 1990**

	% of Central Government Revenue				Total current revenue as % of GNP	% of GNP			
	Taxes on income	Social security contrib.	Taxes on goods & services	Trade taxes		Taxes on income	Social security contrib.	Taxes on goods & services	Trade taxes
Low Income									
Sri Lanka	10.8	0.0	46.4	28.6	21.1	2.3	0.0	9.8	6.0
Lower Mid. Inc.									
Zimbabwe	44.9	0.0	26.3	17.5	35.6	16.0	0.0	9.4	6.2
Thailand	24.2	0.1	41.1	22.1	19.9	4.8	0.0	8.2	4.4
Tunisia	12.9	11.1	20.1	27.9	31.8	4.1	3.5	6.4	8.9
Turkey	43.3	0.0	32.1	6.2	19.3	8.4	0.0	6.2	1.2
Chile	23.3	6.0	37.1	9.8	31.1	7.2	1.9	11.5	3.0
Botswana	38.6	0.0	1.5	13.2	60.9	23.5	0.0	0.9	8.0
Mauritius	13.9	4.1	20.9	46.0	24.2	3.4	1.0	5.1	11.1
Malaysia	30.5	0.8	24.3	16.7	28.9	8.8	0.2	7.0	4.8
Argentina	4.3	43.4	22.4	11.4	13.3	0.6	5.8	3.0	1.5
Upper Mid. Inc.									
Mexico	36.5	13.6	56.0	4.6	14.9	5.4	2.0	8.3	0.7
South Africa	48.6	1.7	34.1	4.9	30.9	15.0	0.5	10.5	1.5
Hungary	17.9	29.2	31.3	5.8	55.6	10.00	16.2	17.4	3.2
Portugal	23.8	25.9	36.9	2.5	36.6	8.7	9.5	13.5	0.9
High Income									
Singapore	24.3	0.0	19.6	2.5	27.9	6.8	0.0	5.5	0.7
U.K.	40.3	17.1	30.8	0.1	35.5	14.3	6.1	10.9	0.0
Canada	53.7	14.2	19.6	3.5	20.5	11.0	2.9	4.0	0.7
U.S.	51.6	34.6	3.2	1.6	20.0	10.3	6.9	0.6	0.3
Sweden	18.1	30.5	28.9	0.5	45.3	8.2	13.8	13.1	0.2
Japan	71.2	0.0	12.0	1.3	13.9	9.9	0.0	1.7	0.2

Source: World Development Report, 1992

Table 2.6 Tax revenue from different sources in South Africa (as a percentage of GDP)

Source of revenue	1980/1 %	1985/6 %	1990/1 %	1991/2 %	1992/3 %
Customs and excise					
Customs duty	1.31	1.05	1.06	1.02	1.01
Surcharge	0.00	0.44	0.88	0.54	0.52
Excise duty	2.21	1.64	1.41	1.43	1.48
Fuel levy	0.00	0.00	1.66	1.94	2.30
Ordinary levy	0.00	0.00	0.05	0.03	0.03
Miscellaneous	0.08	0.09	0.00	0.02	0.03
Subtotal	3.59	3.21	5.05	4.98	5.36
Less Namibia: CRF	0.07	0.27	0.05	0.00	0.00
Custom Union Agreement	0.90	1.08	1.39	1.68	1.74
Total	2.62	1.86	3.62	3.30	3.61
Inland revenue					
Income Tax					
Companies (non-mine)	4.29	4.27	4.92	4.58	3.65
Individuals	3.71	7.44	9.33	10.30	10.56
Gold mines	4.96	2.18	0.27	0.20	0.16
Other Mines	0.38	0.43	0.66	0.27	0.20
Sales Tax/Value Added Tax	2.93	7.16	7.60	6.79	5.61
Gold mining leases	1.49	0.53	0.08	0.06	0.06
Non-res. shareholders tax	0.53	0.31	0.18	0.12	0.09
Stamp duties, fees	0.24	0.24	0.27	0.26	0.25
Transfer duty & estate duty	0.38	0.36	0.32	0.31	0.29
Interests & dividends	1.01	0.32	0.03	0.03	0.29
Other	1.07	0.97	0.91	0.77	0.86
Total	20.99	24.21	24.57	23.68	21.80
Total ordinary revenue	23.61	26.07	28.19	26.98	25.41
Direct taxes	13.10	14.71	15.46	15.57	14.79
Indirect taxes	6.96	9.74	11.92	10.74	9.82
Miscellaneous	3.55	1.62	0.81	0.67	0.80
Other tiers of govt - tax (est)	2.27	3.03	3.02	3.12	3.28
Other tiers of govt - other rev	3.25	3.74	3.60	3.77	4.37
Total General Govt Revenue	29.13	32.84	34.80	33.88	33.06
GDP	100.00	100.00	100.00	100.00	100.00

Source: South African Reserve Bank

Table 2.7 Impact of income tax on real per capita income in South Africa

	1970	1980	1985	1990	1991	1992
Real Income Per Capita	4344.74	4897.81	4828.37	4818.64	4779.78	4702.55
Real Direct Taxes Per Capita	280.35	308.71	546.05	634.73	654.73	655.38
(Direct Taxes as % of Per Capita Income)	(6.5)	(6.3)	(11.3)	(13.2)	(13.7)	(13.9)
Real Personal Disposable Income Per Capita	4064.39	4589.11	4282.33	4183.71	4125.05	4047.17

Source: Based on data from CSS

Table 2.8 Estimates of tax elasticity for South Africa

Actual Income and Tax -1991/2			10% Increase in Income - Rates Constant				Tax elasticity (for 1 %)
Taxable income	Tax paid	Average rate (%)	Taxable income	Tax paid	Average rate %	Growth in tax. income	
17000	770	4.5	18700	1127	6.0	46.5	4.64
25000	2550	10.2	27500	3200	11.6	25.5	2.55
35000	5300	15.1	38500	6420	16.7	21.1	2.11
45000	8650	19.2	49500	10360	20.9	19.8	1.98
55000	12500	22.7	60500	14705	24.3	17.6	1.76
65000	16550	25.5	71500	19230	26.9	16.2	1.62
80000	22800	28.5	88000	26240	29.8	15.1	1.51
100000	31400	31.4	110000	35700	32.5	13.7	1.37
150000	52900	35.3	165000	59350	36.0	12.2	1.22

Source: Department of Finance

Table 2.9 Estimate of 'avoidance' of personal income tax in South Africa, 1990

% of House holds	% of Gross income	% of Taxable income	% of House-holds	Cum. % of gross income	Cum. % of taxable income	H/holds gross income rmn	H/holds taxable income rmn	Difference gross-taxable income	Difference % of gross income
10	0.83	0.00	10.00	0.83	0.00	1471.50	0.00	1471.50	-
10	1.55	0.00	20.00	2.38	0.00	2751.53	0.00	2751.53	-
10	2.85	0.00	30.00	5.23	0.00	5056.32	0.00	5056.32	-
10	3.70	5.07	40.00	8.92	5.07	6564.58	6466.46	98.11	1.49
10	4.53	6.34	50.00	13.45	11.41	8051.37	8088.71	-37.35	-0.46
10	7.01	7.63	60.00	20.46	19.04	12448.07	9729.06	2719.01	21.84
10	9.68	10.10	70.00	30.14	29.14	17185.13	12884.66	4300.47	25.02
10	13.07	13.71	80.00	43.22	42.84	23220.16	17485.05	5735.12	24.70
10	20.02	19.68	90.00	63.23	62.52	35548.78	25101.49	10447.29	29.39
5	13.48	13.40	95.00	76.71	75.92	23931.52	17098.49	6833.03	28.55
5	23.29	24.08	100.00	100.00	100.00	41365.88	30713.80	10652.06	25.75
100	100.00	100.00				177594.81	127567.72	50027.09	28.17
0-30	5.23	0.00				9279.35	0.00	9279.35	
30-80	37.99	42.84				67469.30	54653.94	12815.36	
80-100	56.78	57.16				100646.16	72913.78	27932.38	

Source: Estimated from CSS Household Survey (Metropolitan Areas only) and Statistical Bulletin, Inland Revenue: both 1990

Table 2.10   Personal income tax as a percentage of GDP in South Africa and selected developing countries, 1987

Developing countries	Total tax revenue: % GDP	Personal tax: % GDP
Upper-middle-income:		
Portugal	29.26	1.79
Malaysia	21.03	2.27
Mexico	17.88	1.96
Uruguay	17.12	0.44
Korea	15.39	2.63
Lower-middle-income:		
Zimbabwe	31.35	9.71
Chile	23.49	1.01
Egypt	21.71	0.51
Turkey	15.56	5.31
Indonesia	14.68	0.59
South Africa — 1987	28.11	8.72
South Africa — 1992	30.15	11.46

Source: Dept. of Finance; and South African Reserve Bank

Table 2.11   Average effective company tax rates for South Africa, 1979 to 1992

Year	Effective co. rate	Year	Effective co. rate
1979	21.0	1986	27.2
1980	21.3	1987	25.8
1981	22.9	1988	26.4
1982	26.1	1989	24.9
1983	23.1	1990	33.6
1984	21.2	1991	30.1
1985	25.4	1992	28.4

Source: SARB

Table 2.12   Projected tax revenue from companies (including mines), 1993 to 2003

Year	Revenue (Rm)	Share total revenue (%)	Share GDP (%)
1993	12402	13.95	3.74
1994	12676	13.64	3.75
1995	13062	13.39	3.75
1996	13595	13.16	3.75
1997	14293	12.93	3.75
1998	15025	12.71	3.75
1999	15796	12.50	3.75
2000	16606	12.30	3.75
2001	17457	12.10	3.75
2002	18352	11.90	3.75
2003	19293	11.72	3.75

Source: MERG simulations

Table 2.13   Estimates of the effect of higher VAT rate on luxury goods, 1993 to 2003

Year	VAT revenue	Share total revenue	Share of GDP	VAT rate normal	VAT rate on luxury goods	Luxury goods/ VAT base	Growth in GDP	Full VAT base	GDP	Normal VAT base	Luxury VAT base
	Rm	%	%	%	%	%	%	Rm	Rm	Rm	Rm
1993	24858	27.96	7.5	14.00	14.00	12.00		177557	331342	161577	15980
1994	25353	27.27	7.5	14.00	14.00	12.00	2.00	181144	338036	164841	16303
1995	26125	26.79	7.5	14.00	14.00	12.00	3.00	186661	348330	169861	16800
1996	27191	26.32	7.5	14.00	14.00	12.00	4.00	194278	362546	176793	17485
1997	30491	27.59	8.0	15.00	14.00	12.00	5.00	204239	381134	185858	18382
1998	34057	28.81	8.5	15.00	22.00	12.00	5.00	214711	400675	195387	19324
1999	37910	30.00	9.0	15.00	30.00	12.00	5.00	225719	421218	198633	27086
2000	39853	29.51	9.0	15.00	30.00	12.00	5.00	237292	442815	208817	28475
2001	41897	29.03	9.0	15.00	30.00	12.00	5.00	249458	465518	219523	29935
2002	44045	28.57	9.0	15.00	30.00	12.00	5.00	262248	489386	230779	31470
2003	46303	28.13	9.0	15.00	30.00	12.00	5.00	275694	514477	242611	33083

Note: 'VAT Bases' are only proxies for effective bases.

Source: MERG simulations

CHAPTER 3
Macroeconomic balance, monetary policy and exchange rate policy

In Chapter One, the consequences of continuing with present policies were discussed. If the goals of economic growth, employment creation and redistribution are to be achieved, there will have to be significant changes in economic policy. The need for change however, does not reduce the commitment to a stable macroeconomic environment, which is an important precondition for sustained economic growth. The history of macroeconomic instability in some Latin American countries has demonstrated the self-defeating nature of ignoring macroeconomic balances, even though macroeconomic stability should not be seen as an end in itself, since stability does not guarantee growth. Macroeconomic policy should be growth-oriented, with priority given to variables such as employment creation and export promotion.

There are inevitably trade-offs that have to be made in macroeconomic management. For example, there could be a conflict between real exchange rate stability and the control of inflation, or between the reduction of inflation and employment creation. This chapter discusses some of the macroeconomic choices facing the economy and sets out proposals for monetary and exchange rate policy. In what follows, the expression 'exchange rate appreciation' will mean that the value of the local currency is rising.

The 1980s saw a decline in the growth rate, a decline in investment, rising levels of unemployment and falling productivity. Since the early 1990s, there have been increased macroeconomic pressures, some of which are likely to be intensified in the future. There has been a significant rise in the fiscal deficit, a rising debt/GDP ratio, negative real growth rates and continued balance of payments problems. On the other hand, the inflation rate has started to decline, due in part to tight monetary policies and the continuing recession. This decline in the inflation rate has had serious consequences for certain sections of the population.

There will be increased pressure to raise the level of government expenditure in order to achieve the goals of the democratic government. This will inevitably put further pressure on the budget deficit. As argued in more detail in Chapter Two, there are limits to which taxation can be increased. What is critical is the extent to which fiscal deficits can be sustained without having negative consequences for macroeconomic stability.

3.1 Saving — investment balances in South Africa

The trend in Gross Domestic Saving (GDS) and Investment (GDI) since 1981 can be seen in Table 3.1. The ratio of GDS to GDP has been declining gradually since 1985 and has now fallen to about 16 per cent, compared to an average of about 23 per cent during the 1980s. The ratio of gross domestic investment to GDP declined from 28 per cent in 1981 to 16 per cent in 1992.

This decline in gross domestic investment poses a dilemma, because economic growth requires an increase in investment. However, higher levels of investment inevitably result in higher levels of imports. If the foreign borrowing position of the economy remains unchanged, higher levels of domestic saving will be required, which in turn puts pressure on the government to reduce the budget deficit and increase saving.

The relationship between the fiscal deficit and saving is given by the saving – investment identity. The excess of government investment over saving must be financed by foreign saving and/or the excess of private sector saving relative to investment; i.e. the public deficit must be financed by the private sector excess of saving over investment and/or a current account deficit. Whether or not a fiscal deficit is sustainable will depend on the level of private saving, the desired level of private investment and the desired current account deficit.

Since the 1985 debt crisis, South Africa has had to repay foreign debt, which has resulted in lower savings than otherwise being available domestically to finance domestic private investment and the public sector deficit. The availability of foreign funds or reduced repayment commitments allows for larger public sector deficits to be covered when there are insufficient private sector saving surpluses in the domestic economy.

Restricted access to foreign funds and the need to repay previous debt requires adjustment either in the form of lower public sector deficits, higher private savings or lower investment spending. The adjustment typically takes place through cutbacks in investment. As can be seen, the decline in investment has exceeded the decline in saving, with negative consequences for both current and future growth. The implication is that, given the pressure for the fiscal deficit to increase and the need for domestic investment to rise, there will have to be a change in the foreign constraint.

Table 3.2 disaggregates the saving-investment identity to distinguish between public corporations, private corporations and the household sector (which includes unincorporated business enterprises). The general government sector includes central government, the provincial administrations and local authorities. In 1981 and 1982, capital inflows were a major source for financing the saving shortfalls of both general government and the public corporations. Since 1985, saving surpluses of the private corporate sector in particular have financed general government deficits and capital outflows, achieved through declines in domestic investment relative to saving. A significant feature is the emergence of a positive saving gap in the public corporations since 1987 due to the decline in investment by these corporations. If investment by the public corporations in social and economic infrastructure had been sustained in the 1980s, more growth would have been achieved, crowding in private investment in the process.

The above trends point to the problem of financing future growth and budget deficits if the economic structure remains unchanged. The saving surplus that was generated in the economy and the net accumulation of assets abroad has resulted in declining domestic investment. This surplus was used to repay foreign debt commitments. Any major resumption of investment expenditure will put pressure on the balance of payments (because of its impact on imports) and on the balance between domestic saving and domestic investment.

The 1985 experience shows how important access to foreign capital has been to the economy. After the debt standstill, there was no need on the part of the authorities to apply deflationary policies, as the required current account surpluses were achieved through the collapse of domestic investment induced by a loss of investor confidence. This position was maintained until 1988, when economic growth began to rise for the first time since 1984, and resulted in a 20 per cent increase in imports. This reduced the current account surplus to less than 1.5 per cent of GDP at a time when capital outflows were over 4 per cent of GDP. The policy response was a sharp increase in interest rates and the imposition of import surcharges. Since then, high interest rates and low levels of investment and growth have maintained the current account surplus at a level high enough to accommodate debt repayment.

The above illustrates the problem posed by balance of payments for the economy. On the one hand, current levels of employment and the success of any form of redistributive policies in the future depend on sustainable high rates of growth. On the other hand, the maintenance of current account surpluses has required low levels of investment. Expenditure reduction involves not only a decline in future growth, but also of current output (as income has to decline by the inverse of the marginal propensity to import times the required improvement in the trade balance). Growth declines to the extent that investment is a component of the decline in output.

The 1988 experience also illustrates how quickly a current account surplus can disappear. For future growth, the current balance of payments position is not sustainable. Thus the future stability of the balance of payments will depend on access to international borrowing and future export prospects. The simulations reported in Chapter One show that the employment creation initiative and a programme of investment in economic and social infrastructure are feasible from a fiscal perspective, but run the risk, after a few years, of running into the foreign exchange constraint.

A critical issue, therefore, is the level of access to foreign funds. This is discussed more fully in the section on exchange rate policy below. Because of low South African debt ratios, higher levels of borrowing are sustainable. If the outstanding debt in the net is rolled over, and if there is access to World Bank funds, capital inflows of between 1 and 2 per cent of GDP can be expected, compared with the current situation of outflows of between 2 and 3 per cent.

3.2 Sustainability of fiscal deficits

Table 3.3 shows how the fiscal deficit has been increasing in size over the past few years, having been at moderate levels before 1991.

The impact of these higher deficits has been to raise the debt/GDP ratio, which in turn has caused the interest burden on public debt to increase. It is difficult to assess whether or not a given size of the deficit is sustainable, since this depends partly on the state of the domestic capital markets and private sector investment. Similarly, the optimal debt/GDP ratio is difficult to assess. Calculations by the World Bank (see Kahn et al, 1992) show that a deficit of about 6 per cent of GDP is sustainable under conditions of moderate real growth. However, the sustainability criteria are defined in terms of maintaining a debt/GDP ratio of 35 per cent. The South African debt/GDP ratios are relatively low. Since there has been little problem financing the deficit through borrowing, there is some scope for maintaining higher levels of outstanding debt. In the European Monetary System, an upper limit of 60 per cent has been placed on the debt/GDP ratio. While this helps to put the South African ratio into perspective, the differences between European economies and ours prevent direct comparison.

The major issues have been the lack of investment, and the lack of access to foreign funds to finance imports, that the high levels of investment would have entailed. Private sector saving has not been the major constraint — in fact as shown earlier, corporate saving has been at a high level and has financed the gaps of the government and the foreign sector. The immediate problem is the lack of investment (both public sector and private) and not a lack of saving. Hence it is clear that poor macroeconomic management, including a failure to maintain appropriate levels of public sector investment, has been at the root of the recent macroeconomic imbalance.

It can be concluded from the above that fiscal deficits have not been excessive. However, any substantial increase in borrowing affects the real interest rate and reduces the sustainable deficit. In addition, any sustained increase in private sector investment which puts upward pressure on interest rates would affect the sustainable deficit.

In Chapter Two the effects of increasing real government spending were shown. Excluding interest payments, real government expenditure grows by 3.8 per cent per annum while the GDP growth rate is initially 2 per cent (rising to 5 per cent by 1997). On these assumptions and associated assumptions about tax growth, the fiscal deficit will at first grow and then decline. The resulting increase in public sector debt will initially cause interest payments to increase as a proportion of public spending, but the deficit will be sustainable and will subsequently decline.

3.3 Policy directions

3.3.1 Exchange rate policy

Exchange rate policy can be directed towards three objectives. These are balance of payments stability, internal stability (either the control of inflation or employment considerations) and microeconomic efficiency. The conduct of exchange rate policy in South Africa over the past two decades has reflected major shifts in objectives.

In line with the recommendations of the de Kock Commission, the foreign exchange markets were liberalised from 1979, with the introduction of a policy of variable dollar pegging, whereby the Reserve Bank announced the rate each day. In 1983 the Bank ceased this policy and the rate became market determined. Nevertheless, the Bank maintained its influence on the exchange rate not only indirectly through its overall macroeconomic policies, but also through direct intervention in the markets. Although the Reserve Bank claimed that it has intervened only to iron out excessive fluctuations of the exchange rate, exchange rate policy has been directed towards maintaining a constant real rand gold price. Some of the reasons for this include the political dominance of gold mining interests and the importance of gold export earnings, particularly in the light of the sanctions that were intensified against South Africa during this period. At the same time, the exchange rate was affected by real shocks, particularly changes in the gold price and the capital account shock of 1985 following the debt crisis. This can be seen in Figure 3.1.

The nominal effective exchange rate was allowed to appreciate during the gold price rises in the early eighties and to fall when the gold price declined. Between 1983 to 85, there was a precipitous decline in the nominal effective exchange rate, due in part to the gold price decline and the abolition of the financial rand mechanism.

During this period the real effective exchange rate was highly variable. The competitive position of South African manufacturing exporters was subject to the same high degree of variability. During this period, there was inconsistency between various macroeconomic objectives. During 1983 to 85, monetary policy was aimed at controlling inflation through high interest rates. Despite these historically high real interest rates, the exchange rate continued to depreciate.

Since 1988, the exchange rate has shown a greater degree of stability. This has been partly due to the fact that real shocks facing the economy became less severe, and that there was a change in direction of monetary policy, which was now more clearly directed towards the control of inflation through maintaining fairly stable but positive real interest rates. Monetary policy was at times dictated by balance of payments developments, although generally this was in the same direction as needed in terms of the monetary objectives. Thus, for example, there was an increase in domestic investment in 1988 which resulted in a large increase in imports, which put pressure on the current account. Given the need to maintain a current account surplus to meet debt repayment commitments, the Reserve Bank was forced to raise interest rates to protect the balance of payments, and thereby clamp down on the increase in expenditure.

Stabilising the real effective exchange rate within a target zone

MERG proposes that the appropriate policy for the Reserve Bank to adopt is a real effective exchange rate rule. This would imply a policy that is directed towards maintaining a fairly constant and predictable real effective exchange rate. The advantage of such a rule is that it would give the manufacturing sector some information concerning the likely evolution of relative prices, and avoids production decisions based on incorrect expectations and incentives to speculate. Although this type of approach is an important element in an export promotion strategy, it is relevant not only to exporters, but to import-substituting industries as well. A real exchange rate appreciation not only makes exports more expensive, but also reduces the price of imports relative to domestically produced goods.

A real exchange rate rule of the crawling peg variety is maintained by allowing the nominal effective exchange rate to depreciate in line with inflation differentials between South Africa and its major trading partners. Because such a rule limits the effectiveness of monetary policy, it is proposed that a target zone approach be adopted, whereby the real exchange rate is kept within a band around a central rate. This will give greater scope for monetary policy, as well as helping to adjust to transitory shocks.

The rule should not be of an inflexible nature. Change in economic circumstances requires an adjustment in the real exchange rate. Changes in the real exchange rate target should be consistent with changes in the fundamentals. Realignments would need to reflect only changes in these fundamental determinants in order not to undermine the policy itself. This is particularly the case when the shocks are of a negative nature.

One of the reasons that organisations such as the IMF are ambivalent about real rules, is that these may be consistent with undisciplined monetary and fiscal policies. It is argued that such policies leave a small open economy without a nominal anchor for domestic prices, and may lead to hyperinflation. Crawling pegs in Latin America have suffered from this problem of being consistent with hyperinflation, but it is argued that such occurrences stem from the undisciplined nature of macroeconomic policies, particularly the financing of excessive public sector deficits through money creation. To use the exchange rate as a nominal anchor will not help if monetary and fiscal policies remain expansionary, as evidenced by the massive real appreciation in Chile during the early 1980s. The Chilean experience illustrates that if the constraints are not binding, the economy will suffer, whatever the nature of the exchange rate regime. Thus exchange rate policy should influence the structure of the entire economy and should promote the objectives of economic reconstruction and macroeconomic stability. Given the extremely high levels of unemployment prevailing in the economy, an exchange rate that results in a decline in unemployment and an acceptable increase in nontraditional exports should be aimed for.

A real exchange rate rule has to be consistent with other macroeconomic policies. If there is a perceived need for a real depreciation of the real exchange rate, this will require a tightening of fiscal policies in order to prevent inflationary pressures that would offset the real depreciation.

The policy also affects the degree to which monetary policy can be directed to the control of monetary aggregates. For example, if there is downward pressure on the exchange rate, the appropriate monetary policy response would be to raise interest rates, which would curb inflationary tendencies. However, there could be situations when the economy requires a lower interest rate, particularly if it is in a recessionary phase. Upward pressure on the real exchange rate requires an increase in the money supply, or lower interest rates, which could be inflationary.

Alternatively there could be sterilised intervention which would require the Reserve Bank to engage in open market purchases when there is downward pressure on the exchange rate, and sales when the pressure is in the opposite direction. There are of course limits to sterilisation, particularly in the case where the pressure is in a downward direction, since international reserves are finite. A real devaluation or revaluation could also be considered. This is consistent with the rule that there should be a realignment of the target real exchange rate if the pressures are of an enduring nature. Such realignment is particularly necessary in cases of negative shocks. A change in fiscal policy could also be envisaged. The important principle is to avoid any major sacrifice of either competitiveness or macroeconomic stability.

A real exchange rate policy may not be favourable to the gold mining industry. The recent move towards more stable real exchange rates has resulted in a lower real rand gold price. Clearly the gold mining industry is better off with a real rule than a constant nominal rule, but it will not be afforded the same degree of protection as under the previous regime. As the industry is still an important part of the South African economy, it is important that this sector is not neglected.

One possibility would be to use a domestic commodity price stabilisation scheme, such as is used in Malaysia. Such a scheme should be separated from general government revenue, and possibly held offshore. Although the current tax system does tend to operate in a similar fashion, by increasing taxation during times of high profitability and reducing it when profitability is falling, this tends to move procyclically with the state of the economy and the budget. When the gold price is high, tax revenues increase at a time when the economy is in a relatively healthy position. The converse is true with low gold prices. (This assumes that there is a positive relationship between the economy and the dollar gold prices.) A price stabilisation scheme would have a neutral effect on the budget. The other advantage of this scheme is that it could to some extent reduce the impact of gold price fluctuations on the exchange rate, particularly during phases of increased gold prices.

Controls on capital movements

At present the exchange control environment is one which restricts all movements of resident capital and subjects certain categories of nonresident flows to the financial rand mechanism. The financial rand mechanism insulates the capital account from the exchange rate effects of non-resident sales and purchases of South African assets.

The de Kock Commission proposed a liberalisation of exchange control regulations, calling for the abolition of the financial rand mechanism and the gradual relaxation of exchange controls on residents. The financial rand was abolished in 1983 but reimposed again in 1985 after the debt crisis. The current view as expressed in the

Normative Economic Model (NEM) is to phase out controls 'in due course …from a position of strength'.

This implies that:

- The gold and foreign exchange reserves will first be built up to adequate levels;

- Domestic financial stability, including low inflation, will have to be attained and consolidated;

- The interim debt arrangements will have to be replaced by normal arrangements;

- The flexibility of the South African foreign exchange market will have to be developed by allowing wider ownership of foreign exchange in the hands of accredited domestic financial institutions and corporations.

There is no timetable given for this process. It is intimated that progress has been made with the first two provisions. No indication is given as to the sequencing of reforms. The literature indicates that economies in the process of undertaking liberalising reforms should liberalise the capital account last. It is widely believed that the failures of capital account liberalisations in Latin America in the early 1980s arose because the sequencing of reforms was incorrect, i.e. the capital accounts were liberalised before current account and financial sector reforms. Capital account liberalisations should be undertaken only once the necessary domestic adjustments have been made following trade reforms.

The MERG approach is to be extremely cautious with moves towards capital account liberalisation. However, the criteria set by the NEM are insufficient to guarantee a desirable orderly transition to free capital movements. The lifting of exchange controls should be seen against a background of years of tight controls, a high degree of political instability and economic instability, and the need for domestic saving to finance a large volume of new investment in the industrial, agricultural and infrastructural sectors.

The fact that exchange controls have been a feature of the financial system for so long means that investment decisions have been dictated by this fact. This is particularly true of insurance companies and pension funds. A sudden lifting of exchange controls would result in major portfolio reallocations, even if there was stability in the economic and political sphere. It could also have a major impact on the domestic capital markets. The effect on interest rates could be severe.

The fact that a period of political and economic uncertainty is inevitable, means that capital flight will take place should controls be lifted. The lifting of such controls could result in increased volatility in exchange rates and interest rates.

There will be a need to finance new fixed investment and the increased provision of social and economic infrastructure through both domestic and foreign saving. The bulk of this requirement will have to be borne by domestic saving. (The issue of foreign saving is discussed below.) Because of this pressing need, all domestic saving should be applied domestically and not abroad. It is recognised that capital kept inside the country may not be applied to investment. However, the aim is to encourage domestic investment through creating a stable political and economic climate.

The latter can be achieved through disciplined macroeconomic policies and feasible growth strategies.

There is a need to broaden and increase the efficiency of the foreign exchange market. There should not be a regressive step towards a system of exchange control allocation. An efficient foreign exchange market supports the needs of foreign trade, and priority should be given to such a market.

Exchange controls are alleged to be a deterrent to foreign investment, but it is the nature of the controls, rather than their existence, that deters foreign investment. The focus of controls will continue to be on domestic residents. Controls that are directed towards prohibiting profit remittances will inevitably act as a deterrent to foreign investment, as has been the Zimbabwean experience.

Controls on foreign investors will not be tightened in any way, nor will restrictions will be placed on profit remittances. Means will be sought to encourage foreign investment by streamlining the bureaucratic procedures involved. The encouragement of foreign direct investment results in inflows of long term capital which directly affects domestic production. The removal of the threat of controls on foreign investment, coupled with a commitment to a stable real exchange rate, will enhance the attractiveness of South Africa as a site for investment (although these are by no means the only criteria for investment).

Controls should not be used to maintain overvalued exchange rates. There is, however, a need for exchange rates to reflect the underlying competitiveness and productivity of the economy. They should not be determined by volatile capital flows.

Foreign capital inflows

There has been much speculation as to how much foreign capital South Africa might expect to receive in the future. Although it is difficult to judge what the extent of capital inflows might be, certain issues should be raised.

The impact of financial sanctions on the South African economy has been severe. Macroeconomic mismanagement prior to 1985 exacerbated the effects of financial sanctions. Since 1985, the capital account has placed a constraint on growth in the economy. What growth could have been achieved over this period had to be stifled because of the need to maintain a current account surplus in order to be able to meet foreign debt commitments. It has been estimated by various analysts that the economy could not sustain a real growth rate greater than about 1 per cent because of this lack of access to finance.

With a democratic government in place the situation is likely to ease, although finance will not be available to the degree that it was during the 1970s. In part, this is because the nature of foreign lending has changed. South Africa will need to become more reliant on foreign bond issues. There will, however, be some easing of the current situation. The advent of a democratic government could reduce the reluctance of banks to lend to South Africa, and to roll over existing credits.

South Africa has a relatively low debt ratio. Foreign debt totalled R52.8 billion ($17.3 billion) at the end of 1992, compared to R52.5 billion ($20.6 billion) when the standstill was imposed in August 1985. Behind this relatively small drop was a more significant fall in economic measures of the debt burden: the ratio of external debt to GDP fell from 43 per cent in 1985 to 15 per cent in 1992, and the ratio of interest payments to total export earnings fell from 10.8 per cent to 6.7 per cent over the same period. Foreign debt to export earnings fell from 128 per cent in 1985 to 61 per cent in 1992 whilst interest and dividend payments to total export earnings fell from 14.6 per cent to 10.7 per cent.

These are not the only criteria applied by the banks. South Africa continues to face repayment obligations in its existing debt, both within the standstill and outside of it. Moreover, the total amount raised in 1991 was, as a share of GDP, less than one-fifth as much as the average amount raised in the early 1970s and early 1980s. Any significant increase in the amount raised will depend on three factors: a continuation of the current worldwide trend of increased investor interest in highyielding assets from emerging market countries, a further relaxation of current legal and political restrictions on lending to South Africa, and, most important of all, a sustained reduction in the level of political and economic uncertainty in South Africa.

Inflows from the World Bank could also be forthcoming together with amounts from other bilateral and multilateral agencies. IMF loans which are a necessary condition for increased private bank lending may also become available in the near future.

The desirability of foreign capital, and the terms under which foreign loans are made available, are another matter. When the issue of exchange controls is considered, reliance must be placed on domestic resources. This is not to say that these resources should not be supplemented by foreign capital. However, the current situation places a constraint on growth. Even if existing commitments are rolled over, this could have a significant impact on the balance of payments, as it could turn the current account around by about 4 per cent of GDP i.e. instead of having to maintain a current account surplus of about 3 per cent of GDP a deficit of between 0 and 1 per cent could be sustained.

Over the next few years, commitments which came about as a result of the debt rescheduling agreements, will be falling due. In terms of these agreements, one of the exit clauses for affected debt, was that creditors could convert this debt into ten-year debt outside the net. To avoid the impact of possible debt build-up on the balance of payments, there will be a need to roll over this debt when it matures, or a need to negotiate new loans.

Even if access to foreign borrowing were to be eased, there are inherent dangers in excessive borrowing. Although foreign capital is required for growth, such borrowing must be used productively in order to ensure the ability to repay in the future. The international debt crisis has shown that borrowing used to finance excessive consumption expenditure will lead to a debt crisis. Even if foreign borrowing is used to finance investment it carries risks. If it finances inefficient investment, the problem is obvious, but there are many other types of investment that can generate debt problems. If the rate of return on the investment is positive and greater than the interest cost of the debt, it will be difficult to service the foreign debt unless the returns on the investment increase foreign exchange revenue through improving exports. If the debt is government debt, and the return on the investment does not give rise to tax receipts which are greater than the interest cost, debt servicing problems will arise. For example, government borrowing from abroad to build low-income housing will generate social and economic benefits, but since they do not directly take the form of foreign exchange revenues, and are not directly or fully captured by tax receipts, they will not facilitate the servicing of the debt. Problems would arise even if real interest rates were to remain constant. As the international debt crisis showed, rising real interest rates in creditor countries have had destabilising impacts on debtor countries whose loans were subject to floating rates. Foreign borrowing can be an expensive option and the extent of, and changes in debt obligations, can limit the options of borrowing countries.

The objective would be to try to limit the degree of reliance on direct borrowing. Careful monitoring will be required to ensure that there is not an uncontrolled buildup of debt, particularly of short-term maturity in order to ensure that there is not a bunching of maturities. The uncontrolled accumulation of short-term debt in the early 1980s has made a major contribution to the severity of the debt crisis. The Reserve Bank appeared to have had no idea of the extent of foreign debt, or the nature of the maturity structure.

Much has been said in political and economic debates about the problems of reliance on World Bank and IMF loans. South Africa should bargain with these institutions from a position of strength and negotiate terms which support a strategy of development. The importance of both parliamentary and wider public awareness and participation in this process of bargaining with the international financial institutions, cannot be overemphasized.

The other form of foreign capital which is advantageous, is direct foreign investment. Although these inflows should be encouraged, they should be seen as desirable not for narrow balance of payments purposes, but rather for the transfers of technology, opportunities to develop new markets, and the real investment growth that they may facilitate.

Easier access to foreign borrowing will also allow for a more rational operation of the forward market. At present the Reserve Bank continues to offer favourable forward cover rates to traders, in order to encourage borrowing abroad for trade financing purposes. The results of such an imprudent policy have been enormous forward cover losses which have to be met by the account of the Treasury. At present the debt of the Treasury to the Reserve Bank in respect of such losses is over R8 billion.

There is a further danger in excessive borrowing related to the effect on the real exchange rate. Latin American evidence has shown that capital flows have become more important determinants of the real exchange rate than flows of goods and services, and that capital inflows have been associated with a marked appreciation of real exchange rates in many Latin American countries. Attempts to avoid currency appreciation have caused problems for monetary and fiscal policy, as the desire to attenuate the degree of real exchange rate appreciation leads to intervention by central banks to purchase the inflow of foreign currency. To avoid the domestic monetisation of these purchases, the authorities are forced to conduct sterilising open market operations, which perpetuate the high interest rate differentials and give rise to increased fiscal burdens. While capital inflows are to be preferred to the alternative of outflows, excessive inflows can become a source of concern because appreciation erodes the competitiveness of the export sector. It may also not be possible to sustain such inflows.

3.3.2   *Monetary policy*

The central issues for monetary policy concern the role of interest rates in the economy and the control of inflation. Some of these issues are also discussed in Chapter Eight.

The role of interest rates

This section will not deal with problems of access to finance. However, the cost of finance (interest rate policy) is important for monetary policy.

The Reserve Bank influences interest rates through its control of the bank rate (rediscount rate) which is the rate at which the Bank provides accommodation to the banking sector. Banks are required to hold minimum levels of cash reserves in the form of vault cash and as balances on their reserve accounts at the Reserve Bank. If the banks find themselves short of reserves, they are able to borrow from the Reserve Bank by rediscounting acceptable shortterm assets at the discount window. The value of the indebtedness of the banking system to the Bank is the money market shortage or accommodation. If banks need to offset a loss of reserves, they will borrow from the Reserve Bank, thereby increasing the money market shortage.

By maintaining the shortage at a positive level (i.e. by keeping the banks indebted to it) the Reserve Bank is able to determine short-term interest rates, as accommodation is always available at a cost chosen by the Bank. The Reserve Bank maintains a positive money market shortage through open market operations, by changing the amount of treasury bills offered at its weekly tender, and by varying minimum cash balance requirements. If the money market shortage were reduced to zero, the relevant rate would be the rate at which the Bank was prepared to sell paper to create a shortage. Either way it is the Bank that determines the rates.

Because accommodation is extended automatically and unconditionally, money market rates for a given rediscountable instrument will approximate the rediscount rate of the Reserve Bank. Because longterm rates are an approximate average of expected future shortterm rates, longterm rates will also be affected by the change in shortterm rates.

The Bank affects the economy through its influence on interest rates, which in turn affect the money supply. If the bank rate is reduced, commercial bank rates will fall, resulting in increased demands for credit. This causes an increase in bank deposits and larger required reserves, which are obtained through accommodation. The lower interest rates cause the money supply to rise because of increased demands for bank credit, which are then accommodated. The Reserve Bank influence on the economy comes directly through its choice of interest rate, which in turn affects the general level of spending in the economy.

Reserve Bank policy during the 1970s generally aimed at keeping nominal interest rates low, which resulted in negative real interest rates. During the 1980s, Reserve Bank interest rate policy was subject to wide swings following changing objectives. In 1980, for example, Bank Rate was 7 per cent and the inflation rate was 14 per cent (a negative real rate of 7 per cent). In 1983, following the de Kock Commission report, the Bank changed its stated objective to the control of inflation and encouraged a substantial rise in interest rates, which exacerbated the recession.

By January 1985 the prime overdraft rate was 25 per cent which implied a real interest rate to prime borrowers of 13 per cent. Because of the impact of these high rates on the real economy, this policy was reversed, and by the end of 1986 prime had fallen to 12 per cent. Interest rates remained low and negative in real terms, until the increase in domestic investment in late 1987 started putting pressure on the current account of the balance of payments. Then the stated objective of interest rate policy switched to balance of payments concerns. Although during 1990, the large current account surpluses and the loosening of the pressure on the capital account eased the balance of payments constraint, the stated current interest rate policy is now again directed at further reducing the rate of inflation.

The current policy of the Reserve Bank is to control the money supply with the interest rate as the main instrument, and with the objective of maintaining the external and internal value of the rand. As noted earlier, however, there are conflicts between maintaining the real value of the rand and the desire to maintain a constant nominal exchange rate for antiinflationary purposes. At times, there has been direct intervention in the market to prevent a real exchange rate appreciation despite the impact on the money supply.

Monetary policy since 1989 has been too singlemindedly focused on inflation. Although there have been times when policy was constrained by balance of payments considerations, monetary policy has been excessively tight in the face of a severe recession and extremely high rates of unemployment. Under such circumstances, high interest rates merely exacerbate a recession, particularly in the face of inflation inertia. Monetary policy should show some sensitivity to the state of the real economy. Lowering interest rates in a recession is unlikely to cause an acceleration in the inflation rate, but could help in getting the economy out of the recession. This does not imply that the economy should be stimulated through excessively low interest rates; the MERG model calls for a positive long-term interest rate of 2 per cent.

Control of inflation

The inflation rate in South Africa during the 1980s was moderate. As can be seen from Table 3.4, for most of the period, the inflation rate hovered around the 15 per cent level. A major factor contributing to the recent inflation rate has been the extremely high rises in food prices.

The table shows that the CPI and PPI have diverged over the past two years. This has raised the expectation that consumer prices would fall. Whilst it is not clear why this divergence has come about, it does suggest some structural inertia in the retail sector. What is also of interest is the role of imported prices, which have a weighting of 19.5 per cent in the PPI. These figures show the effect of the changing exchange rate regime. The precipitous decline in the value of the rand in 1984 to 86 had a substantial impact on the PPI while the more stable nominal exchange rate in recent years has had a moderating influence.

Recently, there has been a significant decline in the inflation rate from the 15 per cent level of the 1980s, and for the first three months of 1993, it remained below 10 per cent. While it is one thing to bring down inflation during a recession, it is another to maintain a low level of inflation during an upswing. It would make no sense to stifle an upswing by raising interest rates simply to prevent the inflation rate from rising.

This raises the question of whether or not antiinflation policy is in conflict with growth and employment objectives. There are many examples of countries with moderate inflation that have experienced high growth, and many examples also of countries with low inflation that have experienced low growth. Low inflation is not a prerequisite for growth. While lower inflation is to be preferred to higher inflation, the costs of reducing moderate inflation to low inflation must be taken into account. This must be seen in the light of the fact that despite tight monetary policies since 1988, inflation has taken a long time to respond. The major problem with reducing moderate inflation is the impact it has on unemployment.

MERG does not recommend that attempts to control inflation should not be given priority. The biggest problem with moderate inflation is that it could easily lead to hyperinflation, if not kept in check. Although there must be a commitment to maintaining as low an inflation rate as possible, care must be taken not to do this at the expense of production and employment.

Whether or not the current decline in inflation can be sustained through an upswing will depend to a large extent on the causes of inflation. More research has yet to be done on this, but there have been a series of shocks that have helped to maintain the rate at the levels that prevailed until recently. These included oil price shocks; the precipitous depreciation of the rand during 1983 to 85, coupled with the historically high interest rates over that period which caused mortgage rates to rise; the impact of the drought on food prices; and the impact of the introduction of VAT, and the subsequent increase in the rate. Some of these shocks are of a one-off nature and pass through the index after a year.

No policy to control inflation can be successful if increased wage rates are singled out as the cause of inflation. Since inflation is a process involving the pricing power of firms, foreign trade prices, interest rates and asset prices and workers should not be forced to bear the brunt of reducing inflation.

3.4 Conclusion

Monetary policy and exchange rate policy have important roles in the transformation of the economy. The National Party government has used them to depress the economy and finance both a rising government deficit on current account, and a flow of capital abroad. The resulting low investment in productive capacity has weakened the economic base. The MERG policy is designed to ensure that while public and private investment increases, macroeconomic balance is maintained by reducing interest rates while keeping them at a positive real level, and by maintaining the real effective exchange rate stable within a target zone. The exchange rate target is designed to achieve stability on the current account of the balance of payments. For the capital account, MERG proposes continuation of exchange controls on residents, and an increase in foreign capital inflows, including a limited expansion of foreign credit.

Macroeconomic policies affect different people and different groups in different ways. In recent years, high interest rates have affected small businesses and small farmers directly and disproportionately. Increases in the real exchange rate have hurt workers in export industries, while sharp devaluatiqns have severely increased the input costs of some industries and the living costs of some people. The macro economic policy targets MERG proposes should be implemented with a full examination of their implications for different groups, and as part of a development strategy which is transparent and democratically evaluated.

Δ

Table 3.1   Gross domestic saving and investment as a percentage of GDP, 1981 to 1992

Year	GDS	GDI	Year	GDS	GDI
1981	27.2	27.8	1987	23.4	19.1
1982	20.8	27.9	1988	23.2	19.9
1983	25.3	26.8	1989	22.7	20.8
1984	22.5	24.4	1990	21.1	20.0
1985	24.5	23.3	1991	18.2	18.0
1986	23.5	20.2	1992	16.3	15.9

Source: Derived from SA Reserve Bank Quarterly Bulletins

Table 3.2   Saving–investment gaps as a percentage of GDP, 1981 to 1991

Year	General govt (S-I)	Public corps (S-I)	Private corps (S-I)	Households (S-I)	Foreign savings
1981	-0.49	-7.80	3.69	-0.92	5.20
1982	-1.81	-6.10	3.69	0.60	3.62
1983	-3.75	-4.07	5.46	2.05	0.31
1984	-5.41	-1.90	4.80	1.20	1.31
1985	-3.77	-2.94	8.62	2.90	-4.81
1986	4.79	-1.10	8.78	2.18	-5.07
1987	-5.39	0.88	4.96	3.30	-3.75
1988	-3.22	0.86	2.25	1.58	-1.47
1989	-3.57	0.91	2.74	1.26	-1.34
1990	-1.43	0.42	2.40	0.80	-2.19
1991	-5.02	0.70	4.97	1.84	-2.49

Source: Derived from SA Reserve Bank Quarterly Bulletins

Table 3.3   Central government deficits and debt as a percentage of GDP, 1981/2 to 1993/4

Year	Deficit	Debt	Year	Deficit	Debt
1981/2	2.8	30.6	1988/9	4.0	33.9
1982/3	2.5	33.1	1989/90	1.9	34.9
1983/4	3.5	33.5	1990/1	2.8	34.8
1984/5	3.5	33.5	1991/2	4.3	38.6
1985/6	2.9	33.0	1992/3	8.6	41.2
1986/7	4.3	33.4	1993/4 (est)	6.8	
1987/8	5.8	33.7			

Source: Statistical/Economic Review, various issues and SA Reserve Bank Quarterly Bulletins

Figure 3.1: Real and nominal effective rand exchange rates (1979 = 100)

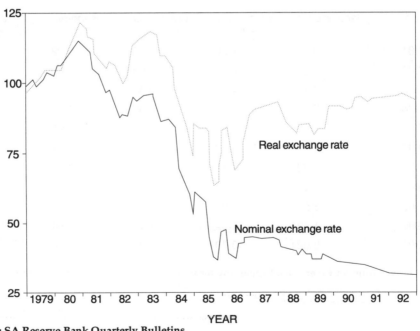

Source: SA Reserve Bank Quarterly Bulletins

C H A P T E R   4

Social and physical infrastructure

·

This chapter is divided into four sections, covering housing, schooling, basic health services and electrification. A summary of the major proposals for expenditure and policy reforms in these areas is provided at the end of each of these sections. The issues discussed are complex, and are not confined to macroeconomic questions of how much to spend on housing, schooling etc., and how to finance this spending. Each section addresses a series of microeconomic questions concerning the capacity to deliver rapid and appropriate improvements in social and physical infrastructure.

4.1 Housing

4.1.1   The poverty of housing

The South African housing system is dominated by the physical and socioeconomic structures inherited from the past. Separate development, influx control and forced removals have bestowed a particular spatial order on both the nature of, and access to, housing. Who has housing, where, at what cost and of what quality, with what security of tenure, and with what communal amenities — these are all marked by the racial divisions characteristic of South African society. Nor is it simply that there are huge inequalities in provision between racial groups, with a massive backlog of homeless, variously estimated to lie between 1.3 and three million units. There is an equivalent inequality and backlog in infrastructural provision. The apartheid city is characterised by a low-density urban sprawl segregated, often at a long distance, from high-density townships. Migrant workers' hostels are as much a product of apartheid as squatter camps and informal settlements. And the whole range of activities associated with housing, from design and construction, to the availability of finance, reflect and reproduce the skewed patterns of housing provision.

Inner city sprawl has been intensified by policies to deconcentrate and decentral-ise industry, together with the one-house-on-a-plot design that has been favoured by white housing provision. It has also led to inefficiencies in infrastructural provision, with the need for public services to function over wide areas, making basic amenities such as water, electricity, rubbish collection and communal facilities hard to provide effectively, and in increasing travelling time for goods, services and workers. Outside white areas, the absence of amenities is often most striking and, where they are available, orientation is more towards consumption than production facilities, thereby undermining the scope for informal, let alone formal, employment prospects. Constructed as residential dormitories to serve white employers from a distance, black townships have been deprived of the wherewithal to serve their own direct household needs, let alone provide the commercial facilities and infrastructure that are vital to economic sustainability. Such considerations apply even more so to the various forms of informal housing.

It is generally recognised that housing plays an important role in the economy. It is a significant sector itself in generating income and employment, and can act as a stimulus to growth in kick-start scenarios — with construction generating demand across sectors with high levels of employment-intensity, with limited demands on the balance of payments and with the potential, in South Africa, to be non-inflationary, since there is ample excess capacity.

Housing is also integrated into the economy in other ways, over and above simple multiplier effects. The availability of housing interacts with the functioning of the labour market, the money market and saving rates. Access to jobs and the ease of travel to and from them is dependent on the availability, cost and mobility within the labour market. Mortgage finance plays a considerable role in mobilising and applying savings, which may be encouraged or not, according to the state of the housing market. Housing provision is also heavily implicated in political processes, especially in South Africa where the control of, and conflict within, communities often focuses on housing issues, not least in rent boycotts, service charges and access to land.

Housing provision has a number of features which, taken together, appear to set it apart from other goods and services. The housing market accommodates both a stock of old and a flow of new dwellings. There is a variety of forms of tenure, whether rented or owned, and these are variously financed and subsidised. The housing market tends to be particularly susceptible and sensitive to cyclical movement, but is also subject to speculative activity — whether in buying and selling by the individual, or in developing or financing sites by the finance house or builder. Housing is tied to the availability of land in specific locations. Public intervention is inevitable although the extent and form has varied considerably.

Over the past few years, housing policy has shifted considerably, not least in response to the formal commitment to dismantle apartheid. As a consequence, it has been acknowledged that increased responsibility for housing provision is necessary. The de Loor Report (1992) recommends that state spending on housing should increase to R3.5 billion by 1995 (or 5 per cent of GDP) from a level of R1.6 billion (or 2.1 per cent of GDP) in 1990/91. This is in part a response to World Bank observations that, across different countries, housing investment typically accounts for 2 to 8 per cent of GNP, and the flow of housing services for a further 5 to 10 per cent.

Whatever level of expenditure South Africa achieves relative to these norms, the current delivery system excludes the vast majority from the possibility of formal housing altogether. For, although the de Loor report perceives a need for 328 000 new units per year over the next decade to meet the housing backlog and formation of new households, it finds that even 200 000 new houses per year would prove unaffordable given the funding available. The issue is seen as one in which there is a trade-off between the cost of housing subsidies, the number of houses that can be built, their quality, and the number of households that are able to afford subsidised housing. With a higher subsidy, more housing is affordable or of higher quality, but fewer houses can be covered, or larger government expenditure is involved.

Not only is there a backlog in housing for blacks but, where they are housed, the accommodation is very much worse than for whites. This is illustrated in Table 4.1 which provides information on living space per person in the PWV area. Conditions are particularly poor in rural areas where 42 per cent of housing does not on average provide adequate health protection, and 50 per cent of the rural population are without sufficient sleeping space (see Table 4.2).

As Planact (1993) observes, the de Loor Report suffers from a number of deficiencies. Firstly, its approach is characterised by a dualism in which provision for upper-income (white) households is seen as unproblematic and independent of the lower-income (black) housing problem. Because the former's housing is seen as largely satisfactory, policy need only be directed at the latter. However, the two housing systems are not independent of one another. By international comparison, standards of delivery are highly variable relative to expenditure, and are variable within South Africa itself, because of differential access to land and finance, for example. Although simplistic arguments concerning crowding out should not be too readily employed, the existence of a continuum of housing markets implies that they are functionally related to one another. In short, government thinking continues to be determined by racial dichotomies because it fails to address the housing system as a whole. By adopting a piecemeal approach of targeting the provision of numbers of houses through numbers of housing sites and serviced stands, it separates out the hard-to-house as if they are to be accommodated independently of any connection to the easy-to-house, and as if they did indeed belong to separate (building) developments.

Whilst the separating out and targeting of the hard-to-house is a common, if unsatisfactory, approach to housing policy across a number of countries, current government thinking continues to reflect past concerns, even though it seeks a shift in policy. Its preoccupation with creating subsidised owner-occupation, with limited attention to alternative forms of tenure, is consistent with the earlier goal of stabilising black residence outside the homelands subject to availability of permanent employment. As such, it is oblivious to the continuing needs of a large migrant labour force which seeks satisfactory rented accommodation. Similarly, in providing for housing, the specific needs of rural communities and the role to be played by informal housing are scarcely addressed, despite their weight in numbers. Significantly, these are often the conditions in which women are disproportionately represented as head of households.

Squatters are not necessarily illegal and informal housing is not always cheap despite its low standards and impermanence. A study of the Durban area found that 35 per cent of squatters rented land from a landlord, a further 24 per cent had access to some form of shack, 20 per cent were allocated tribal land, and 12 per cent had bought their land. Land invasions, however, are more common and are becoming more frequent elsewhere. Squatters and informal tenants are often highly exploited in terms of the charges they face, whether it be for rent as such or for water, etc. Some informal tenants in the Durban area are reported to be paying R50 per month for water. Sapire (1992) finds that inhabitants of informal housing in the PWV area are not necessarily recent arrivals, 60 per cent having been born there and 30 per cent without dependants outside of the area. There is, however, substantial movement from one site to another and from one form of accommodation to another. In general, inhabitants of informal housing are poorer, with higher unemployment and lower education levels. Table 4.3 provides some indication of the distribution of informal housing in the major urban areas of South Africa.

Even where the backlog in housing is currently being addressed, little attempt is made to meet the needs of households over and above the accommodation provided; also overlooked is the wider economic and social role to be played by housing in economic and social reconstruction. Housing by itself is of limited worth in the absence of jobs, infrastructure and communal facilities. It must respond to the specific needs of the homeless or informally housed, whether in developing new sites, which must be properly serviced with access to a means of livelihood, or in upgrading existing sites, whose location may or may not be motivated by the availability of work (depending on whether controls have been exercised over access to more convenient sites).

Government policies have not been able to deliver housing as demonstrated in Tables 4.4 and 4.5, which reveal both the failure to supply and the skewness of supply to the upper end of the market.

The recent initiative to remedy this situation through the IDT has not proved successful, not least because the process of approving sites can take five times as long as it does to build upon them. The IDT intended from March 1991 to subsidise 100 000 first-time buyers by R7 500 each to provide for site and service. Within a year, less than 5 000 stands had been completed. After eighteen months, 109 842 stands had been approved, 81 842 in greenfield sites, but only 45 per cent of schemes had completed servicing and 20 per cent completed altogether.

Secondly, and not just in government circles, policy focus has primarily been upon funding and, in particular, upon the necessary level and form of subsidy required to support the end-user. This focus has been at the expense of adequate consideration of a range of crucial factors determining the ultimate delivery of housing. As Planact puts it:

> *In contrast to the delivery of housing products, the report explicitly constructs a finance delivery system which is a structured relationship between the state, the commercial banking sector, pension funds and grassroots community structures.*

To put it bluntly, throwing money at, or making finance available to, the housing sector, does not guarantee that the impact will trickle down into the provision of the appropriate housing. Walker (1993) notes that the housing strategy of the Urban Foundation fails to recognise the different motives and capabilities of those engaged in the delivery of housing. It presumes a common cost structure across the sector, depends upon a single policy instrument (subsidy), fails to address the problems of urban sprawl and the restructuring of apartheid cities, and only allows for minimal community participation by the recipients of a housing scheme.

What is also often notably absent is any strategy for housing in terms of urbanisation and levels of density, hardly surprising in view of the way in which the housing system is not considered as a whole. The National Housing Forum (1993, p. 2) summarises the situation as follows:

> *Except for the White Paper on Urbanisation adopted in 1986, the government has not devised a new urbanisation policy that takes into account the reforms that have taken place since de Klerk came into power. Despite the much publicised release of the de Loor Report ... the government has not adopted it as an official policy. This lack of policy is an important constraining factor in the overall delivery of land. These constraints happen in the following way:*
>
> - *public authorities experience great difficulty in shifting away from old apartheid policies in the absence of new ones;*
>
> - *there is duplication of functions with regard to planning by various racially created government institutions resulting in delays, confusion and increased costs;*
>
> - *there is no direct accountability by the government for meeting the housing backlogs and other requirements such as land delivery because of the absence of a single ministry of housing or urbanisation with one Minister accountable to Parliament;*
>
> - *there is inconsistency of policy positions across government departments and at different tiers of government;*
>
> - *there are no clearly defined roles for the public, private and community-based sectors, and this reduces the effectiveness of each to deliver to it full capacity.*

Thus, current policies do very little to enable, let alone facilitate, housing delivery except in the area of finance, where there is a proliferation of agencies with limited funds and powers at their disposal. The National Housing Forum (1992b, p. 2) observes:

> *What emerges is that the problem is not so much the availability of resources as the availability of mechanisms to channel funds into development of a viable, and therefore sustainable, basis.*

Moreover, the components of housing delivery are taken to be more or less automatic, subject only to funding. This is despite the highly cartelized building supplies industry, for example. Nor is the capacity to deliver the separate components of housing properly examined, from land availability through to final finishing. Speculative purchase or retention of land is overlooked, for example, even though 'the Black Communities Development Act had the effect of allowing black people greater mobility, and speculators capitalised accordingly by bidding up the price of land where they anticipated that location would take place', National Housing Forum

(1993, p. 6). There are those who will seek to profit from the increased availability of funds directed at housing, and they will not necessarily do so by contributing to the provision of housing. Consequently, public provision of finance and subsidies alone will not suffice. It may even worsen the situation by raising costs in some locations by even more than the subsidies as attempts are made to appropriate development gains, leading to delays in provision.

> *Instead of funding home-builder activities, the IDT's scheme had created 'islands of privilege' for certain developers. Where IDT's subsidies applied to a piece of land adjoining another piece of land for which there was no subsidy, the owners of the latter found it impossible to sell sites because of unequal access to the subsidy scheme (SAIRR 1993, pp. 224-5, attributed to Simon Brand).*

In short, the subsidy does not necessarily accrue in the form of a cheaper house, and it can lead to the withholding of land until a subsidy can be obtained.

In addition, apart from the economic conditions under which housing is delivered, the situation in South Africa is such that the legitimacy of provision is of considerable importance in terms of community participation in the formulation, implementation and monitoring of a housing programme. Whilst those who are to gain by the housing programme cannot reasonably be allowed to determine themselves the levels and forms of support without reference to broader issues and constituencies, collective forms of tenure (such as housing associations) and public housing for rental cannot reasonably be precluded at the outset through an ideological commitment to owner-occupation. Indeed, the housing programme should be driven by the imperatives of supply, given that the backlog in provision is the major target, rather than preference for particular forms of tenure. The failure to promote a variety of forms of tenure is an imposition on black households of what is perceived to be the ideal form of white housing tenure.

Each of the various issues involved in housing delivery cannot be addressed in detail. That they have been neglected by the current government, even as it seeks to shift its policy orientation, is a consequence of two crucial aspects of its vision for housing. It is wedded to a notion of housing provision policy as the funding of a certain number of dwellings of a certain quality within a system of owner-occupation. Therefore, it simply needs to determine what level of funding is available and to allocate this to some of those who are currently unable to afford their own housing. Drawing support uncritically from the recent stances of the World Bank, it perceives state intervention as necessary to correct market imperfections and to make the market work in the specific form of creating owner-occupation.

As a system of provision, housing is tied to specific conditions governing access to land and to finance, and it necessarily establishes prices which reflect the relationship between the existing housing stock and the new dwellings becoming available. Prices respond to quality and to location of housing, but also to general economic and social conditions, each of which can vary considerably in time and place. Such conditions can also change rapidly, either elevating or depressing corresponding house prices (as migration occurs, for example).

Suppose that a price increase does occur. An ideally functioning market would bring forth an increase in supply since price now exceeds previous construction and other costs, and price should later fall to around its previous level. However, this might not occur if the price increase is, for example, consolidated into the cost of obtaining the land on which to build. Thus, providing greater incentives to build (in this case through price, but it could equally be through subsidy or easier credit) does not necessarily succeed in generating new supply. The extra funding available may be channelled into the form of higher prices, which then apply to the whole stock and not just to the new housing stock, absorbing finance and saving throughout the sector. A subsidy to building costs might increase the profits of the recipients, not reduce their prices. Thus, the 'development gains' associated with housing programmes may accrue to the landowner rather than to the putative householder.

The issues involved here are extremely complex. A number of considerations will not be fully taken into account. A rise in house prices may lead some householders to trade up in anticipation of further capital gains and lead others to trade down to obtain income for expenditure or other investments. How much trading up or down takes place can depend upon the age structure of the (home-owning) population and their actual and anticipated incomes. So, whether price changes are sustained or not depends quite heavily upon those already within the housing market whose real asset position is essentially unaffected by the price changes (unless they exit from home ownership, since their house may be more expensive, but they nevertheless have to own it). Thus, the prospects of those seeking to enter the housing market can be heavily circumscribed by trading within the existing stock, with price increases being consolidated in the price of new houses (cost of land, for example). Further, an increase in trading either up or down tends to lead to demands upon the building industry, with alterations crowding out new buildings. Whilst these arguments are hypothetical, they illustrate how varied and perverse supply and price movements in the housing market are liable to be if left unregulated.

Three further points need to be added. Firstly, housing provision is extremely complex and involves a large number of functions, with corresponding economic agents. It is not necessarily the landowner to whom the developmental gains accrue. Potentially, any agent can benefit — from the corrupt official granting planning permission, to the builder engaged in subsidised construction. In short, providing financial incentives to build can only succeed after they have trickled down through the housing system as a whole — by which time they may have evaporated away. Nor is this conclusion affected by who the recipient of the subsidy or incentive is. The householder might confront an unscrupulous builder; the subsidised builder may be confronted by higher prices for land or building materials, etc.

Secondly, the pursuit of gains in these circumstances can create an impediment to a housing programme. These might appear as a bottleneck but, for example, landowners will speculate on the price they can obtain for their land, withholding it from use until prices or subsidies rise sufficiently; builders may tender only at inflated prices, being prepared to operate at less than full capacity (laying off casual workers), or to deliver poor quality products. Oligopolistic material suppliers or distributors can raise prices to obtain profits higher than normal.

Thirdly, such imperfections in the housing market tend to persist in their effects rather than being eroded quickly by competitive forces. Price increases due to what appear to be temporary factors become consolidated into future prices which can be sustained by increasing shares of income and saving being devoted to housing expenditure.

The significance of these remarks lies in highlighting the varied ways in which the housing market might develop in South Africa in view of what is likely to be an extensive housing programme. Some of the consequences, in diverse forms, are already apparent for those inner city areas where desegregation has altered the conditions of access to housing. Whilst the MERG arguments address the conditions in which prospects are favourable to expansion, the functioning of the labour market can also be associated with decline and degradation.

Consider, for example, 'blockbusting', in which estate agents encourage blacks to enter previously exclusively white areas in order to drive down prices so that they can gain commission or speculative profits from the turnover of sales as desegregation proceeds. Alternatively, as land is taken up for cheaper, high-density housing, so it exists cheek-by-jowl with low-density, expensive housing. Private mortgage finance is 'redlined' so as to be confined to the more exclusive areas, whose inhabitants accrue capital gains from the price of their land (incorporated into the value of their houses). Consequently, a bimodal form of housing can emerge as high land prices are associated both with low- and high-density housing, with overcrowding and poor quality necessary to compensate for the high cost of land in providing subsidised housing.

Such developments are already apparent in Johannesburg and even Soweto, where a housing market has in part been promoted by the sale of state-owned accommodation that was previously rented. Paradoxically, there is the possibility that the removal of market restrictions will lead to a general increase in house prices, and to a sharpening of segregation (together with expensive house security measures). Quite clearly, the private housing finance system can reflect and support such developments, since it is concerned with directing finance towards the upper end of the market, thereby inflating (land) prices. SAIRR (1993, p. 214) reports:

> When measured against other developing countries of comparable per capita income, South Africa had the highest proportion of consolidated assets of the banking sector devoted to residential mortgages (almost 40 per cent). However, only 12 per cent to 15 per cent of such funds were allocated to black township borrowers.

The redirection of mortgage finance to black housing has often been recommended, as this could lead to greater availability of funding for a housing programme, and could also reduce pressure on land prices in urban areas, as the capital value of existing white housing stock is reduced by the withdrawal of such extensive mortgaging. It has been suggested that mortgage finance for low-income housing be devolved to local small-scale saving institutions in view of the reluctance of larger finance houses to be involved. This is simply a form of passing the buck, and does not address the issues involved. There is no reason to believe that the inability to pay can be resolved by changing the lender that calls the tune, and smaller institutions will be less capable of bearing and managing the risks involved. Rather than attempt to solicit a housing programme through indirect financial mechanisms, it makes more sense to use the finance that can be made available to fund a public housing programme directly, so that the poor can be housed at subsidised rents.

4.1.2   *Policies for housing provision*

An appropriate starting point for discussing the economic role of the state in housing policy must be the dismal failure of what have often been genuine attempts to remedy at least some elements of the housing problem. Three inter-related features of this failure are highlighted. These obstacles to a housing programme are being further entrenched in the thinking and practice of the current government and other agencies, rather than being rooted out and addressed.

Firstly, there is the continuing commitment to the long-term goal of owner-occupation, a symbol of the reliance upon market forces, and the associated mechanism of intervening primarily through end-user subsidy. This is all predicated upon the leading role being played by the private sector. Particularly disturbing, in the wake of the de Loor Report, is the alliance formed on this basis by the Development Bank of South Africa, the Independent Development Trust, the South African Housing Trust and the Urban Foundation. They propose in their document (DBSA et al, 1992) to divide up and share various functions of housing delivery amongst themselves. Significantly, in an Annexure listing twenty-one such functions, there is no place for regulation of the housing market, the operation of the labour market both as a whole and within the housing sector, control of building materials supplies, training, and research and development. Moreover, they propose that the state be excluded from land and service delivery on the grounds that it would crowd out their own role:

> The involvement of government authorities in the purchase of land, and the servicing thereof, is inherently undesirable and has a fundamentally negative impact on the ability of the private, state corporate and NGO sectors to deliver. The institutions are of the opinion that this function is best and most effectively handled outside the government sphere (p.12).

Secondly, current proposals, whilst seeking to rationalise and even centralise some of the activities associated with housing delivery, do not encompass the full range of institutional reforms that will be necessary. Quite apart from state acquisition and development of land, a number of essential elements in the functioning of housing delivery have been overlooked or, in a kinder interpretation, abandoned to the vagaries of market forces.

Thirdly, there is simply no provision made for housing the poorest households who are caught in the net of finding even subsidised provision too expensive. Dependence upon end-user subsidy alone leads to a desperate but futile attempt to deal with two separate but intimately related issues — bond boycotts/failures and affordability. Neither of these can be solved by efforts to devise the appropriate structure and form of financial instruments. If households cannot afford, they cannot pay. And if those to whom they are obliged to pay are seen as illegitimate, they will not pay even if they are able to.

A solution to these problems can be found in state provision of rented housing. The degree of state intervention can vary over the range of functions involved — it can be a builder itself, or subcontract to an audited private sector; it can provide or guarantee loans; it can subsidise rents or charge at market value. Nor does extensive state intervention now preclude a more market-oriented stance in the future. The British government, for example, has privatised much of the publicly-owned housing stock that was successfully constructed by local authorities in the post war period, mainly through private contractors.

It is imperative to recognise that the housing programme is part of a transitional period. As the World Bank (1993, Feb 12, p. 12) puts it:

> *The task facing South Africa is similar to that of the reconstruc-*
> *tion of post-war Europe, or the unification of Germany in the*
> *1990s. In both South Africa's and these cases, it may be argued*
> *that a short-term reduction in gross inequities is required for*
> *medium- to long-term economic growth to reach its potential, in*
> *an equitable manner. Therefore, a strategy for a significant trans-*
> *fer of resources during the critical transition period should be*
> *considered. This strategy would require policy instruments that*
> *would not necessarily be appropriate for medium- and long-term*
> *vertical and horizontal fiscal balance.*

Only by state delivery of rented accommodation is there a realistic chance of meeting the housing needs of those most in need. This, however, does not have to be at the expense of the continuing role of existing forms of provision, but these must not be allowed to obstruct a major programme to expand supply through commitment to greater or lesser reliance upon the 'market'.

To pinpoint a role for the state sector is not to define in detail how this will be carried out. It is necessary that the policy framework employed to confront the housing system be comprehensive, since any component of the housing system is potentially able to prove obstructive, either as a bottleneck, or as a sponge for financial support and subsidy directed at housing provision. How the system as a whole functions is important, reflecting the interactions between the various economic and social agents involved. State intervention will be necessary not only to address market imperfections, but also to ensure equitable distribution of development gains (and to ensure that their pursuit does not prove an obstacle to provision), effective function-ing of housing supply, and urban and regional planning. There are many different ways in which this can be done, reflecting different institutional structures, at different levels of government, and with different mixes between the roles played by the public and the private sectors. It is inappropriate to provide a blueprint or model for housing provision, since much will depend upon local economic and political circumstances. Rather, a programme for housing and infrastructural provision is presented whose implementation is dependent upon institutional reform and capacity-building, and the priorities chosen politically in the light of economic circumstances. This will involve potential trade-offs with other expenditure programmes, as well as between those who can make a greater or lesser contribution to the funding of their dwellings, whether this takes the form of subsidised purchase or rental.

As a central goal, with macroeconomic implications incorporated into the projec-tions discussed in Chapter One, it is planned that the number of formal houses completed will rise from 38 000 to 350 000 per year by the turn of the century. Of these, 180 000 will be provided by the public sector, rented at half imputed cost, at an overall cost of R32 000 per unit in 1992 prices.

It is essential to ensure effective and efficient delivery. At various tiers of government, this requires the presence and coordination of sites, builders, materials, finance, infrastructure, tenure and community participation. The requirement that each of these be present and act co-operatively, is liable to be more of a constraint on a housing programme than the cost of the programme. It is necessary to ensure genuine and effective community participation in housing provision rather than the superimposition of pre-conceived schemes through, or upon, the community.

The housing programme will require land. Currently, there are over 390 000 hectares of vacant or developable land in the six major metropolitan regions. Of this, over 70 000 hectares is already held by various arms of the state. For a backlog of 1.8 million units, it has been estimated that 65 000 hectares of building land would be required. Subject to mismatch, etc, and compulsory purchase of adjacent, privately owned land, it would appear that there is no obstacle to the provisions of sufficient land for the housing programme. But, as in other areas, the institutional capability to deliver this land and to use it, is what is at issue. As the National Housing Forum observes:

> *The lack of an appropriate, broadly acceptable and legitimate policy approach is an important constraining factor in the overall delivery of land. This is because:*
>
> - *public authorities experience great difficulty in shifting away from old apartheid policies in the absence of new ones. This also hampers decision-making;*
>
> - *there is considerable duplication of functions with regard to planning, by government institutions which were originally established to offer services to different race groups. This causes delays, confusion and increases the cost of development;*
>
> - *there is no direct accountability by the government for meeting the tremendous backlogs and present requirements in housing (and hence land) delivery. What this means is that there is no one single Ministry of Housing (or Urbanisation) with one Minister accountable to Parliament for meeting objectively derived housing targets and that money is not specifically dedicated in the national budget for this;*
>
> - *there is inconsistency in policy positions across government departments (e.g. between own affairs departments) and at different tiers of government. The different types of subsidy policies is a clear example of this; and*
>
> - *there are no clearly defined roles for the public, private and community-based sectors, reducing the effectiveness of each of these to deliver to its full capacity.*

There are numerous agencies at various levels of government which have control over land use. These do not have sufficient powers to promote housing construction adequately. They do not have clearly defined functions and goals, and their lingering past practices and orientation lead them to obstruct the release of land for a progressive housing programme.

Provision of infrastructure associated with housing and housing development involves a number of separate activities, each with its own characteristics. Electrification is discussed elsewhere. Table 4.6 shows the low level of provision of water supply and sanitation in black rural areas. The DBSA estimates that the capital requirement for water supply for the TBVC and self-governing territories would be R7.2 billion (1990 prices). This would cover the supply of piped water, but alternative, cheaper methods of supply are feasible through use of boreholes and hand pumps. The total cost for water supply for the entire unserved South African population has been estimated at R28 billion in capital expenditure with a recurrent cost of R1.6 billion per year. However, with the use of simpler, more localised technology — especially spring and well protection, rather than large-scale regional piping — costs could be reduced to R11 billion in capital expenditure and R600 million per annum in recurrent expenditure. It is estimated by Pearson (1991) that:

> *The present rate of implementation of rural water schemes is far from adequate, and rural sanitation programmes have hardly been considered — with one or two notable exceptions. If the present rate continues unchanged then it could take 20 – 30 years for an improved water supply to reach the majority (say 80 per cent) of rural inhabitants.*

Quite apart from its role as an input to production, the availability of water is essential to health, safety and comfort. It also represents a saving on arduous (female) labour.

Like many other aspects of South African infrastructure, the transport system both reflects and consolidates the functioning of the apartheid system. Black commuters have faced an expenditure on average of 8 per cent of their income on transport — with 35 per cent of commuters spending more than 10 per cent of their income. This is hardly surprising given the distances between home and work — 65 kilometres between Sebokeng/Evaton and Sasolburg and between Atlantis and Cape Town, 39 kilometres between Khayelitsha and Claremont and Bellville, 76 kilometres between Pretoria and towns in Bophuthatswana, 68 kilometres from Botshabelo to Bloemfontein, and up to 190 kilometres from KwaNdebele to Pretoria (McCaul 1991). Around Cape Town, a survey of black households (World Bank, 1991, p.18) found that 8.6 per cent of income was spent on housing and electricity, less than the 10.5 per cent spent on transport, which was itself heavily subsidised. This is a consequence of the increase in density of population as one moves away from the City centre — in contrast to the more typical pattern (see Figure 4.1). Greater Cape Town has a land area that is more than double the size of Mexico City, even though the populations are 3 and 25 million!

Increasing travel distances for Cape Town commuters over time are indicated in Tables 4.7 and 4.8, together with subsidised bus commuter distances for a selection of other cities. In responding to the rising cost of subsidising transport, and blatant corruption in the allocation of subsidies, government policy has been to cut capital expenditure and to privatise where possible. To some extent, the problems involved have been alleviated by the rise in the use of taxis. Taxi transport now accounts for a third of commuter traffic in the Johannesburg area. Travel times have been reduced by one third to two hours on average, and passengers have been more comfortable, and have been able to reduce transfers between modes of transport.

Whilst the success of the taxi-system should not be overlooked, it is not without serious problems such as overwork, speeding, dangerous vehicles, and violent conflict over routes. It is estimated that there are 1.2 million taxi-drivers countrywide. Kombis were involved in over 55 000 accidents in 1991 (14 per cent of all accidents), with over 700 deaths through collisions (7 per cent of the total). 34 per cent of those entering the industry have done so as casual employees without previous driving jobs. The taxi war in the western Cape, for example, has led to 66 deaths and R3.6 million of damage. Externalities in road wear and tear, crowding and pollution also need to be taken into account. It should not be presumed that rail, coach, and other forms of public transport should be neglected as in current policy, which is attempting to cut the subsidies and capital expenditure predominantly allotted to those who cannot rely upon a private motor vehicle.

Government expenditure on roads has declined significantly — from about R3 billion in 1975 to R1.8 billion in 1990 (in 1990 prices), with the proportion spent on construction declining from 73 to 41 per cent, i.e. from R2.2 billion to R0.7 billion (DOT, 1991). It has been calculated that there are road construction and maintenance programmes at a cost of R3.2 billion per year which could achieve an internal rate of return of 15 per cent. For a rate of return of 8 per cent, the amount is R4.6 billion per year (SARB, 1991).

Such calculations, however, tend to reflect the interests of the 'road lobby' and the existing geographical distribution of economic activity. Figure 4.2 illustrates the skewed pattern of paved as opposed to unpaved roads. Yet there is quite a close relationship between geographical gross product and level of road provision, which means that rural areas and townships have poor roads because they are poor and vice-versa. Limited access to transport facilities confines black residential areas to dormitory towns, so that expenditure and employment accrue to what are already more affluent areas.

Road provision (and investment in transport) must be integrated into social and economic planning as is standard to a greater or lesser extent throughout the world. This should apply to new sites, city centres, and up-graded townships, informal settlements and squatter camps. Yet this has only happened to any extent in white areas. Only the barest attention has been directed towards residential functions in most black areas. Consequently, while some account has been taken of water and sewage facilities as comprising essential personal services, the economic benefits of roads have been neglected. Indeed, a major part of the problem is the failure to constitute a proper authority to deal with the issues involved. Thus, not only has the apartheid system created a backlog of transport needs, it has also bequeathed a system of administration that is incapable of confronting the rapidly evolving demands associated with the transition to a democratic economy. Indeed, even the simple expedient of creating lay-bys and stopping places for taxis to facilitate traffic flow has proved too demanding. The most urgent task is create an appropriate authority to remedy the situation in which:

> *There is no systematic monitoring of or planning for access roads to urbanising areas in South Africa, undertaken by one specific institution. Many different organisations, at varying levels of government, are involved in the construction and maintenance of these roads ... In other cases there seems to be serious neglect of these roads outside local authority jurisdictions, possibly because of uncertainty as to which party is responsible for the maintenance (DOT, n. d., pp. 2-3).*

In much of its Urban Reconnaissance Programme, the World Bank has taken a geographical focus across sectors. It finds that in the Witwatersrand region, two million (or 40 per cent of the population) suffer seriously deficient provision of all basic infrastructural facilities. It would cost R10 billion over five years to upgrade these facilities fully. Such a programme could be financed by a 4 per cent increase in rates, falling predominantly upon white local authorities, without requiring capital cost recovery from black local authorities or newly serviced greenfield sites. The World Bank considers this an appropriate redistributive tax. Although the potential may be less for other major urban areas, there is substantial scope to fund infrastructural provision through local taxation.

In terms of building materials, the two most important inputs are cement and bricks. The cement industry operated at a capacity of 71 per cent during the 1980s, but was at only 59 per cent of capacity in 1991. A housing programme of 350 000 units per year could be accommodated by raising capacity to 85 per cent. There will, however, be other demands upon supply from other forms of construction, with civil engineering output having declined to half its 1980 level). A major problem, however, with relying upon full capacity production of cement, is the high degree of concentration with just three companies monopolising the sector. They have operated a price-fixing and market-sharing cartel which has been unregulated by the state. Intervention will be necessary to ensure that the industry delivers at prices reflecting costs of production, and that the current organisation of distribution is reoriented to serve newly-located markets efficiently. Presently, availability of building materials (especially their transport) is a crucial constraint on informal housing supply. It has been found that migrant workers will transport materials obtained in urban areas to a rural site, where they prefer to establish a more permanent dwelling.

In the brick industry, there is less concentration and more limited economies of scale. Capacity utilisation has been between 50 per cent and 60 per cent, and a housing programme of 350 000 units would raise this to about 65 per cent. Unlike the cement industry, however, there is scope for small-scale plants to be developed commercially, which has not been exploited in the past. In the meantime, as for cement, it will be necessary to guarantee adequate distribution of materials and regulation of prices.

For building firms, there are a number of dangers to be avoided, if there is a construction boom. Firstly, tenders may be inflated, work may be of poor quality and completion may be delayed as firms contract for as much work as possible, even if they do not have capacity to deliver. Secondly, this potentially reinforces the drive to casualisation and subcontracting in employment as workers are taken on or dismissed by large firms with relatively limited numbers of permanent employees. Thirdly, these factors tend to raise costs, undermine training and working conditions, and pre-empt the development of black building businesses, other than as dependent subcontractors with a weak bargaining position. To deal with these issues, there is a need for strong contract compliance in managing housing (and other construction) programmes, and even a case for municipal construction units. It is transparent that subsidies to individual owner-occupiers is an ineffective response, for the head of household is likely to be totally inexperienced in handling the different agents responsible for housing supply. Indeed, bond boycotts and defaults have been reported as the response to quality deficiency in new buildings, even though the builder, and not the finance company, is the culprit. The problems for small-scale, black builders include lack of skills, deficiencies in accounting techniques, limited availability of materials, and insufficient and insufficiently regular work, partly as a consequence of preference for white contractors, and white monopoly over local authority work. These issues will need to be addressed in order to promote black businesses that are both efficient and independent of white-controlled, large-scale corporate contractors.

4.1.3   A summary

The housing system is complex and subject to pervasive market imperfections, as a result of the way in which price movements and developmental gains can be consolidated into housing costs and, as such, prove an obstacle to housing delivery. It is proposed that:

1. A unitary national housing authority with corresponding institutions at lower tiers of government be established. Its responsibilities will include:

    *   urban and regional planning;

    *   infrastructural provision;

    *   restructuring of the apartheid city;

    *   coordination of all aspects of housing delivery;

    *   formulating and monitoring planning regulations and ensuring their effective functioning;

    *   liaison with other bodies involved in economic and social policy;

    *   facilitating the release of land for housing.

2. A variety of forms of housing tenure, delivery, upgrading and products be encouraged to reflect the variety of housing needs, and to allow for the fullest appropriate democratic community participation in policy formulation.

3. The housing market be regulated.

4. Building supplies be regulated to ensure cheap and widespread availability.

5. Support be given to small-scale builders to ensure availability of skills, continuous workload, and freedom from exploitative subcontracting.

6. An access and feeder road-building programme of R3.2 billion per annum be established.

7. A water supply programme of R1 billion per annum be started with recurrent expenditure rising to R600 million per annum within ten years.

8. A house building programme rising to at least 350 000 units per annum be commenced, with attention to the needs of the rural population, and with government expenditure depending upon the extent of self-financing owner- occupation as opposed to state rented accommodation.

4.2 Schooling

4.2.1 The continuing crisis

Under apartheid, education has proved to be a particularly intense focus both for dissent and in the struggle for change. The crisis of apartheid has been reflected in, and has in part been a product of, the crisis in education. The crisis within the education system has to be understood as a cascade of mutually reinforcing factors. Within education itself, the issues have included inequality in access and provision together with the content and language of the curriculum. These issues have been properly identified as concerning the illegitimate exercise of power and control and, as such, have given rise to a multifaceted culture of resistance and the formulation of educational alternatives. The schooling that has been available to the majority has been heavily circumscribed. This educational environment has not been conducive to communicating traditional skills, or to employing them in later life, given the high levels of unemployment and general instability of daily life. Pupils, teachers, administrators and parents have been caught up in conflicting tensions as they have sought both to function within and to transform, or (in some instances) to preserve the society in which they teach and learn.

These tensions are extremely complex. The framework of principles emanating from the democratic movement is, however, both simple and compelling. It calls for a process of policy formulation governed by the pursuit of equality, non-racism, non-sexism, affirmative action and democracy. But such goals are necessarily confronted by a general economic and social environment in which the practices and consequences of apartheid persist and continue to thwart the formulation and implementation of new educational policies, as well as the broader aims and objectives to which they are attached. From day-to-day activity through to policymaking itself, the majority of South Africans currently involved in, and previously often excluded from educational practices, are faced with a dilemma. This is the inherent contradiction of working for their goals through the very institutions and powers that have oppressively deprived them in the past, and which still deprive them in the present. For example, a significant and symbolic example of this situation is the way in which the ANC 'back to school' campaign was appropriated and represented as an issue of law and order by the authorities. Such conundrums are not unique to education, given the more general process of embarking upon the transition from apartheid, before a legitimate government is in place and able to function effectively. The issues have been particularly prominent in the attempts to enhance educational provision, even as the struggle is engaged in restructuring the education system itself. The strength of the tensions involved is partly explained by the extent to which education has played such a central role as a symbol of the lack of the legitimacy of the government, both practically and ideologically.

While the present government suggests that it has accepted that educational provision should not be based upon racial discrimination, such claims are open to doubt. First, the educational problem is defined in terms of low economic growth, and hence availability of resources, set against the high growth of, and backlog in, pupil numbers. As such, there is an implicit and continuing division of the schooling system between races, in which the white system is regarded as satisfactory and the black system is perceived to be a problem of excessive need in relation to available expenditure. Consequently, there is no recognition of, let alone any attempt to remedy, the iniquitous legacy of apartheid in having created the separate and unequal educational systems. Indeed, there is no commitment even to equality of per capita funding between the systems of provision, nor are the institutional mechanisms specified through which a unitary and egalitarian system might be created. On the contrary, there is a continuing commitment to the retention of whites-only schools. This must be rejected. Segregated schooling must not be allowed.

Government policies (and often those of other agencies) remain too focused on vocational requirements, or the need for skills, thereby skewing priorities between different levels of education, and between different parts of the curriculum. The broader alternative is to embrace the role of educational provision as a means for all to participate equitably and democratically within society — rather than promoting a smaller number into elite labour market positions, whilst condemning others to unemployment and minimal skills.

Unfortunately, the immediate concerns of those who have been actively involved in the struggle over education have scarcely been addressed by the more narrowly defined issues raised by traditional treatments within the economics of education, which are unacceptably technicist in scope. Here, education is seen as an asset, so-called human capital, with a greater or lesser rate of return. The latter varies according to the extent that education is provided, and according to the skills that are imparted, with the potential to increase productivity for the economy and wages for the individual employee. It is generally recognised that the education and training system has given rise to a shortage of skills, and that this deficiency is compounded by the greater demands that will be made upon the capacity of the work-force in the future.

This view of a skills shortage as a starting point to the role of education and training should, however, be approached with considerable caution, even if schooling should play a major role in supporting those who are to enter the labour market. Apart from the narrowly defined goals of education in terms of vocational capability (rather than social participation), it is also important to stress that the South African education system is a product not only of apartheid, with its heavy restrictions on access to education for the majority of the population, but has also responded to economic and other socially defined needs and practices. In many respects, the apartheid economy generated the education and skills that it required — with an abundant, low-wage, nominally unskilled, black work-force complemented by a skilled, highly educated, white work-force which was further supplemented through immigration. The apartheid system generated both a demand for places within a skill structure, and the means with which to fill those places. As in all economies, especially when in transition, the impression arises of a general and even specific shortage of skills, undermining present and future competitiveness. Consequently, if it had survived, the apartheid system would have responded to its skills shortages no doubt by building selectively upon the educational provision that it had already made available for the black population. The prospect of a democratic society poses not so much the problem of bridging the skills gap that has previously developed, than of transforming the way in which both the demand for, and supply of, skills are generated, although it bears repeating that economic functions are neither the primary nor the sole determinants of educational provision.

A society in which 'unemployment' has been in the region of 40 per cent, in which formal or informal job reservation has been endemic, and in which access to urban life and the franchise has been systematically denied, is not one that generates a universally educated work-force. The most telling indictment of the apartheid education system is the inequality in provision in terms of per capita expenditure by racial group. At one extreme, school expenditure per white pupil (including capital expenditure) stood at R4 448 in 1991/2 compared to R1 248 for Africans (SAIRR, 1993). But these simple indices of inequality are themselves averages which conceal further and, at times, even greater inequalities caused by the divisions which are the direct or indirect consequences of apartheid. It has been estimated that over two million children do not even attend school. Per capita provision of education is highly unequal between rural and urban areas, and between one homeland and another, whether these be self-governing or independent. The extent of the inequality differs according to the type of education, but generally worsens at higher levels, whether these be academic and/or vocational.

Qualitative dimensions of poverty and privilege in South African education include the following:

- Average education attainment of the adult population is seven years of schooling, while for whites it is thirteen years.

- White and Indian school enrolments are about 100% of population at the primary level and over 90% in secondary schooling. African children spend an average of eleven years enrolled at school, but average attainment of African school-leavers is Std 7, or nine years.

- African secondary enrolments relative to population are highest in the Transvaal regions, and lowest in the Transkei and KwaZulu-Natal areas, Ciskei, Bophuthatswana, and the DET Cape regions.

- Total senior certificate passes were 190 000 in 1990, technikon diplomas awarded about 10 000, and university degrees and diplomas about 45 000. In 1990, Africans were 71% of all senior certificate (Std 10) candidates, but accounted for 49% of passes and 35% of successful matriculants. Overall, about

40% of African children now reach Std 10, less than half of these pass, and about 10% reach the standard required for admission to higher education. Whereas 40% of the population of school-leaving age obtain senior certificates in Lebowa, Venda and Gazankulu, less than 155 pass Std 10 in the Transkei and KwaZulu and under 10% in several regions administered by the DET. African students account for about 6% of technikon diplomas awarded and 21% of university degrees and diplomas.

- Technikon and technical college enrolments came to under 160 000 in 1990, and were about two-thirds white. Other training activities enrolled over 400 000, largely in non-formal, industry-managed courses or training for the unemployed (NEPI, 1992/93, p. 135).

Table 4.9 indicates expenditure on education both by the public and the private sector. Whites benefit from 33 per cent of government education spending and 45 per cent of private spending, approximately 36 per cent of total expenditure. This uneven incidence of provision both within and between racial groups, and at different levels of the education system, is itself associated with an administrative crisis within education. It is not simply a matter of the inefficient replication of education departments and the failure to co-ordinate and systematise provision. There is general recognition of the extreme fragmentation in administration. The processes by which funding is both allocated and employed are unduly influenced by the inherited political structures and the imperatives through which they operate. Both the objectives of any rational educational policy, and the levels of funding by which they might be achieved, have been swamped by other factors. Fragmentation and replication are a source of inefficiency because of the unnecessary duplication of costs and loss of economies of scale. In the form that decentralisation of expenditure has taken, it is open to ineffective targeting and to abuse in under- and in over-funding. It leads to what Crouch and Healey (1992, p. 8) term, 'the current system of "perverse" decentralisation, and hence "perverse" centralisation' in which the lack of co-ordination of the constituent administrations for education is superimposed by the exercise of the powers of central government.

This can best be understood by close examination of the formal and informal mechanisms through which educational finance has been organised. Different racial groups have been funded through the three separate Houses, the Department of Education and Training, and the TBVC governments, with subsidies being transferred to the latter through the South African Department of Foreign Affairs. Each of these conduits has contained its own fragmented aspects, and each has been driven to a greater or lesser extent by a genuine commitment to educational provision. Whilst there has been a token recognition of the allocation of funding in response to need as dictated by pupil numbers, for example, the data involved is far from reliable, the formula used to determine funding levels remains shrouded in secrecy to cloak its inadequacy, and actual levels of expenditure are revised in the light of informal bargaining and influence, and off-budget allocations. This is most transparent in the case of the TBVC states, where funds allocated for education can be reallocated under other headings. Ciskei diverted R300 million to the road-building programme in one year in this way. A common practice has been for funding levels to be marked up in nominal terms from one year to the next. Under-funding has led to increasing reliance upon overdraft facilities. Moreover, corruption and inefficiency is often cited as endemic within educational administration.

Irrespective of the level of funding allocated to education, the system of administration is in urgent need of reconstruction in order to make delivery effective. Gestures in this direction by the current government are counterproductive. Their strategy has been: to preserve the privileges of the white minority, even if allowing for the token incorporation of a few black students. Thus, in 1992, only 7 932 African pupils had been admitted to previously whites-only schools, even though there were 47 286 vacancies at white primary and 82 046 vacancies at white secondary schools (see Table 4.10). In addition, 174 white schools have been closed down, with a proposal at one point to retrench 11 000 teachers. MERG opposes the continuance of whites-only schools, and observes that the policies and machinations to preserve them are severely undermining the provision of schooling to the majority.

There have been attempts to pass on some of the costs of education to the white population, by devolving ownership and control of capital assets (notably schools) in return for the taking on of responsibility for a greater proportion of current expenditure, through reliance upon higher levels of fee income. In the short term, this has reduced the recurrent state subsidy to white education, but only at the long term expense of entrenching control over admissions (to those who are acceptable and can afford fees) and over capital expenditure.

This façade of devolving and democratising schooling has been accompanied by minimal measures for equalising expenditure. Indeed, the fact that the gap in provision has narrowed is because of falling subsidies to white education, rather than any rise in the real per capita expenditure for black pupils. Thus, the government is employing the language of decentralisation and democratisation as a means of justifying both cutting of budgets and the consolidation of the existing privilege. It does not genuinely embrace a system of education in which secure and adequate central state funding is used to restructure provision to create greater equity and democratic participation at all levels of decisionmaking.

In view of the levels of, and mechanisms for, allocating expenditure, it is hardly surprising that educational outputs have been disastrous in many respects. It has been estimated that over 1.5 million children between the ages of 6 and 17 did not attend school in the late 1980s; 300 000 of those leaving school each year do so without functional literacy or numeracy. Pass rates for African candidates for senior certificate or matriculation (with enrolment levels of only 25 per cent for secondary school) have hovered around 50 per cent over the past decade, and plummeted to 42 per cent in 1989 when the corresponding figures for coloureds, Indians, and whites were 73, 94 and 96 per cent, respectively. Table 4.11 indicates further deterioration for African scholars in 1990.

It is commonly accepted that one of the largest sources of efficiency gains in education could be obtained through a reduction in repetition and drop-out rates (PESA, 1992). The hierarchy of privilege across education departments is evident both in the small numbers of African children who reach senior classes, and in the time it takes them to complete different phases of the school programme. The published drop-out figures are difficult to interpret and unreliable. However, it is likely that only half of all children now reach Standard Eight, while only 40 per cent of African children reach Standard Ten; about half of these children pass.

A major problem of repetition exists in lower primary education and this is associated with very slow progress from one grade to the next. One of the consequences is that a bottleneck arises in lower primary schools, with enrolments being 50 per cent higher than otherwise, which places additional burdens on an already under-resourced system.

Although both repetition and survival have shown some marginal improvement in recent years in some departments, analysing why repetition and drop-out occur is hampered by lack of adequate research. Both in- and out-of-school factors have been identified as causes. In her research on farm schools, Gordon (1986) argues that family financial considerations and employment conditions have a greater influence on school drop-out than factors such as teacher upgrading and supply of books. In contrast, Nyikana (1982) calls for an improvement in education variables such as teacher in-service training, in order to reduce repeater rates in the Ciskei. A major problem in the analysis of drop-out and repetition is that the data available is widely believed to be less than accurate and difficult to obtain. It has proved impossible to assess with any accuracy whether dropouts are permanent, or whether they reappear as new enrolments and should really be counted as repetitions or re-enrolments, depending on the level at which they resume. The most recent research revises down the extent of drop-out, suggesting that 99 per cent of those who leave school do return, but that over 30 per cent repeat the grade at which they left. Such high repetition rates are unacceptable. Clearly, improvements in the quality and scope of the education system, and improvements in the socioeconomic environment in which education functions, will reap the benefit of previously unmeasured efficiency gains arising out of reductions in repetition and drop-out.

Repetition rates are indicative of an interrupted and prematurely completed education. But even the time that is spent in school is undermined by the poor conditions experienced there. Only in 1986 were textbooks nominally funded out of the state budget, and by 1990/91 they were in acute short supply. Many African teachers are without formal qualifications. Almost 20 per cent and 10 per cent are without the professional qualifications required for teaching primary and secondary schools respectively. The shortages in qualifications in mathematics and the sciences are particularly extreme (see Table 4.12).

Pupil : teacher ratios for the homelands are shown in Table 4.13. They should be compared with ratios of less than 20:1 for white pupils in primary schools and 15:1 in secondary schools, although all of these figures must be treated with caution for a variety of reasons. Backlogs in the provision of classrooms are indicated in Tables 4.14 and 4.15.

Absenteeism is also high for a variety of reasons (not least due to the need to supplement family income through child labour) and the ability to learn is itself seriously hampered by poor nutrition.

In short, the crisis in education is multidimensional, and policy will need to address a number of different issues simultaneously. But it would be a mistake to overlook many of the positive features of the South African education system. Over the past fifteen years, average pupil : teacher ratios have been falling, from 54:1 to

42:1 for Africans, despite an increase in student numbers from under three to over seven million. The ratio of male to female pupils is fairly even, in contrast with a male bias in most other developing countries. This reflects a number of factors, the most important being child labour for family income, and the career prospects for girls in nursing, social work and education. Thus, there has been considerable and a growing capacity to deliver educational services over the last 15 years.

4.2.2   Policy perspectives

The priority in schooling is to provide for ten years of universal education. To a large extent, this is uncontroversial in view of what are estimated to be the high rates of return to education, especially primary. These are taken to be at least 10 per cent and as high as 20 per cent, with substantial impact upon other factors such as fertility (World Bank, 1988). There are, however, serious deficiencies in the argument for education purely on the grounds of the calculated rates of return. Apart from the value of education in its own right, as a basic need allowing for fuller social participation, such calculations necessarily presume an extrapolation from the estimated results of educational achievement from the past. This is not to doubt that such benefits, or even greater ones, can be replicated. But for them to materialise requires much more than the allocation of funding to education and its effective use. To some extent, this is recognised by the World Bank (1988, p. 3):

> *Expanding access to primary education should remain a high priority in most African countries. To maintain the high economic and social returns that have accrued to this investment in the past, however, parallel efforts are required to combat the incidence of disease and malnutrition among young children.*

The issues involved go far beyond the important ones of disease and malnutrition which clearly impede the receptivity to schooling and the benefits that can accrue. Familial economic and social deprivation undermines learning — as in the availability of basic needs. Subsequent job prospects are an important component in raising the incentive to learn as well as in utilising what has been learnt.

Apart from economic and social returns to education, a standard approach to reform of the South African education system has been in terms of assessing the cost and finance of providing black education at equivalent levels to that of white education. This is an unsatisfactory exercise in principle and in practice. The goal is not to deliver white educational standards to the whole population but, rather, to offer a different, and more equitable educational system for all. Moreover, in practice, funding is only one influence on the provision and consequences of education. In failing to address the issue of delivery and how education interacts with other economic and social factors, the goal of equalising funding essentially puts aside the advantages that a minority already enjoy, and overlooks the obstacles that are faced by the majority in terms of the environment within which education is both received and employed. Whilst employment, income, housing, communication, household stability, child nutrition and other such factors remain problem areas for the majority, there is unlikely to be equality within education. Parity in funding cannot of itself deliver equal access to, and benefit from, education.

This raises some doubts over the use of formula funding by which finance is allocated to education according to numbers of pupils, schools to be built, etc, even if higher compensatory payments are made where economic and social deprivation exists (broadly, the opposite of present practice in South Africa). Such measures go far, but not far enough in providing for education. While educational provision cannot be expected to put right all of those factors that influence its impact, it is essential to recognise that providing extra funding to make up for missing schools, for high levels of unemployment, and for nutritional programmes, etc, will only succeed to the extent that they are accompanied by programmes that provide for employment, housing and transport (and even the more immediate capacity to build and maintain the schooling system).

With this discussion in mind, how are educational services to be delivered? Consider first the availability of teachers. Here, in terms of overall numbers, some of the evidence is encouraging. Over the period 1960 to 1990, the number of black teachers has increased from just under 30 000 to nearly 200 000. Overall, there are well over 50 000 students on teacher training courses, of which fewer than 10 000 are white. There are 31 teacher training colleges in the homelands, and these have 23 997 students enrolled, even though there are places for only 17 776 students. Meanwhile, five colleges for white students closed between 1990 and 1992, and only 8 930 places were filled out of the 13 609 available. In 1988, R40 million could have been saved by allowing black enrolment to fill empty places in white teacher training colleges.

It is possible to provide teachers for universal primary education within a few years if the maximum capacity for training is utilised at 16 000 new teachers per year, and this capacity is supplemented by an extra 3 000 to 4 000 teachers in each year, to peak at 34 000 new teachers per year by the end of the century before settling down to 20 000 new teachers per year. This presumes a pupil-teacher ratio of at most 40:1. Although such claims should be treated with caution, the World Bank reckons that the loss in educational effectiveness would not be significant if this ratio were to rise to a ratio of 50:1. This gives a 20 per cent margin with which to allow for under-provision of teaching staff in the short term, and a swelling of pupil numbers from those children not currently attending school, in addition to the 7.3 million who are.

A difficulty in providing for universal primary education is that while the overall numbers of teachers may just suffice, they may be extremely unevenly distributed. Orbach (1992) reports a prospective oversupply of teachers in TBVCs together with a combined shortage of 20 000 in the other homelands (with KwaZulu responsible for 11 000 of these). To some extent, such mismatches will be remedied by the greater mobility arising out of the reincorporation of the homelands. But there will continue to be limitations on the flow of teachers in the light of personal motivation and language differences. The surplus of teachers in some of the homelands has occurred because of their having heavily subsidised training in conjunction with low entry qualifications. This has been in order to hold out the promise of greater employment opportunities in general, and not just within education, for which the training acquired may be inadequate.

The provision of primary school teachers points to a number of policy issues. First, in training itself, there is the need to provide for some permanent and for some temporary increase in capacity. This needs to be complemented by the training of those already teaching, who do not have professional qualifications. The situation can best be remedied by creating distance learning programmes for teacher-training, as well as building upon existing capacity.

But distance learning cannot be seen as a cheap panacea for the training problem. Apart from cost, it does have advantages — it is relatively easily open to all, it enjoys a degree of flexibility, and it has the ability to draw upon a variety of teaching media. However, the learner suffers from isolation. South Africa has been characterised by a conservative and technicist approach that is inappropriate for the changing character of educational provision. Accordingly, the use of distance learning must be part of a more general programme of life-long pre- and in-service training, drawing upon the range of media available and suitable (the radio in rural areas, for example). It must allow for face-to-face learning with provision for feedback, it must command the highest quality materials in exploiting economies of scale, and it must be seen as part of a programme to develop the media skills of both teachers and trainers. These imperatives should be felt throughout the education system, a matter to which we will return below.

The problem of mobility and matching teacher supply with demand has to be considered within the context of restructuring the salary system. In 1987, the average salary for a black teacher outside the homelands was R22 000 per annum, and as little as R16 200 in the self-governing territories, compared with R30 100 for white teachers. The new salary system will have to respond powerfully to what are perceived to be the priorities within the newly structured educational system. As this will include the geographical redistribution of the teaching staff, the need to develop new curricula and multiracial teaching skills, and the upgrading of qualifications, these criteria should figure prominently in determining salary levels, along with other more traditional rewards for merit, skills, qualifications and dealing with difficult working conditions. Donaldson (1992, p. 20) estimates that the salary cost of providing primary, middle and secondary schooling for all by the year 2000 will be R5.0, R4.5 and R3.5 billion respectively; this adds up a total salary bill of R14 billion at 1990 prices.

The provision of teachers for secondary schooling presents greater problems than the provision for primary schooling, because the present level of provision is so much less, with a bigger backlog to make up, as is the corresponding capacity to train teachers. If current trends continue, only one-third of primary pupils will be able to attend secondary school. Currently there are just over 100 000 secondary school teachers, many without adequate qualifications, and the capacity to train is as little as 3 000 per year. There is an urgent need to expand training provision through distance learning programmes and through a change in priorities within universities. In planning targets, funding and salary structures, the institutions of higher education must be directed towards teacher training and curriculum development, even if these are not the most popular goals for those oriented towards more academic research, or teaching within elite institutions. Donaldson (1992, p. 20) makes an estimate of R1 billion per annum for this purpose by 2000.

Even if adequate numbers of teachers can be supplied there is, paradoxically, a problem in providing adequately for the numbers of pupils. Even with sufficient schools, there is the need to provide for transport. Krige (1989), for example, finds that in some areas of Natal, nearly 25 per cent of secondary school pupils need to walk more than 12 kilometres to and from school each day. Moreover, 26 per cent of the population in the age group 5-15 years live more than ten kilometres from the nearest primary school (32 per cent and 1 per cent for rural and urban areas respectively). One of the factors underlying this is the dependence on farm schools, run by some white farmers for their employees' children through a subsidy from the state. They are, on average, the source of the poorest forms of schooling, but are also especially variable in quality. Outside the homelands, farm schools take one in five of all black pupils. But the schools are often small, with one or two teachers for children of all ages, so that a third of all primary teachers are on farm schools, which make up two-thirds of all schools. It is imperative, as one example of the fragmentation of the education system, that they be abolished as soon as possible.

Pupils also face problems of poverty, malnutrition, the need to work and to migrate. These issues need to be addressed through effective legislation against child labour. They need to be addressed by adequate nutrition programmes and a curriculum that is sufficiently standardised to allow pupils to move relatively freely between schools. Account must also be taken in education programmes, of the high rate of pregnancy amongst female teenagers, especially the large number under the age of 19. Such issues should be an acknowledged priority within teacher training. More generally, support services to teaching are extremely important, ranging from furniture to textbooks; Donaldson (1992, p. 20) estimates these as costing R1 billion per year by 2000.

According to Taylor and Smoor (1992), while the capacity exists to build the necessary 14 000 new classrooms needed per annum for ten years of education for all, only 6 000 are currently being added annually to existing stock. Together with a programme for the rehabilitation of existing schools (which are often without water taps, sanitation and electricity), they estimate that the total building programme for universal education through to secondary level would cost R4.1 billion.

In rural areas, much school construction has been funded on a rand-for-rand basis through the joint participation of quasi-governmental bodies and communities. Taylor and Smoor observe that this has probably had the effect of consolidating the very backlogs it was purported to address, 'because relatively poor people cannot find or raise the resources from within their own communities to build enough classrooms to keep pace with the increases in school-age population and the demand for school places' (p. 34). In addition, one consequence would be an uneven and uncertain timing of any school building programme, as an individual project would be required to wait for the community to raise adequate finance.

Reducing the community's responsibility to 10 to 20 per cent of costs, as some have proposed, may moderate such negative effects and may engender a sense of responsibility for, and commitment to, the school building programme that would otherwise be absent. But MERG doubts whether the principle that 'you value what you pay for' is either a strong or even a primary issue to be resolved in generating the appropriate environment within which to create and use the educational infrastructure. The legitimacy of local government will require that many lessons are learnt, but will not require an effort to teach the virtues of the market. As in other areas of public provision, how education should be funded is a fiscal judgement to be made in the light of alternative options, with the goal of minimising any impediments to the delivery of services.

As important as funding is the manner in which school building is integrated into the economic and social life of the community. The project itself must gain legitimacy. It must form part of a coherent construction programme that generates employment in building and through multiplier effects. Appropriate technology must be employed and developed and the school should ultimately serve a number of community purposes over and above those of schooling alone. To the extent that there is a trade-off between quality and quantity in the programme for school building, there is a case for leaning towards quality, and doubting the presence of a hard trade-off between quality and equality, as suggested by P. Moll (1991). This is reinforced to the extent that the administration of the building programme may be a constraint, and reduction in quality at one site may release funds without them necessarily being taken up at another site.

While there will be some saving in administering a unitary education system, there will still be a need for a substantial programme to develop and restructure administrative capability. This is especially true in light of the uneven distribution of pupils per professional, non-teaching staff and per clerical staff (see Tables 4.16, 4.17 and 4.18).

Fehnel et al (1993) estimates that the cost of handling the backlog in administrative staff and in making provision for the future will vary between R50 and R60 million. This is to provide, amongst other things, for 2 400 staff as soon as possible and for another 700 per annum for the next four years. Once again, as with teachers, but on a lesser scale, account needs to be taken of potential wastage and mismatch, as administrative resources are relocated and oriented according to the new goals of a democratic education system. The wage bill required to cover the extended administration is liable to be approximately R100 million, but the necessity of redeploying the administration where it is excessive and of regrading employees according to the work that they undertake, will be of crucial importance. The administration of Indian education has been less labour-absorbing than for whites, but with very little difference in achievement (Crouch and Healey 1992, p. 6); and the varying ratios in the homelands is indicative not only of wasteful duplication of functions, but also (apart from uneven access to resources), of corrupt or vested interest-group job creation.

To finance such an education programme, Donaldson (1992) suggests a policy that would involve higher user charges the higher a student progresses in the educational hierarchy, and higher charges to (white) pupils in better, predominantly urban, schools. He finds that the schooling programme can be funded, albeit with the imposition of user charges upon the newly up-graded and extended schooling. The issue, then, is not whether or not the schooling programme can be funded, but how.

Donaldson envisages fees (or other private contributions) making up the shortfall arising out of a growth in the education budget by 4 per cent per year in real terms. By the year 2000, per capita charges to township and rural residents are calculated at R10 for primary schooling, R210 for middle schooling (12-14 years), and R640 for higher secondary schooling (15-17 years). These charges are designed to raise R80 million (1 per cent), R530 million (12 per cent), and R960 million (26 per cent) of the costs respectively, across the three levels of schooling. Thus, out of a total cost of R15 billion, little more than 10 per cent will be provided by fees.

Donaldson's case for user charges rests on affordability and equity, since the proposed programme has to be financed, and will allow for equal subsidy to all in school. State spending could even be skewed in favour of the disadvantaged. However, MERG questions the validity of these justifications for a number of reasons.

Firstly, it accepts that schooling, and subsequent education, will remain unequal either because of the more beneficial socioeconomic circumstances in which the privileged receive their education, or because they will be able to secure more resources through private spending over and above the fees charged. To some extent, this has been justified on the grounds of the need to sustain quality in education at the expense of quantity. But it is almost inevitable that the survival of the quality will be primarily attached to whites, as a consequence of their higher incomes. They will be able to afford to pay and, in doing so, will bid away resources such as teachers from those dependent upon free state education. And privileged education will tend to reproduce intergenerational privilege.

The quality argument must also be treated with extreme caution. The calculations under which quality is perceived to generate greater returns than quantity are extremely crude, and are extrapolated from the past organisation of both education and apartheid. If repetition and drop-out problems are addressed properly, educational provision can be improved dramatically. This achieves improvement in quality and quantity within the disadvantaged educational sector, rather than supporting quality for the advantaged at the expense of the quantity for the disadvantaged. The cost trade-off between quality and quantity may not be as sharp as implied, since the ability to deliver services rather than to raise finance may prove a major constraint.

Secondly, dependence upon user charges is liable to induce inefficiency at all levels of educational delivery. At one extreme, authorities may be unable to secure sufficient pupils, or may not make sufficient effort to do so, and may delay the building of facilities and the hiring of teachers. At the other extreme, children may be denied access to existing school facilities for want of the available fee, itself a source of inefficiency for the capacity utilisation of the school, as well as for the child's education. The latter is too important to leave to the vagaries of pseudo-market forces.

Thirdly, it is only with considerable caution that the principle of universal free education (or other welfare services) should be abandoned. The government will be subject to pressure to extend the scope of user charges and to cut subsidies, with much of the pressure coming from those who are both privileged within the education system, and also better placed to withstand increased user charges. In short, the principle of equitable subsidy is liable to be subject to increasing erosion in practice. Universal provision without fees is some guarantee of continuing commitment to provision, even against the swings in the balance of economic and political fortunes. The income generated has to be set against the costs of collecting it, the lower disposable income available to poor households, and the potential loss of children from schooling due to unwillingness or inability to pay.

Fourthly, there is no rationale in using the schooling system as a fiscal unit, as is implicitly recognised by allowing for growing state subsidy. The balancing of books is for accounting purposes only. Whether or not user charges should be levied can be judged only in the context of the fiscal system as a whole. The relative impact of raising finance, or cutting expenditure in other areas, has to be taken into account. At the very least, the funding of the whole educational system should be assessed, and user charges for schooling should be compared with other forms of raising revenue at higher levels in the educational hierarchy.

Finally, the principles of equity involved need to be carefully assessed for their practical implications. In any proposal for an equal per capita subsidy for schooling, the impact upon households is dramatically different, depending upon the number and age composition of its children — an issue that Donaldson does not address, even though it is central to affordability. black households are often larger than those of whites, so they face higher charges for equal service. Even though the proposed charges are skewed towards higher levels of education, where pupil numbers per household will be less, a household with two children in middle school and one in secondary school would pay over R1 000 in annual fees (at 1990 prices). Some 60 per cent of African households have an income of less than R700 per month, and the average African household income is a mere R779 per month (1991 prices). It might even be argued that such charges are liable to consolidate educational inequality within the black family, with at most one child being selected for advancement. Furthermore, Donaldson does not consider the impact on fertility, with user charges and lower educational attainment liable to result in larger families. In short, there must be a general presumption against user charges for schooling, both on equity and efficiency grounds.

Central to the reconstruction programme is the provision of universal, state-funded schooling. The highest priority must be given to putting this into place. User charges are just one form in which the relationship between public and private provision is raised. It is inevitable that there will be continuing individual and collective attempts to grant certain children private provision, whatever the success of the public school programme. Those already receiving advantages will benefit most. The continuing relationship between public and private provision must be monitored to ensure that the former commands priority, and that clear policies are formulated to regulate the role of the private sector (in terms of how it may and may not operate), with administrative responsibilities being allocated to the various tiers of government.

This section has been almost exclusively concerned with schooling. It has neglected other areas of education, and their overall integration with one another. To some extent, these are considered in Chapter Five on labour markets, and provision is made for other expenditures on education in the overall budgeting discussions in Chapters One and Two.

4.2.3   *A summary*

It is beyond the scope of this contribution to address the issues of educational policy as such. But these are themselves so intimately related to economic issues, that the two must be considered in conjunction with one another as well as with other factors. MERG proposes that:

- The whole system of educational administration be reconstructed in order to meet the goal of unitary provision through the principles of equality, non-racism, non-sexism, affirmative action and democracy;

- A universal education programme be implemented in conjunction with policies to ensure delivery of schools, books and teachers, etc;

- Educational policy be assessed in the light of the delivery of other basic needs such as employment, housing, transport and nutritional and health programmes;

- Training of teachers be in part met through the use of a distance learning programme, which must itself be situated within a broader strategy, both for lifelong pre- and in-service training, and for the development of media skills throughout the educational system;

- The institutions of higher education be re-oriented towards making a much greater contribution to promoting the universal education programme;

- The reason for drop-out and repetition should be thoroughly researched, and appropriate policies directed towards reducing these sources of educational inefficiency;

- User charges for education should be avoided unless shown to be more effective and advantageous within the functioning of the fiscal system as a whole;

- A programme for training and providing personnel for educational administration should be an urgent priority;

- Salaries and grades be restructured throughout the educational system to reflect not only qualifications and experience, but also the priorities in the restructuring of the educational system;

- The funds to provide ten years of universal education be made available as rapidly as educational delivery allows. The major items of expenditure are:

    - *a salary bill of R14 billion per annum*

    - *a teacher training programme costing R1 billion per annum*

    - *expenditure on school supplies of R1 billion per annum*

    - *a school building programme of approximately R0.5 billion per year.*

4.3 Health

Health is often a precise reflection of individual economic and social welfare. It is an important component in creating, and not just in enjoying, well-being. Those who are unwell cannot work or cannot work efficiently, whether for wages or otherwise; and those who do not work are often the most unhealthy — even in developed countries, where the psychological and social stigma attached to unemployment reinforces the lowered levels of income that prove disastrous in a developing country. The effects of individual ill-health are also experienced by others through worry, care and the disruption of daily life — costs that are difficult to quantify. The direct impact of ill-health on lost working days is, for example, much more significant than those lost due to industrial action. Health expenditure, efficiently employed and effectively targeted, is not a drain on economic resources, but a positive guarantor of economic performance.

The link between health and employment is not the only economic interaction, although the most important general determinant of health among the poor, is access to a steady and adequate source of income. Health, fertility, education, urbanisation, and household income, for example, are all known to be intimately related to one another. Yach (1992), for example, finds that both mortality and fertility decline within a stable urban environment, but that in rural areas, fertility decline has been delayed, and migration contributes to an ageing population structure.

The costs of health care filter through the economic system in their own particular ways — in drugs and medical supplies, training, construction and in the salaries of the medical work-force. It has been said that if the cost of education is thought to be too high, then consider the cost of ignorance. The same argument applies to health.

A particularly important feature of health care is that it can be extended to individual patients almost indefinitely. A consequence is that inequalities in provision take on the most dramatic forms — hugely expensive cosmetic surgery for one, alongside the chronic and acute illnesses and deaths of many — for lack of the simplest and cheapest forms of health care, and the basic amenities that are its precondition. Unfortunately, the limitless application of medicine to a minority of the healthy and wealthy has popularised the belief that better health is the consequence of more curative treatment, and the complex scientific advances and intensive treatments that have made it possible.

Nothing could be further from the truth in both developed and developing countries. With the partial exception of vaccination programmes which have long been available, the most important determinants of health are to be found in levels of nutrition and provision for water, sanitation, housing and other basic needs.

4.3.1 The inadequacy of current health provision

In a sample of African urban households, it was found that less than 50 per cent had an inside tap, less than 70 per cent an inside flush toilet, less than 40 per cent their own refuse receptacle, and less than 40 per cent their own electricity supply. Conditions in rural areas are considerably worse. Nearly one-third of South Africa children are underweight due to malnutrition. In a sample of KwaZulu households, it was found that half of all illnesses were gastro-intestinal, reflecting the absence of a hygienic water supply, and the inconvenience of boiling the water that was available. Only 4 per cent of households had access to a latrine at their homesteads. A programme to extend water and sanitation infrastructure as quickly and extensively as possible, especially to rural areas, is an urgent priority. (This is discussed further in the section on housing.)

Poorer countries have been able to achieve superior records for life expectancy and infant mortality because of a public commitment to address these issues. Inequalities in health mean that whites live for almost a decade longer than Africans, with almost a quarter of the latters' children failing to survive beyond the age of five years. (see Table 4.19).

Inequalities between racial groups in both health and health expenditure are compounded by the fragmentation of administration by the apartheid system. But much more than the replication and proliferation of administrative authorities is involved. Many aspects of ill health, not least the spread of infectious diseases or the positive externalities to be gained from immunisation programmes, are affected by the geographical, legal or administrative restrictions that have been placed upon their treatment. This is especially so in a country where migration is the norm. Tuberculosis, for example, a treatable and preventable disease, is being recorded as increasing in incidence as a result of migration and overcrowding. Failure of patients to be able to afford to complete treatment is also leading to drug-resistant strains of the disease.

There are economies of scale in both general and specialist health care, so that co-ordination and pooling of resources are required that cut across those structures of apartheid which have obstructed such co-operation.

Administration inefficiencies created by apartheid include:

- The cost of maintaining, staffing and equipping fourteen departments of health;

- The cost of attempting to co-ordinate the activities of all the different authorities;

- The cost of building, staffing and maintaining segregated institutions. In many small towns there are three or four clinics to serve different races, when one is all that is required to provide adequately for the needs of the population;

- The cost of maintaining separate sets of patient records in the provincial, state and local authority facilities;

- The waste of health worker time and the costs involved in travelling the long distances necessitated by the geographical fragmentation of services, particularly in the homelands;

- The costs involved in transporting patients long distances for secondary or tertiary care when there are closer referral facilities that are racially segregated (Source: Centre for Health Policy, 1988)

Such fragmentation is itself a source of inequalities according to the funding that is made available and how it is employed. It is illustrated, for example, by the health indicators by regions given in Table 4.20.

The number of people served per available clinic ranges across the homelands to levels as high as 30 000, even though 10 000 is considered an absolute maximum as a norm — the appropriate number being subject to density of population and ease of access. It was found in Natal that 30 per cent of the rural population lives more than five kilometres from a mobile clinic. This figure is 7 per cent for black urban dwellers. For permanent health care facilities, almost half of the black rural population is at a distance of more than ten kilometres. Yet there is continuing pressure upon the current government to appease its favoured constituencies by building more high-powered hospitals, rather than to provide basic clinic services. Inequality and fragmentation are also associated with surplus capacity alongside desperate shortages, most notably in the under-utilisation of hospital beds, especially in white own-affairs hospitals, as shown in Table 4.21.

On the other hand, desegregated hospitals have also suffered from unused beds due to lack of funding to carry out treatments, rather than lack of the patients of the 'appropriate' race requiring treatment.

In 1992/93, government expenditure on health was just below R10 billion. The proposed budget for 1993/94 of R11 billion represents a real cut in expenditure, since the medical price index increased by 13.2 per cent over the year (see Table 4.22). The private sector spends about the same on health as the government, although private expenditure in absolute and in per capita terms has been rising very rapidly. Little more than 2 per cent of government expenditure is devoted to primary health care, although the figure is about 15 per cent in Natal. Although South Africa spends approximately 6 per cent of its GNP on health care, above the WHO norm of 5 per cent for developing countries, this splits roughly down to 13 per cent of per capita income in the private sector for whites, and just 2 per cent for blacks through the public sector.

Given the failure to resolve health problems by increasing expenditure, the government purports to be addressing them by a dual strategy of desegregating facilities and privatising health care. The one proceeds as slowly as the other gathers pace. The arguments and empirical evidence against privatisation of health care are overwhelming. It leads to the consolidation of inequality, creaming off the capacity that is available at the expense of the increasingly marginalised public sector, which is intended to serve as the safety net for those without sufficient funds to go private. The private sector is never self-sufficient, but often benefits from direct subsidies, and is totally dependent upon medical personnel whose training has been publicly funded. Nor does the dependence upon private practice necessarily release funds for the use of the public sector; apart from the economic and political pressures that the private sector will place upon the public sector, it itself suffers from the diseases of modern commercial medicine — over-treatment, over-charging and over-administration, not to mention (in the US) over-litigation. An index of the over-treatment, the inequality and the predominance of curative over preventative medicine is provided by the figures on the use of drugs. The private sector accounts for 80 per cent of the R2 billion spent on drugs, but the public sector uses 60 per cent to 70 per cent by volume (and pays 40 to 50 per cent less for drugs through bulk purchase).

Although broadly correct, the discussion of the previous paragraph suffers from too sharp and unrefined a distinction between public and private provision of health services. As already indicated, the two necessarily interact with one another (in provision and use of personnel, for example) and private provision (and privatisation) can take on a number of different forms. At one extreme, the state might take full responsibility for financing and providing services without levying charges. But any one or more of these features is open to privatisation. The state might provide funding, but contract out to the private sector for the services involved (whether for personnel or other costs). This is potentially independent of whether the state charges for the services directly on a treatment-by-treatment basis, through a registration charge, through general taxation, or an ear-marked health payroll tax.

The different ways in which public and private provision interact with one another, and the exact balance of provision between the two will vary according to the medical service concerned. Not necessarily, but commonly in practice, the more advanced, specialised, expensive and individualised a treatment, the more it is likely to be both privately provided and set apart from the public sector. Thus, patients will often go private once they have used the public sector to its limits. On the other hand, at the opposite extreme of primary and preventative health services, the public sector is more likely to be exclusively responsible.

This general discussion of the relationship between the public and the private provision of medical services is particularly pertinent in South Africa for a number of reasons. Firstly, health is a merit good with considerable externalities, and for which individual demands can be disproportionate relative to available resources. Because of apartheid, inequalities in income are particularly highly correlated with other indices of socio-economic well-being. Consequently, the extreme incidence of ill-health will be further compounded by differentiation in access to treatment, the more so to the extent that this depends upon the ability to pay.

In the light of the extreme inequalities in the distribution of income, privatisation inevitably tends to the over-treatment of the wealthy and, by the criteria of social efficiency and equity, the inefficient crowding-out of the treatment of the impoverished. Moreover, privatisation is often linked to occupational insurance schemes, which widen existing inequalities between the employed and the unemployed. Similarly health provision amongst the employed will be unequal, as health care as a form of fringe benefits will reflect and magnify occupational stratification. With unemployment currently said to be at 40 per cent or more, and with employment itself insecure, health provision becomes equally uncertain. It may also lead to various forms of screening of employees' health status in order to reduce insurance premiums and liability, creating incentives to conceal illnesses (with subsequent neglect of treatment) in order to obtain or retain work. In other words, privatisation will benefit the rich over the poor, and similarly benefit the urban over the rural, men over women and children and employed over the unemployed.

A second feature which distinguishes South Africa from other countries (especially those in the developed world where privatisation has been adopted) is that their starting point has often been one of extensive, even universal, public provision from which the market has taken over some responsibility. In South Africa, by contrast, the situation is one of relatively full public provision for only a minority and negligible provision for the majority. The introduction of market forces is inevitably biased towards customers for whom there is already a service in place, especially as commercial medicine has high fixed costs for which certain and rapid returns are required. It is far from clear that the social benefits of a healthier population could accrue fast enough in the form of the profits required by commercial health companies.

Thirdly, the South African medical system is already more than usually distorted in the direction of what is commonly regarded as an endemic feature of western medicine — overemphasis on curative treatment at the expense of preventative medicine. Despite a longstanding recognition of this deficiency and good intentions to remedy it, the imbalance has persisted throughout the world, not least in South Africa. Van Rensburg et al (1992, p. 57) note that:

> *The shift in emphasis towards primary, preventative and commu-*
> *nity health which was propagated continually and from various*
> *quarters — inter alia, by the Loram Commission in 1928, the*
> *Gluckman Commission in 1944, the 1977 legislation, the Na-*
> *tional Health Service Facilities Plan of 1980 and the Browne*
> *Commission of 1986 — was time and again abortive.*

Privatisation does not usually lend itself to preventative programmes (immunisation, nutrition, sanitation, etc), although these can be contracted out. Privatisation reinforces those distortions towards curative medicine, since it is primarily concerned with the provision of services to the individual paying patient (who, by definition, will already be ill). The predominance of curative over preventative treatment operates at all levels. The poorest seek expert medical advice, especially for the youngest members of their households, often at great expense to themselves. Employed collectively for preventative measures, such funding could be more effective many times over. Where concerted programmes of preventative health care (often linked to literacy programmes) have been implemented, as in Sri Lanka and Kerala, for example, they have proved extremely successful, with beneficial impacts on fertility also.

A particularly dramatic example of the neglect of preventative medicine is seen in the development of AIDS. It is not simply that preventative measures should be taken in sexual relations, which themselves depend on socially determined circumstances. The ideology of cure as opposed to prevention is instilled in popular ideas about health, with ill-health often perceived as an accident or misfortune, and this makes effective campaigns around AIDS more difficult to conduct. But no one doubts that the economic impact of AIDS could be extensive. Estimates are highly speculative since they depend upon a variety of uncertain factors — how fast AIDS will spread and to which sections of the population, what impact it will have on morbidity and fertility, how the direct costs of treatment will evolve and be borne, and the methods used to predict and calculate the indirect costs of AIDS to the economy in terms of shortened working lives. The Centre for Health Policy (CHP, 1991) reviews various estimates of the economic costs of AIDS and suggests that its direct burden will lie (in 1991 prices) between R0.7 and R1.3 billion by 1995, and between R4 and R10 billion by 2000. The indirect costs, in terms of lost employment and output, are calculated to fall from 3.2 to 1.3 times direct costs — although international estimates tend to use a factor of 5 or 6 because they estimate lost (individual) earnings, implicitly taking no account of high levels of unemployment. Thus, AIDS demonstrates both the complex relation between health and the economy, and the urgent need for preventative health care (and consciousness around it), for which public rather than private provision is most appropriate.

Fourthly, privatisation would encourage a further commonly neglected area in western medicine, one that again takes an extreme form in South Africa. This is the failure to take adequate account of industrial health and safety. Occupational health schemes at work could encourage neglect since the insurance company would foot the bill for ill-health (and charge premiums accordingly). Whatever the provision for health through employment, it is essential that health provision incorporate a strong work-based component (in conjunction with legislation with effective enforcement) rather than functioning through the more traditional reliance upon residentially-based health services. Paradoxically, in some instances, South African employers (especially those engaging migrant workers) have developed their own medical facilities because of the compound system. These facilities are generally inadequate and function for work reasons rather than for health reasons. To press for health provision through the workplace is not, however, to suggest that employers must have their own fully developed range of medical facilities, but that these should be appropriately provided in and around the workplace. This goal would be under-mined by privatised provision which would seek out lucrative, curative markets, usually displaced from the work environment, especially if health insurance is selectively and unequally extended to those in employment as a fringe benefit.

The impact of privatisation cannot be assessed as if an all-powerful government or public sector is able to reconcile the gains of self-financing derived from private provision with a safety net of public provision for the needy. Privatisation itself creates or reinforces those interest groups (whether in the service of, or served by the system), who also have the economic and political power and voice to undermine and shift government intent. The medical profession has proved itself to be powerful, as have the insurance companies that organise the finance for private schemes. In addition, there will always be economic and political pressures from those who receive or benefit from private medicine to be the beneficiaries of direct or indirect subsidies equivalent, or even preferential to, those allocated to the public sector, and for the latter to be a target for reduced expenditure and further privatisation to the degree that the public sector continues to expand provision. Of course, there is no guarantee that a future government would not capitulate to pressures to reduce health expen-diture even if a system of public provision was in place. But the previously developed presence of, and commitment to, a public health service would prove a major obstacle to such retrenchment, and the associated forms of resistance to cutbacks would otherwise be absent to the degree that privatisation had been already accomplished. In particular, medical and other employees would have an interest in working to defend the health service, not just its funding.

In short, privatised medicine is more than a system of provision of health services in conjunction with, and at the expense of, public provision. It reflects and consoli-dates economic and political empowerment, almost inevitably at the expense of those who are already disadvantageously placed by a range of socio-economic indicators. The apparently attractive argument that the private sector pays for itself and relieves the state of some of its responsibility, is not convincing. For the private sector can render public sector provision more expensive by bidding up the price of scarce resources, those paying for the private sector can seek economic redress through the wage (fringe benefits) and political system (direct or indirect subsidies to the private sector), and inequalities in health may even be widened. Furthermore, arguments concerning the favourable fiscal implications of privatised health services in reducing expenditure, need to be seen in the context of alternative methods of raising or saving government finance. The financial advantages of private (or privatising) health services must be weighed against the negative impacts on the provision of health services more generally. As a result, public provision for a well-defined package of basic health services warrants full government funding.

These arguments are borne out by empirical analysis of the shifting balance between and within public and private health care. As Kelly (1990) documents, many concerned and progressive personnel within the health system have been combatting the restrictions imposed by apartheid. Their ability to do so has been dependent upon the fragmentation within administration and the uneven resistance that they have encountered. Whilst their efforts are to be applauded, greater access to medical facilities for blacks must not be allowed to be contingent upon the ethics and benevolence of what is primarily a medical hierarchy dominated by whites. More-over, such personal and collective commitments are not general across the medical profession, so that privatisation offers the opportunity to pursue private gain by treating the minority at the expense of public service for the majority. Currently, the private sector employs half the doctors, 80 to 90 per cent of dentists, nearly 20 per cent of nurses and absorbs half the money spent on health. Most of this expenditure arises out of private insurance, yet only 16 per cent of the population are covered — 70 per cent of whites and under 4 per cent of blacks. The rapid growth for the latter, from a negligible base, indicates the inadequacies of resources devoted to public provision, rather than the superiority of a private health care system.

As previously observed, the private depends upon, and crowds out, the public sector as illustrated over the past decade by the relative movements in medical personnel per capita. These have decreased for the private, but increased for the public sector, as shown in Table 4.23.

Consequently, it is hardly surprising that nurses are described as leaving the public sector in droves; 10 per cent resigned from provincial hospitals in 1991. Yet the private system is estimated to suffer from abuse and fraud to the extent of R240 million per annum and, when estimates of over-utilisation of facilities are added, this rises to R1 billion per annum or 25 per cent of medical aid contributions (SAIRR 1993). However, it is also necessary to acknowledge that the public service does not always itself have a clean bill of health, in terms of wages and working conditions, availability of facilities and efficient and honest administration. This tends to push staff into the private sector. Whatever role it plays, the functioning of the public sector must itself be regularly monitored for performance in delivery according to resources allocated.

4.3.2 Healthy alternatives

It is necessary to recognise that the public sector will continue to function in symbiosis with the private sector for the foreseeable future — not only because the public sector is currently unable either to deliver or to afford a sufficient spread of health services, but also because many potential patients, whether rich or poor, will continue to purchase medical services over and above, and even in place of, public provision. A long-term accommodation between public and private provision must be reached, even if the goal is to achieve a leap forward and sustain a momentum in public provision.

The issues involved are complex and cannot be worked out in detail here, partly because of the unevenness with which services are already provided, some of which might be lost if subject to generalised rules and policies. Nor can the principle which favours public provision of health-related needs be permitted to undermine the provision for those in most need. A private hospital bed charged at R350 per night, for example, but state-subsidised to the tune of R50, might lead to a net saving of R100 if the subsidy allowed a public sector bed at R150 per night to be reserved for a poorer patient. Attempts to enforce public service from medical personnel, to charge for training, to withdraw all subsidies from, and even tax, the private system may curtail provision to the needy by even more than any support that might be appropriated for a more equitable public provision.

There are a number of ways of strengthening and securing the role of the public sector. One is to guarantee a proportion of national income and/or government expenditure to the public health programme. This might be reinforced by a payroll tax committed to the creation of a health system, or for social security more generally (although this may induce either overspending or underspending, given the uncertainties around both health needs and economic performance). Another is to have a rolling programme of services to be provided through the public health sector; these might build upon and incorporate, initially on a piecemeal basis, some of those services in which the private sector is also increasingly active. A choice might be made to charge for these services, even if subsidised, and/or a system of rationing could be implemented through referral. However, the main thrust of the public sector health programme should be the growing provision of primary and preventative care, with this providing the basis for utilising and expanding into other areas of public provision at higher levels of treatment.

Alternatives for health must, however, begin with basic needs, especially in rural areas. Primary health services must be targeted as a high priority, with emphasis on the low-cost preventative and curative measures that serve the majority of the population and which accrue substantial social rates of return. South Africa spends less than 5 per cent of its health budget on preventative medicine, and basic health care has also been neglected. Yet, the per capita running costs of providing high-impact, primary health care may be as low as R25 per year. This could provide for vaccinations, essential drugs, oral dehydration salts for treatment of digestive tract infections, and vitamin and other supplements to address micro-nutrient deficiencies. About R500 million would provide food for two million infants and pre-school children in need, although the infrastructure for this would need to be put in place.

The backlog in clinics must be addressed. To meet World Health Organisation (WHO) norms of one clinic per 10 000 population, 2 000 extra clinics are required. These would require a building programme costing about R300 million. Extra running costs would be approximately R1.5 billion per year. MERG has not calculated estimates of medical personnel needed, but a training programme would also have to be initiated, with emphasis upon the skills needed for the targeted service to be provided.

Delivery of health services depends upon the creation of an environment free from the threat of violence. In Soweto, for example, for Africans, 60 per cent of all non-fatal injuries for males and 40 per cent of those for women, are due to interpersonal violence. Physicians for Human Rights (1992) report that in Alexandra, roughly half the women below the age of 26 have been raped at least once. Violence, and the threat of it, not only creates ill-health, it also undermines the ability to deliver basic health services, given the insecurity of personnel and facilities.

4.3.3   A summary

South Africa requires a unitary national health service available to all citizens without user charges, and based on a rolling programme of basic health services, which will be extended over time to include more services, as well as specialist treatment at higher levels on a selective basis. In the interim, these will continue to depend upon a mix of private and public provision. MERG recommends that:

1. The creation of a single department of health be implemented, responsible for planning health services and providing basic health care. Government expenditure and health policy should be directed towards preventative measures and primary health care — with immediate attention to neo-natal services, family planning, serious childhood illnesses (including malnutrition), gastro-intestinal disorders, TB and sexually transmitted diseases, and the provision of facilities to meet minor and acute health problems. A basic health care and nutrition programme must be implemented as soon as possible at a cost of R1 billion per annum;

2. The role of the private sector must be regularly reviewed; and current trends towards the privatisation of health services must be strongly discouraged and, where appropriate, reversed;

3. The health service be funded out of general government revenue, although an earmarked payroll tax and level of expenditure may be beneficial;

4. A programme be implemented immediately to assess and respond fully to the economic and social implications of AIDS;

5. While trade unions are seeking to negotiate private health cover for their members, an attempt should be made to negotiate consolidation of these schemes across all COSATU affiliates, with the ultimate objective of integrating them into the developing national health service;

6. Legislation be drawn up and facilities be made available for a more comprehensive and enforceable scheme for health and safety at work;

7. A programme be initiated to provide water and sanitation, together with 2 000 clinics as rapidly as is feasible, at a capital cost of R300 million and a recurrent cost of R1.5 million per annum. The priorities for construction should be rural areas, especially those suffering the greatest deprivation;

8. The department of health should have the responsibility of developing and strengthening the health information system so that health planners have access to a valid set of data for policy evaluation and the setting of priorities.

4.4 Electrification

4.4.1   *The current scene*

South Africa has one of the most extraordinary electricity supply industries in the world. It is a mixture of extremes in both achievement and failure. It has achieved, for example, a per capita consumption of electricity that is comparable to that of the UK. But, while household consumption is provided to over three million households, well over twenty million of the population are without access to electricity. Table 4.24 gives some indication of the limited extent of electrification across a selection of black townships.

Whilst the white population is well-served in its homes, a key role played by electricity has been in industry, particularly mineral extraction and processing. South Africa has not only used a very high proportion of energy in the form of electricity — no doubt, in part, in response to oil sanctions and as a result of its secure domestic supply of coal from which the vast majority of electric power has been generated; it is a uniquely energy-intensive economy. For each unit of output, it uses three times as much energy as the United States and six times that of Japan.

This is predominantly because of the high energy use of large-scale mining and processing. Mining accounts for 25 per cent of all electricity consumed, with more than half of this taken by the eleven largest users. Mining, together with the eight largest nonmining users (including a chemical firm and six metallurgical firms) use as much as 30 per cent of all electricity consumed in South Africa.

Large-scale use of electricity has gone hand-in-hand with large-scale generation. Eskom is able to rely upon the largest and most advanced power stations in the world. It is the fourth largest electricity utility worldwide (see Table 4.25), and it has been engaged in a building programme of six power stations which could have been completed in the mid-nineties, were it not for self-imposed delays in response to slower than anticipated growth in electricity demand. The strength of the electricity supply industry in South Africa is indicated by its consuming as much electricity as the rest of the continent put together.

Eskom is extremely technically advanced in three areas in particular, apart from power-station construction. These are in the use of dry-cooling of power-stations in order to reduce dependence on scarce water supplies; in the burning of low-grade coal in power stations in order to maximise usage of ore extracted and to reserve higher grade coal for export; and in long-distance cabling so that power supplies can be sent over long distances with minimal energy loss. In these and other areas, South Africa holds a leading position in world technology. It also has the ability to undertake large-scale construction and infrastructural projects. The flow of the Vaal River, for example, was reversed over 200 kilometres to provide water for the power-stations on the Eastern Transvaal coalfields and to serve the SASOL complex.

These features of the electricity supply industry are indicative of its economic capability across a broad range of activities. The industry is associated with huge power-stations to serve industrial plants dependent upon massive electricity usage, or to serve the white population, predominantly concentrated in urban centres (although remote white farms have also been connected to the grid at the expense of its extension to the homelands). When a programme to meet the electricity needs of the majority is embarked upon, a number of distinct advantages will be inherited by a democratic government. Firstly, there is already in place a highly sophisticated system of power supply and distribution network. Secondly, there is a high level of technological expertise across a broad range of activities. Thirdly, there is considerable excess capacity, with little need for new capacity before the next century even with a major programme of electrification. Indeed, power-stations that could have been built or completed have been delayed and the older, less efficient stations have been retired or mothballed prior to the end of their potential working lives. This has been a result of the economic crisis of apartheid and the inability to sustain growth and hence the anticipated increase in the level of electricity demand. It is anticipated that existing generating capacity is sufficient into the next century. Fourthly, there are huge coal supplies with which to fuel power-stations. Fifthly, Eskom has considerable skill and experience in raising finance on domestic and international money markets.

There is general agreement on the desirability of a major programme of electrification. Eskom has already achieved a level of 160 000 new connections in 1992 (from a base of only 38 000 in 1991), and this has been complemented by 40 000 new connections through local authorities (the exact figure is uncertain). The electricity department of Durban is credited with responsibility for almost half of these connections.

This is indicative of the unevenness with which electrification is currently proceeding. It reflects the inherited control over a major part of distribution, with extremely limited generation capacity, by a large number of local authorities. Eskom itself has direct access to less than a million outlets, although it is able to negotiate access or assist in electrification with the designated local authority. Figure 4.3 shows the anticipated electrification programme of Eskom, and distinguishes between connections that it will make as opposed to those falling under the responsibility of local authorities. Table 4.26 reveals how this programme will close the gap in electrification from 44 per cent to 65 per cent of all households, despite an increase in the number of new dwellings to be supplied.

There is an apparent perversity in these projections in that the institution which has proved most effective in bringing about electrification, namely Eskom, is designated to occupy a diminishing direct role in the future programme. To a large extent, this reflects the use by Eskom of a five year planning period from which major unanticipated changes in activity (such as greater involvement in electrification) are precluded. But an increasing role for Eskom in conjunction with local authorities is not to be relied upon, from the evidence of the past. Eskom would have to negotiate with a highly fragmented distribution system, comprising hundreds of separate authorities. Many of these have numbers of customers which would fall well below the level necessary to accrue scale economies in distribution. At the end of the 1980s, more than 520 white and 260 black authorities had the sole right to distribute electricity. It is estimated that a distributor serving less than at least 10 000 customers is not cost-effective. For the distributors in South Africa, the average number of customers is 4 350, with a third handling less than 1 000 customers, and 89 per cent handling less than 10 000. The impact on labour productivity is striking. The four largest municipal distributors serve 750 000 customers with a work-force of 6 000. The rest of the system, excluding Eskom, uses 24 000 workers to handle approximately 1.5 million customers — half the ratio of customers to work-force. Eskom serves 250 000 customers with 18 000 distribution workers but it handles large-scale users, and remote farms make up half of its connections.

There is a significant inverse relation between distributor size and charges for electricity, with tariffs ranging from 9.6 to 16.5 cents per kwh in 1989, although this might reflect proportionately greater taxation in smaller local authorities, as well as lower productivity as a result of older equipment or less capital equipment. As shown in Figure 4.4, Eskom has proved its ability to provide for electrification most rapidly, and although the large white local authorities are in a position, by virtue of their market size, to distribute efficiently, this capacity does not necessarily translate automatically into an electrification programme to new customers.

This is especially so for black households, as the position of black and white local authorities has been quite different in the fragmentation of distribution. For the white local authorities, with supply in place, monopoly of distribution has proved an invaluable source of revenue through generous price-cost margins. In this way, white municipalities as a whole benefited to the tune of R600 million in 1989 (R60 million in Johannesburg and R125 million in Pretoria). DMEA (1992, p. 19) finds that electricity accounted for 39 per cent of the revenue of all white local authorities (R4 684 million) but only 24 per cent of expenditure (R2 900 million), even if wage and salary costs are taken into account. The estimate of surplus after wages and salary costs, etc., is R1 786 million. In effect, electricity distribution has constituted a major form of local taxation.

For black local authorities, rent-seeking behaviour has led to attempts to emulate such outcomes, with a number of undesirable results: firstly, it has obstructed electrification due to the higher charges involved and the need to incorporate local government officials (whose salaries are linked to service provision and revenue raised). Secondly, it has been associated with mismanagement, corruption and inefficiency. Thirdly, it has led to non-payment of bills in part as a protest against the abuse of power and ineffectiveness of local authorities. Tables 4.27 and 4.28 demonstrate the contrasting position of a selection of black and white local authorities in terms of their electricity accounts.

A further result of apartheid is that black townships are heavily residential in their pattern of electricity use, because of the relative absence of major productive activity in these areas. Consequently, the smoothing of peak demand between domestic and commercial use is absent (see Figures 4.6 and 4.7), skewing load factors and, potentially, average system or tariff charges.

This by no means exhausts an account of the deficiencies of the currently fragmented system of distribution, but it does bring home the need for institutional reform, without which the macroeconomic benefits of an electrification programme will be either delayed or lost. Eskom has to take the leading role in this programme. Local authority control of distribution is an anomaly from the past, will impede the programme, and does not reflect an effective form of decentralised democracy. The skewed provision of electricity infrastructure inherited from the past has endowed white local authorities with inequitable powers for appropriating revenue through tariff policy. A standardised national policy for electrification should be designed, with Eskom taking the lead, even if there is some provision for variation in the form of implementation at local authority level. But local authorities should not take charge of the conditions of finance and pricing. There will be powerful resistance to these measures from those local authority officials who have benefitted unduly from the past system. However they are compensated, their interests cannot be allowed to block the spread of electrification. It is doubtful if hard-pressed local authorities will be in the best position to raise or make available the finance for the capital expenditure required for electricity distribution.

4.4.2   Macroeconomic implications of electrification

The average cost of an electricity connection is in the region of R3 000 rand per unit, although this varies considerably between dense, urban and dispersed, rural connections. With the rate of connections rising to over 400 000 units per annum and with an allowance for some reductions in real costs, the annual cost is approximately R1 billion. The costs break down as follows; materials, 60 per cent; labour, 25 per cent; transport, 4 per cent; and overheads, 11 per cent. Of these, import costs are liable to be approximately 15 per cent or R150 million. However, electrification will probably be based upon pre-paid meter systems. Although these are import-dependent, there is scope to exploit economies of scale and serve export markets sufficiently to meet the direct import cost of electrification.

These direct effects on the balance of trade are small compared to those which are liable to be generated by the multiplier effects of electrification. These can be divided into two components. One concerns the overall impact on the growth rate of the economy, and should be assessed against the background of macroeconomic balance. The other derives specifically from the induced demand for electrical appliances.

For the latter, it is estimated that expenditure on durables will be in the region of R1 000 for each connection. Whilst there is substantial excess capacity to produce electricity durables in the domestic industry, these are not internationally competitive. Even if imports are used to meet demand, they are unlikely to make up more than 2 per cent of the current import bill. However, the electrification programme creates the potential to promote the domestic durables industry, and this should be considered an urgent priority in industrial policy, together with an appropriate training strategy.

More generally, the electricity industry has an impact upon macroeconomic performance in terms of investment levels, inflation, etc. Currently, for example, Eskom is a major actor in domestic and foreign capital markets, to such an extent that it should not be allowed to operate independently of government. Macroeconomic impacts have to be taken into account by central government, but there are also certain dangers to be considered. In the UK, for example, electricity and other utility price increases, and borrowing for investment, have at times been disproportionately curtailed in order to reduce inflation and the budget deficit, even at the expense of long-term damage to the public sector industries concerned. For this reason, a careful balance must be struck between the development of the industry and broader macroeconomic objectives.

4.4.3 *The broader impact*

Although the commitment to a programme of electrification is uncontroversial, it is worth rehearsing the arguments in its favour, in order to bring out the implications for financing, tariff and other policy issues. The social rates of return from electrification far exceed the private rates of return. One of the reasons is because of the multiplier effects to other economic activities, particularly important in conditions of excess capacity and high unemployment. De Wet, for example, employing input-output analysis, has argued that with 7.5 million customers being connected between 1991 and 2015, GDP would increase by 5.8 per cent by 1995, 10.9 per cent by 2000 and 23.5 per cent by 2015. In addition, over two million new jobs would be created and black disposable income would be increased by 5.2 per cent per annum. One indication of the returns to electrification can be gauged by the loss to GDP that results from insecurity of electricity supply when it is in place. It is estimated for India and Pakistan that power cuts result in 1.5 per cent to 2 per cent loss in GDP over and above spoilage. By the same token, the impact effect of availability of supply might be expected to raise income for those concerned by at least the same amount. How much more must be the significance of the total absence of electricity altogether!

Such estimates are highly speculative since they extrapolate from the current production coefficients for the economy, and they are generally regarded as overly optimistic. At the opposite extreme, one could confine employment prospects to those jobs generated by the electrification programme itself, in the region of 10000 including material supplies, and adopt pessimistic assumptions about the prospects for further employment creation other than in the informal sector, because of excess supply and import competition in electrical appliances. This does, however, leave aside the employment arising out of the multiplier effect of increased incomes. The informal sector effects are difficult to quantify; Figure 4.8 indicates an apparently exemplary outcome within a year, with extraordinary implications if replicated across the country — but it was dependent upon credit assistance and other infrastructural provision that would not normally be part of an electrification programme.

Such growth in employment in the informal sector may itself reduce the work that some are able to do. This does not imply that it becomes no longer worthwhile but the overall effects have to be carefully considered. Electrification will, for example, reduce individual time spent on wood-fuel collection by as much as 16 hours per week, with a total saving of some 500 million person hours per annum, quite apart from any beneficial effects on the environment. But whilst this impact on (unpaid) labour will be primarily felt by women, the employment generation associated with electrification may well be more heavily skewed towards men. Accordingly, the gender implications of the programme are complex in terms of the workload and work availability for women. However, such impacts are most likely only within rural areas which may to be the last to benefit from connection given the relatively high costs involved — although a case can be made for accelerating the rural electrification programme not only to correct urban bias, but also to prompt learning by doing at an early stage.

Other benefits of electrification are less easy to quantify. They essentially reflect the readier access to heat, light and power, and the support these give to every activity, whether for production or consumption. Improvements are to be expected in literacy, education more generally, and levels of fertility will drop. A quantifiable example of this sort is provided by the impact on health. It has been estimated that the costs of burns, poisoning and respiratory illnesses from the use of coal, wood and paraffin use will be reduced by R100 million with fuel-switching to electricity. Surveys of energy use have shown how expensive alternatives to electricity (such as paraffin) are.

In the previous paragraphs, attention has been given to an assortment of what are essentially potential microeconomic impacts of an electrification programme. None the less, these do belong in the discussion of the macroeconomic implications because, even though highly diverse, they are significant in aggregate. In order to capture this analytically, they will be referred to as the developmental gains of electrification. The notion is familiar within geography. It can be associated with the externalities that arise from infrastructural or other economic progress, the classic example being the arrival of the railroad. In the previous section, it has already been shown how the attempt by local authorities to appropriate such developmental gains in advance can lead to a delay, or even prevent their accruing at all. For reasons of equity and efficiency, institutional mechanisms must be found that facilitate not only electrification, but also the benefits that follow as a consequence. In addition to ensuring that developmental gains do accrue, it is essential to target those to whom they accrue as an important component of redistribution.

Consider for example, the financing of the electrification programme. Eskom has taken the view that the developmental costs of the programme should be rolled up into electricity charges so that, on average, fixed costs will be recouped as electricity is used over the years. As shown below, this might add between four and five cents per kwh, or around a third of the unit price. There are, of course, many arguments against such a pricing scheme on efficiency and equity grounds — not least because those who use more electricity will subsidise the capital costs of those who use less, and new (black) customers will pay more than old (white) customers. Eskom estimates that those who use less than 350 kwh per month gain by using the S1 tariff (in view of the lower, implied capital costs in the per unit cost for consumption). It follows that the tariff structure will have the effect of sorting consumers by level of use rather than affordability of fixed charges. Of course, a further complication is that use is liable to change with occupancy.

A range of different tariff structures could be charged, but these are liable to impede the electrification programme if they involve excessively expensive running costs for poorer households, or if there are inefficient disincentives to use electricity when connections are made. Table 4.29 indicates the current tariff structure of Eskom and how it responds to the capital costs covered by consumer or community. Effectively, it demonstrates that Eskom seeks to function as a rough and ready source of credit to those who cannot afford the fixed costs of connection; only the interest paid back to Eskom for providing the capital costs of connection on credit takes the form of higher tariffs.

The essential feature of this scheme lies in the attempt to fund the electrification programme out of tariff revenue. This was the policy employed in the 1970s when Eskom prices rose much faster than inflation in order to finance their power-station construction programme. The same policy has been used in South Korea. It cannot be justified on grounds of efficiency (given that price exceeds marginal cost)-or equity (since capital costs are being borne by those who have previously been denied connection, and who are worse-off than those who are already connected, and whose capital charges have been written off). There is no reason to fund the electrification programme out of tariff revenue. However, it is possible that higher electricity prices might serve as a form of indirect taxation, taking into account the objectives of the fiscal regime to be equitable, effective and efficient. These goals and the scope for raising revenue through electricity pricing will have to be set against one another, and the impact upon electrification and electricity use, and the alternative sources of revenue considered. There is even a strong case for cross-subsidisation in electricity pricing as a mechanism for raising revenue for electrification, and as a means of redistributing to the worse-off through lowering their prices and charges for connection (if any).

It is not necessarily desirable for the electrification programme to be self-financing through pricing. Even within the electricity industry itself, there is scope for funding the electrification programme from other sources. One of these is by cross-subsidisation from those distributors who are creaming off a surplus from the prices they charge; and the other is from the potential of Eskom to raise finance on the money markets, if it is not appropriate to draw upon its own surplus. The latter indicates a further potential source of funding — higher electricity prices than otherwise — especially in the light of the proposed commitment by Eskom to cut the real price of electricity by 20 per cent over the next five years; it already has some of the lowest electricity prices in the world (see Figures 4.9 and 4.10). Surely, a stronger case can be made for taxing those already connected rather than imposing higher prices on those most recently connected? In terms of raising capital costs, Eskom currently has total assets of R42.5 billion, a turnover of R12.6 billion and a net surplus of R1.5 billion. It is anticipating raising R3 billion on the money markets in 1993, but only partly in order to finance its electrification programme — to the tune of R500 million alone. A further source of funding could be through lower prices for the coal used to generate electricity, much of it from collieries tied to power stations and with guaranteed profits. It may be worthwhile developing a National Electrification Fund as a conduit for finance, if this can prove an effective institutional mechanism for gathering and disbursing funds. This, however, carries the danger of added bureaucracy, dereliction of governmental responsibility, uncertainty of secure funding to sustain the programme, and the diversion of funds from other areas of application that are less attractive to potential donors.

This point on financing can be made by linking the electrification programme to the housing programme. Necessarily, the two go hand-in-hand, since the new dwellings to be electrified will make up as much as half of all new connections. In real resource terms, the fixed costs of electrification are part and parcel of the costs of housing construction. Therefore, those who argue that electricity prices should cover the costs of connection, should accept that they should also cover other parts of housing construction costs and land costs as well. Yet, the affordability of housing is already known to be beyond the reach of the personal finances of those most in need. A solution does not lie in splitting off the costs of electricity connection and adding them to recurrent charges which, in the form of bond payments, have already proved not to be affordable. If (new) housing is too expensive, separating out its constituent costs does not make it any less so — although it may both impede delivery, through fragmentation of the agencies involved, and give some charges priority over others.

An additional point concerning developmental gains arises here. The relationship between (new) housing and electrification highlights the interdependence between different sectors of the economy, and different agencies and institutions involved in the provision and in the use of infrastructure. This is of crucial importance not only to the housing programme, but also in guaranteeing that the activities that can potentially spin off from electrification do materialise in practice. As Muguerza et al (1990, p. 592) conclude:

> *Despite the difficulties in the past, two issues seem clear: first, it seems likely that to be effective investment in rural electrification requires additional, complementary investment in other productive activities, particularly those that can benefit from electricity. Second, it also seems likely that many attempts to enhance rural conditions will themselves have a greater chance of success if they can utilize electrical energy. Frequently, policies for the supply of electricity are missing from rural development plans.*

Electrification schemes must be co-ordinated with development plans. This applies at all levels of economic policymaking, from the national industrial strategy for electricity-using consumer durables, to the detailed support to the small businesses in the smaller townships or rural areas. A wide variety of factors are involved. Barnett (1990, p. 551) draws up a number of lessons to be learnt:

- Invest more than in the past in understanding the needs of potential users of technology in rural areas;

- Consider a wide range of options for meeting each of these needs in the particular location in which they arise;

- Allocate greater efforts than in the past to understanding how the macro policy environment will affect the introduction of technology;

- Develop simple and reliable technology that is robust across a number of users, needs and locations, avoid experimental and untried technology unless it is part of a genuine, evaluative programme that can monitor progress and draw the necessary lessons;

- Ensure a longterm commitment to meeting the chosen energy use (this is not necessarily the same as a commitment to a particular energy conversion technology);

- Harmonize the diffusion strategy with local physical, human and institutional resources. At the outset, plan specific action to build local technical and institutional capabilities;

- Build up a production, delivery and maintenance system that is willing to monitor progress honestly and can adapt to changing circumstances.

In South Africa these goals need to be supplemented, modified and targeted in greater detail. This is especially so for both townships and rural areas where formal and informal economic activity has been chronically limited. Effective developmental institutions have to be put in place in full recognition of the fact that they have been almost entirely absent in the past, despite the extraordinary capacity and capability that the industry has been able to create.

Eskom has been driven in the past to support white domestic supplies and large-scale industrial users. Its current strategy and immediate proposals inevitably reflect this. Attention continues to be devoted to the imperatives of big business. Whilst the control of Eskom is being institutionally reformed (through wider participation of trade unionists and other representatives of civil society, for example, in its governing Electricity Council) it appears to remain firmly wedded to the pursuit of commercial criteria (although these are rarely clear-cut in practice), rather than developmental goals for which social rates of return exceed those that could accrue to the balance sheet of Eskom. It also appears to be seeking as independent a position from government as possible.

Although adopting commercial criteria, Eskom has not functioned like a private corporation. If it had done so, it would inevitably have employed its command of resources to diversify into a range of electricity- and energy-related activities, and become much more like the present conglomerates that dominate the economy. Eskom does have accumulated reserves of about R12 billion, and its investments in subsidiary, associate and other companies have risen from R432 million in 1991 to R869 million in 1992. The returns on these reserves and investments amounted to about R1.5 billion in 1992, compared to R4.6 billion in net operating income and R12.6 billion in electricity sales. The evidence from the privatisation of electricity in the UK is revealing. There it has led to inappropriate choice of fuel and generating technology at the expense of jobs, the balance of payments and indigenous skills — in order to reap quick returns and establish a strong competitive position. Fortunately, privatisation of Eskom seems to have been taken off the agenda.

While the price of electricity should be regulated, MERG opposes the institutional restructuring of electricity supply so that it can be governed by an independent regulator nominated by government, with the primary function of reviewing fair prices. This is for three main reasons. Firstly, the powers of a regulator are generally insufficient to encompass all developmental goals. They are unlikely to take account of matters that do not affect price directly. Consequently, issues such as industrial policy, protection of the environment, macroeconomic and distributional goals, and the strategic restructuring of energy supply within the southern African region, would probably fall outside the remit of the regulator. The integration of the hydro-electric power of the region with South African generating capacity is essential, but raises issues and conflicts that cannot be satisfactorily devolved to a regulated Eskom.

Secondly, regulation is a blunt instrument even for the factors that it can influence. There will always be room for doubt and flexibility around the targets set, and the information and detail of regulation otherwise required would be excessive. In short, even with regulation in place, this would remain a contested area in terms of both the interpretation of what lies within its scope, and in terms of implementation. There is every reason to believe that a utility will evade regulation.

Thirdly, regulation is not a particularly democratic mode of conducting policy, although there can be advantages to arms-length control. Indeed, government can be seen as devolving its responsibilities rather than embracing them. Thus, regulation leads to the conduct of policy by a relatively unaccountable body with limited powers and objectives.

To direct Eskom is particularly important, as it is so well-placed to take a leading role in electrification (and other areas). It is experienced in a wide variety of activities, including negotiating with local authorities and engaging in joint ventures. It is an institution that is already up and running, with a proven record of being able to deliver, despite its past record of discriminatory delivery.

Eskom has accelerated its activities around urban domestic provision over the past few months. By taking over black local authority distribution rights, it has become the largest retail distributor in terms of numbers of customers, with its base rising from 278 033 in 1991 to 542 866 in 1992 (including 145 522 new connections). 38 black local authorities, including Soweto, came over to Eskom in 1992, and a further 25 signed over to Eskom between January and May, 1993. Eskom connections have risen to 30 000 per month.

Apart from playing a greater role in electrification, Eskom needs to initiate and support the economic activities that spin off from the availability of electricity. Such mechanisms are by no means novel. In the UK, both the steel and the coal industries have been involved in job creation in order to ease the problems of unemployment associated with retrenchments; and there is some experience of this in South Africa, both at the mines and at power-stations. It is crucial that institutions be developed to harness electrification into a positive and broader developmental programme, and that Eskom be used and transformed along these lines.

The rationale for proposing a greater role for Eskom, is to ensure that ex ante distributional conflict over the developmental gains associated with electrification do not obstruct or distort its implementation, and that the ex post gains are equitably distributed. Eskom must not only remain in public ownership, but must also extend its range of activities. But there must be a redefinition of its conditions of operation in conjunction with a more open and representative determination of its policy formulation, implementation and monitoring.

State enterprises and institutions such as Eskom are able to develop their own goals and ethos; and these can be captured by others with which they are closely associated (such as subsidised connection for Afrikaner farmers, or close attention to the needs of mining and mega-projects). This has been particularly marked in the electricity supply industries around the world. It is endemic around the development of nuclear power and the pursuit of narrowly defined and expensive research interests with limited pay-offs. The South African government has spent only R4 million on R&D into renewable energy technology (including small-scale hydro, for example) but as much as R750 million through the Atomic Energy Corporation. As seen from British experience, there are dangers to which Eskom has been, and could be susceptible, particularly those associated with giantism in generation. The electricity supply of Eskom has been driven by a power-station programme which locks the corporation into raising finance, awarding profitable coal mining and construction contracts, and paying more attention to the creation of the demand for electricity, than to its efficient use and pricing. To some extent, such deficiencies of the past have been recognised and remedied, not least by revising the tariff structure to even out peak loading. But much more needs to be done in addressing issues related to energy efficiency and the environment. And, in ways which reflect new goals and constituencies, institutional restructuring of Eskom is essential in order to address the issues of electrification, decision-making over large-scale projects, finance, international developments, training, joint ventures, developmental initiatives, distribution, contracting to suppliers, and technological progress in electricity supply and use.

The electricity supply industry is experiencing a major institutional restructuring. From experience around the world, often in the wake of privatisation, there is a multitude of different structures from which to learn and to choose. These necessarily cut across functions (generation, transmission, distribution, diversification and spin-off), corporate responsibility (public and private), strategic planning (macroeconomic and industrial policy) and responsibilities both geographically and by tiers of government. It is beyond the scope of this report to recommend the form that institutional restructuring should take, although the principles and goals involved have been mentioned. The institutional structure should be subject to statutory review both in the light of performance and changing objectives and circumstances as reconstruction proceeds.

4.4.4   A summary

Electrification and electricity have a major role to play in the democratic economy. They will provide heat, light and power, and the opportunity to support a range of developmental goals. MERG proposes that:

1. Eskom remain in public ownership and be used as a major instrument for electrification and the development of spin-off economic activity;

2. Industrial policy be targeted to meet the growth in demand for electrical durables;

3. User charges for electricity should avoid the capital costs of connection;

4. An electrification programme rising rapidly to at least 400 000 new connections per year be implemented — annual cost of approximately R1 billion per year;

5. An institutional restructuring of distribution be introduced to eliminate rent-seeking by (white) local authorities and to accrue economies of scale in distribution;

6. An electrification programme be developed for the southern African region as a whole as part of an overall energy plan.

Δ

Table 4.1   Floor area per person, by racial group (square metres)

Racial group	Floor area per person (m^2)
White	33.2
Coloured	12.0
Asian	18.2
Black (formal housing)	8.9
Black (backyard shacks)	4.8
Black (squatter settlements)	4.2

Source: World Bank, 1991

Table 4.2   Proportion of rural population in different regions occupying housing providing 'health protection', 1991

Region	Proportion of rural population (%)
Eastern Cape	27
Northern Cape	33
Western Cape	52
Natal	39
Orange Free State	45
Northern Transvaal	41
Southern Transvaal	16

Source: SAIRR, 1993

Table 4.3   **Distribution of informal housing in major urban areas, 1990**

Area	Total African population	Informally housed African population	Proportion informally housed (%)
Bloemfontein	470 100	150 100	34
Cape Town	570 000	330 000	58
Durban	2 600 000	1 800 000	69
East London	342 800	105 000	31
Port Elizabeth	580 000	320 000	55
PWV	5 213 000	2 260 000	3
Total	9 775 900	4 975 100	51

Source: SAIRR, 1993

Table 4.4   **Formal houses completed by the private sector, 1986 to 1991**

Year	African	Coloured	Indian	White	Total
1986	4 248	4 127	2 586	16 649	27 610
1987	7 330	5 493	2 795	17 443	33 061
1988	11 168	7 512	2 874	18 226	39 780
1989	12 067	8 521	3 377	15 301	39 266
1990	14 631	6 951	2 737	11 789	36 108
1991 (by June)	4 364	2 744	1 016	6 094	14 218

Source: SAIRR, 1993

Table 4.5   Percentage of houses built in 1991 in different price ranges

Cost of house	Proportion of houses built (%)
Less than R12 500	3
R12 500 – R35 000	7
R35 001 – R65 000	17
R65 001 – R100 000	19
R100 001 – R175 000	24
R175 001 and above	30
Total	100

Source: SAIRR, 1993

Table 4.6   Estimated coverage of water supply and sanitation in rural areas

	Water supply		Sanitation	
	%	Number	%	Number
Gazankulu	95	712 500	20	150 000
KaNgwane	75	262 500	20	70 000
KwaNdebele	90	270 000	30	90 000
KwaZulu	25	875 000	10	350 000
Lebowa	50	1 250 000	10	250 000
Qwaqwa	90	270 000	20	60 000
Bophuthatswana	60	780 000	20	260 000
Ciskei	60	300 000	20	100 000
Transkei	25	625 000	10	250 000
Venda	80	320 000	10	40 000
SA Dev. Trust	60	120 000	10	20 000
Provincial land	50	250 000	10	50 000
Commercial farms	80	2 800 000	10	70 000
Total	53	8 835 000	14	2 390 000

Source: Pearson, 1991

Table 4.7   Average travel distance for the journey to work in Cape Town

Year	1975	1980	1985	1990
Distance (km)	14.9	15.2	15.8	16.7

Source: National Housing Forum, 1992

Table 4.8   Average travel distances for subsidised bus commuters (August 1986)

Metropolitan area	Average one-way travel distance (km)
Witwatersrand	20.0
Pretoria	52.0
Durban/Pinetown	20.0
Bloemfontein	58.4
Port Elizabeth	16.1
East London	21.4

Source: National Housing Forum, 1992

Table 4.9   Estimated total expenditure on education, 1990

	Total spending		White share
	R million	%	%
Government spending	17 600		33
CURRENT EXPENDITURE	16 470	100.0	35
Pre-primary education	130	0.8	69
Primary schooling	6 480	39.3	24
Secondary schooling	5 140	31.2	31
Teacher training	560	3.4	29
Special education	490	3.0	64
Technical and vocational education	680	4.0	65
University education	1 730	10.5	65
Administration, and auxiliary and associated services	1 260	7.7	31
CAPITAL EXPENDITURE	1 130		18
Private education spending	5 000	100.0	45
Fees & other household/student outlays:			
Pre-primary	100	2.0	80
Primary	1 500	30.0	25
Secondary	1 600	32.0	42
Tertiary and other education	1 000	20.0	75
Corporate grants, investment income of universities, foreign aid, & other sources	800	16.0	50
Total	22 600		36
Govt. education expend. as % of tot. govt spending			23.6
Govt. education expend. as % of gross nat. product			7.1
Total education expend. as % of gross nat. product			9.0

Source: Donaldson, 1992

Table 4.10　Surplus capacity in 'white schools', 1992

	Transvaal	Cape	Natal	OFS	Total
Primary:					
Surplus places	9 954	27 984	19 512	9 744	47 286
Surplus classrooms	249	700	488	244	1 183
Secondary:					
Surplus places	27 041	27 935	21 020	6 010	82 006
Surplus classrooms	773	798	601	172	2 344

Source: Taylor & Smoor, 1992

Table 4.11　Standard 10 exam results for all racial groups as indicated by per cent passing, 1986 to 1990

Year	Blacks	Whites	Coloureds	Asians
1986	51.6	93.1	67.6	87.1
1987	56.1	95.1	72.7	95.2
1988	56.7	96.1	66.0	95.1
1989	41.8	96.0	72.7	93.6
1990	36.7	95.8	79.4	95.0

Source: Fehnel et al, 1993

Table 4.12 Teacher qualifications according to racial groups, 1990

Population group	School stage	Without professional qualifications		With professional qualifications		Total
		Number	%	Number	%	
Blacks	Primary	19 819	16	10 5659	84	125 478
	Secondary	5 112	8	59 651	92	64 763
	Total	24 931	13	165 310	87	190 241
Whites	Primary					
	Secondary					
	Total					53 101
Coloureds	Primary	921	4	23 150	96	24 071
	Secondary	650	5	11 633	95	12 283
	Total	1 571	4	34 783	96	36 354
Asians	Primary	61	1	5 872	99	5 933
	Secondary	115	2	5 474	98	5 589
	Total	176	1.5	11 346	98.5	11 522

Source: Fehnel, 1993

Table 4.13 Pupil : teacher ratios in the homelands, 1992

	Primary	Secondary
Bophuthatswana	32.6:1	30.1:1
Ciskei	38.9:1	32.2:1
Gazankulu	43.0:1	33.7:1
KaNgwane	40.3:1	35.6:1
KwaNdebele	39.9:1	36.7:1
KwaZulu	52.5:1	41.3:1
Lebowa	40.4:1	33.8:1
QwaQwa	33.7:1	31.4:1
Transkei	72.5:1	18.0:1
Venda	35.1:1	27.1:1

Source: SAIRR, 1993

Table 4.14   Classroom backlogs (secondary) for a pupil : teacher ratio of 35 : 1

	Total backlog 1990 (DBSA)	Pupil: classroom ratio 1990 (DBSA)	Total backlog 1991 (RIEP)	Pupil: classroom ratio 1991 (RIEP)
Transkei	-3 205	22	-2 164	26
Bophuthatswana	-885	30	-753	30
Venda	418	43	439	43
Ciskei	547	47	464	45
Sub-total (TBVC)	-3 125	29	-2 109	31
Gazankulu	1 112	65	828	51
Lebowa	3 636	58	4 011	59
KaNgwane	772	62	829	59
KwaNdebele	561	60	533	54
KwaZulu	3 668	53	3 725	51
Qwaqwa	360	51	291	46
Sub-total (SGTs)	10 109	57	10 217	54
Cape			1 326	63
Diamondfields			558	59
Highveld			1 016	50
Johannesburg			192	38
Natal			321	45
Northern Transvaal			728	50
Orange Free State			689	55
Orange-Vaal			1 071	60
Sub-total (DET)	5 919	55	5901	51
Total (TBVC, SGTs, DET)	12 902	45	14 099	47
Cape Province	-3 943	13		
Natal	-1 657	14		
Orange Free State	-1 438	13		
Transvaal	-6 441	16		
Sub-total (Hse of Assembly)	-14 934	15		
House of Delegates	-790	27	872	26
House of Representatives	-3 589	23	-2 698	25

Note: Negative numbers relate to apparent surpluses of classrooms in some areas, rather than backlogs

Source: Taylor & Smoor, 1992

Table 4.15   Classroom backlogs (primary)
for a pupil : teacher ratio of 40 : 1

	Total backlog 1990 (DBSA)	Pupil: classroom ratio 1990 (DBSA)	Total backlog 1991 (RIEP)	Pupil: classroom ratio 1991 (RIEP)
Transkei	8638	65	10 593	70
Bophuthatswana	1 691	48	1 429	46
Venda	178	42	387	44
Ciskei	307	43	242	42
Sub-total (TBVC)	10 184	54	12 651	56
Gazankulu	1 734	57	2 223	62
Lebowa	4 923	59	4 047	54
KaNgwane	1 524	63	1 699	65
KwaNdebele	192	44	170	43
KwaZulu	8 637	56	8 636	56
Qwaqwa	-631	29	-593	30
Sub-total (SGTs)	16 108	55	16 182	56
Cape			734	45
Diamondfields			44	40
Highveld			370	42
Johannesburg			-615	34
Natal			-342	37
Northern Transvaal			-208	38
Orange Free State			-23	40
Orange-Vaal			320	42
Sub-total (DET)	-1 053	39	280	40
Total (TBVC, SGTs, DET)	25 869	49	29 113	51
Cape Province	-3 943	18		
Natal	-1 657	19		
Orange Free State	-1 438	17		
Transvaal	-6 441	22		
Sub-total (Hse of Assembly)	-13 478	20		
House of Delegates	-1 296	29	-1 400	29
House of Representatives	-8 612	26	-10 436	24

Note: Negative numbers relate to apparent surpluses of classrooms in some areas, rather than backlogs
Source: Taylor & Smoor, 1992

Table 4.16 Pupil : professional staff ratio by departments

Departments	Professional staff	Enrollment	PPSR
Lebowa	85	929 043	10930
Ciskei	58	287 453	4956
Transkei	266	1 161 664	4367
KaNgwane	63	226 809	3600
KwaZulu	453	1 540 852	3400
Venda	71	231 839	3265
Gazankulu	148	318 667	2153
Bophuthatswana	277	573 664	2070
Representatives	475	841 387	1771
Delegates	165	233 101	1413
KwaNdebele	109	141 126	1295
QwaQwa	77	106 9.720	1390
Natal	127	120 973	953
DET	2 675	2 249 340	841
Cape	297	249 994	841
OFS	98	82 335	840
Transvaal	790	605 931	767

Source: Fehnel et al, 1993

Table: 4.17 Pupil : non-teaching staff ratio (based on current staffing less vacancies)

Departments	Pupils : executive	Pupils : middle management	Pupils : supervisory
SGTs (combined)	466 213	17 471	4 404
TBVC (combined)	125 256	13 831	5 737
DET	124 963	3 824	1 109
Representatives	420 692	5 194	2 705
Delegates	77 700	4 757	2 062
Assembly (combined)	62 397	2 847	832

Source: Fehnel et al, 1993

**Table 4.18   Pupil : clerical staff ratio
(based on current staffing less vacancies)**

Departments	Ratio : pupil/clerical staff
Representatives	4,065
SGTs (combined)	3,734
TBVC (combined)	3,573
Delegates	2,619
DET	984
Assembly (combined)	713

Source: Fehnel et al, 1993

Table 4.19   Basic indicators for health in South Africa

	African	White	Coloured	Asian
Population (million) (1)	29.0	5.0	3.2	1.0
Per cent of population (1)	75.5	13.5	8.6	2.6
Total fertility 1988 (1)	3.9	1.8	3.0	2.4
IMR (1000) 1988 (1)	80.0	11.9	46.3	19.0
Per cent of population under 5 years (3)	15.9	7.9	11.9	10.3
Per capita health expenditure 1987 (1)	R95	R596	R339	R356
Per capita child welfare expenditure 1988 (2)	R22	R176	R227	R171
Per capita educational expenditure 1988 (1)	R276	R3 080	R1 358	R2 225
Life expectancy 1985 (3)	62	71	61	67
Per cent of death before 1 year 1987 (3)	15.7	1.3	10.8	5.4
Per cent of death before 5 years 1987 (3)	22.5	2.1	16.3	7.3

Source: Weir, 1992

Table 4.20   Health indicators by development region: facilities per thousand members of the population, 1989

Development region	Hospital beds[a]	Doctors[b]	Nurses[c]	Treatment points[d]
A (Western Cape)	5.7	1.3	6.9	0.1
B (Northern Cape/ Western Tvl)	3.8	0.3	4.1	0.2
Non-homeland area	4.5	0.4	4.1	0.2
Bophuthatswana	2.2	0.0	4.1	0.1
C (Orange Free State)	3.6	0.4	3.7	0.1
Non-homeland area	3.7	0.5	3.8	0.1
Bophuthatswana	5.7	0.2	5.8	0.2
QwaQwa	2.8	0.1	2.8	0.1
D (Eastern Cape)	4.1	0.4	3.9	0.1
Non-homeland area	6.0	0.7	5.8	0.1
Ciskei	4.2	0.4	3.3	0.1
Transkei	2.2	0.1	2.2	0.1
E (Natal)	4.0	0.5	4.6	0.1
Non-homeland area	8.7	1.3	11.0	0.1
KwaZulu	2.0	0.1	1.7	0.0
Transkei	2.1	0.1	2.3	0.1
F (Eastern Transvaal)	2.8	0.3	3.1	0.1
Non-homeland area	3.1	0.3	3.7	0.1
KaNgwane	1.8	0.1	1.5	0.1
G (Northern Transvaal)	2.6	0.1	3.8	0.1
Non-homeland area	3.8	0.7	15.4	0.1
Gazankulu	3.1	0.1	4.2	0.1
Lebowa	2.1	0.0	1.9	0.2
Venda	2.8	0.1	2.1	0.1
H (PWV[e])	4.0	0.9	4.7	0.1
Non-homeland area	4.6	1.1	5.6	0.0
Bophuthatswana	0.7	0.1	2.0	0.1
KwaNdebele	0.05	0.0	0.4	0.1
J (Western Transvaal)	4.6	0.3	3.7	0.1
Non-homeland area	5.4	0.4	3.7	0.1
Bophuthatswana	3.5	0.1	3.6	0.1
South Africa[f]	4.0	0.8	4.5	0.1

a   Excluding beds at mental and dental institutions
b   Including doctors in private practice
c   Including registered nurses, enrolled nurses and nursing assistants
d   Includes hospitals, health centres and clinics, but excludes mobile clinics
e   Pretoria/Witwatersrand/Vereeniging
f   Includes all ten homelands   **Source: SAIRR, 1993**

Table 4.21   Unutilised hospital beds, 1991

	Provincial hospitals	White own affairs hospitals
Cape Province	5 443	6
Natal	462	10
Orange Free State	237	12
Transvaal	861	613
Total	7 003	641

Source: SAIRR, 1993

Table 4.22   Departmental distribution of budgeted government health expenditure, 1992/93 and 1993/94

Department	1993/94 (R'000)	1992/93 (R'000)	% Increase
CPA			
Health	2 277 384	2 065 342	10.3
Other[a]	85 802	80 267	6.9
Total	2 363 186	2 145 609	10.1
NPA			
Health	1 373 820	1 155 601	18.9
Other	39 000	30 814	26.6
Total	1 412 820	1 186 415	19.1
OFSPA			
Health	739 481	617 063	19.8
Other	42 400	51 246	-17.3
Total	781 881	668 309	17.0
TPA			
Health	2 927 930	2 690 889	8.8
Other	252 778	167 575	50.8
Total	3 180 708	2 858 464	11.3
DNHPD[b]			
	2 177 343	1 110 078	
(Own Affairs)		880 477	
Total	2 177 343	1990 555	9.4
Self-governing	1 020 344	988 234	3.3
Public Works[c]	134 037	83 754	
	11 070 319	9 921 340	11.6

a.   'Other' consists largely of proposed works and capital expenditure
b.   The budgets of the three 'own affairs' health departments have been amalgamated with the Department of National Health and Population Development's (DNHPD) budget, reflecting administrative integration scheduled for 1 April 1993
c.   This was a new category in the 1993/94 budget summary and appears to include capital and works expenditure for the 'own affairs' health departments and the DNHPD. It is uncertain as to whether or not the estimated 1992/93 figure is directly comparable with that for 1993/94

Source: McIntyre & Strachan, 1993

Table 4.23   Doctors, dentists and nurses in the private and public sector, 1979 and 1990

	Total on register			Total in practice			Private sector			Public sector		
	1979	*1990*	*%Inc*	*1979*	*1990*	*%Inc*	*1979*	*1990*	*%Inc*	*1979*	*1990*	*%Inc*
Doctors	14 966	24 391	63.0	11 650	19 736	69.4	5 502	11 651	111.8	6 148	8 085	31.5
Pop/Dr				2 428	1 917	-21	957	564	-41.1	3 745	3 838	2.5
Dentists	2 509	3 775	50.5	1715	3 111	81.4	1337	2 883	115.6	378	228	-39.7
Pop/Dntst				16 496	12 162	-26.3	3941	2 213	-43.8	60 905	137 970	126.5
Nurses	135 151	163 036	20.6	90 551	109 236	20.6	15 131	22 939	51.6	75 420	89 296	14.4
Pop/Nrse				314	346	10.2	348	265	-23.9	307	368	19.9

Source: Masobe, 1992

Table 4.24   African townships without access to electricity, February 1992

Proportion of households without electricity (%)	Number of townships
0	8
1-9	9
10-19	10
20-29	6
30-39	7
40-49	15
50-59	20
60-69	11
70-79	19
80-89	27
90-99	93
100	50
Total	275

Source: SAIRR, 1993

Table 4.25   Major electricity utilities in the world

Utility	Country	Sales (GWh)	Rating	Nominal capacity (MW)	Rating
EDF	France	312 100	1	93 290	1
Tepco	Japan	219 942	2	46 550	3
ENEL	Italy	182 399	3	47 293	2
Eskom	South Africa	136 168	4	35 673	4
Hydro-Quebec	Canada	135 237	5	25 682	10
Ontario Hydro	Canada	130 875	6	31 150	7
National Power	United Kingdom	121 800	7	28 300	8
RWE	Germany	121 698	8	26 059	9
Kansai Elec Power Co	Japan	120 585	9	31 378	6
TVA	USA	116 483	10	32 110	5

Source: Tokyo Electric Power Company Statistical Review — September 1991

Table 4.26   Planned number of new connections in relation to number of households in South Africa and unelectrified portion, 1992 to 1997

	1992	1993	1994	1995	1996	1997	Total
	(Thousand households)						
Total	6 714	6 882	7 045	7 230	7 411	7 596	-
Newly formed	168	172	176	181	185	190	1 072
Newly electrified	-200	-300	-350	-450	-450	-450	2 200
Not electrified	3 727	3 599	3 425	3 156	2 891	2 631	-
% Electrified	44	48	51	56	61	65	-

Source: Eskom

Table 4.27   Contribution of income from electricty to the gross income of white local authorities

	Gross income	Rate income	Income from electricity	Surplus on electricity
	(R millions)			
Jo'burg (1989/90)	1 453.9 (100%)	247.4 (17%)	650.5 (44.8%)	204.3 (14%)
Alberton (1989/90)	130.5 (100%)	15.3 (11.7%)	81.4 (62.4%)	14.6 (11.2%)
Springs (1989/90)	103.9 (100%)	14.2 (13.7%)	67.4 (64.9%)	10.7 (10.3%)
Benoni (1988/89)	145.9 (100%)	25.2 (17.2%)	83.7 (57.4%)	11.5 (7.9%)
Brakpan (1987/88)	76.4 (100%)	11.2 (14.6%)	42.0 (55.0%)	6.4 (8.4%)

Note: These figures have been calculated from the information provided by these local authorities in their financial statements for the years cited
Source: Swilling et al, 1991

Table 4.28   Contribution of income from electricity to the gross income of black local authorities

	Gross income	Income from electricity	Deficit on electricity
	(R millions)		
Tsakane (1988/89)	7.5 (100%)	1.05 (14%)	0.36 (4.8%)
Wattville (1987/88)	3.37 (100%)	0.92 (27.3%)	0.37 (10.8%)
Daveyton (1987/88)	22.91 (100%)	8.3 (34.7%)	1.03 (4.5%)
Tembisa (1988/89)	33.4 (100%)	10.9 (32.6%)	0.4 (1.2%)
Duduza (1989/90)	2.22 (100%)	0.16 (7%)	0.3 (13.4%)
Tokoza (1989/90)	17.87 (100%)	4.36 (24.4%)	0.68 (3.8%)

Note: These figures have been derived from the financial statements of the local authorities referred to as well as supplementary documents provided by the local authorities where necessary to complete the picture
Source: Swilling et al, 1991

Table 4.29   Electricity tariffs and capital outlays

Tariff	Capital outlay	Charge/kWh
S1	0	22.38
S2	At least R1200[a]	19.13
S3	Full Connection[b]	16.79

a   To cover connection to town of residence.
b   To cover all connection costs, as for S2 plus to house

Source: Eskom

Figure 4.1   Distribution of population densities in Cape Town's built-up area

PEOPLE PER HECTARE
WITHIN 1 KM INTERVAL

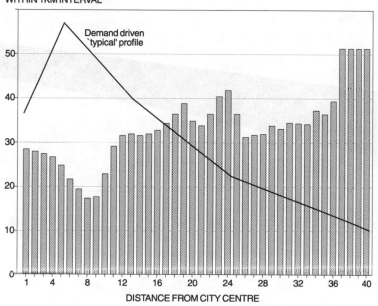

Figure 4.2   Road utilisation by region

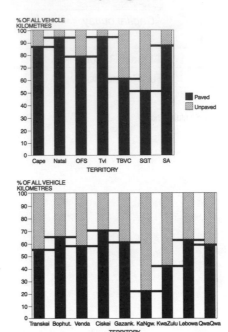

Source: Department of Transport 1991

Figure 4.3   A national electrification programme
1992 to 2007

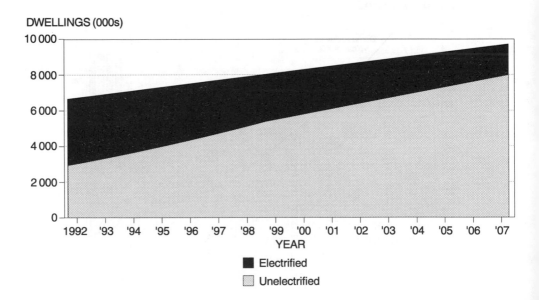

Source: Eskom

**Figure 4.4   A national electrification programme
1992 to 2007**

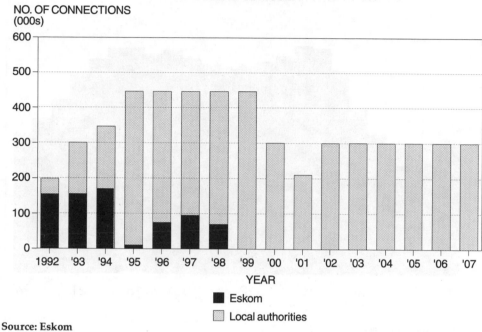

Source: Eskom

Figure 4.5   Eskom electrification, monthly connections

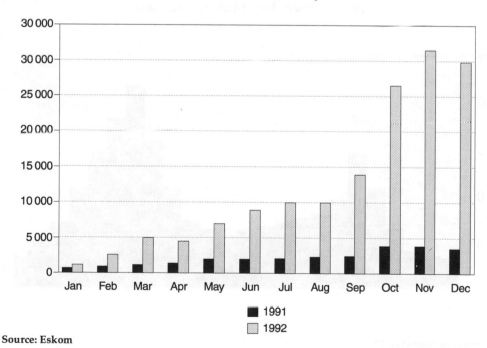

Source: Eskom

**Figure 4.6   The daily electricity consumption profile
of the municipality of Durban**

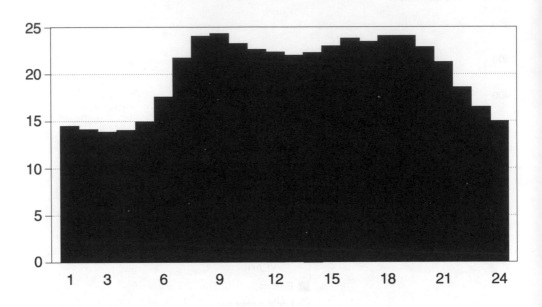

Source: Swilling et al, 1991

**Figure 4.7   The daily electricity consumption profile
of the township Mabopane East**

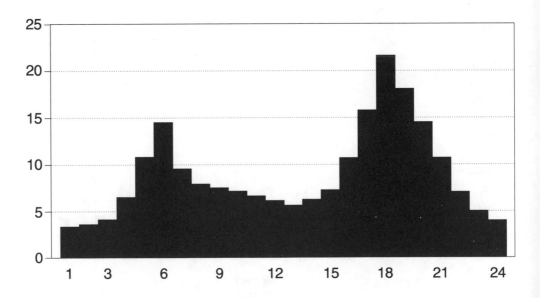

Source: Swilling et al, 1991

Figure 4.8   Growth of business activity after electrification

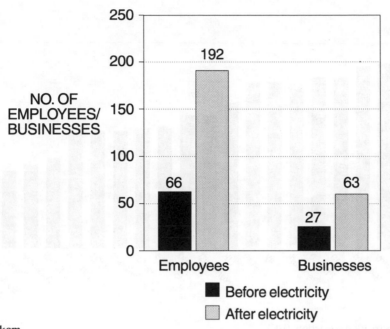

Source: Eskom

Figure 4.9   Industrial electricity prices in selected economies

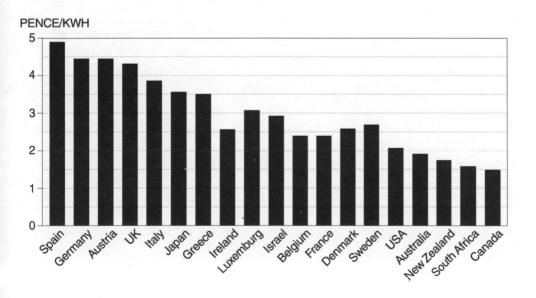

Source: Electricity Association, (UK)

Figure 4.10 Domestic electricity prices in selected economies

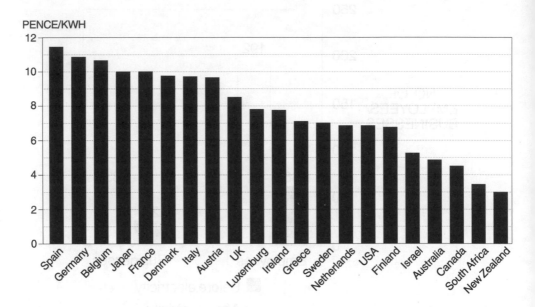

Source: Electricity Association, (UK)

C H A P T E R 5
Labour market policies

.

5.1 Performance of the labour market: the impact of past policies

5.1.1 The data required to assess performance

The problems in assessing trends in employment and wages in the South African labour market are immense. They stem largely from the dereliction of duty of the state agencies responsible for collecting the relevant data. Hardly any information at all is available concerning the economically active population not registered as employed in the enumerated or formal sector of the economy. The information that has been published on employment in the unenumerated sector is inconsistent, suggesting that either 19.9 per cent of the black labour force is involved in this 'informal' sector (CSS, 1989), or 28 per cent (Kirsten, 1988) or 24.5 per cent (Fallon, 1992). Rather than undertaking regular and detailed surveys of workers in the unenumerated sector, where the majority of people are engaged, the size and features of this sector are usually estimated as a residual from the little that is known about the enumerated or formal sector. Moreover, these residual estimates depend upon unreliable and gender-biased definitions and measurements of the economically active population. In addition, the published estimates provide no accurate time series on the sectoral or geographical breakdown of employment in the unenumerated sector, and do not analyse the role of wage employment, despite the fact that pilot surveys by the CSS indicate that a higher proportion of those engaged full-time in the unenumerated sector are wage employees than are workers on their own account (CSS, 1990, p. 1).

Improved statistical data on trends in wage employment for the majority of the poorest South Africans, who depend on unenumerated jobs in domestic service, farm labour, trade and hawking, transport, etc., or as child labourers, are an urgent priority for the democratic movement.

The statistics covering those employed in the enumerated sector are only slightly more reliable. Their defects are well known and have been discussed quite thoroughly by South African economists, who have concluded that current estimates of absolute levels of employment are likely to be out by a considerable margin; that information available on employment in the TVBC states is tenuous and often contradictory; and that the CSS has been guilty of changing the criteria according to which employment series are compiled without applying the adjustment retroactively, which creates great difficulties when analysis of long-term trends is required (Roukens de Lange and van Eeghen, 1990). The available sources, i.e. CSS periodic Censuses of the Industrial and Service Sectors, South African Labour Statistics, the Population Census, the Current Population Survey and the Manpower Survey, give inconsistent results concerning the number of employees, particularly at the sectoral level.

Moreover, there is no single aggregate wage series available for enumerated workers in South Africa. Even the data on government sector wages over time are unreliable, because of reclassification between government and parastatals and the creation of the TVBC states. While the Manpower Surveys published by the CSS provide some data on employment by occupation and by race, which has been used as the basis for publishing time series of employment by skill level, there are no directly comparable wage series. Besides, the occupational groupings are so broad that they often hide differences between important occupations (Crankshaw, 1989).

5.1.2   Trends in employment

Despite these data problems, the corrected standardised employment series for the enumerated sector which covers the years 1946 to 1988, does reveal distinct shifts in the employment growth rate in the mid–1970s, with a breakpoint between 1974 and 1976 and a further decline in the growth rate of employment between 1982 and 1988 (Roukens de Lange and van Eeghen, 1990). Thus, although many of the absolute numbers are unreliable, when the data is consistently compiled, it is possible to be confident about the direction of the national trend in enumerated employment, which has been unambiguously downwards since the mid–1970s and was stagnant between 1982 and 1988.

It is also possible to establish a marked shift in the distribution of enumerated employees between sectors since 1960, reflecting the fact that enumerated employment growth has declined far more rapidly in some sectors than others. The fastest rates of decline in employment since 1980 have been in the agricultural, transport and mining sectors, and manufacturing employment hardly increased at all over this period. Regions B, J and F had the worst employment growth record (see Table 5.1). If it had not been for substantial growth in public sector employment in the period between 1986 and 1990, total enumerated employment growth would have been negative in that period.

The evidence concerning enumerated employment in more recent years, although not available in the corrected form of long-term standardised employment series, suggests a severe worsening of the trend. Over the period 1989 to 92, total employment in the enumerated non-agricultural sectors of the economy declined by 4.8 per cent, equivalent to the loss of about 286 000 jobs; the slight positive growth in employment in the public sector was not sufficient to reverse the overall decline. There have, of course, been substantial further declines in enumerated employment in the period since the end of 1992. In the current recession (1989–1993), the rate of decline of enumerated employment has been of an unprecedented order of magnitude, and has affected a wider range of sectors of the economy than recorded in any previous recession since 1970. Between February 1989 and December 1992, total private sector non-agricultural enumerated employment declined by 7.8 per cent, while employment declines in the electricity generation, mining, private road transportation and construction sectors were 18.5 per cent, 18 per cent, 16.3 per cent and 13.6 per cent respectively.

The consequences of this disastrous record have been that an ever smaller proportion of new entrants to the labour market have been able to secure unenumerated wage employment, and that a large number of those previously in enumerated employment have lost their jobs. The mismatch between available enumerated jobs and the size of the economically active population is undoubtedly very large, but cannot be analysed in the absence of satisfactory data for the economically active population (Meth, 1988). However, it is possible to conclude that only a small proportion of the two million or so new entrants to the labour market have been able to secure enumerated employment over the last five years, and that a very large number of workers have lost their enumerated sector jobs over the same period.

The rate of growth of productive employment opportunities in the unenumerated sector, where on average the returns to labour are lower, is unlikely to have kept pace with the growth in the number of those denied access to enumerated employment. With rapid declines in enumerated employment, the demand for unenumerated activities will also deteriorate. While no satisfactory estimates of unemployment covering the majority of the population are available,[1] it can confidently be stated that a large and rapidly increasing gap exists between the number of people requiring employment and the capacity of any sector of the economy to provide employment.

The aggregate data conceals the fact that the capacity to create or maintain employment has deteriorated more rapidly and is far weaker in some regions than others. The proportion of the labour force employed in the formal economy in 1989, according to DBSA definitions and estimates, ranges from 61 per cent in the PWV area to only 22 per cent in region G (covering the northern Transvaal, Venda, Lebowa and Gazankulu). The fall in this proportion over the period 1985 to 1989 has been far greater in some regions than others; the worst-affected regions show a fall in the proportion of the labour force employed in the formal sector by over five percentage points, compared with a fall of under two percentage points in the least affected regions (DBSA, 1991b, p. 24).

It cannot be assumed that the large and growing proportion of the economically active population that has failed to find enumerated employment has been absorbed in self-employment in homeland agriculture. A relatively small and declining proportion of the economically active population is reported in the population censuses to be engaged in the agricultural sector (currently amounting to approximately 10 per cent) of which probably less than a quarter is in full-time agricultural self employment (DBSA, 1991b, p. 47 and Chapter Six).

5.1.3 Trends in real wages

Those responsible for economic policy have not only failed to avert a dramatic and accelerating decline in the creation of enumerated jobs, but this decline has also been accompanied by an inadequate rate of growth of real wages for the majority of those employed in the enumerated sector, as well as by sharp declines in real wages in particular regions and sectors. Since 1980, the average rate of growth of real wages for African workers has declined dramatically. In the manufacturing sector, it fell to 0.6 per cent in 1986 to 89, compared to 4.6 per cent in 1971 to 89 (Fallon, 1992, p. 16). In the construction sector, African real wage growth was negative, at -1.45 per cent over the period 1986 to 90, while in the agricultural sector real wages had fallen to below 1975 levels by 1987 (World Bank, 1993, p. 109). Falls in real wages in the transport and communications sector have also been substantial (CSS, 1992b, p. 4.44).

The trend in average real wages conceals wide variation in wages for different African workers. The majority of African working-class employees in the enumerated sector fall into the occupational categories 'unskilled' (40.4 per cent) and 'menial' (10 per cent), with a further 8.4 per cent classified as 'drivers' (Hindson and Crankshaw, 1990, Table 11). The demand for these occupational categories has been falling particularly rapidly since 1965. The absolute number of semi-skilled and unskilled workers in the enumerated sector (excluding agriculture) fell from 3.12 million in 1981 to 2.99 million in 1990, equivalent to a fall in the share of these occupations in total enumerated non-agricultural employment from 57 to 50 per cent (CEAS, 1993, p. 177). The growth in real wages for male unskilled employees has been negative for many years. There have been increasing occupational differentials between enumerated African employees (Hofmeyer, 1990; Knight and McGrath, 1987). Although trade-union membership appears to have been successful in suppressing some of the effects of occupational differentials, by no means all unskilled enumerated employees have been recruited as trade-union members, and in non-unionised sectors, wage differentials have probably been rising particularly rapidly (P. Moll, 1993).

The economic status of those African males in the lowest educational and occupational categories has therefore been deteriorating; they suffered from falls in their real wages between 1975 and 1985 at a rate of 3 per cent per year (Hofmeyer, 1990). In 1991, an estimated 77 per cent of the economically active African population had not completed standard seven (CEAS, 1993, p. 175). These lower-paid unskilled African workers, whose real wages have been falling since 1980, have also been the first to lose their jobs in the current recession (SARB, 1993b, p. 20). Hindson summarises the similar impact of an earlier recession: 'the impact of the economic recession in terms of employment growth was far less severe on coloured and Asian employment, substantial in the case of whites and devastating in the case of African workers' (1988, p. 6).

5.1.4   *The employment and remuneration of women*

The generation of employment and the remuneration of female workers has also been far from satisfactory. Women are severely under-represented amongst those in enumerated employment, although the available statistics do not allow precise statements concerning trends. However, women do appear to be over-represented in the segments of the enumerated labour market with the worst records for employment and wage growth. Between 1965 and 1987, while the proportion of African working-class enumerated employees in 'unskilled' and 'menial' occupational categories decreased, the proportion of females in these categories increased (Hindson and Crankshaw, 1990, Table 12). As noted above, the ability of the economy to provide enumerated wage employment to unskilled workers, whether male or female, has been declining over time.

The over-representation of females in menial occupations has been reinforced by fact that more females than males are illiterate, while the literacy gap between females and males appears to be widening (Budlender, 1991, p. 12). With rapidly declining training facilities in industry, the number of apprenticeships filled by women in the engineering industry in 1992 amounted to a grand total of eight (Bird and Lloyd, 1992, p.3; Wood, 1993, p. 19).[2] At the lowest levels of the skills grade, where most black females are concentrated, male : female wage differentials are particularly great, with females earning less than three-quarters of the wage earned by males in equivalent grades (Budlender, 1991; see also Chapter Six).

Female workers are overwhelmingly concentrated in those sectors and occupations where wage rates are particularly low (Ginwala, Mackintosh and Massey, 1991); and female members of COSATU unions are clustered in the lowest-grade jobs (Dove, 1993; Budlender, 1991). By the end of the 1980s, women, mainly teachers and nurses, accounted for only 29 per cent of high-level and middle-level employment, with white males dominating all high-level positions. Black females constitute a negligible percentage of high-level occupations as defined by the Manpower Commission and only 6 per cent of all medium-level occupations (excluding teaching and nursing professions) (NMC, 1990, p. 41). Although women have made some inroads into semi-professional and routine white collar occupations, constituting 50 per cent and 56 per cent of these occupational categories in 1987, the majority of these women are still white (Hindson and Crankshaw, 1990). Moreover, middle-class black women in these categories of employment represent a tiny proportion of the total number of black women in wage employment, and male employees with similar qualifications are still likely to receive higher levels of remuneration (Budlender, 1991, p. 22).

The upgrading of the skills of some black workers has given rise to a floating colour bar, rather than a breach in the colour bar; white/black hierarchies have remained substantially untouched, and a very large percentage of black employees, especially female employees, continue to receive poverty wages (see Chapter 6). This is confirmed at the aggregate level by the fact that, although the black labour force grew a great deal more (by over 15 per cent) between 1985 and 1990 than the white labour force (which grew by approximately 4 per cent over this period), the racial shares in total wages and salaries changed far less. The white share fell slowly and remained at over 50 per cent in 1990 (Urban Foundation, 1991, Table 2). Within the manufacturing sector, there appear to be differences of 10 per cent between black and white workers in the same skill positions, and of 15 per cent in unskilled positions (Joffee, 1993, p.7).

Both with respect to the generation of employment and the maintenance of real wage growth, the South African economy has performed extremely badly for some time. The net outcome of the labour market processes described above has been an increase in the number of black people who are struggling to survive in households with income levels which are below the minimum living level. The number of black people experiencing poverty increased from 14.6 million in 1985 to 16.3 million in 1990.[3] The majority of the population, especially unskilled and female members of the labour force, have experienced severe and rapidly worsening difficulties in the labour market over the last decade. These difficulties have become so acute and are affecting so many, that few would now deny the existence of a major employment crisis in the economy.

5.2 The government and orthodox responses to the employment crisis

There is a consensus that the failure of the economy to generate large-scale and sustained increases in employment undermines the possibility of social progress. However, the MERG analysis of the causes of this failure, and its policies to address the crisis differ radically from those promoted by the government and the Washington-based international financial agencies. The differences start at the theoretical level. The MERG view is that government, IMF and IBRD conclusions are analytically incoherent, coloured by an ideological anti-worker bias, and unsupported by the available empirical evidence.

The Normative Economic Model (1993) asserts that employment problems have been 'caused by the high cost of labour', and that the source of the capital intensive structure of the economy is the high unit cost of labour (p. 158). In this model, the rate of growth of enumerated employment is determined by the changes in the cost of labour relative to capital (p. 52). Thus, the prolonged policy-induced depression is effectively ignored and no account is taken of the fact that an expansion of demand would lead to fuller employment of both labour and capital. In more sophisticated and standard macroeconomic models developed in other countries, the real wage (as an outcome of money wages and prices) would be simultaneously determined along with employment — rather than there being a direct and inverse relation between real wages and employment.

The NEM policy conclusion, that 'increases in real wages should be limited to the growth in (total factor) productivity' (p. 54), amounts to abandoning government responsibility for achieving an adequate rate of growth of employment. The growth in total factor productivity, which is taken as the constraint on real wage growth, and hence on employment growth, is assumed to be given. It is projected to rise by 0.75 per cent per year from 1992 to 2000, on the basis that even lower (in fact, negative) rates have been observed in recent years. However, the abysmal recent record of total factor productivity growth is in itself an indictment of government policy, an indication of technological stagnation, and the misallocation of public expenditure. It acts as a pointer to the public investment priorities which the government economic policy makers should now be setting. If the problems of stagnation in output and declining productivity performance were to be addressed by competent economic policy makers, then the extrapolation of historic economic relations (such as the elasticities of substitution between capital and labour) would become inappropriate.

The policy conclusions of the IMF are virtually identical to the NEM ones, and open to the same criticisms. In fact, the NEM derives its approach from the standard IMF arguments for wage flexibility, so as to realign the relative prices of capital and labour in order to effect a more efficient allocation of resources. The IMF argues that, 'if employment growth is to rise enough to begin alleviating the existing, severe underemployment problem, real wage growth must be contained' (IMF, 1992, p. 9). The argument is based on a Cobb-Douglas production function and assumed rates of multi-factor productivity growth. The model leads tautologically to the conclusion that if average real wage growth is about 1.25 per cent per year, employment growth would be very much slower than if real wage growth were at 0.25 per cent per year, all other things being equal. The IMF ignores the fact that there has never been a stable inverse relationship between real wages and the level of employment in South Africa.

The World Bank has recently developed more sophisticated, but essentially similar arguments. Fallon (1992) estimates employment levels, dividing the work-force into Africans (who, in direct contradiction to empirical evidence, are arbitrarily designated unskilled and in excess supply), whites (skilled and in short supply), and Asians and coloureds (somewhere in between). African employment is determined by an efficiency-wage argument in which employers choose, or are forced, to pay a wage above the market-clearing level (to avoid high turnover, poor work effort, and industrial action). white wages, on the other hand, are perceived to be more respon-sive to market forces or the level of overall demand, so that they vary inversely with the level of employment. As whites are close to being fully employed, their levels of employment are even taken as an index of capacity utilisation.

Four possible factors — bottlenecks in the supply of white labour, excessive capital-labour ratios due to high wages and low user-costs of capital (interest rates), recession, and black wage increases — are investigated in terms of their impact on black employment. It is concluded that:

> *Changes in factor prices have had an important effect on black employment. The empirical results indicate that this can over-whelmingly be traced to upward movements in black wages ...the elasticity of black employment with respect to the real wage is of the order of - 0.25 (pages 27– 8).*

The analysis is riddled with arbitrary assumptions which may have been introduced to make the model tractable, or because of the desire to obtain qualitatively and quantitatively acceptable results. Although the model is concerned with macroe-conomic relations, it has no international nor monetary sectors. Two issues must therefore be addressed.

The first concerns excess capacity. During the 1970s, investment in the South African economy was dominated by the public sector, giving rise to considerable excess capacity in some sectors in the 1980s, especially in electricity generation, for example. This was prompted by the expansion of mining, especially gold. This excess capacity continues to persist. It suggests that aggregate production functions are at best appropriate only if they do not ignore extensive lags (since investments have long gestation periods). In South Africa, capital-labour ratios have been heavily determined by a few sectors which can only respond sluggishly to price signals, and which are in any case heavily influenced by other considerations, such as strategic political decision-making. Given the weight of such public investment in the 1970s, and the stagnation of both public and private investment in the 1980s, the quantitative relations discovered by the World Bank or others for this period (between capital-la-bour ratios and factor prices), must be treated with considerable scepticism.

Secondly, analysis of labour markets must be sensitive to the variety of conditions that prevail across them, whether these be indirect as in differences in investment, technology and excess capacity, or direct as in overt racial or gender discrimination between different sections of the work-force. Indeed, if the hypotheses put forward by Fallon (1992) are examined at a disaggregated level, they are inconsistent with the evidence. Unemployment appears to be highest amongst those sections of the work-force (women and youth) with the lowest levels of wages. In rural areas, unemployment is comparable to the level in urban areas even though wages are driven down to levels as low as four rand per day. Similar anomalies emerge for the occupational, sectoral and geographical distribution of wage rates and unemployment.

Of course, such evidence could be reinterpreted by incorporating further explanatory factors specific to the particular disaggregated labour market concerned. But this merely serves to confirm the need to identify how labour markets function, and how they are structurally related to one another and the economy and society. Fallon does distinguish labour markets by race (and occasionally by other socio-economic factors such as gender, age, skill and education). However, these have not been adequately addressed in confronting the relationship between wages and employment, and the other determinants of labour market outcomes.

Other attempts made by the World Bank to model the effects on agricultural employment of changes in real wage rates are based on flimsy assumptions. For example:

> *Based on the assumption of competitive labour markets and wage rate equalisation across sectors, the variance in off-farm earnings is a good proxy for the variance in farm wage rates. An increase in wages (in the manufacturing sector) should theoretically have a negative effect on farm labour employment though....the substitution of machinery for labour as farm labour costs rise relative to farm machinery costs. (Roth et al, 1992, p. 90)*

The econometric results do not support the existence of a link between the decline in black farm employment levels and rising wage rates in agriculture (Roth et al, p. 91). Indeed, the available regional and crop specific data on changes in farm wages and employment clearly show that employment growth is not determined by changes in real wages in the agricultural (or non-agricultural) sectors (see World Bank, 1993a, Table 5.6, p. 110).

The MERG analysis of causes of the poor employment record of the South African economy focuses on the failure of the government to sustain reasonable levels of aggregate demand, and of public sector investment in appropriate projects and the education of the labour force. The MERG macroeconomic model also highlights the fact that the available supply of saving has not been channelled into domestic investment to boost the level of demand. There remains considerable capacity to increase the level of demand and of employment. The assertion that increases in the real wages of the lowest paid and in average black real wages are, in the medium term, inconsistent with fast rates of growth of output and employment, is not valid. International comparative evidence supports the MERG argument that in growing economies, real wages and employment are not inversely related, and that employment is a function of aggregate demand and output, rather than of wage flexibility in the labour market.

5.3 New policies for employment, wages, working conditions and training

The rapid implementation of a set of policies specifically designed to create employment, to foster training and to improve the wages and working conditions of a substantial number of the most disadvantaged people in the labour market, is an immediate objective of the democratic movement. Some increase in the demand for labour and the rate of growth of employment may be expected as a consequence of improved macroeconomic management, leading to higher sustained levels of aggregate demand, GDP growth and investment (see Chapter One). However, the trickle-down effects on labour market conditions of a more favourable macroeconomic environment, although necessary, are not sufficient to achieve either the medium or long-term labour market outcomes which are a priority of the democratic movement.

Reliance on trickle-down cannot achieve the expansion on the supply side of the skills-base necessary for an internationally successful manufacturing economy; nor will it raise the levels of wages of the poorest employees at a rate sufficient to ensure a large domestic market for manufacturing as a secure platform for export growth. In the absence of a set of interventions designed to achieve the labour-market objectives of the democratic movement, the social, political and human costs of labour, under-utilisation and poverty wages will escalate, and the prospects for a reduction in endemic violence will recede.

The range of interventions and institutional innovations which must be put in place, is extensive and not all the policy goals of the democratic movement for the labour market can be described in this chapter. In particular, the reform of the social security system, which is an urgent priority of the democratic movement, is not discussed here. Nevertheless, three major policy initiatives will be outlined, which are anticipated to have a substantial impact on employment, productivity, output and public expenditure. The first consists of interventions aimed at addressing the current deficiencies in the training of labour, or in human resource investment.

5.3.1 Investment in human resources

The interventions required in this area cover not merely changes in public expenditure, but legislative reform of the entire industrial relations and educational system. Government legislation has limited the overall numbers of qualified artisan workers in South Africa, raised the cost of training and employing artisans, and adversely affected the quality of all technical education for the labour force. In the current recession, there has been a sharp decline in private sector involvement in technical training, which has had a severely negative effect on the number of black apprenticeships. According to Bot, 'In 1982, for example, 10 659 new white and 3 838 black apprenticeship contracts were registered, while in 1986 the corresponding figures were 8 032 and 1 628; thus black apprenticeship contracts decreased from 26 per cent to 17 per cent of the total' (1988, p. 27). The number of people acquiring artisan status fell from 12 933 in 1985 to 7 132 in 1990 (Langa, 1993, p. 10).

By 1989 only 6 per cent of artisans (and 14 per cent of apprentices) were African. The bulk of these artisans and apprentices are concentrated in the building sector; the numbers engaged in the more technologically advanced metal and engineering sectors are few (Joffee, 1993, p. 5). Private sector expenditure on training is extremely low by international standards. Moreover, black semi-skilled workers, such as artisan aides, suffer overt discrimination in both the public and private sector. Although they develop advanced skills, these are not recognised by employers. When unskilled and semi-skilled workers do receive any training, it is mostly job-specific and does not lay the basis for further training, career advancement or mobility.

Currently, the mean education level of the work-force is only seven years, and a very high proportion of economically active black people are not literate or numerate. At the post-secondary level, education in science and technology is more racially discriminatory in outcome than other post-secondary education, since most Africans matriculate without maths and science. The proportion of matriculants passing maths and science has declined in the 1980s, with less than 2 per cent of African matriculants passing maths in the 1990s, and 0.02 per cent passing both Maths and Science (Langa, 1993, p. 10).

The deficiencies in education are discussed in Chapter Four, together with the MERG policy proposals. Here, the policies developed by COSATU and the Industrial Strategy Project with respect to skills acquisition and training for those already in the work-force, are described. It is proposed that a large scale and sustained programme to promote skill acquisition and training should be put in place. Skills acquisition should occur through training modules (accredited by tripartite institutions) and career-paths designed to enable workers to move from one skill level to the next on the basis of competence. Appropriate standards will be maintained by constantly up-dating the skills themselves, in line with changing sectoral needs, the strategic objectives of firms, and changes in technology and work organisation.

The provision of career paths enabling workers to achieve continuous training, and gain skills which are transferable to other sectors, will provide a new and important incentive to those workers who are currently the lowest paid. If skill upgrading and improvements in productivity are regularly accompanied by improvements in employment security and increases in real wages, further incentives will be provided to all workers. These proposals recognise that behind the label of unskilled (black) work, there exists a large pool of unrecognised skill and a poorly motivated labour force, which has experienced many years of adversarial industrial relations during a period of macroeconomic mismanagement and rapidly increasing job insecurity. The MERG proposals address these problems, and argue that the talents of this pool can contribute to productivity growth in the economy in the second half of the 1990s.

Proposals to introduce such a nexus between wages, training, skills-grading and work reorganisation have recently made headway; NUMSA and SEIFSA are successfully negotiating a three-year programme along these lines. Negotiations on such long-term plans at an industry level hold out the promise of replacing annual rounds of narrow adversarial bargaining over wages with more socially productive interactions between employers and workers. If targeted government support (tariffs, depreciation allowances, subsidies, tax relief, etc.) for new investment in plant and machinery is made conditional on associated investments in human resources and (re)skilling, tripartite negotiations on the appropriate schedule of conditions could provide the institutional framework for substantial improvements in industrial productivity. Models for the application of such training conditions have recently been agreed upon for labour-based construction and public works at the National Economic Forum.

The majority of the current work-force is unlikely to be able to take advantage of new opportunities for skill enhancement and the state funded incentives discussed above, without a further commitment by the state, calling on financial and other contributions from employers, to provide adult basic education (ABE). The priority accorded to ABE should be integrated together with the programme designed to provide a universal general certificate of education accrediting ten years of schooling. This education certificate, or an equivalent ABE qualification, should be made available to all existing and new entrants to the labour force, especially those in rural areas, as soon as possible, and as a matter of the highest priority. The democratic movement is committed to ensuring that the education and training of women receives a substantial share of the allocation of funding in the programme of investment in human resources. The public expenditure implications of this policy are discussed below.

In the longer run, the ANC and COSATU are committed to promote lifelong learning. 'Education and training should continue throughout a worker's life to enable him/her to keep pace with technological change and develop his/her abilities.' (COSATU, 1991). This commitment recognises the fact that the ability to learn while off the job reinforces the ability to learn on the job, and vice versa. Training without lifelong education and access to further education is unlikely to produce a skilled and motivated work-force.

MERG has simulated the results of the recommended programmes of investment in human resources in order to estimate their impact on the skill composition, and hence wage-earning capacity, of the work-force over the period 1990 to 2010. In the analysis, the economically active population in South Africa is divided into four educational or skill categories:

Level I: Standard 10 plus diploma or degree
Level II: Standard 8 — 10
Level III: Standard 2 — 7
Level IV: Lower than Standard 2

Currently, black people dominate the most unskilled group, level IV, and have decreasing representation at levels III and II, with only marginal representation at level I. White members of the economically active population constitute only a small share of level III and a negligible share of level IV, although they make up a significantly higher proportion of level I than all other workers (see Figure 5.1).

The next step is to examine the available projections for the growth of the labour force. Labour force estimates for each year between 1990 and 2010 are presented in Table A.14. The black labour force obviously accounts for an increasing share of the total economically active population over the projection period. The key question is, what proportion of the growing labour force can be expected to fall into each of the education/skill categories in future years? MERG has undertaken simulations to provide two different answers to this question: the results depend on whether or not the MERG policy recommendations concerning investment in human resources are implemented.

The first simulation assumes that none of the recommended policy initiatives are adopted. Tables A.15, A.16, A.17 and A.18 contain the estimates for this scenario. This simulation is also based on the following important additional assumptions:

- that the net addition to the labour force in each year (as determined by the differences in the yearly totals from Table A.14) is the result of the sum of new entrants, less the number of retirements;

- that the ratio of new entrants to the black labour force with education levels I, II, III and IV remains constant, i.e. that the current proportions of children entering school, proceeding to Standard 6 and then progressing through secondary school and higher education remain unchanged in the future. Thus, it is assumed that the relevant educational ratios to be applied to new black entrants should be 10:25:40:25 for levels I:II:III:IV;

- that those people already in the labour force do not have any significant access to programmes of further/continuing education which would promote them from a lower education/skill level to a higher level.

Based on these assumptions, the percentage of the black labour force in the highest education/skill categories (level I and II) increases very slowly and the percentage in the categories III and IV decreases correspondingly slowly. For example, in 1990, 2.6 per cent of the black economically active population was at level I; by 2003, this proportion rises to only 5.6 per cent.

It is also possible to estimate the earnings of each educational/skill category of worker. For this purpose, a wage earnings capacity index was calculated, based on the current ratio of the relative earnings of people in each of the four education/skills categories. The relative earnings for level I, II, III, and IV were then set at 11.7:6.7:2.3:1, which means that those workers educated to level I continue to earn approximately 12 times as much as those educated to level IV.

The wage earnings capacity index captures the ability of all members of the economically active labour force to command earnings corresponding to their education/skill level. Thus, if the entire labour force is at level IV, the index is set at 100. On this basis, the wage earning capacity index for the black labour force is found to be 306 in 1990, rising to only 360 by 2010 if there are no substantial policy changes leading to greater investment in education and training (see Table A.15).

The corresponding wage earning capacity index for economically active whites in 1990 is 766, rising to 783 by 2010. By the end of the projection period, the wage earnings capacity index for economically active Asians is 643, and 471 for coloureds.

The implications of a failure to effect a radical change in education and training policy are presented in Figure 5.2, which plots the wage earning capacity indices of the different population groups under current policy. The gap between white and black earning capacity hardly narrows at all between 1990 and 2010. Another way of expressing the point made in Figure 5.2, is to express the projected wage earning capacity of the black labour force as a percentage of that of the white labour force over time. This shows that by 2010, the wage earning capacity of the black economically active population would rise to only 47 per cent of that of the white population, up from about 40 per cent in 1990. Such an outcome would of course, be unacceptable to the democratic movement, which is committed to achieving a substantial shift towards equality of opportunity for those who have been oppressed by apartheid.

The alternative policy recommended by MERG (see Tables A.19 to A.24) has been modelled on the assumptions that all children will receive a minimum of ten years of schooling; that a programme of Adult Basic Education/Training for those in employment is implemented; and that a programme of Adult Basic Education/Training for new employees on public works projects and labour-based civil engineering projects, is put into practice. Some of the detailed assumptions underlying the projection exercise are the following:

- The ratio of new entrants to the labour force at levels I, II, III and IV changes yearly to reflect the impact of increased participation rates in primary school and secondary school as a result of the policy of providing ten years of schooling;

- An Adult Basic Education/Training programme begins in 1994 with 50 000 current employees who fall into the Education/Skill level IV. These employees enter a programme of one day per week of Adult Basic Education equivalent to approximately 400 hours per year. Each year after 1994 a further 50 000 persons enter the programme. The 50 000 who began their training in 1994 progress to a second level of training, also consisting of about 400 hours per year, and finally to a third and fourth level of training in 1996/7, which is designed to bring participants up to the level of Standard 8, in addition to providing them with portable skills training. Under this system, those employees with the greatest educational deficiencies will receive a total of 1 600 hours of training. Those with minor problems with numeracy and literacy will be offered 400 hours over one year. All employees will be given the opportunity to increase their basic education up to a level equivalent to Standard 8 and will, in addition, receive some skills training. MERG recommends that workers who have already achieved basic numeracy and literacy should be able to move into a skills training programme which will amount to a further 800 hours of training, spread over an additional two years. Unfortunately there are likely to be delays in ensuring an adequate supply of lecturers/trainers for this ambitious programme, as well as in the supply of appropriate educational facilities and infrastructure. Therefore, the MERG calculations assume that the programme will be staggered, so that in 1995 the first 50 000 trainees enter level III, and this cohort only enters level II in 1997. The process of a gradual depletion at the lower end of the education/training scale and a corresponding net addition to the numbers at the higher end continues throughout the projection period. By 2004, the proportion of the economically active black population in level IV will have fallen to below 20 per cent, compared to the current proportion of over 30 per cent;

- The third component of the MERG policy recommendations involves providing Adult Basic Education/Training to an additional 100 000 unemployed persons per annum who will be engaged to work on physical infrastructure projects at the same time as they are being trained. The education/training programme for these employees on labour-based construction projects will take the same form as that proposed for those already in employment, i.e. they will be entitled to one day per week of education/training to bring them up to the educational equivalent of Standard 8. The results of the addition of this third component of the MERG programme, in terms of changes in the education/skill composition of the economically active black population over the period up to 2010, are given in Tables A.23 and A.24.

The simulation suggests that the investments in education and training proposed by MERG raise the wage earning capacity index of the economically active black population to 536 by 2010, in comparison with a projected rise to only 360 if no such initiatives are taken. By the end of the projection period (2010), only about 5 per cent of the economically active black population is confined to the lowest education/skill category (level IV), compared to almost 28 per cent if policies remain unchanged. The wage earning capacity of black people in the labour force rises to close to 70 per cent of that white people by the end of the projection period, compared to approximately 47 per cent if policies remain unchanged.

The public expenditure implications of the investment programme in human resources described above have been integrated into the MERG macroeconomic framework. The costs of providing 10 years of education to all children have been estimated at R5 billion in annual recurrent and teacher training expenditures. Annual capital expenditure to provide this education will have to increase from the current level of R0.5 billion to R1 billion in order to provide the necessary infrastructure. The Adult Basic Education programme for employees will require the government to employ additional teachers/trainers, which is estimated to cost R80 million per year (1992 prices). The employees involved in this programme will not be expected to take a cut in their wages, which means that their employers would face additional labour costs of about R360 million per year (1992 prices). However, it is anticipated that the government will offset these additional costs to employers by granting a 150 per cent tax reduction for the wage bill covering the time spent in training. Employers will be expected to recover only a part of the costs of the programme through the benefits they derive from the greater productivity of their better educated workers.

Incentives will be provided to a wide range of employers to participate in the training/employment of those new entrants employed on the infrastructure projects proposed by MERG. Firms will be encouraged to participate in the government-funded programme of infrastructure construction, provided that they fulfil employment and training conditions. Thus, firms will be required to take on a number of new female and male employees/trainees from the pool of currently unemployed, with the number set in relation to the current employment and skills base of the firm. Once this requirement has been fulfilled, these enterprises would be eligible to bid for construction contracts from the public sector, subject to certain local content and employment maximising rules. The trainees/new employees in these firms would be expected to embark on a four-year training scheme along the lines outlined above.

The total costs of this scheme for job creation and training linked to infrastructure provision would be about twice those of the Adult Basic Education programme for employed workers. The training costs have been included in the MERG estimates for the education budget above. However, these employers would be compensated for their additional training and employment efforts by offering them a margin on their successful bids for construction projects, which would compensate for the increased labour costs they have borne as a result of production time sacrificed for training. This margin would be paid for by the government, but would represent only a small proportion of the total costs of each construction project. MERG estimates that, with normal income tax deductions, a state subsidy of between 20 and 30 per cent of the firm's training costs would be appropriate.

Considerable effort will have to go into the detailed design and administration of this complex and large-scale programme. Without an effort on the scale proposed by MERG, the prospects for achieving the restructuring of the labour market required for sustained growth are very dim indeed.

The institutional reforms required to implement these proposals are far-reaching. They go beyond those reforms required to implement the programme of investment in human resources. A tripartite task committee of the National Manpower Commission is currently considering an appropriate legislative framework in detail. MERG supports the view that the industrial relations system needs to be recast, so that it is comprehensive in its coverage, establishes permanent and transparent bargaining opportunities for every industry, and encourages the emergence of strong centralised union and employer bodies. (This is in marked contrast to the recommendations of the NEM, which advocates decentralised wage negotiations.)

Wage bargaining, as currently organisèd, is voluntary, partial and non-comprehensive. Since 1990, centralised bargaining has been a core demand of the trade union movement, with industrial councils being viewed as the most appropriate forum for such bargaining. At the moment, the coverage of industrial councils is low (837 000 out of approximately eight million enumerated employees) and key sectors of manufacturing, i.e. chemicals, paper and food, are still without a centralised negotiating forum. Some industrial councils operate only at sub-national levels, such as the clothing, building and furniture industries which have regional industrial councils. Other councils operate only at the local level, or cover only one manufacturing plant.

Where industrial councils have been established, the scope of bargaining remains too narrow. The proposed reforms of the industrial relations system would widen the scope of such industry level negotiations to relate wages to skill formation, training, investment, technological change and work re-organisation.

The restructuring of the National Training Board, as proposed by COSATU, will be essential if a nationally coherent system is to be achieved. The Board should set the framework for a massive training effort, for occupational certifications and standards for training involving progression criteria, credit transfer and clear linkages between different providers in the formal education, the Adult Basic Education, and the training systems. The ANC and COSATU propose a nationally integrated system (of training/education) built around a single qualification structure which requires learners to complete a compulsory core of subjects, plus a specified number of options, within the requirements set by the national framework, in order to achieve a nationally recognised qualification at a particular level (Joffee 1993, p. 10). The role of the government will be to ensure that the policies of the departments of education and training are co-ordinated and integrated with those of departments responsible for employment and labour; and to mobilise adequate levels of funding for this programme of investment in human resources.

Legislation is required to cover the rights of trade union members and, more generally, those of employees in every sector and region of the economy. This legislation should cover trade union recognition, organisation and recruitment of membership, as well as the legitimate scope of collective bargaining and industrial action. The government must actively promote trade unionism and the scope of collective bargaining on training and work organisation, as well as wage issues amongst its own employees. This will strengthen the base of white collar unions from which greater inroads will, it is hoped, be made in organising the private services sector. Finally, the democratic government must be committed to consulting and negotiating with trade unions over its proposed policies within the framework of an institution such as the National Economic Forum. This will enhance the capacity of working people to participate positively in the formulation, implementation and monitoring of the full array of economic and social policies.

The MERG analysis does not support the view that an enhanced role for trade unions and, more generally, for all working people in economic decision-making, education and training policy, and industrial restructuring and investment policy, will lead to excessive real wage increases, or to an unsustainable social wage accompanied by macroeconomic instability. On the contrary, centralised bargaining can facilitate responsible macroeconomic management, since the key economic agents are integrated into an institutionalised management process. The MERG results query the argument that assigns a major responsibility for inflation to wage increases. All too frequently, policies aimed at reducing money wage rates merely feed through into higher profits and stagnant productivity, allowing firms to continue to use out-dated equipment, and primitive methods of production organisation which would otherwise have had to be replaced. The roots of poor macroeconomic performance and declining international price competitiveness lie less in the alleged automatic inflationary pressures arising from wage increases, than in the structural determinants of productivity and growth (including the skills and motivation of workers), which have been so dismally managed over the past decade or more.

5.3.2   A living wage

The above analysis suggests that the increased costs faced by employers participating in training programmes will rapidly be offset by a variety of micro- and macroeconomic benefits. These programmes and institutional reforms will be designed to force employers to use their more highly skilled labour in an efficient manner, and to invest in technologies which increase labour productivity and the competitive position of the enterprises concerned. The economic arguments in favour of the second major MERG recommendation for labour market intervention are similar.

MERG recommends the introduction of a national minimum wage, which the democratic movement has aspired to since 1953. The general grounds for this recommendation are that growth is unlikely to be achieved on the basis of the poverty wages received by significant numbers of working people. Nor will it be achieved if the labour force is divided between small, well-trained, well-paid and unionised segments, and other market segments in which labour is under-utilised and denied access to wage levels sufficient to ensure adequate standards of work efficiency. Reliance cannot be placed on huge wage differentials to restructure production and transfer labour from very low wage to higher wage and productivity employment. Direct labour market intervention is required to act as a spur for many enterprises throughout the economy to restructure, innovate, and provide their workers with transferable skills. Unprofitable and inefficient enterprises should not receive long-term subsidies from the poor, i.e. from those of their employees who are accepting very low wages.

The primary aim of the national minimum wage is not to achieve a rapid general rise in wages, but to improve the wages and productivity of the lowest-paid members of the work-force, say the bottom 10 per cent of the current wage distribution. Productivity gains will be achieved by reducing absenteeism, illness and labour turnover; they will also be achieved by sending out a clear signal to inefficient enterprises that they can no longer expect to compete by paying their workers a tiny fraction of the wage offered by more efficient firms. As long as very low wages prevail, there is little incentive for employers to undertake the necessary adjustments to make human resources more productive.

To calculate the number of employees who will be directly affected is a complex task, given the state of wage statistics. Very low wages are common in farm labour (especially female and casual/seasonal labour), domestic work, work for sub-contractors, temporary work, and work in regions and industries in which union densities are low. Wage survey data covers samples of workers mainly outside these poverty wage sub-sectors.

This data suggests that a minimum wage set as low as R550 (1990 prices) would affect 12 per cent of surveyed workers, amounting to about 710 000 employees who are paid less than this amount (Young, 1990, p.6). The Minimum Living Level, which is far from a generous estimate of 'the lowest sum possible on which a household (usually a household of five people) can live', was calculated to be approximately R590 per month in 1990. In that year, full-time farm workers received on average only approximately R250 per month, and casual/seasonal workers approximately R50 per month (Directorate of Agricultural Statistics 1993). An attempt to set the national minimum wage at a level close to the MLL would affect far more than 10 per cent of employees. If the aim of the intervention is to focus on the lowest paid, then a national minimum wage set at approximately two-thirds of the MLL, would be a readily achievable initial target for the democratic movement. This translates into a daily wage which considerably exceeds that currently achieved by millions of farm workers, domestic servants, and participants in public works/drought relief programmes.

A conservative and cautious initial approach to setting the national minimum wage, which takes a fraction of the MLL as its starting point (and explicitly attempts to confine the resulting enforced wage increases to the bottom end of the wage distribution) would have a number of advantages. First, this approach would limit the degree of evasion; it would dilute the strength of the political opposition to minimum wages by the most reactionary and politically volatile employers, since large numbers of the major employers already pay well above the minimum rate and will not be affected. Secondly, the macroeconomic consequences are likely to be positive.

Increased expenditures by the lowest paid have a very low import content; their expenditures will raise the overall level of demand for domestic agro-industrial output (food and processed food), building materials and housing, which are all particularly labour intensive sectors operating at well below capacity. The national minimum wage will increase demand for those goods and services which are most likely to lead to further demand for labour. The longer production runs to meet the increased consumer demand are likely to reduce average costs, creating the possibility of an even wider market amongst the mass of low-income consumers for lower priced manufactured goods.

There are no grounds for believing that export price competitiveness will be directly eroded, since the major export producing sectors, including the fruit and horticulture sub-sector within agriculture, are characterised by relatively high wages. Besides, the demand for South African exports, including tourism, is likely to be positively affected if it is widely recognised that internationally acceptable minimum standards are applied to workers in South African enterprises.

Neither theoretical arguments nor international empirical evidence suggests that minimum wage legislation makes a significant difference to the rate of inflation (Wilkinson, 1992; Edkins, 1993). However, if perceptions and expectations concerning the inflationary impact of such legislation are considered to be widespread in South Africa, then the cautious and focused approach advocated here should help to neutralise anxieties and inflationary expectations.

There is no reason to believe that the national minimum wage will induce employers in those sectors most affected to shed labour. The level and rate of growth of employment in the lowest wage sectors, such as agriculture, are obviously affected by a range of factors other than the price of labour. Falls in real wages in recent years have not been associated with employment growth, which is hardly surprising, given the small percentage of agricultural costs accounted for by labour. The evidence for the 1980s, derived from neoclassical production functions, suggests that in every region of South Africa farm labour has been both underutilised and underpaid, not that it has been underutilised because it has been overpaid (Van Schalkwyk and Groenewald, 1992).[4]

Those who argue that higher wages for the lowest paid will necessarily lead to reduced employment rarely spell out the argument. However, their position usually depends on the naïve assumption that machinery can always substitute for labour in production, if the price of the latter becomes too high. The technological possibilities for such substitution in the agricultural sector are often limited. Thus, the price of labour would have to become extraordinarily high before it was economically (and technically) feasible to substitute for certain types of fruit-picking labour by machinery.

The extension (in May 1993) of the Basic Conditions of Employment Act to the agricultural sector is insufficient to meet the objectives of the democratic movement. The new Act has several positive features concerning regulation of normal hours of work, the employment of children, and the application of the Unemployment Insurance Act to agriculture. However, farm workers, as well as other very poorly paid workers, still require the protection of additional legislation to introduce a minimum wage, as well as legislation that positively promotes trade union organisation. The advantages of a statutory national minimum wage include the ease of administering and monitoring compliance, and stem from a single, well-advertised norm. MERG recommends a thorough reform of the existing Wages Act in order to achieve the following objectives:

- The establishment of a national Wage Board, with a duty to set a national minimum wage;

- Membership of the Board should be tripartite, with equal representation from trade unions, employers, and appointed members representing consumer or other non-aligned interests;

- The establishment of sectoral Wage Boards with tripartite representation to cover those sectors/spheres of employment in which unions and collective bargaining are known to be weak. These sectoral Boards would not be permitted to set wages lower than the national minimum, but would be able to set higher wages, would be able to recommend the phased implementation of the national minimum wage, and would be encouraged to transform themselves into Industrial Councils as soon as trade union membership in their sector was sufficiently strong;

- Trade unions should have the power, under the reformed Wages Act, to take legal action against employers who pay less than the national minimum wage or the sectoral wage determinations. The Department of Manpower has been incapable of enforcing existing legislation;

- The reformed Act should make provision for the possibility of a phasing-in period for the national minimum wage in some sectors of the economy on the recommendation of the sectoral Wage Boards. The maximum length of the phasing in period in any sector should not exceed two to three years;

- The national Wage Board will be required to undertake regular, frequent reviews of the level of the minimum wage, which should be indexed to the MLL and to average industrial wages in a formula designed to increase the standard of living of the bottom 10 per cent of wage distribution, without threatening macroeconomic stability;

- The national Wage Board will require sufficient, well-qualified staff to disseminate national publicity concerning the statutory minimum wage, promote enforcement, and evaluate the impact of the minimum wage on the employment levels and standards of living of the lowest paid, particularly those in unenumerated wage employment, and vulnerable migrant workers from neighbouring states. Clear guidelines regarding the treatment of payment in kind when calculating minimum wages will have to be established.

5.3.3   Labour-based infrastructural investment

Despite agreement in principle on the necessity to ensure that state expenditure on public works be used as an instrument to create employment and upgrade workers' skills, progress in providing such employment is unacceptably slow. While the government has agreed to fund pre-investment research to develop a medium term public works programme as a matter of urgency, at this stage even the terms of reference for the research have not been agreed upon.

Crucial economic questions remain unanswered, such as questions concerning feasible targets for person-hours of employment in each year of the programme; the maximum total cost anticipated per person-day of employment generated; the gender mix and geographic location of worker beneficiaries; the breakdown of the portfolio of projects between roads, housing, water supply, sewerage, schools, clinics, and so forth; and the institutional requirements for efficient project design, selection, implementation and monitoring, and the longer-run recurrent budget implications of maintaining/operating the new infrastructure. MERG believes that the preparation of detailed answers to such questions and of a viable medium term plan cannot be the task of an ad hoc committee, but should be made the responsibility of a powerful, adequately staffed and funded government department, supervised by the TEC and the NEF, and subsequently scrutinised by the new legislative body.

The investment programme will have to combine the mixed objectives of delivering well-designed physical structures to the most deprived, increasing the casual employment opportunities available to women and the poorest people, and ensuring that all expenditures result in genuine investments in human resource development with high rates of return, rather than in additions to the number of poorly maintained and socially wasteful monuments in the veld.

The dangers of massive and unforeseen leakages of state public works expenditures into the hands of contractors, material suppliers, and the local male elites who claim to speak for community interests, are obvious in South Africa, and have been a major feature of such programmes elsewhere in the world. Minimisation of such leakage requires a powerful central organisation with national credibility, and a large cadre of technical experts, who are well co-ordinated at the national level in a permanent state department. The scope for local-level consultation and participation in the detailed design and implementation of the projects is very wide, but national co-ordination and monitoring is certainly necessary if the employment gains and macroeconomic viability of the programme are not to be dissipated.

The constraints on implementing a medium term public works programme in 1994/5 are unlikely to be financial. The slow record of the NEF in disbursing their 1993/94 budget, as well as the considerable underspending of the R1 billion allocation in 1991 for labour intensive projects by government departments, and the problems affecting the drought relief projects, point to the need for institutional reform. Recent calculations indicate that there is ample scope for reallocating existing departmental budgets to make funds available for a public works programme. At least R6 billion could readily be made available within the expenditure estimates for 1993/94. Under reasonable assumptions concerning the ratio of unskilled wage costs to total expenditures and the rate of pay on public works projects, such expenditure would be sufficient to create one million jobs (Teixeira, 1993).

MERG recommends that a phased programme of public works be implemented over the years 1994 to 2004, so that the overall share of general government capital expenditure (excluding public enterprises) rises from the current level of 1.3 per cent of GDP to 3 per cent by the end of the period. The initial disbursement rate in 1994/5 should be considerably slower than in subsequent years, in order to allow co-ordinated planning and competent technical design of a portfolio of sustainable projects, strategically located to reduce the worst aspects of female poverty, and to ensure that the skills/training component of the projects is more than a gesture.

MERG simulations suggest that it will be possible to create a total of 2.5 million jobs between 1992 and 2004, if the full range of MERG recommendations are implemented. This model also suggests that it is feasible to aim for the creation of 300 000 new enumerated jobs per year by 1996.

Δ

Endnotes

1. White unemployment rates are recorded with reasonable accuracy and have risen since 1985 and accelerated during the current recession.

2. The failure to achieve adequate rates of expansion in training and education for the majority of South African workers will be discussed further in Section 4 of this chapter.

3. One explanation for this increase in the number of black people experiencing poverty is that the decline in the index of white real per capita personal income and the roughly similar rise in real per capita personal income for blacks between 1985 and 1990 was accompanied by an increase in income inequality amongst blacks (Urban Foundation, 1991.)

4. The authors are obliged to examine non-economic factors such as the mental attitude of farmers and influx controls in order to explain the observed deviations from profit maximising behaviour.

Table 5.1   Employment in 1990, by economic sector and development region (1980 =100)

Region	Agric	Mining	Manuf	Elec	Constr	Comm	Trans	Fin	Serv	Total
A	97	80	102	103	118	119	76	145	117	109
B	77	63	99	75	74	97	71	134	123	91
C	75	106	120	135	124	107	89	155	117	105
D	82	117	107	106	118	102	75	139	119	105
E	88	87	102	105	127	102	85	149	117	105
F	86	101	106	120	56	109	90	175	120	99
G	77	78	123	212	165	113	108	192	140	111
H	88	96	103	119	138	108	98	158	118	112
J	73	85	116	98	112	107	92	151	125	98
Total	83	93	104	115	117	108	87	153	119	107

Source: DBSA, 1991c and MERG calculations

Figure 5.1   Comparative education levels of economically active persons, 1991 (per cent)

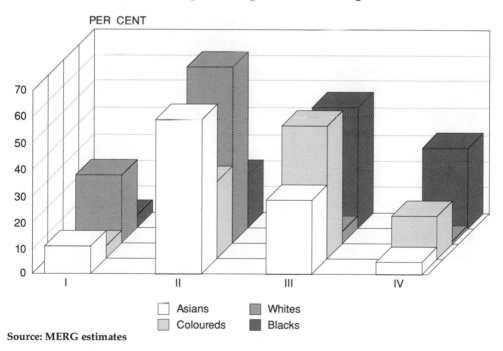

Source: MERG estimates

Figure 5.2 **Comparison of wage-earning capacity indices between population groups, with current policy settings**

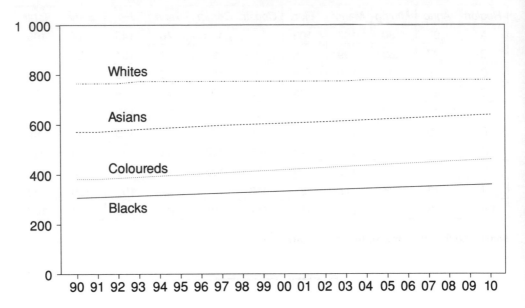

Source: MERG estimates

C H A P T E R 6

Rural development and food policy

.

6.1 The role of rural development in an economic programme for a democratic South Africa

> *Rural development forms an essential component of the ANC's programme for redistribution and growth.... The rural development policy will give emphasis to generating a viable, productive rural economy through activities such as agro-industry (ANC, 1992b, p. 22).*

The degree to which poverty, and especially female poverty is concentrated in rural areas (see section 6.3) has obvious implications for the reallocation of social infrastructure investment expenditure, as well as for an expanded and redirected flow of social welfare expenditure. However, the macroeconomic importance of the performance of agriculture —in terms of its contribution to the growth of total output, employment and exports — is perhaps less immediately obvious, and requires some analysis.

In terms of the conventional national income accounts analysis, the importance of agriculture, forestry and fishing is quite small and has rapidly been diminishing. Having accounted for 21 per cent of GDP in 1911, the share of this sector had declined to 5.2 per cent by 1990 and to 4.7 per cent by 1991 (Directorate of Agricultural Information, 1993, p. 81). As a result of the drought in 1992, agricultural contribution to GDP (at current prices) was only 3.9 per cent; the 24 per cent fall in the real value added by agriculture between 1991 and 1992 is believed to explain a large proportion of the 5 per cent decline in GDP which occurred in the fourth quarter of 1992 (SARB, March 1993, p.30). Although agriculture accounts for a rather small percentage of total output, the fact that agricultural output is subject to large fluctuations means that the performance of this sector has a significant effect on the rate of change of total output.

The contribution of this sector to the employment of the economically active population, as measured in the standard official statistical publications, fell from approximately 33 per cent in 1951, to less than 14 per cent in 1985, and about 10 per cent in 1991.[1] It is also argued that agricultural exports contribute a rather small percentage to total export earnings, especially if only exports of primary animal and vegetable products are considered (Roth et al, 1992, p. 59). Trends in the share of agricultural exports in total exports are shown in Table 6.1. All of the indices of agricultural export performance suggest that it is a small contributor to total exports (less than 5 per cent) and that its importance has been declining.

However, rather different estimates of the importance of agriculture to the South African economy are available, which point to the need to develop a new policy perspective concerning the actual and potential contribution of agricultural production to the growth of output, employment and exports. An examination of the input-output tables for 1988 shows that only 34 per cent of agricultural output is directly consumed, while 66 per cent takes the form of intermediates, which means that the downstream or forward linkages from the agricultural sector are relatively high. (Only 26 per cent of mining output is of an intermediate nature.)

The bulk of the intermediate outputs from agriculture are destined for the manufacturing sector (84 per cent). About 58 per cent of agricultural inputs of goods and services are sourced from manufacturing sector, principally chemical and fuel based inputs, although prepared animal feeds and agricultural and transport equipment are also important. It is, therefore, reasonable to depart from the standard sectoral classifications and identify a range of linked production activities, which involve not only the direct production of certain agricultural commodities, but also a large number of other production activities, especially a set of manufacturing sub-activities, which are closely linked to and dependent on agriculture. This manufacturing-agricultural complex, or agro-industrial sector, plays an extremely important role in the South African economy (Rustomjee, Z, 1993a).

The sectoral boundaries of the agro-industrial sector could be drawn in different ways. Rustomjee, Z, (1993a) has proposed that the sector could include:

ISIC 3100 (food products, beverages, liquor and tobacco)
ISIC 3200 (textiles, garments, leather products)
ISIC 3300 (wood, wood products, furniture)
ISIC 3400 (pulp, paper, printing, publishing)
ISIC 3512 (fertilizer and pesticides)[2]

This aggregated group of economic activities constitutes a large proportion of the manufacturing sector in South Africa. Table 6.2 shows that the manufacturing-agricultural complex (MAC) accounted for about 402 000 jobs in 1988, or 28 per cent of total recorded employment in manufacturing, 31 per cent of manufacturing production, 21 per cent of its capital stock and almost a quarter of the contribution of the manufacturing sector to GDP. Moreover, the MAC accounted for 23 per cent of manufacturing exports, while absorbing only 9 per cent of the imported inputs of the manufacturing sector.

The contribution of the MAC to GDP is more than double the contribution of agriculture to GDP. Its contribution to GDP appears to have been both larger and more stable than the contribution made by those miscellaneous manufacturing activities which fall outside the mineral-energy core (MEC, see Chapter 7). Thus, while the contribution of the MAC to GDP declined gradually from 13 per cent to 11 per cent between 1972 and 1990, the contribution of all the other non-MEC manufacturing sub-sectors fluctuated at levels which were largely below 10 per cent of GDP over the same period (see Figure 6.1). A few of the largest component sub-sectors of the MAC, such as food, beverages, paper and wood products were making an increasing contribution to GDP over the same period (see Figure 6.2). Since the mid – 1970s, the food, paper and wood products components of the MAC have also been making a growing contribution to the value of South African exports (Rustomjee, Z, 1993a).

Several possible policy implications may be drawn from the above analysis. It appears that outside the MEC and the MAC (i.e. outside the natural resource-based industrial production areas), the remaining sub-sectors of manufacturing have failed to make much of a contribution to the economy, at least until the late 1980s. On the other hand, some components of agro-industry have been playing quite a significant and growing role in the economy, and have considerable potential to make an even greater contribution to employment, output and exports. One example of this potential is based on the finding that agro-industries, as well as the agricultural sub-activities to which they are linked, are far more labour-intensive than the non-agricultural activities in the South African economy. Sugar, tobacco, fibre crops, animal fibres, clothing, oil-seeds, grapes, citrus, fruit, vegetables, forestry, furniture and tea, all have higher than average employment : output ratios (Van Seventer, Faux, Van Zyl, 1992, p. 16).

Because of the urgent need to expand wage employment, such findings have considerable policy significance. They underpin the declared policy of targeting investment in agro-industry. Furthermore, such a policy is certainly consistent with a macroeconomic strategy which aims at increasing the real income of poor and black people, since black households in general have much higher income elasticities of demand for the commodities supplied by agro-industry than other households (BMR, 1990, p. 20). Anticipated shifts in the pattern of demand in the second half of the 1990s will have a positive impact on the agro-industry in South Africa. An agro-industrialisation strategy is also likely to be consistent with maintaining a balance between import requirements and available export revenues, partly because such a low percentage of agro-industry inputs have to be imported.

An increase in rural incomes would not only have a positive impact on agricultural processing industries and employment because of the demand elasticities and employment : output ratios noted above, but could be beneficial for the long-run growth of the manufacturing sector as a whole. This is clear in the case of those sub-sectors of manufacturing which are currently very dependent on agriculture, i.e. fertilizers and pesticides, agricultural machinery and prepared animal feeds. For the manufacturing sector as a whole, however, it is striking how small a percentage of its output (less than 3 per cent) now finds a market in agriculture. This tiny contribution to the market for manufactured goods can be considered to be a direct consequence of inadequate rates of growth of investment in agriculture, the extremely skewed pattern of income distribution in the economy, and the extremely low levels of consumption by the overwhelming majority of the rural population. To the extent that investment, output and employment growth in manufacturing have been constrained by domestic demand deficiencies in recent years, an increase in demand, accompanied by a shift in the structure of demand for manufacturing output towards rural mass markets, which is achieved on the basis of a widespread increase in incomes in the agricultural sector, would have positive economy-wide consequences.[3]

Dynamic interactions may be anticipated between expanded demand in the agricultural sector, increased agro-industry output and increased output from a range of other manufacturing sub-sectors. Growing output and rates of capacity utilisation, especially in the food processing components of agro-industry, should lower the real price of basic goods, resulting in an increase in the proportion of their income that the mass of the rural population can devote to the purchase of manufactures. This increase in effective demand could lead in a virtuous circle to higher output and faster productivity growth in manufacturing, which would benefit productivity growth in agriculture through the provision of lower priced modern inputs and incentive goods. An appropriately formulated national food policy, designed to have the effect of lowering and stabilizing basic food prices (see section 6.2), would also make an important contribution to this growth strategy.

Some further support for the strategy outlined above, and for the argument that agriculture has the potential to play a major role, is to be found in Van Zyl and Vink (1988), who estimate the impact of changes in agricultural production on the rest of the economy based on older CSS input-output tables (1976, 1979, 1982 and 1986). They conclude that, because of its strong linkages with the rest of the economy, the total impact of a change in agricultural production on the economy is more than twice that of the direct impact. They also provide estimates of the degree to which additions to production or capital in agriculture have multiplier effects on employment and income in the economy as a whole. Within the framework of the 1985 production structure, an increase in agricultural production would result in the creation of relatively more jobs throughout the economy than could be achieved by an increase of the same order in any other sector. For every additional unit of capital invested, agriculture ultimately yields a larger number of job opportunities than all other sectors, with the exception of construction. These findings underpin the MERG policy recommendations on rural infrastructure construction and increased investment in agricultural production.

The list of economic arguments for according the agriculture sector a high degree of priority could be extended; some of these arguments will be outlined in subsequent sections. However, at this stage, it is important to note that there is a certain amount of spare capacity in South African agriculture, especially in the areas of high and medium arable potential. It has been estimated that in the white farming areas of regions E and F, cropping intensities are only approximately 51 per cent. There are, therefore, up to three million hectares of high/medium potential land in these areas, which are not currently producing high-value arable crops (McKenzie, Weiner, Vink, n.d. p. 5). There is an even larger amount of available agricultural production capacity in the southern African region as a whole (Davies et al, 1993; African Development Bank, 1993, ch. 5). The degree of spare capacity should not only be measured in terms of under-utilised land, water and installed manufacturing resources, but also in terms of the under-utilisation of the productive potential of the rural population. The poor education, ill-health, low life-expectancy and consequent low productivity of the rural labour force is not only an indictment of apartheid policy; it also provides the major opportunity for, and indicates the potential of, the agro-industrial growth strategy proposed by the democratic movement.

Past and current economic policies of the government are severely limiting the prospects for the growth of the rural sector. The following section describes the failures of these policies. The outlines of a new rural development and food policy emerge naturally from this critique.

6.2 The failure and unsustainability of government policy

One clear indication of the neglect of rural development by the current regime is the lack of attention this issue receives in the Normative Economic Model (1993). In a document of 305 pages, one page is devoted to rural development. There is no justification for this neglect. The rural population will amount to more than 21 million people in 1995, approximately half of the total population.

Apart from a brief and mealy-mouthed phrase concerning the possibility that rural development could contribute to economic growth and development, the document recommends a continuation of present policies and the stabilisation of the commercial agricultural sector on a market-orientated basis (CEAS, 1993, p. 243). Proposals for a more market-orientated or deregulated policy environment for white farms have been surfacing repeatedly since the early 1980s. Nevertheless, the degree to which perverse state interventions, controls on agricultural markets and the state subsidisation of white farms remain central features of policy, should not be under-estimated. This array of interventions will be the focus of much of the following discussion.

6.2.1 Deregulation?

The forms of state intervention practised by the current regime have resulted in unacceptable outcomes, but this does not constitute a powerful argument for rapid, indiscriminate deregulation and the abdication of state responsibility for rural development and food security. Although the World Bank critique of current policy (1993a) is a useful starting point, the policy conclusions rest too heavily on an almost religious faith in the welfare and growth-optimising characteristics of free agricultural markets, upon the assumed inevitability of state failure, and the policy irrelevance of market failures. The World Bank prescriptions also ignore the role played by pervasive state intervention in the agricultural sectors of all of the now developed economies, and in the agricultural sectors of the most rapidly industrialising economies in the second half of the twentieth century.

The main government policy initiatives affecting agricultural marketing and pricing since the mid-1980s have been described under six main headings (LAPC, 1993a):

- Deregulation of the control schemes: Table 6.3 summarises the most important deregulatory measures. Marketing decontrol has, to date, left some of the major schemes intact, including those concerning maize, winter cereals and livestock. In 1990, 67 per cent of the gross value of agricultural production was accounted for by commodities still marketed under various control schemes; the legislative basis of the old marketing system originally established in the

1930s remains largely intact. Control boards still raise levies on the sale of a large number of products falling under the marketing schemes, which are used to finance the bureaucracy of the control boards. These bureaucracies are notorious for their actions in favour of 'certain organisations, companies or co-operatives to the detriment of other parties' (Kassier, 1993, p. 33);

- Reduction in the extent of price controls: this policy started in the early 1980s with the removal of price control on milk, butter and cheese. In 1991, price controls on bread and flour were abolished, with devastating consequences for the poor. The system of price and quality control previously in operation had engendered an efficient bread industry and, coupled with the bread subsidy, resulted in a relatively cheap standard loaf. Moreover, during the control period the price of bread did not fluctuate widely. Following the deregulation of the baking industry in March 1991, the price of white bread rose by more than 46 per cent in the 12 months from November 1991 to November 1992. Prior to deregulation, the retail profit margin had been fixed at 4 cents a loaf; when retailers were freed from statutory control the margin increased by 256 per cent, to 14.5 cents per loaf by November 1992. Some retailers are now selling bread at margins of 20 – 25 cents per loaf, especially in rural areas where there is less competition and the largest low-income market (Frost, 1992, p. vi);

- The replacement of quantitative controls on external trade in agricultural commodities by tariffs: since 1990, tariffs have been established for poultry, tobacco, vegetable oils, oilcake and red meat. However a great many agricultural commodities are still subject to quantitative external trade controls, and others remain covered by formula tariff protection. The most important commodities for which the government has still not developed tariff proposals are maize and wheat, which continue to be marketed through single channel systems with a unified domestic price;

- The removal of subsidies provided through administered marketing schemes: the key policies have been the total elimination of the bread subsidy, and the removal of the maize subsidy (discussed further below). A large acreage of marginal land on white farms is still being used for arable crops as a result of price/subsidy policies, while land of much higher arable potential in some of the homelands, and in the Eastern Transvaal in particular, is being used for livestock or forestry (Van Zyl and Van Rooyen, 1991, p. 188 – 9). Cropping on technically non-arable land is particularly prevalent in the white farming areas of the western and northern Cape (McKenzie, Weiner and Vink, n.d.);

- Reforms to the Co-operative Act: the combined effects of these reforms, together with the introduction of new rules governing minimum business levels or farm sizes as qualifications for co-operative membership, have been to increase the degree to which co-operative membership and control is restricted to the (white) owners of larger farms;

- Interest rate policy: interest rates for agriculture have been affected both directly, by the implementation of the recommendations of the 1983 de Kock

Commission, which led to higher interest rates for agricultural borrowers from the Land Bank and the co-operatives, and indirectly by the general tightening of monetary policy as the government began its inconsistent adherence to monetarist orthodoxy in the second half of the 1980s. Some effects of these policies on farm debt and levels of investment will be referred to below.

6.2.2   *Government expenditure benefitting white farmers*

It is important to highlight certain other features of recent interventions and patterns of state expenditure in the agricultural sector. The main recent policy initiative to emphasize is the massive and unsustainable expenditure programme (amounting to well over R3 billion), which was designed to alleviate the debt burden of some white farmers in the fiscal year 1992/3, although it was ostensibly undertaken in the name of drought relief (LAPC,1993b).

The rise in farm debt since the early 1980s has been largely a consequence of policy failures over the last decade, in particular, government failure to address the problems arising from the structural characteristics of uncompetitive grain farming. The background to the large-scale and economically indefensible intervention in 1993 is the critical insolvency position of a number of white large-scale grain farmers in the summer and winter rainfall areas. A growing proportion of the liabilities of these farmers has been in the form of short-term debt, and there has been a marked deterioration in the ratio between net farm profit and short-term debt. The relatively slow rate of growth in these farmers' nominal output prices, which was partly a result of the changes in marketing and pricing policies described above, was accompanied by a far more rapid increase in input prices (see Table 6.4), and an increase in the real cost of credit as a result of changes in interest rate policy. The drought of 1991/2 made the viability of these farms more precarious, but played a relatively minor role in their accumulation of debt.

While achieving reasonable harvests between the early 1980s and 1991/2, these farmers were nevertheless unable to reduce substantially the carry-over debt levels which the government had originally subsidised (through guarantees to the tune of R800 million) after the 1982/3 and 1983/4 droughts. Some farmers found themselves in the position of being unable to repay carry-over debt, even in years with fairly good harvests.

Their incentive to repay this form of debt was small, as it was held at a lower rate of interest than other farm debts, i.e. those held at commercial banks. The state guarantee had for many years encouraged the co-operatives to continue lending without taking changing relative prices and commercial risk into account; thus, government policy contributed directly to the accumulation of short-term debt. After the very poor 1991/2 cropping year, carry-over debt rose to R2.4 billion; the government paid the Land Bank the full amount of R2.4 billion in March 1993, and the farmers owning the largest farms were the major beneficiaries.

In addition to this huge transfer payment of R2.4 billion under the heading 'drought relief', there have been other substantial forms of state financial assistance to white farmers, some of which have been calculated to amount to R355 million in 1992/3. The complex array of loan and subsidy schemes currently available to white farmers is illustrated in Table 6.5.[4] Moreover, these farmers also benefited from yet another package of drought-related state expenditures, which amounted to R870 million in 1992/3 (see Table 6.6).

In contrast, black farmers received a mere R130 million in the recent drought assistance programme, only 72 per cent of which was actually disbursed, as a result of the extremely poor administration of the programme in the homelands.

Apart from being open to criticism on grounds of fiscal irresponsibility, (70 per cent of the amount by which government expenditure exceeded the budget estimate in 1992/3 is accounted for by the debt relief and other 'drought' schemes for white farmers), it is clear that government policies over the last decade have left a large number of heavily indebted arable farmers on land which they have proved incapable of managing profitably. These costly policies have by no means removed the financial problems of the co-operatives, many of which remain in financial difficulties; nor have they allowed land prices in these marginal areas to fall to the full extent required to reflect more accurately their potential revenue from arable activities. These policies illustrate the degree to which the present regime has failed to reallocate state resources away from a tiny minority of the rural population. The government has also refused to evaluate the impact on the most vulnerable rural people of the meagre resources actually devoted to alleviating the effects of the 1992 drought in the black rural areas. There is little doubt, however, that these resources were poorly administered and inefficiently targeted.

A longer-run, detailed analysis of the pattern of government expenditure on agriculture is being undertaken by MERG. Preliminary results confirm the degree to which the government has recently refocused its expenditures on white farmers. Table 6.7 provides a more accurate and up-to date account of the trends in agricultural expenditure than that of Vink and Kassier (1991), in that it is based on actual as opposed to budgeted expenditure. This table suggests that, although the proportion of expenditure on white agriculture fell somewhat between 1989/90 and 1991/2, by 1993 more than three-quarters of government expenditure on agriculture was again directed towards white farmers, i.e. approximately the same proportion as prevailed in the period 1985/6 to 1987/8. The absolute level of real expenditure on black agriculture did increase between 1986/6 and 1992/3, rising from R555 million to R833 million (in 1989/90 prices), but real expenditure on white agriculture also increased from R2 billion to R2.71 billion over the same period.

Unfortunately, the most reliable data on total government expenditure on agriculture, based on IMF government finance statistics classification, is available only up to 1991. This measure shows a fluctuating but declining real value of expenditure on agriculture and a similar decline in expenditure on Agriculture as a percentage of total expenditure (see Figure 3).[5] Most of the 1992/3 increase in agricultural expenditure has benefitted white farmers, and the general conclusion remains that the government has, over the last decade, failed to accord the agricultural sector as a whole the degree of priority that its contribution warrants. The mean percentage of total government expenditure on agriculture in South Africa between 1989 and 1991 was only 2.5 per cent, i.e. about the same proportion as that observed in New Zealand, which has a far smaller proportion of the labour force in agriculture. By contrast, the comparative percentage in more successful economies with similar structural characteristics to South Africa, such as Malaysia, Thailand, Indonesia and Korea, was between 7 and 10 per cent, i.e. more than double the proportion spent in South Africa (IMF 1992). The government has wastefully misdirected expenditures to a small minority of white grain farmers.

While government productive investment in the agricultural sector has been declining as suggested in Figure 6.3, there is no indication that the private sector has taken up the slack. On the contrary, all the evidence suggests that the impact of incoherent government policies with respect to marketing, pricing, subsidisation, interest and exchange rates, not to mention the cost-increasing effects of protecting agricultural input supply industries such as ADE (diesel engines) and SASOL,[6] have adversely affected the agricultural terms of trade and, therefore, farmers' incentives to invest. The consequences have been a decline in the real value of farm expenditures on intermediate goods and services since 1985; a decline in real levels of capital investment in fixed improvements (from a peak of R693.3 million in 1973 to R344 million in 1990); and a decline in real levels of investment in tractors, machines and implements from a peak of R1.7 billion in 1981 to R389 million by 1990 (Roth et al, 1992, pp. 72 and 81).

These adverse effects of government policy have not been uniformly distributed among the white farmers. For example, producers of some of the most important field crops, i.e. maize, wheat, grain sorghum, barley, cotton and sunflowers, have all faced a very marked deterioration in their terms of trade between 1982 and 1991, with real producer prices for these commodities falling by between 49 per cent and 21 per cent over the decade (AgriReview, Jan 1992). On the other hand, the terms of trade for tomatoes, oranges, grapefruit, lemons, apples and avocadoes, for example, have all moved quite favourably for farm producers since 1982 (AgriReview, October 1992). This has been reflected to some extent by changes in the pattern of investment, with output of horticultural products increasing by 25 per cent between 1985 and 1991, while field crop production stagnated, and the area planted to maize decreased by almost a million hectares between the early 1980s and the turn of the decade (LAPC, Jones, 1993, p. 12). [7]

These very large shifts in the terms of trade, in investment and in the pattern of production and employment have not been the outcome of a coherent rural development strategy or food policy. They reflect, rather, the peculiar and combined outcome of vacillating responses to the pressures of particular white rural vested interests,[8] market liberalizing and monetarist ideologies, rainfall and unanticipated fluctuations in international price and exchange rate movements.

This record of economic policy mismanagement highlights the urgency of adopting a rational and consistent set of state interventions to promote the development of the agricultural and agro-industry sectors. The continuation of recent policies promised in the NEM would be rejected by a democratic government.

6.2.3 Government policy in the homelands

It will be necessary to increase the real level of government expenditure on agriculture within and without the homelands. Two MERG research projects will soon provide more detailed analyses of the trends in the pattern of government expenditure on agriculture within the homelands. These will constitute the basis for a more rigorous evaluation of the deficiencies of current policy in these areas and the magnitude and direction of the changes required.

Two points can meanwhile be emphasised: firstly, within the ten homelands, a meagre 6 per cent of budgetary allocations were, on average, directed towards 'Agriculture, Forestry and Environment' in 1990/91, with the developmentally irrelevant categories of 'Defence', 'Chief Minister', 'Military Council', 'Presidency', 'Internal Affairs', 'Foreign Affairs' and 'Other' collectively absorbing double this amount (see Table 6.8 and Daphne, 1993). Data for 1989/90 suggests that these expenditures translated into flows of less than R50 per cultivated hectare, or about R70 per head of the homeland rural population (Rimmer, 1993).

As much as 40 per cent of this expenditure on the agricultural sub-head is devoted to the payment of salaries.[9] The contribution of homeland bureaucrats to increasing agricultural production, or the levels of income of the rural poor, is probably very small and has certainly never been evaluated. There exists considerable scope within the existing homeland budgets for expanding and reallocating expenditure for agricultural development.

Secondly, the major state initiatives to promote rural development in the homelands have, over the past decade, been co-ordinated through the quasi-state agency of the Development Bank of South Africa (DBSA). The expenditures of the DBSA on rural and agricultural investment, totalling R392 million between 1982 and 1992 (see Table 6.9), have had very limited success and have been, for the most part, misconceived. The DBSA itself admits that its capital-intensive agricultural projects in the period before the mid–1980s were undertaken by homeland parastatal companies and external consultants at high cost, with low productivity outcomes, and that its approach during this period was 'financially unviable and economically unsustainable' (Van Rooyen 1993, p.22). It does not, however, recognise the deficiencies of the farmer support programme (FSP) projects which it has been vigorously promoting since 1987. Nor has it identified the dramatic decrease in its agricultural loan portfolio between 1987 and 1991 as an indication of its failure.

Approximately 25 000 farmers have been the beneficiaries of DBSA farmer support programme since its inception. The fixed cost per farmer has reached an average level of approximately R5 000 on irrigation schemes, while the annual variable cost has been about R2 000 per farmer. Total expenditure to date by the DBSA on these 25 000 farmers has been about R145 million, which pales into insignificance when the amount of state support per white farmer is considered, but which nevertheless represents an expenditure of close to R6 000 per beneficiary.

Some simple arithmetic exposes the limitations of this approach. If it is assumed that there are about 1.25 million rural households in the homelands who are now cultivating at least some land (Roth et al, 1992, p. 100), to extend the FSP programme to all of these would cost R7.5 billion. Even if the FSP were to be extended to the so-called 'progressive small-scale farmers' in the homelands, say 250 000 enterprises, the costs would exceed DBSA total loans to the rural sector over the last ten years by a factor of five. Of course, the number of rural households which could reasonably expect some support in improving their farming from a democratic government, is likely to be far higher than the largest of the figures quoted above, especially if one were to include at least some workers on white farms (1.2 million people), and some of those currently landless in the homelands, amounting to more than half a million households.

Even if it were to be established that the FSP has been a cost-effective means of raising agricultural output and the incomes of the poorest rural households, its costs per beneficiary are too high to make the programme replicable on a reasonable scale in the short-term. Besides, there is evidence that FSP has not been focused on the poor, or on women, and that the majority of its subsidised credit, ploughing services and other excessively high-cost and high-tech inputs have been allocated to relatively wealthy male rural households, with the other major beneficiaries being local contractors (Kirsten, Van Zyl, 1993). Few of the 35 FSP projects have been evaluated, and it is impossible to determine the percentage output which has been a direct result of programme expenditure on the basis of these evaluations, since no adequate benchmark surveys are available.

The most serious difficulties in using the FSP as a replicable model for rural development in the future are institutional and political. Whether in its FSP, or its small business development programme, or its large-scale agricultural projects, the DBSA has co-operated closely with illegitimate and corrupt homeland agencies, development corporations or departments of agriculture, which have used DBSA resources to build up networks of patronage around tribal and other homeland institutions, which will (it is hoped) have little influence in a democratic South Africa.

The redirection and reform of rural development policy will require not only the re-allocation of resources within a new expenditure plan, but the radical reform of the central, regional and local state and quasi-state enterprises which have been responsible for the mismanagement of such resources in the past. The model for such an expenditure programme should be neither the costly current support packages to white farmers, nor the less costly but non-replicable and narrowly focused support to black farmers through the FSP. MERG recommends instead a far more tightly targeted set of lower cost interventions, which are especially designed to improve the living standards of the very poorest rural households wishing to undertake part-time agricultural production as a supplementary activity. The scope for financing such state intervention through a reduction in state expenditure on white farmers and the homeland and other bureaucracies is obviously considerable.

The resources for the proposed poverty-targeted interventions will prove inadequate if a growing number of black capitalist farmers stake their claim to the excessive level of state resources currently received by their white counterparts. The political economy of rural South Africa and the weakness or absence of appropriate rural development institutions and experienced personnel, means that it will be difficult to prevent such inefficient hand-outs of state resources. This suggests that there is likely to be a role for efficient agri-business to expand its recent efforts to incorporate small black producers into nucleus estates or contract production. More importantly, the argument above implies that there is an urgent need to define with a great deal of precision, the needs and targets to be addressed by the agrarian transformation strategy of the democratic movement. The following section of this chapter draws an outline of these needs, and identifies some targets.

There remains an important strand of policy which has not been sufficiently discussed. The recent record of the government in meeting the food needs of the poor is, as indicated in the discussion of the removal of the bread subsidy, open to serious criticism.

6.2.4   Food Policy

The overwhelming majority of the population in the urban and rural areas are net purchasers of staple foods. This is particularly true for poor rural households, who are also likely to remain net purchasers of food in the post-land reform period (Van Zyl and Van Rooyen, 1991, p. 195). Therefore, policies to ensure low and stable food prices are of crucial importance to the standard of living of the poor. The poor always devote a high proportion of their income to food purchases, and they lack the bargaining power to achieve rapid increases in their real wage/income in response to increases in consumer prices. Low and stable basic food prices can also promote the rate of growth of manufacturing output, by minimising the wage costs of repro-ducing a healthy labour force, and by ensuring that a domestic mass market for manufactured goods is not constrained by fluctuating or limited discretionary pur-chasing power.

Maize and wheat are by far the most important cereals for human consumption, although approximately half of South Africa's maize production is used for animal feed. Trends in per capita human consumption of maize have been consistently downwards since the mid–1960s. However, per capita wheat consumption has been increasing since the mid–1980s (see Figure 6.4), while levels of domestic wheat production have roughly kept in line with this increase. The self-sufficiency index for wheat averaged 116 between 1985 and 1990, fluctuating around 100 with no apparent trend. Maize self-sufficiency has been much more variable, although the average self-sufficiency index between 1985 and 1990 was higher, at 121. There appears to have been a sharp downward trend in maize self-sufficiency in recent years, which has been accompanied by a reduction of exportable surpluses.

These trends for maize and wheat net exports reflect the fact that government food pricing and food production policy has been excessively geared towards the dual objectives of sanctions busting (or self-sufficiency within fortress South Africa) and catering to the needs of a small white group of grain producers. This policy generated 'surpluses', particularly of maize, which were not absorbed on the domestic market and which were exported at a loss. A significant proportion of the welfare costs of the policy were borne by low-income consumers of basic agricultural products.

In order to illustrate the scale of these costs to low-income consumers, it must be noted that wheat can be delivered at Durban from Argentina (generally the lowest cost producer in the world) at prices which are approximately half the cost of production and transport from within South Africa itself. Similarly, imported yellow maize can be delivered to the coastal areas at a price that is below domestic production and transport costs. The high protected price of yellow maize in animal feed has an adverse impact on the domestic price of chicken, which is an important component of low-income diet. A more telling indictment of government food policy is provided by the indices of malnutrition in South Africa (see Section 6.3 below).

It is not proposed that there should be a rapid convergence to a one-to-one link between world and domestic staple grain prices. The more efficient domestic produc-ers and all low-income consumers of staple grains should be cushioned from world market price fluctuations. A variable tariff rule could be adopted, and tariff levels adjusted to offset violent world price or exchange rate fluctuations. The MERG research project on food policy will shortly be presenting proposals along these lines.

There can be no assumption that a policy of greater reliance on imported wheat would have serious balance of payments consequences for South Africa; firstly, because the value of food imports is an insignificant proportion of the total value of imports; secondly, because land released from wheat production is likely to be used for livestock production, and will thus generate import saving on meat (the average SSI for beef between 1985 and 1990 was only 89 per cent) to offset the higher cereal import costs, or the loss of cereal export revenues.

A number of additional food policy options have been discussed by the democratic movement, which are of particular relevance to the poor:

- A relatively high-cost option would be for the state to introduce or reintroduce subsidies on those foods with low-income elasticities of demand which are bought mainly by the poor. The costs of such an option would be high because a significant number of the non-poor would also benefit, so that a substantial portion of the budgetary cost of such a food policy would simply increase the consumption of the already well-nourished. Moreover, if budgetary resources are constrained or liable to periodic cuts, the benefits of such a policy for the really poor and nutritionally vulnerable might be limited, because the benefits would be too thinly distributed to achieve much increase in their food-intake. MERG does not recommend this option;

- Another option would be to expand the provision of particular types of subsidised food to targeted groups of women and children through rural health and nutrition clinics. However, the existing location of clinics in the rural areas, as well as their limited coverage of vulnerable rural households, can act to discriminate against the poor in remote regions. The MERG recommendations for a substantial investment programme in clinics in rural areas will help to avoid these targeting problems;

- Alternative policies rest on the finding that inadequate access to food should be understood as stemming from a lack of purchasing power, so that a food policy is best and most directly pursued through raising the real incomes of the poorest households, for example, through direct, targeted income transfers, such as pensions and through the introduction of a statutory minimum wage (see Chapter 5).

Some combination of the latter two options, as well as others (see Bosman, 1992), should be introduced in a phased and flexible way to replace the irrationalities of present government food policies. The new interventions should be flexible, and concentrate on the most vulnerable people in those rural areas with the worst indices of malnutrition.

6.3 The needs to be addressed by an agrarian transformation policy

The central goal of the economic policy of the democratic movement is to eliminate poverty and extreme inequalities (ANC, 1992b, p. 19). There is overwhelming evidence that it is the rural sector which contains the largest relative proportion of poor people, as well as the largest absolute number of people struggling to survive on low incomes, nutritionally at risk, poorly educated, and without sufficient access to the sanitation, health and other services necessary for leading a productive, let alone a dignified life. In addition, the most severe inequalities in standards of living and in access to the means of production are a pervasive characteristic of the rural areas.

This section aims to provide a sketch of the magnitude of the problems to be addressed. Precise quantification of the targets for policy is severely limited by the history of neglect of the issues concerned. The government has demonstrated gross incompetence and irresponsibility in a sphere which requires, uncontroversially, direct and continuous state attention and expenditures; it has failed to collect and publish reliable and disaggregated time series data covering rural vital statistics, malnutrition, employment, incomes and output (Meth,1988; Glatthaar,1992; Simkins,1985; Roth et al,1992). There is an immediate requirement to restructure the state institutions concerned with the production and dissemination of statistics, so that rural needs can be more precisely identified, policies refined and policy outcomes monitored (see section 6.4). It must be emphasized that the data presented here concerning the dimensions and characteristics of rural poverty are far from reliable; indeed, they are barely adequate for the purpose of developing appropriate policy.

6.3.1   Some characteristics of the poor

The scattered and inconsistent surveys covering the incomes of rural households, the majority of which have been undertaken by non-governmental agencies, cannot be used as a basis for analysing national, or geographically disaggregated, or male–female trends over time in per capita real incomes.[10] These surveys do, however, agree in drawing a few, quite firmly based conclusions:

- Black people living in rural areas in general have much lower incomes than black or, of course, white people in urban areas;

- The degree of black rural poverty, in both 'white' and other rural areas, is much more acute in some regions and some districts than in others. There is probably a growing degree of spatial and within-district inequality in the distribution of rural black incomes;

- The incomes earned by black women in rural areas, or by female-headed or female-dominated households, are much lower than those earned by black men, or by male-dominated rural households;

- A large proportion of rural households only survive, or finance their consumption of basic goods such as food, through wage employment. Quite apart from employment in the mines and in manufacturing, rural wage employment, both on-farm and off-farm, is, and has been for many decades, a critical source of income for a very large number of poor rural households.

The last point concerning rural wage employment has important consequences for the design of economic policy and for the MERG proposals on agrarian reform. It will be the focus of much of the following discussion. However, it is useful to outline in a little more detail the characteristics of rural poverty relative to other forms of poverty in the country, before returning to the need to increase the effective demand for and the remuneration of rural wage workers, especially female rural wage workers.

One broad, but in many ways unsatisfactory, headcount measure of poverty suggests that over 16 million people in South Africa had incomes lower than the minimum subsistence level in 1989. Over 93 per cent of these people were black (Department of Agriculture, 1990). Excluding the TVBC, the same source estimates that no less than 74 per cent of the poor black population were living in rural areas. The Urban Foundation has published a similar headcount measure, covering the number of people in households living below the minimum living level (R8 500 per year), and estimates that in 1990, 17.1 million people were in such households, of whom 16.3 million (96 per cent) were black. It estimates that twice as many of these poor black people lived in rural areas (11 million) than in urban areas (5.3 million). The Urban Foundation concluded that 'Among poor black people poverty is both more widespread and more severe in rural areas' (p. 12). It also notes that income inequality is more acute among black rural than black urban households (Urban Foundation, 1991, Table 7).[11]

Apart from poverty estimates based on dubious household income data, it should be noted that rural indices of black illiteracy and inadequate access to educational facilities are far worse than those found in urban areas. There is a difference of about 30 per cent between the literacy of urban and rural dwellers, with the difference between urban and rural women greater than that for men (Budlender, 1991, p. 12). The nutritional status of black rural children appears, despite the profound inadequacy of the national data base, to be far worse than that of urban black children. Infant mortality and the under-five mortality rates show broadly the same pattern. Moreover, there are large disparities in these proxy indices of poverty within urban and rural areas. For example, the infant mortality rate in Grahamstown was 204 in the mid-1980s, while the comparable black rate in Johannesburg was 27 (Glatthaar, 1992, p. 1332). Rural Africans and coloureds have been estimated to suffer from infant mortality rates at least 2.6 times higher than those living in urban areas. (Centre for Health Policy, n.d., pp. 15 and 27). A proximate cause for these differences in infant mortality rates may be the fact that vaccination coverage in rural areas is far lower than in urban areas. Total fertility rates and maternal mortality rates, which are fairly good proxies for the status of women, are much higher in rural than in urban areas (Klugman and Weiner, 1992, pp. 26 and 49).

The broad dimensions of the rural malnutrition problem in the mid-1980s can be illustrated by reference to the first national study of protein energy malnutrition (PEM) in South Africa. Up to 15 per cent of black pre-school children were underweight for age; and 25–33 per cent were stunted or chronically undernourished, although in some areas the figure exceeded 50 per cent for four to five year olds (RHOSA, 1991). The survey evidence is scattered, but the worst PEM indicators are found in the homelands, while the children of well-established black urban residents in the Cape Town and Soweto areas are far less likely to be nutritionally at risk. There are well-known links between diarrhoeal disease, nutritional status and the availability of adequate water supplies. Since about 50 per cent of black rural households lack reasonable access to safe water (compared to 30 per cent of black urban households), the number of rural black children whose health and life expectancy is threatened is large (Schur, 1993). This point is reinforced by the estimate that only 14 per cent of rural dwellers have access to adequate sanitation, whereas 62 per cent of urban dwellers have access to waterborne sewerage systems (Centre for Health Policy, 1992, p. 11).

The proportion of black rural households which are female-headed or female-dominated, or the number of the rural poor who are women, cannot be identified precisely. However, there are several indications of the degree to which black rural women are over-represented amongst the poor. Firstly, the black rural population, which constitutes more than two-thirds of the national total of poor black people, contains many more women than men. In the rural areas as a whole in 1991, the female : male ratio was 1.06:1, while the ratio of adult (aged between 20 and 64 years) females to males was 1.38:1 (BMR, 1993; DBSA, 1991a). There are indications that in the poorest of the rural areas the percentage of males is even lower; for example, the adult female to male ratio in Region G is 1.58:1 (DBSA, 1991b, p. 10).

Secondly, there is evidence of very large gaps between the wages received by rural women and rural men for comparable work. It is common for women to receive only two-thirds of the male wage in non-farm rural employment (Sender, 1992; Kotze, n.d.). The occupational categories of seasonal agricultural workers and domestic workers on commercial farms are probably the lowest paid forms of recorded wage employment in South Africa. These occupational categories are dominated by women. The daily wage rate of these women is approximately one-third of that received by, for instance, permanent/male farm workers (de Klerk, 1984, p. 26). Moreover, female seasonal agricultural workers face the difficulty of surviving for five to six months of each year with no access to wage employment (Louw and Graaf, 1993, p. 24).

Thirdly, both the patriarchal culture on white farms (Van Onselen, 1991) and the oppressive invented legal traditions in the homelands place severe limitations on women's access to the means of agricultural production, whether as labour/share-cropping tenants or as homeland farmers (Roth et al, 1992, p. 138). Finally, the most rigorous micro-survey data, collected by social anthropologists, has clearly established the extreme vulnerability and poverty of women bringing up children in rural areas with no or only tenuous access to a male income, i.e. separated, divorced and widowed women (James, 1985; Sharp and Spiegel, 1986; Kotze, 1992).

6.3.2   The need for rural wage employment

Rural households have, for many decades, been able to survive only because of access to wage employment. Of the poor black rural population, which is estimated above to amount to about 11 million people, a significant proportion are surviving in the so-called white rural areas, either as employees on white farms or as dependents of these employees. The officially recorded number of black farm employees and domestic servants on farms in the white areas has fluctuated over the period 1985 to 1991, but has averaged just over one million, of which about one-third are domestic workers. If coloured and Asian farm employees are included, the figure is close to 1.2 million (Directorate of Agricultural Information, 1993, p. 6). The total number of people relying on these wages could be between five and six million.

No up-to-date and appropriately deflated wage series exists for these employ-ees,[12] but there are indications that their real wages are considerably lower than the real wages received by recorded urban black employees, probably amounting to less than one-third of the urban level (Urban Foundation, 1991). Movements in the real wages of farm workers have not, of course, been uniform across farms, crops and geographical districts. The permanent farm workers in regions J, C, B, D, and G receive only about half the monthly cash wage received by farm workers in region A (Farm Workers Research and Resource Project, May 1993; Graaf, Louw, and van der Merwe, 1989, p. 37-8). Moreover, many of the 1.5 million children of farm employees receive very poor education with about 40 per cent of the relevant age group not attending primary school (Gordon 1991).

The official data on farm employees in white rural areas is almost certainly extremely misleading. The recorded wage rates appear to be rather higher than those observed in micro-surveys, and the number of employees, especially casual and seasonal employees commuting or temporarily migrating from the homelands and from neighbouring countries in southern Africa, appears to be under-estimated in the CSS publications. Therefore, the number of rural people dependent on wage employ-ment on these farms is probably considerably larger than the estimate of five to six million given above.

Agricultural wage employment within the 'black' rural areas should be added to this total when an estimate is made of the national importance of agricultural wage employment. This calculation is problematic, since statistics on formal, i.e. recorded wage employment, have not been collected on a geographically disaggregated basis (DBSA, 1991c, p. 19). The DBSA estimates that roughly 1.45 million people were in wage employment in the 'outer peripheral area of South Africa'(1991c, p. 44). These are largely rural areas.[13] While this total includes employees on the large scale agricultural projects of the development corporations (perhaps amounting to a fifth of all employees) and government employees, it does not include all domestic workers in these areas, nor does it include the large number of farm workers employed for wages by small black farmers. In particular, casual/seasonal agricul-tural wage employment for black farmers, which is extremely important as a source of income for poor black rural women who are unable to commute or migrate to white rural areas, is ignored. The degree to which poor rural people depend on wages received from farm (or from off-farm) rural employment within the homeland areas cannot be estimated with any degree of precision.

Nonetheless, micro-surveys covering the sources of income of rural households suggest that wage employment is an extremely important source of income (Nattrass and May, 1986; de Wet et al, 1989, p. 66; Leibbrandt, 1993, p. 54; and Bromberger and Antonie, 1993). Unfortunately, far too few of these surveys give any indication of the sector from which these crucial flows of wage (and remittance) income are derived. Neither the current nor the potential role of farm employment in providing an income for poor rural people (in particular, poor rural women) can be estimated with confidence. Nevertheless, it would probably not be unrealistic to assume that well over half of the rural poor depend on agricultural wage employment for their survival. The sale of labour services represents their only means of surviving, since even if they have some arable land, the opportunity cost of devoting labour to that land in terms of wage earnings foregone, is very high.

The impact of rural development policy on the demand for agricultural wage labour should not be ignored. Policies which reduce the level of demand for farm workers, or reduce their wages, including ill-conceived redistributions of land, would have a devastating effect on large numbers of the poorest people in South Africa. Some policies designed to have the opposite effect are discussed below in Section 6.4.

6.3.3   The need for access to land

The number of people now living in rural, peri-urban and urban areas who wish to acquire rights to land for the first time, or to re-acquire previously held rights to land, or to acquire rights to additional extents of land is undoubtedly very high indeed. The democratic movement is committed to providing land to the landless in a programme of land redistribution. It has also stated that the major beneficiaries of such a redistribution programme should be the rural poor and women (ANC, 1992b, p. 26).

One of the problems in designing a land redistribution policy, is that the available data does not distinguish adequately between the number of landless rural households in the homelands, and those rural households which already have some limited access to land for residential purposes, but lack access to sufficient land of an appropriate quality to undertake agricultural production. Nor is it clear whether the ANC is politically committed to providing all possible claimants with access to land as a means of production, or whether it is committed to policies which would provide every citizen with sufficient land to establish a secure residential base.[14] In this section, the focus will not be on land for residential purposes, but on providing broad quantitative indicators of the availability of productive agricultural land, and some feasible short-term targets for the redistribution of that land.

The MERG estimate of the need for land will be confined to a preliminary assessment of how poor rural households and poor rural women could benefit through state intervention in redistributing productive land. The goals of such an intervention would be to increase the standard of living of the rural poor by ensuring their direct access to the means of agricultural production, and by redistributing land to more wage-employment intensive agricultural enterprises, which have the capacity to offer rising real wages.

State intervention in the land market is required for two distinct purposes: firstly, to redistribute land directly to poor rural people; and secondly, to reallocate land to those employers capable of achieving the technological dynamism required for the macroeconomic goals of raising employment, real wages, agro-industrial output and exports.

The first of these goals, i.e. the allocation of land to some of the poorest rural households must be regarded as an urgent priority, which should be achieved in the short-run. The policy changes required for the second goal are no less urgently required, but hasty or ill-considered state interventions could easily disrupt existing agricultural production and wage employment, with harsh consequences for the retrenched and for the poorest rural households. The appropriate package of price incentives, tariffs, subsidies, taxes and legislation designed to avoid such disruption, while steadily reorganising cropping patterns to meet sectoral employment and output targets, will be briefly described in section 6.4 below. A crude, medium-term target for the restructuring goal would be the elimination of the degree to which rural labour force : arable land ratios are currently skewed in South Africa. The amount of arable land per capita in the white rural areas is currently 12 times greater than in the black rural areas (McKenzie, Weiner and Vink, n.d.). These figures indicate that there is considerable scope for policies which encourage more labour-intensive forms of production in white rural areas. These policies could include a greater role for nucleus estates, along the lines pioneered by the sugar, timber and tea industries, and contract-farming or similar tenancy arrangements in many white rural areas.

The amount of reasonably productive arable land which could be transferred to the rural poor in the short-run is likely to be constrained by several factors:

- The need to avoid sharp falls in demand for rural wage labour;

- The lack of appropriate rural institutions staffed by trained personnel who are committed to ensure that the eligibility criteria (poverty, gender) are strictly followed in the land allocation process;

- The fiscal costs associated with such transfers, which might include some compensation to previous owners, the costs of resettling beneficiaries, and the costs of providing adequate amounts of seed, fertilizers, implements, credit and marketing services to the beneficiaries. Of these costs, the most significant would probably be those associated with resettlement, particularly if this does not take the form of spontaneous migration, but relies on state provision of expensive infrastructure for planned small farms such as those planned by the DBSA;

- The availability of reasonably productive land which is not a major source of wage employment income, and which is sufficiently close to the current concentrations of poor rural households to minimise the trauma and costs of resettlement. Whether or not sufficient land of an appropriate quality is available will depend on the assumptions made concerning the purpose of allocating land to poor households. Thus, if the primary purpose is to provide land for part-time farming as a marginal supplement to other income sources, or to the diet, relatively little land will be required. However, if this land is supposed to provide for all, or the majority of a household's income, far more will be necessary.

Some of the land required for redistribution to poor households is already owned by state or quasi-state agencies. Comprehensive figures on total state holdings have not been officially compiled; a detailed analysis of the distribution of these holdings should obviously be an urgent priority for a democratic government. The DBSA estimates that the state currently holds 13 million hectares outside the homelands, of which eight million hectares are devoted to conservation, forestry and waterworks. No information is available on the quality and distribution of the remaining five million hectares.

Of the 17.6 million hectares acquired by the state over the years for segregationist purposes and the consolidation of the homelands, 1.25 million hectares were never transferred, and now remain under the control of the Minister of Regional and Land Affairs. It is not exactly clear how the land is geographically located. Nor is it known what proportion of it is unoccupied, leased to white farmers, productively utilized, of high to medium arable potential, or the subject of on-going claims by individuals and groups who would dispute the right of the State to dispose of this land (McKenzie, Van Rooyen and Matsetela, 1993).

In addition, the illegitimate homeland states control large extents of land which have been allocated to 'projects', managed by homeland parastatals or by white management consultants. Neither the extent of such land holdings, nor their agronomic characteristics, nor their current cropping intensities/utilization rates have been accurately estimated.[15] One estimate of the total extent of arable land allocated for projects in the homelands is that it amounts to between 10 per cent and 12 per cent of the total homeland arable area, i.e. about 300 000 hectares. A significant proportion of this land is not cultivated, or is extremely inefficiently cultivated (McKenzie, Weiner and Vink, Table 9).

The classification of this supply of about six to seven million hectares of state controlled land into categories of land quality — high, medium and low arable potential — and by geographical area, is clearly an urgent task for a democratic government, and a prerequisite for the planning of a redistributive strategy. However, it is also important to begin a more detailed analysis of the dimensions and nature of the demand for land which the redistributive strategy aims to address. On the demand side, the data base for planning is at least as inadequate as the data on supply side. Even if it is assumed that only the land needs of poor rural households and women are to be met in the short-term, and it is assumed that all these households are currently living in the rural homelands, there are serious difficulties in quantifying the number of people or households involved, and their geographical distribution.

A significant proportion of the population of the homelands is established in urban settlements, and expresses no interest in engaging in small-holder agricultural production (Bromberger and Antonie, 1993, p. 44; Tapson, 1990, pp. 563-5). Another important group of rural households in the homelands are currently in possession of some arable land, although the quality and quantity of the land operated by each of these households differs considerably.[16] It has been estimated that between 20 and 54 per cent of the land allocated to these households is not regularly cultivated. One of the reasons for this is that much of the land allocated is low-quality and non-arable. Other rural households in the homelands, perhaps as many as one-third of all rural households in these areas, have no access to any arable land at all (McKenzie, Weiner and Vink, p. 9).

Little is known about the demographic or socio-economic characteristics of these landless households, partly because official statistics do not distinguish on a realistic basis between the urban and rural components of homeland populations. The Urban Foundation estimates that about 45 per cent of the black population lived in the homelands in 1985 (ie. 14.7 million people) of whom two-thirds were rural (7.7 million people). This suggests that about 500 000 rural households are now landless.

In some areas these households consist of those most recently removed from precarious and poorly paid agricultural employment on farms in white areas, for whom no additional land could be found in the homelands. Their landlessness is evidence of poverty, since it suggests weak political access to tribal authorities or the political structures responsible for land allocation. If the women in these households were allocated plots of arable land in their own right, then there is little doubt that an extremely poor group of people would benefit.

The supply of state and quasi-state land available for redistribution would appear to be adequate for a short-term redistribution programme targeted to reach a very large number of these landless households in the rural homelands. The costs of such a programme, including some subsidisation of initial farming inputs and infrastructure costs, at an approximate total capital cost of R2 000 per female beneficiary, could be kept well below the level of 1992/3 expenditures on debt relief for white farmers.

If, however, a more ambitious land redistribution target were to be set, involving a significant proportion of the 1.3 million rural homeland households which already own and cultivate farms, as well as a proportion of the 1.2 million workers on white farms, then it would certainly be necessary for the state to acquire additional land. There are, in addition, further categories of black people whose demands for land have been recognised by the democratic movement. These include small capitalists farming on the borders of the existing homelands, who are currently seeking access to land on neighbouring white farms, as well as the many thousands of people evicted or retrenched from white farms, who are currently living in small towns in white rural areas and, besides requiring wage employment, would also benefit from access to peri-urban land for horticultural purposes. The fiscal, legislative, administrative, income-distributional and other economic consequences of attempting to satisfy the land hunger of such a large group of black households have never been calculated. It is unlikely that a programme of this nature could be implemented within the first year or two of the tenure of a democratic government. However, other needs and aspirations of this much larger group of rural households could and should be addressed in the short-term. The policies required to address these needs will be discussed in section 6.4, where feasible targets for state expenditure on rural productive and social infrastructure will be outlined.

The recommendation here is that the initial aim of direct state intervention to redistribute land should be to benefit adult female members of landless households in the rural homelands. The benefits this group may be expected to experience will consist of improvements to their own and their children's diet, achieved through consumption of the vegetables and other food they produce on their newly acquired land, as well as through the small amounts of additional income they may be able to acquire through sales of agricultural produce or through the leasing out of their new asset. It is not anticipated that they or their dependents will be able to survive on the returns from this land alone. The majority of their consumption needs will continue to be met through their own or their family members' access to wage employment, or through transfer incomes, especially pensions. This recommendation does not, of course, preclude the simultaneous pursuit of land redistribution through the proposed land claims court, which would aim to restore specific parcels of land to all people (whether currently landless or not) illegitimately dispossessed by the apartheid state. The adjudication process, however, may take some time, whereas the MERG proposals should be implemented very rapidly.

An additional source of land for redistribution may be the more productive land owned by white farmers who have accumulated unsustainable levels of debt as a result of the impact of government policy mismanagement, rather than the inherent agro-ecological deficiencies of their land. In some areas it may be cost-effective for the state to foreclose on these debts, and acquire some of this land for redistribution programmes designed to benefit the poorest rural households. Such a policy should not be perceived as punitive. Measures would have to be taken to retrain and redeploy the skills of the farmers affected, or more generally, to avoid the dangers of provoking violent coalitions of white farmers aimed at disrupting rural development initiatives. State acquisition of some farms currently owned by white people must not take a form which discourages a rapid resumption of investment in labour intensive production on other large farms. The MERG policy recommendations focus on poverty elimination, rather than on the reduction of rural inequality in order to achieve equality in poverty.

The MERG recommendations may be contrasted with some recent proposals for a land redistribution programme in 1994 from the World Bank (1992a). Their proposals rest on a 'broadly targeted' (i.e. ill-defined) injection of purchasing power which will allow some black people to purchase land in the existing land market, using state-subsidised credit to make their acquisitions. The criteria for targeting suggested by the Bank exclude those who currently have access to very low incomes, no collateral and poor organisational capacity to represent themselves. The issues of poverty and gender are not taken seriously. Rather, the vision is of a package of state subsidies to a class of male black rural capitalists.

While there can be no objection to the removal of all the apartheid obstacles which have constrained the dynamism of black employers, their access to land, as well as the access of their white counterparts to land, should be conditional upon the economic consequences of structures of ownership for the rural poor. The state should certainly intervene to restructure production on large-scale capitalist farms, but the objectives of such interventions should be broader than to merely achieve a change in the colour of the capitalists concerned. These objectives must include achieving the sectoral employment and output targets of the macroeconomic strategy, as well as the demands of the ANC and COSATU for poverty reduction and rapid improvement in the wages and working conditions of farm labourers.

6.4 Policy recommendations

The MERG recommendation that the state should immediately redistribute land to women living in landless households in the rural homelands has already been outlined. In this section, four further policy recommendations will be discussed.

6.4.1 Investment in rural social and physical infrastructure

The proposed programme of investment in sanitation, water supplies, rural clinics, nutrition intervention, education, adult basic education, training, housing and electrification is described in some detail in the chapters on infrastructure and labour policy, while Chapter One indicates that the costs are consistent with macroeconomic balance. This chapter has already made the argument for concentrating these investments in human resource development on rural women in particular regions, because of their absolute and relative levels of deprivation.

Three further economic arguments in favour of such a strategy need to be made here. Firstly, many rural women are now living in homeland or other rural areas where the medium-term prospects for obtaining local productive employment, whether wage employment or self-employment in agricultural or non-agricultural enterprises, are poor. The resource base of the areas in which they live at present, the agro-ecological characteristics and the non-agricultural installed capacity, are all shaky. Consequently, many of them, together with their children, are already commuting, or seasonally migrating, or moving more permanently to the white rural areas, to small towns throughout rural South Africa and to the major urban areas, in an attempt to obtain wage employment and escape their poverty.

Unfortunately, the labour market for uneducated women, lacking employment experience, skills or capital, and restricted both by the nurturing requirements of their dependents and their own poor health status, is extremely slack. Nor can demand for this category of labour be expected to increase substantially, even when growth resumes. Interventions are required in order to improve the mobility and wage earning capacity of this group. Their educational, health and nutritional status must be improved rapidly if there is to be any hope that they and their children can migrate to enter other labour markets with reasonable prospects of success. Obviously, their ability to obtain income through agricultural or non-agricultural self-employment anywhere in the economy is also severely constrained by their structural aversion to risk and by illiteracy and ill health.

Secondly, if they must remain in the homeland for extended periods, these investments are required for another reason. The proportion of their time that they are now able to devote to earning the cash that they and their children need to survive is severely limited. It is limited by the many hours of drudgery involved in the collection of water and fuel, by the distance they must walk to visit a clinic, an educational facility or even a shop, and by the hours they must spend in domestic labour because housing, lighting, washing and cooking facilities are so seriously inadequate. An important aim of the proposed investments should, therefore, be to reduce this drudgery.

Finally, given the extent to which the poorest rural households are dependent upon rural wage labour, it is important to allocate the bulk of the new employment opportunities generated by proposed investments in water supply, sanitation, clinics, etc., to uneducated rural women in the poorest areas. The MERG programme to create 100 000 jobs and opportunities for training per year in labour-based construction must be designed in such a way that the initial beneficiaries are rural women based in the most deprived regions. The availability of such public works employment, within commuting distance, would directly expand their short-term options for wage employment (currently confined largely to agriculture and domestic service), and indirectly improve both their own and their children's longer-term prospects in the labour market, since their education and quality of life would benefit from the infrastructural facilities created.

The MERG proposals for investment in other types of infrastructure include projects in the following areas:

- The rehabilitation and improved maintenance of existing irrigation facilities, oil conservation works, rural feeder roads and on-farm structures. Rehabilitation and maintenance projects for physical infrastructure are stressed because of their relatively short gestation period;

- The labour-intensive construction of new irrigation and water control structures, soil conservation structures and rural feeder roads.

There are strong arguments for concentrating these public investments in those rural areas with the greatest production and export potential, rather than in the most remote, deprived or least productive homeland areas. Thus, although the condition of roads, for example, in remote rural areas is known to be appalling, MERG questions the value of further investment in those areas which were designed as dumping grounds in the heyday of apartheid (cf. Mbongwa and Muller, 1993). The capital cost of providing and maintaining infrastructure services in rural conditions such as these is relatively high, and if these areas have very limited productive potential, then local communities will face great difficulties in meeting maintenance or recurrent costs.

It will be necessary to plan the programme of rural physical infrastructure projects across wide boundaries which include both white and homeland areas. The plans will have to ensure that the benefits or income streams arising from these investments are not confined to those who already own most of the rural means of production. If the investments involve large inputs of female rural labour, and are also designed to lead to faster rates of growth of wage employment in the rural enterprises which benefit from the output of the projects, reasonable rates of social and economic returns may be expected. It may be necessary to focus the initial phases of the physical infrastructure investment programme on those areas with high-to-medium arable potential that are either within, or near the boundaries of the homelands, in order to maximize the possibility of female labour participation.

6.4.2 *Economic carrots and sticks to elicit the co-operation of capitalist farmers*

Large-scale state funding of investment in physical infrastructure along the lines described above could constitute a carrot to elicit co-operative investments by the most dynamic capitalist farmers or agri-business, i.e. those capable of employing large amounts of productive wage labour at a living wage, and of making a contribution to export revenues. Other forms of state intervention will also be required as inducements to encourage restructuring of agricultural production on these farms in areas of high potential.

For example, the state subsidisation of agricultural or agro-industry exports could and should be made conditional on the meeting of per hectare employment targets. State support for agricultural research should also be directed towards achieving employment targets. Indeed, there are immense possibilities for putting economic pressure on farmers, by expanding, eliminating, and redirecting the array of state expenditures and tariffs affecting their incentives. The purpose of such pressures should be to encourage all farmers to begin to invest in a wage labour intensive, technologically dynamic and internationally-competitive farm production structure.

The accelerated conversion of integrated agricultural estates into nucleus estates or small-holder outgrower or contractor schemes, which tend to use more labour per hectare than the original large-scale units, could also be promoted through judicious state intervention by means of expenditure carrots or the fiscal stick. The level of user charges for irrigation water is another obvious example of an appropriate instrument to assist in achieving employment and export targets on existing farms, as is the structure of rail-freight charges. Few, if any, of these state interventions would require new legislation. However, the introduction of a land tax should also be investigated; not because such a tax would or could contribute significantly to revenue, but because it could be used to create incentives for appropriate levels and forms of investment on capitalist farms.

6.4.3   *The statutory national minimum wage*

The arguments in favour of this policy are presented in the Chapter Five. Here it is simply necessary to note that the proposal includes provision for the phased introduction of a rather low minimum wage. Clearly, negotiations concerning the speed of introduction of the minimum in various rural areas will allow both the state and rural workers to bargain for realistic provisions concerning the total numbers employed by farmers in each period. As in the case of the MERG recommendation for investment in physical infrastructure, this proposal will enable the government to influence both cropping patterns and labour intensity within a framework of co-operative bargaining with farmers. The necessity for such a framework is stressed in the MERG proposals because of the dangers posed to the poorest rural households by potentially violent political reaction by more reactionary white farmers.

6.4.4   *Institutional reform*

The MERG recommendations for rural development will require a range of institutional reforms. The most important of these reforms must be aimed at developing the organisational strength and the political voice of landless rural females. If the proposals for a minimum wage, land reallocation, nutritional interventions, public works employment and training for females are to be implemented effectively, then rural women will need external support, not only in the form of enabling labour legislation, the national and sectoral wages boards, but more directly in order to develop and strengthen trade-unions of farm workers and other nationally powerful rural women's organisations/associations, through which they can demand their rights.

The proposals concerning the minimum wage are intended, in part, to provide an immediate focus for mobilising trade-union organisation for female farm workers. The programme of employment creation linked to the construction of rural social and physical infrastructure should provide further opportunities to strengthen women's ability to form associations of employees/trainees. In fact, the design of these investments must include provision for the establishment of such associations, and funding to promote their work.

NGOs can also play an important role in the development and strengthening of the unions, organisations and associations required. There should be provision for the reallocation of existing public sector expenditure away from agricultural extension and administration carried out by large numbers of state-salaried bureaucrats, and towards NGOs with appropriate track records and viable proposals to support the organisation of poor rural women.

At present, few, if any of the state and semi-state institutions concerned with agriculture and rural development are required to prepare strategic plans and supporting programmes for implementing government agricultural policies. There is a remarkable absence of mechanisms either within the Department of Agriculture, or the homelands for ensuring cost effectiveness. Objectives are extremely vaguely specified, and the outputs from the myriad expenditure programmes currently undertaken in the agriculture sector are not clearly identified (Rimmer, LAPC, 1993). This unsatisfactory situation is partly a consequence of the unacceptable degree to which the budgets for these institutions have been determined by the strength of political lobbies, rather than by a rational planning process.

However, the weakness of existing institutions (including the DBSA and the largest NGOs), as shown by their recent inability to disburse even the limited available funds for rural/nutritional development in homeland areas, also accounts for current practice. The introduction of performance auditing and monitoring against objectives is required throughout the public sector, and is further discussed in Chapter Nine. Many of the institutional reforms required for the implementation of the MERG infrastructural programmes are discussed in some detail in Chapter Four. Here it is necessary only to note that the restructuring of the Department of Agriculture and the Department of Regional Land Affairs in April 1993, is most unlikely to provide an appropriate institutional framework for the implementation of the policies of the democratic movement. Substantial further rationalisation is clearly required (Adams, Ashworth, Raikes, 1993).

Δ

Endnotes

1   It should be noted that the share of employment in agriculture in 1991 is rather higher if only the economically active 'black' population is considered; for this group, employment in agriculture accounted for more than 12 per cent of total employment (CSS, 1992, p.222).

2   Van Seventer, Faux and Van Zyl (1992) provide a more detailed analysis of a sector they call 'agri-business' using an expanded input-output table which includes a disaggregated agriculture. Their concept of agri-business only takes account of the forward linkages of agricultural sub-activities, i.e. mostly food processing sub-activities, although textiles and clothing and paper and printing are also included.

3   An officially recorded 20 000 wholesale and retail businesses, together with a larger number of such businesses whose existence is unrecorded, operate in rural areas and generate considerable wage employment. These businesses may be regarded as directly or indirectly dependent on Agriculture (Roth et al, 1992, p.61).

4   This list does not, however, exhaust the full panoply of support received by white farmers from the state, which has also accorded white farmers a favourable tax status. One estimate is that income tax concessions to farmers amounted to 70 per cent of their theoretical tax bill in 1981– 4 (Vink and Kassier, 1991, p.217). More broadly, legislative barriers erected against competition from black farmers and share-croppers since 1913, and the array of legislation designed to lower the supply price of labour to white farms (Schirmer, 1993, pp. 17–19) should also be considered as subsidising interventions.

5   In most of the self-governing territories, there has also been a decline in agricultural spending as a proportion of total expenditure between 1984/5 and 1991/2 (see Figure 6.5).

6   One estimate of the level of increased input costs faced by farmers as a result of protection policy, is that farmers in the early 1980s would have been able to save about 25 per cent on fertilizer inputs in a tariff-free environment (Vink and Kassier 1991, p.217). Note that exporters of processed agricultural commodities have not been able to benefit from incentives such as GEIS.

7   One of the significant failings of the official statistics is that they do not report areas cultivated for the key growth sectors of white farming, i.e. horticultural crops and vegetables.

8   The latest ad hoc response to such pressures has been the allocation of approximately R50 million in mid–1993 to selected white farmers to compensate them fro the costs of protecting themselves against violence. The regime does not ap-

pear to appreciate the fact that rather more black rural inhabitants than white have been the victims of violence.

9   In 1992–93, 39.1 per cent of total state expenditure in the TVBCs was devoted to salaries (Daphne, 1993).

10 One of the many deficiencies of the available sources is that they have not been able to make use of an appropriate deflator. Low-income rural consumer price indices appropriate for different districts are not available in South Africa.

11 For further evidence, see Wilson and Ramphele, 1989, or Lynne's rural survey, in which the bottom 10 per cent of households received less than 2.4 per cent of the total amount of cash income received by all households.

12 Between 1981 and 1987 the real wages of these workers appear to have fallen quite considerably (Roth et al, 1992, p.105).

13 This includes most of the self-governing territories (with the exception of some districts of Kwazulu which are defined as part of the Durban/Pine-town/Inanda metropole), as well as the TVBC states.

14 Some rural households without access to productive land have no intention of at-tempting to survive by farming and may have no desire to devote their labour to the production of agricultural commodities.

15 In particular, the extent of land allocated to 'projects' in Bophutatswana, Ciskei, Kwazulu, Lebowa and the Transkei is not known. Apart from land allocated to projects, land has also been allocated to 'private commercial farmers' in the homelands. The extent of such land is unknown.

16 Estimates of the average size of land holdings in the Transkei range from 1.8 hec-tares and Kwazulu from 0.6 hectares to 3.5 hectares. In Kangwane the esti-mated average was five hectares per household. In the Cheto valley in Ciskei, average land holdings are as low as 0.43 hectares per household (McKenzie, Weiner and Vink, Appendix 4). Of course, these averages conceal the fact that some black households in the homelands are cultivating farms of 20 hectares or more.

Table 6.1   The share of agricultural exports in total South African exports, 1969 to 1991 (percentage)

	1969	1970	1971	1972	1973	1974	1975	1976	1977	1978	1979	1980
Total incl. gold (Current prices)	6.37	6.15	6.05	8.32	5.96	5.24	6.11	5.53	5.28	5.33	3.50	4.37
Total excl. gold (Current prices)	9.25	8.84	8.67	11.74	9.28	8.48	9.25	7.64	7.24	7.67	5.50	8.10
Total incl. gold (Constant 1991 prices)							3.76	3.00	3.36	3.73	2.79	4.16
Total excl. gold (Constant 1991 prices)							7.15	5.59	5.97	6.62	4.81	7.11

	1981	1982	1983	1984	1985	1986	1987	1988	1989	1990	1991	
Total incl. gold (Current prices)	4.20	3.62	1.85	1.60	1.59	1.73	1.82	2.05	3.09	2.52	2.53	
Total excl. gold (Current prices)	7.05	6.00	3.24	2.73	2.60	2.72	2.87	3.13	4.36	3.40	3.43	
Total incl. gold (Constant 1991 prices)	3.54	3.14	1.63	1.36	1.61	1.85	1.83	2.05	3.10	2.52		
Total excl. gold (Constant 1991 prices)	6.16	5.53	3.03	2.48	2.71	2.99	2.87	3.13	4.36	3.40		

Source: CEAS data bank

Table 6.2   Components of a manufacturing–agricultural complex in constant 1990 rands (million), 1988

	Employment	Intermed-iate output	Total production (excl. Imports)	Imports	Exports	Value added	Captital stock	GDP %
Agriculture	1 350 000	15 713	22 451	1 242	1 271	13 914	34 240	5.9
Agro-processing m'facture								
Food	187 900	11 402	31748	1 601	2 292	5 300	8 077	2.2
Beverages	35 100	2 227	6 853	313	191	1 87	4 073	0.8
Tobacco	5 330	44	1 194	59	67	320	285	0.1
Textiles[1]	28 347	1 850	2 398	346	322	714	661	0.3
Leather products	11 000	321	870	195	149	235	105	0.1
Footwear	30 700	150	1 563	240	105	571	196	0.2
Wood & wood prods	57 000	2 635	2 935	279	261	851	955	0.4
Paper & paper prods	39 900	7 897	8 406	839	790	3 116	3 671	1.3
Fertilisers & pesticides	6 630	1 914	2 047	215	238	313	729	0.1
Mac-manufacturing	401 907	28 442	58 015	4 087	4 413	13 299	18 752	5.6
Non-mac manufacturing	1 040 673	98 189	131 328	41 373	15 179	44 543	71 746	18.9
Mac as % of m'facturing	28	22	31	9	23	23	21	23.0
Manufacturing[2]	1 442 580	126 631	189 343	45 459	19 592	57 842	90 498	24.5

1   Since a significant proportion of textiles is produced from synthetic inputs, only 30 per cent of the sector was assumed to fall within the MAC
2   GDP contribution estimates based on 1988 Manufacturing value added of R57842m being equivalent to 24.5 per cent of national GDP

Source: IDC Manufacturing Sector Database, January 1992. All monetary data in constant 1990 Rand. 1988 data inflated by SA-PPI of 1.29

Table 6.3   Recent reforms in selected controlled markets

Scheme/Product	Recent reforms
Single-channel fixed price	
Maize	Shift to pool-type pricing (1987); prohibition on erection of grain silos repealed; grain silo committee scrapped; grain sorghum established as surplus removal scheme (1986); scrapping of control measures on buckwheat under consideration.
Winter cereals	Abolition of restrictive registration of millers and confectioners; elimination of bread subsidy (1990); price control on flour, meal and bread and fixing of millers' margins scrapped (1991); simplification of grading system for wheat (1991).
Single channel pool	
Oilseed	Abolition of import control measures on oilcake and fishmeal; liberalisation of groundnuts under consideration.
Leaf tobacco	Discontinuation of single channel.
Deciduous fruit	Free issue of domestic marketing permits.
Citrus fruit	Domestic market control abolished (1990).
Bananas	In process of conversion to free market and privatisation of Board.
Lucerne seed	Switch to surplus removal scheme rejected (1990); Board permitted allow private import and export (1992).
Surplus disposal schemes	
Slaughter stock	Abolition of restrictions on movement from uncontrolled to controlled areas (1992); abolition of restrictive registration of producers, abattoirs agents, butchers, dealers, processors and importers.
Eggs	Abolition of production control; cancellation of authority to fix market prices.
Milk and butter fat	Consumer price control on fresh milk abolished (1983); price control on butter and cheese abolished (1985); price stabilisation activities ended following court ruling ending levy income (1992).
Supervisory and price regulation	
Canning fruit	Consensus committee established for price determination.
Control in terms of section 84A	
Karakul pelts	Karakul scheme and board abolished.
Control in terms of other legislation	
Sugar cane	Reform of cane quota system (1990).
Fresh produce	Reform of market rules, following report of Marx Committee (1992).
Lucerne hay	Discontinuation of single channel.

Source: Adapted from Department of Agriculture information

Table 6.4   Annual average price increases, selected indices (percentages)

	1981-91	*1981-86*	*1986-91*
Farm machinery	17.1	19.5	14.7
CPI (food only)	15.1	13.2	17.0
CPI (all items)	14.7	14.7	14.7
Fruit	14.3	16.9	11.8
Fertiliser	14.0	16.0	12.0
General Producer Price Index	13.5	13.8	13.1
Animal feed	12.4	14.2	10.7
Summer cereals	11.9	14.7	9.1
Poultry	11.3	10.3	12.3
All agricultural producer prices	10.8	11.4	10.3
Oilseeds	10.4	11.1	9.7
Fuel	9.9	7.9	11.9
Vegetables	9.5	8.9	10.2
Winter cereals	9.4	8.9	10.0
Sugar cane	9.4	9.1	9.7
Dairy	9.3	8.4	10.2
Slaughtered stock	9.0	8.2	9.9
Wool and mohair	8.2	13.6	3.0

Source: **Derived from Directorate of Agriculture Information (1993)**

Table 6.5 **Major loan, emergency and subsidy schemes to commercial farmers, 1991/92**

Name of scheme	Type of assistance	Current status 1992/93	Allocation 1991/92
1. Purchase of agricultural land	loan: ACB	suspended	22 002 400
2. Consolidation of debt	loan: ACB	operational	125 087 200
3. Bringing about improvements	loan: ACB	suspended	-
4. Purchase of implements and vehicles	loan: ACB	suspended	131 300
5. Purchase of livestock	loan: ACB	certain areas only	3 148 700
6. Means of crop production	loan: ACB	operational	159 197 600
7. Erection of waterworks	loan: ACB	suspended	13 600
8. Erection of soil conservation works	loan: ACB	operational	3 501 500
9. Allocation of state land	loan: ACB	operational	4 918 700
10. Flood disaster loans	loan: ACB	emerg. assistance	2 855 300
11. Subsidy on carry-over debts	subsidy	operational	113 856 000
12. Interest subsidy on production credit	subsidy	operational	87 900
13. Subsidy on farm bond interest in consolidated ag. debt	subsidy	operational	61 200
14. Stockfeed purchases and incentives	subsidy	operational	65 122 800
15. Flood/fire disaster subsidies	subsidy	operational	19 943 800
16. Water quota subsidies	subsidy	operational	1 007 600
17. Conversion of marginal lands	subsidy	operational	52 483 900
18. Farm labourer housing	subsidy	operational	25 910 650

Source: Department of Agricultural Development

Table 6.6 **Allocations under the original R1 000 million budget for drought relief**

Scheme implemented	Allocation (R mill)	Description of scheme
1. Retaining the services of full-time labourers	5.0	Subsidy of R150 per month per full-time labourer. Farmers may apply when payment of debt or settlement with creditors will result in dismissals.
2. Emergency assistance to farmers compelled to retire from agriculture	3.6	A welfare payment made to farmers who are forced to retire from agriculture. Monthly payment of R2 000 (married couple) for a maximum of 12 months. No assistance for farm workers forced to retire from agriculture.
3. Checking sequestrations	15.0	Assistance to check foreclosure.

4. Co-ordinated reconstruction of debt	43.35	Assistance to call together creditors, restructure debt and refinance the farm. Includes provision for some of the debt to be written-off.
5. Subsidy: carry-over debt	212.0[1]	The first instalment on the carry-over debt subsidy (described above).
6. Interest subsidy: new production credit	217.0	Subsidised interest rate for new production credit. Subsidy on sliding scale between 4,5% and 7.5%. Upper limit of R750 000.
7. Rebate on transport of fodder	30.0	Subsidy, in addition to normal disaster drought assistance, of the transport costs of fodder. Measure entails a 75% rebate on transport costs.
8. Interest subsidy: long-term loans at commercial banks	10.0	Extension of scheme started in 1991/92. Subsidy of 5% on long-term loans at Land Bank and commercial banks.
9. Direct to co-operatives	110.0[2]	Assistance to help co-operatives survive through amalgamation.
10. Training farm workers	1.0	Payment to farmer of training costs of farm workers.
11. Sundry supporting measures: a) Grain storage b) Emergency water schemes	173.0 20.0	a) Contribution towards the fixed costs of grain storage. Low crop means that fixed costs are not covered. b) Schemes for the transportation of water, installation of emergency water pipelines and the drilling of boreholes.
12. Assistance to a) Sugar industry b) Wool industry c) Mohair industry d) Meat industry	(paid 93/94) 15.0 2.5 2.5	a) Loan assistance for sugar producers - 8 year loans at subsidised rate of 8%. b) Payment to International Wool Secretariat for use against the Wool Board's IWS financing cost. c) A direct payment to the Mohair Board for the promotion of mohair marketing. d) Interest subsidy on finance for the purchase of bredding stock in drought areas
13. To farmers & rural communities in self-governing territories	130.0	Assistance to fund i) Job creation programmes ii) Input cost subsidies to commercial crop farmers iii) Interest subsidy on new production credit iv) Rebates on transport of stockfeed v) Subsidised stock feed vi) Water projects
14. Joint services boards Natal	3.488	
15. Water provision (Dept of Water Affairs and Forestry)	2.973	
16. To Indian farmers To coloured farmers	9.5 2.5	Indian farmers received of a one-off subsidy of R1400 for sugar-cane producers. Coloured farmers helped under the various input subsidy schemes.

1   An additional amount of R2,400 million has been allocated for the subsidy on carry-over debt in March 1993
2   Includes an additional amount of R65 million allocated for financial assistance to co-operatives (WPK & VETSAK) (funded from savings on interest)

Source: Drought Action Co-ordinating Centre (March report: 2/3/93)

Table 6.7 Agricultural expenditure in nominal prices 1985/86 to 1992/93

Year	Total (R billion)	White (R billion – % total budget)	Black (R billion – % total budget)
1985/86	1.45	1.14 (79%)	0.31 (21%)
1986/87	1.31	0.94 (72%)	0.37 (28%)
1987/88	1.69	1.24 (73%)	0.45 (27%)
1988/89	1.76	1.17 (67%)	0.58 (33%)
1989/90	1.67	1.01 (60%)	0.66 (40%)
1990/91	1.79	0.93 (52%)	0.85 (48%)
1991/92	1.97	1.04 (53%)	0.93 (47%)
1992/93	5.24	4.01 (77%)	1.23 (23%)
Av. annual % increase	20%	20%	22%

Notes:

1 'White' agriculture refers to expenditure by the Department of Agriculture (General Affairs — state revenue account) & the Department of Agricultural Development. Data on coloured and Asian agricultural expenditure (small amounts from the Houses of Delegates & Representatives) not yet available
2 All 'white' data is actual expenditure, not the buget vote
3 Outstanding payments due under the revised budgets of the Departments of Agriculture and Agricultural Development and not paid out 92/93 are to be rolled over to 93/94
4 From 93/94, the Department of Agricultural Development has joined the Department of Agriculture, as have Representatives and Delegates
5 For 'black' (TBVC & self-governing states) expenditure, audited accounts have been used if available. If not, budget estimates have been used. Where possible, Ministers' salaries have been included. Forestry expenditure has also been included
6 Figures may not add due to rounding

Table 6.8   Proportion of total homeland budget
allocated to various deparments, 1990/91

Department	Allocation (%)
Education	28.0
Health, welfare, pensions	20.0
Works, transport	15.0
Agriculture, forestry, environment	6.0
Finance	10.0
Post and telecommunications	2.0
Economic affairs, energy, tourism	1.0
Local government and housing	1.0
Justice, police, prisons	5.0
Defence	2.0
Chief minister, military council, presidency	3.0
Internal affairs	2.0
Foreign affairs	0.4
Other	4.6
Total	100.0

Source: Daphne, 1993

Table 6.9   The loan portfolio of DBSA for rural
and agricultural investment, 1982 to 1992

Year	Community support (%)	Development planning	Farmer support (%)	State farming (%)	Settlement projects (%)	Other (%)	Total
1982	-	-	-	-	88.0	12.0	28 907 240
1983	-	-	-	2.0	76.0	22.0	23 121 280
1984	-	-	13.0	3.0	78.0	6.0	25 754 730
1985	-	-	55.0	23.0	22.0	-	11 725 000
1986	55.0	7.0	7.0	14.0	17.0	-	16 953 050
1987	1.0	-	46.0	53.0	-	-	53 788 865
1988	7.0	2.0	-	34.0	57.0	-	50 273 815
1989	-	-	61.0	-	35.0	4.00	24 480 420
1990	15.0	-	24.0	-	53.0	11.0	40 438 820
1991	-	5.0	73.0	-	22.0	-	14 940 780
1992	13.0	0.4	41.0	-	5.0	38.0	96 789 000
Total	22 313 280	3 415 760	144 404 120	23 606 080	132 849 920	64 275 840	391 865 000

Source: Van Rooyen, 1993

Figure 6.1   MAC–contribution to GDP (percentage)

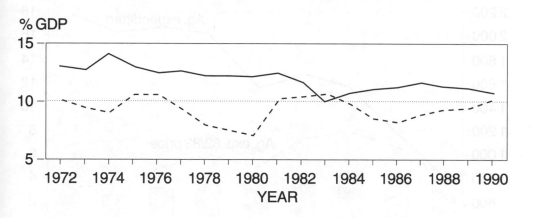

Source: Rustomjee, 1993

Figure 6.2   Agro-manufacturing contribution to GDP (percentage)

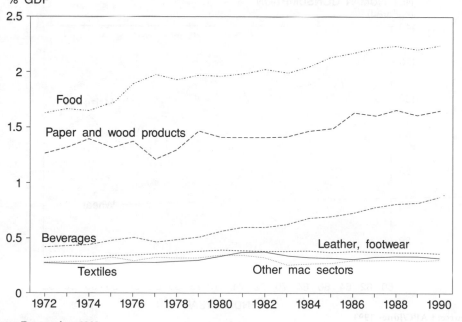

Source: Rustomjee, 1993

Figure 6.3   Total expenditure on agriculture, consolidated general government

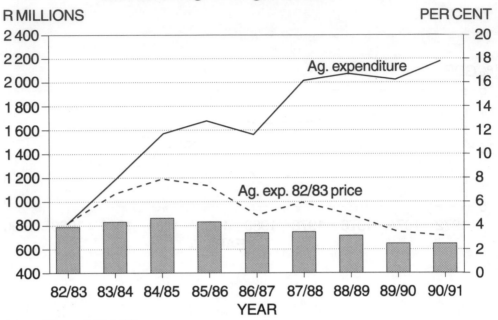

Source: Rimmer/LAPC 1993

Figure 6.4   Per capita consumption of maize and wheat 1960-1992

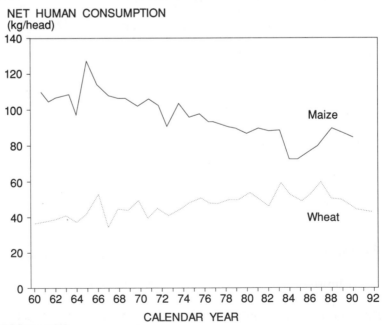

Source: LAPC/Jones 1993

Figure 6.5   Agricultural expenditure as a percentage of total expenditure in self-governing states

PER CENT TOTAL BUDGET

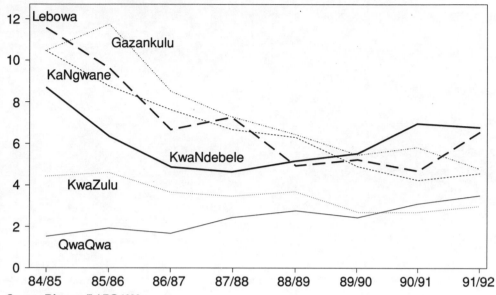

Source: Rimmer/LAPC 1993

C H A P T E R 7
Industrial, corporate and trade policy

•

Industrial development has the capacity to generate employment, to produce basic commodities for domestic consumption, to ease balance of payments constraints through enhancing the balance of trade and encouraging foreign direct investment, and to raise the general level of productivity in the economy. It is important to appreciate the limits of what can be achieved by industrial policy. Whilst industrial growth can contribute to job creation, this may not be substantial in the short-term, as productivity increases, rather than employment growth, absorb demand; and such processes will be uneven across sectors. Support for industrial policy, then, should not detract from the responsibility borne by the state to generate employment through expenditure programmes on physical infrastructure.

Formulation of industrial policy is extremely challenging, partly because industry covers a particularly heterogeneous set of economic activities that have been gathered together under one heading only for the purposes of statistical convenience. Consequently, the differences in the character of certain productive activities that are commonly regarded as belonging to industry, may be greater than the differences between certain industrial and non-industrial activities. This simple observation serves as a sharp warning to those who seek to treat industry as amenable to policy formulation through general principles divorced from their application to the specific activities concerned. It can even be difficult to establish where one industrial activity begins and another ends. For these reasons, MERG supports the approach taken by the industrial strategy project (ISP), sponsored by COSATU, in which careful consideration is given to the sectoral differences within industry, and to how industrial activities are integrated with one another. This chapter draws freely upon ISP work, although it has not adopted the framework of the ISP.

In addition, industrial policy formulation faces difficulties because it is made up of a number of separate components, and these are liable to be employed to a different extent, and in different ways, from one industrial sub-sector to the next. As a result, the present chapter is wide-ranging in scope, but steers a path between general principles and specific policies. It should be seen as representative of a broad set of policy stances towards industrial development, with selected themes examined in greater detail. MERG does not make any claim to comprehensive coverage.

The chapter begins with an overview of the causes and consequences of manufacturing decline, and of industrial policy since the 1930s. There follows an analysis of the central features of South African industry. Mining and mineral processing are identified as lying at the core of the industrial structure. Several key components of MERG strategy are then addressed. These relate to competition policy (where the discussion includes an assessment of market and ownership structures, as well as the role of small, medium and micro-enterprises, and the issue of public ownership); trade policies; and strategies aimed at strengthening the capacities required to revitalise manufacturing, particularly in the area of human resource development and technological capabilities.

7.1 Manufacturing decline: causes and consequences

Investment in the manufacturing sector grew rapidly between the 1930s and the 1960s. The underlying cause was the strength of the mineral economy based on gold. Other important factors included the protective impact of two world wars and the depression of the 1930s; protectionist trade policies implemented since the 1920s; direct state involvement in industrial development through state corporations such as Iscor and the Industrial Development Corporation; foreign investment in manufacturing from the late 1920s to the 1970s; and the drive by mining houses to diversify.

The growth of manufacturing slowed in the late 1960s, and entered an as yet endless spiral of decline. Table 7.1 shows that the growth rates of manufacturing output, manufacturing employment and GDP slowed in each five year period after 1946 to 1991. In the final period, manufacturing output improved slightly, but not by enough to reverse the downward trend in GDP.

There has been some improvement in manufacturing export performance since the mid-1980s, and especially in the late 1980s and early 1990s. The reasons do not suggest a fundamental shift in underlying conditions, and it is most unlikely that such improvements will be sustained. The improvement in manufactured exports appear to have been mainly due to the provision of substantial export incentives, the recession in the domestic economy, and the devaluation of the real value of the rand in the mid-1980s. It is not accounted for by the renewal of growth in productivity that is the prerequisite for a departure from the disastrous outcome of the previous decade.

The weakness of the industrial sector goes far beyond the difficulties that would be experienced by any economy subject to a decade or more of economic stagnation and political and social instability. The World Bank, for example, argues that the relative prices of capital and labour have been artificially distorted in favour of the former, so that capital-intensity of production has been too high at the expense of job creation. SACOB, however, argues that investment has been discouraged by the high cost of capital.

A separate issue has been the role of tariffs and protection, with a commonly held view being that these have been excessive, even if supporting the creation and survival of some domestic capacity for the production of consumption goods. But the outcome appears to have been the featherbedding of inefficient producers, and the failure to develop exports and meet international competition. Together with the high degree of concentration of industry, it has been argued that beneficial competitive pressures or market forces have been dulled.

For these and other reasons associated with the apartheid system, (especially skill levels), many have pointed to the disastrous stagnation in productivity growth, despite high capital-intensity, although separate allowance for the impact of low capacity utilisation has not always been carefully distinguished. Calls for lower real wages as a means both to encourage investment and to create jobs have also been prominent.

The MERG view is that the debate over industrial policy has suffered from a false understanding of the structure of South African industry, and of the economic and political sources of its decline. Structurally, industry has developed most at the two extremes of the range of potential sectoral activities. On the one hand, the heavy dependence upon mining and energy has given rise to substantial downstream activity in sectors such as iron and steel, mineral beneficiation and heavy chemicals. On the other hand, consumer goods industries have been developed largely in response to protection. In both cases, the degree of further integration, in forward linkages from mining and energy, and in backward linkages from consumer goods, has been extremely limited. The result is the narrow base upon which manufacturing has been dependent, especially notable being the absence of capability in capital and many intermediate goods. In the light of limited access to foreign investment, the economy can expand only at the expense of the balance of payments as imports of necessary inputs place pressure on the balance of trade which cannot be ameliorated by domestic sourcing even at higher costs.

It is necessary to recognise these fundamental features of South African industry, because the reasons for the creation of this duality in industrial structure, and the polices to remedy it, are quite different in the case of the heavy industries associated with mining and energy, as opposed to the light industries attached to consumer goods. It will be necessary to target policies that are appropriate to the different types of manufacturing found in South Africa as well as shifting the balance in the composition of output. This will depend upon integration across the different sections where appropriate. The tendency to lump all manufacturing together and consider it as a sector distinct from primary and tertiary economic activity is particularly inappropriate in South Africa. A major part of what is considered to be manufacturing is more accurately analysed in terms of its connections to mining and energy, to which it is more closely related than to other sectors of manufacturing. Thus, the prospects for sectors such as iron and steel, metal fabrication and heavy chemicals are governed by their links to mining and energy, and policy making will be misguided if based upon bundling these particular sectors together with general manufacturing and analysing them in terms of capital-labour ratios, relative prices, etc.

7.1.1 The achievements and failures of industrial policy

The industrial policies that have been adopted, and those that continue to be adopted are discussed briefly below. Throughout the post-war period and before, the role of the state in industrial policy has been paramount. The state has acknowledged three crucial areas of intervention.

Firstly, there has been the growth of state corporations such as Iscor, Eskom and SASOL. These have not only made a major direct contribution to industrial output, but they have been central, at times in joint ventures, to the indirect promotion of large-scale manufacturing by the private sector in and around heavy industry. Secondly, trade policy has been used to stimulate other sectors of manufacturing and has, to a large extent, offered protection more or less on demand, and certainly in response to political pressures, rather than on the basis of rational economic calculation. Thirdly, government policy has been predicated over a long period upon the apartheid principle of separate development, which, in the case of industry, has taken the form of an apparent commitment to decentralisation. In practice, this has been more of an ideological than a real commitment, so that the resources devoted to homeland industrial development have been derisory.

Over the past decade, these three areas of government policy have changed as the state has embraced goals of privatisation and tariff reform, and overtly abandoned the paper exercise of separate homeland development. These most recent developments are discussed in greater detail below. First, however, it is important to recognise that industrial policy ranges over a much wider set of activities. In particular, it needs to incorporate education and training, for the skill levels and composition of the work-force are central both to the levels of productivity with given production methods, and to the capacity to adopt and adapt new technology. Technology policy itself is a crucial component of any industrial policy.

Access to finance and competition policy must also be taken into account in formulating and implementing industrial policy. This is particularly so in South Africa, given that its financial system has not been conducive to investment in industry (as shown in Chapter Eight), and given that industrial activity is itself heavily dominated by what is arguably an industrial structure which is one of the most concentrated in the world by ownership distribution and interlinkages in corporate control. Quite apart from oligopoly in markets, marketing itself is an important aspect in the success of industry. Customers have to be found and serviced effectively. South Africa has borne substantial penalties in marketing because of sanctions. These have entailed lost markets, and/or selling at a discount. In addition, MERG research has found that South African marketing policy for its major exports has been far from satisfactory. Unduly high commissions have been paid for marketing services, opportunities to exploit market power have not been pursued, and insufficient attention has been paid to thwarting capital flight, tax evasion, and avoidance achieved through false invoicing and transfer pricing.

Quite apart from the content of industrial policy across all these areas, there has been an imbalance between them, resulting in the neglect of regional development, competition policy, technology and training. This is symptomatic of a more general failure to adopt coherent long-term objectives for industry. The different components of industrial policy, with a few exceptions, have not been integrated to achieve specific strategies for individual sectors. Such failure has been a major factor in the skewed sectoral composition of industry and the continuing absence of a broader range of manufacturing capability. It has undermined the momentum underlying the competitiveness of those sectors that have been established, since their prospects are often tied to the 'economies of scope' associated with vertical linkages, as well as the economies of scale arising out of horizontal integration within sectors. Attention to such linkages have been vital to the manufacturing successes of the newly industrialised economies.

Against the above background, it is possible to assess the apparent shifts in government policy in which privatisation, trade liberalisation, and the abandonment of separate development have been to the fore. MERG would argue that these have illustrated a remarkable degree of continuity with the past. Regional industrial development continues to be neglected; large-scale interventions through the state in conjunction with private capital are still of central importance; and trade policy remains selective and not coherently tied to long-term objectives, even if there have been some reductions in overall levels of support.

Such conclusions are confirmed by examining the role of the Industrial Development Corporation which, from an initial position of significance in industrial policy making, has strengthened its influence even further over the past few years. This has been as a result of the abolition of the Board of Trade and Industry, which had previously played a major role in setting tariffs and protection.

In the late 1980s the Board of Trade and Industries was attempting to reduce tariff protection by linking it to interventionist (and inappropriately named) structural adjustment programmes (SAPs) sector-by-sector. This was partly to ease the path of adjustment but, more significantly, to secure productivity increases without relying exclusively upon the competitive coercion of the market. It faced, however, considerable opposition from the IDC. It publicly challenged the interventionist approach of the BTI, preferring to rely upon market forces, whilst ignoring its own interventionist role in nurturing a range of heavy industries through support to state corporations. In 1990, the Department of Trade and Industry withdrew ninety personnel seconded to the BTI, crippling the work on existing SAPs, and forbidding any new ones. Subsequently, the BTI was further emasculated by the BTI Amendment Bill of 1992.

With the demise of the BTI, the IDC is implementing the only significant industrial policy remaining, namely the promotion of an industrial trajectory around large-scale mega-projects including SASOL expansions, aluminium smelting, stainless steel and potash. The only difference is that the process is now driven by private-sector interests rather than the parastatals previously supported by the IDC. Furthermore, discretion still remains at the heart of decision-making as in the selection of projects qualifying for Section 37E tax incentives, which has been the subject of opposition from senior officials of the Finance Department. Section 37E incentives initially, in 1991, covered projects beneficiating locally sourced minerals. Its extension, in 1992, to projects beneficiating imported material, in particular the Alusaf project, which did not previously qualify because it utilised imported alumina, is evidence of the ability of coalitions of powerful private sector interests to lobby for favourable discretionary treatment.

This continuity in the narrow scope of industrial policy is confirmed by the Normative Economic Model. This relies on the traditional divisions between primary, secondary and tertiary sectors, which are particularly inappropriate in South Africa. It treats industrialisation as if it has only occurred through backward integration from consumer goods promoted by protection, and fails to address the range of industrial policies that have been employed in the past, let alone those that have been neglected, focusing upon the role of protection alone. Not surprisingly, this leads to simple dependence upon correcting market price distortions, whether for inputs or outputs, without seriously examining how such policies might actually eliminate rather than restructure the industries concerned. In addition, the lack of a coherently formulated industrial policy has been complemented by industrial restructuring that has weakened even further the capacity to implement and monitor the policies that will be necessary.

7.2 The mining and mineral processing industry

The South African economy today is dominated by a highly concentrated system of ownership of corporate capital, straddling mining and finance (and, consequently, many economic activities in between, as investment in the form of acquisitions and mergers has taken precedence over real investment in new capacity). Highly concentrated private capital has had an intimate and integral relationship with the state — in the co-ordination of productive activity with state corporations, both institutionally and in the determination of economic policy. Much of the manufacturing, which is apparently displacing the role of mineral and energy sectors, is directly dependent upon these sectors. This dependence is illustrated by the arguments in the following sections.

An important part of what is defined as manufacturing is in fact the refining of minerals such as iron ore (iron and steel), chromite ore (ferrochrome), manganese ore, (ferromanganese) etc. The further processing of minerals into dimensional products before export has become an important economic activity, and is currently being rapidly expanded through the implementation of three major refining plants with a total escalated capital investment of over R12 billion. Given South Africa's exceptional mineral resource endowment, this sector is likely to expand further in a post-sanctions future, and there are several other major projects in the pipeline. The main mineral refining companies are Iscor (iron, steel, zinc, tin) owned by the IDC, Samancor (ferroalloys, manganese metal) owned by Genmin and Highveld (iron, steel, vanadium products) owned by Anglo.

While existing statistics categorise electricity as an economic activity separate from mining, quarrying and manufacturing, there are extensive linkages between them. More than 90 per cent of electricity is generated from coal, a mining activity, and the balance sourced from hydro-electric and nuclear stations (the latter also ultimately sources its feed from uranium mining and electricity-intensive, coal-powered enrichment). Some 22 per cent of electricity output is consumed in the coal, gold, diamond and other mining sectors. An additional 21 per cent of electricity output is consumed in the energy-intensive smelting and refining processes.

Even though chemicals and petroleum production activities may seem remote from mining, they are linked largely through the coal mining industry, on which the South African economy is heavily reliant. The production of fertilisers, plastics, chemicals and petroleum depends on energy-intensive processes which consume large quantities of electricity, which is in turn generated from coal. The SASOL liquid-fuel-from-coal plants are themselves major users of electricity and in 1991 this sector used some 7GWH (18 per cent of industrial supply). Of the 176 million tons of coal mined in 1989, 47mt was exported. From remaining local sales of 129mt, 70mt was used by Eskom to produce electricity, 35mt was consumed by the three SASOL plants to produce synthetic fuels and chemicals, and 1.1mt was used by AECI to produce ammonia, explosives and methanol at Modderfontein. The AECI/Sentrachem Coalplex plant at Sasolburg produces PVC from coal. A coal-based industrial gas grid supplies industries in the PWV area from the SASOL plant in Sasolburg.

Non-metallic mineral products such as cement and bricks, the inputs to building and construction industries, are immediate downstream activities from mining. In both cases, mined or quarried product such as limestone and gypsum is crushed, mixed and heated, often using coal as the fuel. These plants are usually located close to the quarries which supply their raw materials.

Iron and steel industries are not as numerous as cement- and brick-making plants. Of the three steel producers in South Africa, the recently privatised Iscor dominates the industry. Iron ore, coal and electricity constitute the major inputs to steel manufacture which is produced in the form of shapes, sections, tubes, wire or castings. Other mineral products, such as chrome and vanadium, are also used to produce alloys and various grades of stainless steels, although at present only one plant, Columbus (formally Middleburg Steel and Alloys), currently produces stainless steel.

Copper, silver, aluminium, the platinum group metals, nickel and zinc, are the major components of the non-ferrous metals category. As with steel, the respective ores are smelted and refined to produce the basic sections, castings or refined mattes that are then either sold on commodity markets, or used in subsequent manufacturing activities.

The core of the mining and mineral processing industry is still gold mining which constitutes about 70 per cent of mining exports and employment and 80 per cent of revenue. However, unlike most other minerals for which there are large reserves, the bulk of our gold reserves have already been extracted. Over the last century over 45 thousand tonnes of gold have been removed, constituting over two-thirds of the original resource base, and the 20 thousand tonnes remaining tend to be deep and low grade. Thus the gold mining industry is in long-term decline, and the MERG simulations indicate that at a real price of 350 USD per ounce, output will decline from 614 tonnes in 1992, to 528 tonnes by 2000 and 414 tonnes by 2007. This constitutes a loss of about R8 billion or 15 per cent of total exports, and alternative exports will have to be found if increasing balance of payments contraints are to be avoided. In addition, an average price of 350 USD/oz is not secure and the MERG gold report suggests that a price of 300 USD/oz would be more probable over the period, which would result in production of only 250 tonnes by 2007, representing a forex loss of R15 billion.

Significant expansion of exports of other major minerals (coal, PGMs and ferro-alloys) is unlikely, given South Africa's already high market share and the most probable short- to medium-term expansion will have to come from further processing of minerals before export (beneficiation). The new beneficiation projects (Columbus, Alusaf and Namakwa) will earn about R4 billion per annum net in forex.

Overall, mineral and mineral-based exports are expected to increase from R48 billion (1992 Rand) to R53 billion in 1997 and then fall to R47 billion by 2007. However, this does not include numerous projects that fall into the 'possible' rather than 'probable' category. If these are included, forex earnings could increase to R57 billion (1992 Rand) by 2007.

The industrial orientation is not accurately portrayed by the traditional GDP distribution graph (Figure 7.1). The central role that mining, mineral processing and energy generation (to be termed the broader primary sectors) play in the economy is better represented by Figure 7.2. Since 1960, other manufacturing has stagnated within a narrow band of 15 to 17 per cent of GDP. The relative contribution of the broader primary activities to GDP fell in the 1960s from 22 per cent to about 17 per cent but rose to a high of 32 per cent in 1980, and then settled within a band of 25 to 27 per cent. Eskom power generation, the SASOL petroleum/chemicals complex, and the rise in mineral processing have underpinned the integrated nature of the economy. The largest growth in the contribution of the broader primary sector seems to have taken place in the capital-intensive mineral processing and chemical industries (largely SASOL) in the 1980s, whereas it was the electricity industry that grew in the 1970s.

The growth of the broader primary sector has been accompanied by stagnation of the other manufacturing sectors since 1960. The contribution of the latter sectors to GDP has not risen above 18 per cent (1981) and in fact declined to 15 per cent in 1989. It also exhibits weak forward and backward linkages with the broader primary sector. Forward linkages between the two are, however, stronger than between mining and manufacturing. Some 22 per cent of other manufacturing inputs are drawn from the broader primary sector, mainly from the iron and steel, basic chemicals and petroleum, synthetic resin and plastic and non-ferrous metal sub-sectors. However, backward linkages are relatively weak, almost de-linked from other manufacturing. Only 13.4 per cent of primary inputs were drawn from other manufacturing. This contrasts with the standard analysis of mining versus manufacturing, where 50 per cent of mining inputs are drawn from the 'manufacturing' sector.

The extent of the development of the manufacturing sector has been exaggerated due to failure to recognise how closely related much of it is to the immediate downstream activities of the mining and energy sectors, as in metal-processing, for example. This vertical integration has its counterpart both in the corporate structure and in the close collaboration between the state and private institutions.

Mining and mineral processing lie at the core of the economy. There are a number of reasons for this, and sunsequent implications.

- The principal reason for the size and dominance of the mining and mineral processing sector, is South Africa's exceptional mineral resource endowment. It contains the world's largest reserves of managanese, the platinum group metals, gold, chromium, vanadium and alumino-silicates. It also has huge reserves of iron ore, coal, diamonds, uranium, titanium and nickel;

- Coal is responsible for 80 per cent of primary energy needs. It also provides for 20 per cent of exports (one-third of nongold). But very little coal is used for direct energy needs. The vast majority is either converted into electricity (over 50 per cent) or into oil (over 30 per cent). The South African economy is uniquely dependent on electricity, and is uniquely electricityintensive with levels of consumption per capita comparable to those of the UK, despite limited domestic consumption by the majority of the population. As already observed, this is primarily due to its use in mining and mineral processing, accounting for 40 per cent of consumption. Thus, coal is produced to generate electricity which acts as a major direct and indirect input to the production of gold. In this light, it is not surprising that some estimates put gold as generating 40 per cent of GDP through its direct and indirect effects, (Lombard and Stadler 1980), although the direct and indirect impact of the gold economy has slackened with the decline in its price over the 1980s;

- The roots of the ownership patterns in the mining and mineral processing industry were laid down in the diamond (and later gold) mining industries late last century, followed by strategic investments by the government (Iscor, Sasol). The sector, and indeed most of the economy, is dominated by these players. The most important are the major mining houses, namely, Anglo American, Genmin, Anglovaal and Gold Fields, and the ex-parastatals, particularly Iscor and Sasol. Major cross holdings are common across the industry, constituting a web of interlocking directorships and control that extends to all aspects of the economy;

- As is already apparent from the ownership structure, there is close integration between the state and the private group producers and this is entrenched institutionally. The interests of the group producers are co-ordinated through the century-old Chamber of Mines. Government policy towards mining, minerals and energy is formulated through close co-ordination with the private sector. In addition, the state has depended on tax revenue derived from the mineral sector, which has contributed an average of 8 per cent of government revenue since 1913. In some years, the revenue derived from the mineral sector has been extremely important; for example, gold alone contributed 26 per cent of total tax revenue in 1981;

- The conglomerate structure depends upon, and is reflected in, a close integration with highly developed financial institutions. For each mining house, there is not only a corresponding holding company for its industrial activities, but also a matching set of financial institutions;

- The mineral sector has been particularly dependent upon the apartheid system because of its reliance on migrant and compound labour. This again indicates a close relationship between the state and private capital; and the organisation of labour markets with appropriate state intervention has had a profound influence on the operation and structure of south(ern) African labour markets as a whole.

Such are the immediate and obvious parameters that trace out the core of South African industry. But there is obviously more to it than this, for it has given rise to, and continues to influence a much wider range of economic, as well as political and social phenomena, such as in the labour market system. The current view of both business and government is that the economy should be governed more by market forces and unregulated private capital than it has been in the past. There is a strongly held belief that, as far as industry is concerned, the restructuring of the economy will best be accomplished through a minimum of state intervention. MERG doubts the validity of this argument for a number of reasons that will now be addressed in detail.

The current global recession has provoked a dramatic fall in demand for most minerals and metals, which has been further exacerbated by increasing exports from the ex-USSR and China, particularly of ferroalloys, in their pursuit of hard currency. This has resulted in significant over capacity of several minerals, some of which are indicated in Table 7.3. This has important implications for employment (in case of retrenchment), stockpiling, depletion and marketing policy (and for the balance of payments). It cannot be presumed that the competitive (or collusive) outcome will achieve the most beneficial possible results for the South African economy. Private and social rates of return may differ, producers may engage in competitive over-supply in the attempt to cover sunk fixed costs, and state support for production in other countries, and dumping on international markets will be highly likely.

These are all reason enough to suggest that the state should intervene in output and pricing decisions. There is also a case for the creation of a state mineral marketing auditors office, and the national marketing of certain minerals, such as is already done for gold. MERG research has shown that as a result of the difficulties associated with trading in the sanctions era, and as a consequence of the use of transfer pricing to accommodate capital flight, revenues earned from mineral exports have been considerably depressed, expertise in marketing has been limited, and commissions paid for handling exports have been excessive. In addition, because of the preponderant presence of South African production in some mineral markets, and the capacity to come to arrangements with small numbers of other producers, it will be possible to co-ordinate world markets in some instances, legally if subject to state direction. Excluding gold and coal, it has been estimated that by enforcing changes through national marketing, an extra R3 billion per year could be realised in foreign currency by 1997. Possibly an extra R1 billion could be earned through more and better priced coal exports.

In the case of chrome, ferrochrome alloys, manganese ore and ferro-alloys, zinc, tin, rutile, zircon, titanium slag, pig iron, aluminium, vanadium, nickel, steel and iron ore, MERG research suggests that employment and real foreign exchange earnings are liable to remain stagnant well into the next century. The situation for the country's copper and phosphate production is bleak, as both come from the Phalaborwa open pit mine which is coming to the end of its life, and unless the project for underground mining (currently under investigation), proves viable, both these minerals will have to be imported, as most of the current production is consumed domestically. However, if the project to reduce their waste magnetite to sponge iron (using Pande gas from Mozambique or local coal) goes ahead, then it is likely that an underground operation will be feasible. Prospects are brighter for platinum-based metals, which could increase export earnings by 40 per cent to R8 billion by 2007. Coal output is unlikely to increase, as the main domestic consumers are Eskom and Sasol, neither of which are likely to expand in the next ten years. However, exports, currently running at 50 Mt per year, could grow either through the expansion of the current Richards Bay Coal Terminal, or through the construction of the planned new 'Red' Terminal with a capacity of 12 Mt per annum. The long term prospects for gold are poor, especially in light of declining grades and increases in the depth of ore, the overhang of world gold reserves, and new supplies on the world market. Whatever policies are adopted towards the mineral sectors, these sectors should be used where appropriate as the basis for promoting forward linkages in order to create further employment and foreign exchange earnings.

It is generally acknowledged that beneficiation of minerals has been underdeveloped, and this reflects a number of factors, including the unwillingness of the major corporations to commit themselves to large-scale domestic investment programmes during the sanctions era as, in general, the greater the degree of beneficiation, the more severe the sanctions, as these products competed with industries in the industrialised countries. With the lifting of sanctions, several major beneficiation projects have been given the go-ahead and many more are being reassessed. However, there is no reason to believe that beneficiation will proceed at a socially optimum rate, and there is also a case for promoting indigenous technology, R&D, training and spin-offs into related processing sectors, which will require a degree of state intervention, as has already been the case with the involvement of the IDC in many projects, and an accelerated tax write-off scheme to lower the cost of capital.

Some of these beneficiation processes are extremely capital-intensive. The Alpha project, presently being jointly considered by Iscor and the IDC, would cost R3 billion, but would directly employ only 600 workers; the Columbus plant to produce stainless steel (undertaken by Gencor, Anglo and IDC) will cost approximately R3 billion and employ 5 000 over the three-year construction period, but will employ only 1 500 in the running of the plant (and only 157 new jobs after reorganisation with other plants!); the new Alusaf plant (major participants being Genmin and IDC) will cost R7.2 billion, and provide 6 000 jobs over the three-year construction phase, and 1 900 subsequently. The economic rationale for these plants is that they will provide an economic surplus, particularly of foreign exchange, which will create the potential for many more labour-intensive jobs in other sectors of the economy, compensating for the excessive capital-labour ratios that characterise these mega-projects.

A number of important points need to be made here, all of which support the case for more effective state intervention. Firstly, these are very big projects indeed. While they are microeconomic in the sense of involving an appraisal of a single investment, they are sufficiently large to have macroeconomic implications. They will have an impact on the balance of payments and on money markets, for example. As such, there is no reason to presume that these projects will be prejudiced by a rigorous analysis of their macroeconomic consequences. There has always been an implicit assumption that the foreign exchange generated will accrue to the domestic economy. This is by no means certain and not just because of the need to pay for interest, technology licences and imported equipment. One of the attractions to the participating corporations is undoubtedly the potential generation and appropriation of foreign exchange that they will be under no obligation to use for subsequent generation of domestic employment. It follows that if such large-scale projects are approved on the basis of their foreign exchange potential, precisely because this is simply an intermediate objective, so the indirect generation of labour-intensive employment must be guaranteed. This might be done by making IDC project approval and tax breaks dependent on the elaboration of a plan for further downstream processing of the commodity into elaborate manufactured exports, with guaranteed export parity prices to the local fabricator. If the potential for further processing of the commodity is limited, the project approval should be dependent on the development of other labour-intensive projects.

There are not only future projects to consider. SASOL and, to a lesser extent, Mossgas have been developed as huge oil-producing facilities to safeguard against sanctions. They would certainly not be economic if not already in place. Whether or not they are now, with fixed capital already sunk, is once again a macroeconomic issue in which private and social returns will diverge considerably, particularly in the light of the heavy chemicals industry which SASOL has spawned, and in view of the negative impact that the abandonment of coal-to-oil conversion would have on the balance of payments, given dependence on imported oil and employment. The role of nuclear facilities will also need to be reassessed in light of their huge and distorting command of scientists and R&D expenditure, environmental impact and the R500 million subsidy to the AEC.

In addition, for several electricity-intensive beneficiation processes such as aluminium (Alusaf) and ferrosilicon smelting, Eskom has contracted to supply electricity on a sliding scale with the price of aluminium, so that it has some share in the (mis)fortunes of the industry at a global level. This has the advantage of acting as a cushion to fluctuations in the market, but it is by no means certain that this is the optimal form of participation, given the goals of Eskom and those of macroeconomic policy.

Because the corporate structure is one of interpenetrating ownership and multiple sources of finance and incentives, the competitive advantages and capabilities of each individual mine do not necessarily emerge efficiently. There may be inefficiencies in terms of its own extraction and depletion policies, in relation to the mineral sector as a whole to which it is attached, or for the exercise of macroeconomic policy. Accordingly, it may be necessary to establish a coherent strategy for co-ordinating extraction policy across each of the various minerals. The removal of the obligation to mine at the average grade of the deposit in the new Minerals Act needs to be reassessed in conjunction with the current system of mine ownership through low equity holdings (10 per cent to 30 per cent) and lucrative management contracts, which tends to have the effect of increasing the life of the mine rather than maximising return to shareholders.

For reasons concerning marketing, beneficiation (or vertical integration more generally), efficient depletion and extraction, the macroeconomic impact of megaprojects, and the handling of excess capacity, there are grounds for state intervention, over and above normal competition and regulation policy. Furthermore, there are issues concerning the development of new technology and training in which private and social returns might diverge considerably, and the broader primary sectors have significant potential for, and expertise in, infrastructural provision. State intervention in the industry would most probably be through a tripartite structure involving government, labour and capital, such as the existing (although moribund) Mining Summit. Obvious areas for state intervention are fiscal incentives or disincentives, policing of transfer pricing, optimisation of marketing arrangements, training, downscaling of mining, the monitoring of working conditions, environmental monitoring, R&D and long-term strategic planning for the industry.

7.3 Market and ownership structures

The bimodal structure, of which mining and energy-related activities lie at one pole, has resulted in an industrial base in which exports have been dominated by raw materials and processed raw materials. Their export share rose from 69 per cent to 88 per cent between 1970 and 1988 (see Table 7.4).

While some growth in exports of material-intensive and final-processed products are evident from Table 7.2, these have not been significant enough to alter the broader industrial structure. Furthermore, the investments currently under way in the Alusaf and Columbus projects are likely to skew export dependence further in the traditional direction.

Employment creation through industrial expansion is heavily conditioned by the balance of bimodal activities. The growth of capital-intensive raw material processing industries since 1970 has been accompanied by falling employment in the manufacturing sector (see Table 7.1). Consequently, MERG recognises that one of the major challenges for future industrial policy is to address the growing cleavage between heavy raw material processing and the manufacturing sub-sectors which fall outside the immediate ambit of such industries.

This will be a complex and contested process, considering the powerful state-owned and private sector interests that have evolved around the present industrial structure. This brings the issue of market and ownership issues to the fore. With a more open trading environment for manufactured commodities, as is argued below, competition will be raised in domestic markets. But this could be blunted by high levels of concentration in domestic production. Even in a liberal trading environment, domestic firms are protected by considerable entry barriers. Indeed, just as the highly concentrated ownership structures of South Africa are thought to act as a considerable deterrent to direct foreign investment, so do concentrated and vertically integrated markets deter foreign trade.

It has been argued that anti-trust policy in South Africa is open to criticism on two grounds. Firstly, large, well-resourced firms are said to be necessary if South Africa is to penetrate international markets. In a small economy, large firms inevitably translate into concentrated market structures. Secondly, oligopolistic markets do not necessarily predispose participants to competition-deadening collusion; on the contrary, oligopolistic markets may well constitute the best structure to ensure vigorous competition.

Large firms may be an advantage in international competition, although even this is questionable, considering the increasingly unsuccessful struggles of the great international industrial behemoths against smaller, better focused, and more nimble competitors. Moreover, vigorous competition in domestic markets may well be an equally important factor in successful penetration of international markets. Certainly the internationally successful giant Korean and Japanese conglomerates are forced by state intervention to compete vigorously in some of their domestic markets.

What of the argument that oligopolistic markets may act as a spur to competition? Whilst oligopolies may compete vigorously — and in some South African manufacturing sectors such as cars and consumer electronics, there is evidence of all too vigorous competition — there is considerable evidence of oligopolistic collusion in

South Africa. Most disturbingly, there is considerable evidence that the shape that this collusion takes is the segmenting — by region or product niche — of key product markets, ensuring, not oligopolistic structures, but rather single-firm domination of major product markets.

Single-firm domination that may amount to monopoly but is consistent with smaller market shares, is a particularly worrying phenomenon, in so far as it places firms up- and down-stream of the dominant firms, in acutely dependent positions, with their profitability, indeed their very existence, in the hands of their supplier or customer. The dominance of a single firm over its market and related markets, obviously acts as a considerable deterrent to potential entrants into the dominant firms market.

On balance, MERG supports a more vigorous anti-trust policy, one that would strengthen the resources and punitive power of an anti-trust authority. The dismantling of the conglomerates is not recommended, but MERG suggests that a commission to look into comglomerates be established. The behaviour of participants in oligopolistic markets should be monitored, particularly the behaviour of dominant firms to the extent of defending producers in competition with, and dependent upon, dominant firms. The factors predisposing South African oligopolies to collusion rather than vigorous competition should be dealt with.

The key factors that underpin collusion are found in the ownership structures that dominate South Africa manufacturing, mining and services sectors. A small number of shareholders control a major slice — approximately 90 per cent of the asset value of the Johannesburg Stock Exchange — of corporate South Africa. It is these shareholders, a mixture of founding families such as the Ruperts and Oppenheimers, and financial institutions such as Old Mutual and Sanlam, that effectively control the operating units in the manufacturing sectors. The form that their control takes is that of highly diversified conglomerates spanning the mining, financial and manufacturing sectors.

These ownership structures facilitate collusion partly through a practice known as 'conglomerate forbearance', an agreement, implicit or explicit, to refrain from vigorously competing against the subsidiary of a fellow conglomerate in a particular market, for fear of retaliation in an unrelated market. This practice is strongly underwritten by increasing evidence of inter-conglomerate collusion, reflected in interlocking directorships and cross-and common-shareholdings.

The conglomerates that straddle the South African economy are under increasing attack by the democratic movement, and not only because of their tendency to promote and maintain concentrated market structure. The conglomerates are a particularly stark representation of the inequalities that characterise South African society. A small number of shareholders — frequently families — control the lion's share of the South African economy. The boards that control the strategic direction of these corporations are, without significant exceptions, comprised of a handful of white males, who frequently sit on a number of other boards. There is not one single black or female executive director on any of the main boards of the six corporations that dominate the private sector.

The conglomerates have been defended on a number of grounds. They are said to maximise the sharing of scarce managerial, technical and financial resources. They are also said to overcome the agency problems entailed in the separation of ownership from control. In South Africa, it is argued, strong entrepreneurial shareholders ensure the accountability of management.

ISP research calls these claims into question. There is remarkably little evidence of the conglomerates facilitating the sharing of productive resources amongst their operating subsidiaries. R&D activity, export marketing, training, and other productivity enhancing resources and activities are generally left to individual subsidiaries. The connections between head office and subsidiaries are financial. Nor is it clear that the head office financial resources are utilised to the advantage of the subsidiaries. The manufacturing interests of the conglomerates have (certainly since the original spate of investment in mining related activity) grown by acquisition. The companies acquired represent the cream of South African industry and there is evidence that, far from the conglomerate centre extending their financial largesse to their subsidiaries, they effectively foreclose the independent access of the managers of the subsidiaries to the capital markets or, even, to the cash flow of the subsidiaries themselves. Moreover, the dominance of financial relations accounts for a system of control and accountability that is remarkably narrow in its orientation, and focused on very short-term financial ratios rather than long term competitiveness.

The claims that conglomerates represent superior efficiency are disputed across an increasingly wide range of opinion, including from within the corporate sector itself. This, coupled with the long standing hostility of the democratic movement, has inspired some of the conglomerates to embark upon the unbundling of their interests. This move has been led by the conglomerates controlled by Sanlam — Gencor, Malbak and Murray and Roberts. Recently, the giant Barlows conglomerate, controlled by Old Mutual, has announced its intention to split into three separate companies, leaving Barlows itself with the groups' interests in mining and engineering, and hiving their considerable interests in food processing, textiles, and electronics into two other companies.

This process of de-conglomeration or specialisation should be extended, and there are a variety of policy measures that may be employed to this effect. These include legally prohibiting the formation of pyramid companies, and tightening up and extending controls over corporate mergers and acquisitions.

The formation of corporate groups should not be prohibited. Experience elsewhere has established their potential importance in industrial development. Indeed, ISP research has identified groups constructed to maximise the economies that derive from inter-firm co-operation — these groups tend to be more focused than the portfolio-management oriented groups referred to above, and they tend to be controlled by owner/managers or by managers. In short, powerful owners do not necessarily lead to corporate dynamism. On the contrary, their power has to be circumscribed by other powerful agencies.

How does one ensure a more equitable spread of ownership and a strengthening of the representation of other interests? In the process of deconglomeration sketched above, control has generally come to reside with the large financial institutions, and the time is rapidly approaching where the control of these institutions needs to be carefully examined. Old Mutual and Sanlam are mutual societies, nominally controlled by their policy holders, and in fact controlled by an oligarchy of self-perpetuating managers. It would require only simple legislative amendments to ensure that the boards of these companies represented a wider spread of their policy holders than is currently the case. These institutions should also be encouraged to use their financial resources in support of management and co-operative buy-outs, employee share ownership schemes, and other schemes designed to spread ownership. Unions, on the other hand, should be encouraged to consider the possibility of comprehensive co-determination that includes a share in ownership.

MERG recommends that a new set of institutions be created by law to oversee the implementation of anti-trust policy. MERG is mindful, however, that much anti-trust and related policy often proves reactive or prohibitive — as, for example, would be the reference of an acquisition or merger to the Competition Board to investigate whether it should be allowed to proceed or not. Consequently, it is recommended that the role of the Competition Board be extended so that it may be required to investigate significant mergers or acquisitions and oligopolised markets, with a view to making positive recommendations for industrial policy over the full range of instruments available. This is all the more urgent since there is a close relationship between the bimodal structure of industry and the concentration of corporate power.

7.4 Small, medium and micro enterprises

Comparative industrial performance appears to be significantly influenced by market structure. In some cases — notably Korea, Northern Germany and Japan — large firms seem to be associated with dynamic comparative advantage. Their size provides them with the opportunities to cross-subsidise new areas of activity. Large firms may also obviate co-ordination problems and benefit from the problems of internalising transaction costs. In other cases, large firms show few signs of the flexibility necessary for sustained growth and profitability, for example, as in Peru, where large firms appear to block, rather than to promote, the achievement of dynamic comparative advantage. International experience also provides evidence of the potential offered by small and medium-enterprises (SMEs); both Taiwan and mid-Italy are examples of industrial dynamism achieved by small scale firms.

Thus, the issue is probably less about firm size per se than about the types of small and large firms in existence and the relations between them. For example, Italy has come to dominate a range of sectors which have traditionally been thought of as lying within the industrial competence of lower-wage economies, such as South Africa. It remains one of the largest net exporters in clothing, shoes and furniture, even though during the mid-1980s average plant size in these sectors was, respectively, 5.3, 17 and 5.7 employees. These small firms have managed to compete effectively by co-operating closely in a range of areas which have traditionally been seen as providing the rationale for large-scale ownership. For example, they have incorporated marketing, purchasing and design. At a global level, large firms are also increasingly co-operating with each other, not just in relation to technological collaboration, but also in the co-ordination of production scheduling and in moving from an arms-length and sequential relationship, to one which is organic, and in which production and design occur in parallel process (simultaneous engineering). In many countries there is also a fertile link between large and small firms, although this is not always without tension. The key theme which emerges out of this comparative international experience on firm size is that efficient production cannot only be achieved through market competition; it has to be complemented by appropriate forms of co-operation.

The South Africa market structure is characterised by acutely high levels of concentration, both in terms of ownership and production, and there is evidence of significant collusion with respect to prices and market share. High levels of market concentration are evident in both labour and capital intensive sector. For example, in the shoe industry, four firms account for 70 per cent of output. Less well-known, but probably equally significant, is the concentration of plant size. For example, the average number of employees in South African manufacturing plants is twice as large as in the UK (which is itself well-known for the relative absence of SMEs). In footwear and clothing, the average South African plant employs 175 and 101 workers respectively, whereas in Italy these figures were between 5 and 20 during the mid–1980s.

A second distinctive feature of South African manufacturing is the general weakness of medium-sized industries and the specific absence of high-tech, enumerated sector micro-enterprises. Even in the electronics sector, where international experience suggests that small, flexible firms tend to play an important role in industry development, MERG has observed the existence of a missing middle. A large number of factors contribute to this gap, including the predatory expansion of large conglomerates (usually by acquisition) and the weakness of the financial sector in meeting the specific needs of medium-sized firms.

A third characteristic of the South African corporate sector is the underdeveloped nature of the unenumerated manufacturing sector. The IDC has been and is still concerned with decentralisation and small business support, although its role has been devolved to, or supplemented by, other organisations such as the SBDC (formed in 1983) and the Board for the Decentralisation of Industry, formed in 1960. But its funds and orientation have largely been captured by parastatals, with these acquiring at least half of its investment resources, with an average support of over a hundred times that allocated to other companies.

ISP research has devoted considerable resources to an attempt to identify the size of the informal sector and the constraints to its growth, in part because of its ability to produce cheap wage goods. This sector also has the potential to offer productive employment, as is illustrated by its contribution in many other countries with similar per capita incomes to South Africa. This sector is poorly developed in South Africa, in terms of numbers and in terms of the incomes it offers to entrepreneurship. The absence of civil harmony caused by stagnation in employment, real wages, infrastructure, and the shortage of marketing channels, are all contributory factors, as is the low buying-power of potential consumers. Thus, whilst in many developing countries the owners of micro-enterprises (but not their employees) tend to earn incomes approximately double the levels prevailing in the formal sector, in South Africa, earnings are approximately half those of average industrial wages.

The level of co-operation across these various firm types is predictably poor. The ISP found, for example in the building materials industry, a strong tendency for the characteristically large-scale construction and civil engineering firms engaged in major property developments to rely on inputs provided by brick and cement product suppliers of a similar scale. This example is pertinent because in brick and cement product manufacturing, there is considerable technical scope for small scale, labour intensive production of quality products.

Perhaps more surprising is the lack of evidence of co-operation within the conglomerate groups, or between SMEs. The ISP has suggested that poor intra-group co-operation is accounted for by a corporate governance system characterised by shareholder power and managerial weakness. Poor co-operation between SMEs, on the other hand, appears to reflect institutional failure, in particular the apparent domination of employer and industry associations by the large corporate groups, and the historic preoccupation of these institutions with lobbying for government protection, rather than with grappling with the co-operative requirements of manufacturing competitiveness.

An ISP study has identified a potentially important set of relationships between large enterprise and SMEs, and between large enterprises and micro-enterprises. This refers to the phenomenon of work from home. There is strong evidence of formal sector employers in the clothing industry putting out work to home workers, usually former employees in the garment industry. Earnings from this activity vary, with the entrepreneur better off than his or her formal sector counterparts, whilst the workers receive less than the industrial council minima; working conditions are predictably poor and child labour is significant; and these jobs are undoubtedly at the expense of enumerated employment.

A number of policies are required to correct these deficiencies, although the prosperity of small business is heavily determined by the fortunes of big business and the prosperity of those in formal employment on which it is so dependent. The first challenge is to meet the particular needs of SMEs, including (but not exclusively) those of the informal manufacturing sector. These cannot be met merely in terms of a change in the incentive structure, since these small enterprises often suffer from 'internal' difficulties and require support with respect to the development of managerial and technological capabilities. What is clear — and confirmed by experience elsewhere — is that prohibition of informal sector activities is unlikely to be effective. South Africa is, for a variety of reasons, characterised by a highly segmented labour market, and employment opportunities need to be developed wherever possible.

- Policy will have to be developed that recognises this reality by attempting to move micro-enterprise activity up the value chain, whilst simultaneously retaining as many jobs as possible in the country or region;

- The second set of policies is to place clear limits on the collusive power which is so prevalent in South African industry. It is anti-competitive and dulls the incentive towards technological change;

- Thirdly, it is desirable to promote greater co-operation between firms, including those cases where geographical proximity is apparent (i.e. to promote the development of industrial districts).

MERG is aware of the potential conflict between policies which, on the one hand, are designed to inhibit anti-competitive collusive behaviour, and those which promote closer inter-firm co-operation in production scheduling, in design and in export marketing. However, a clear distinction needs to be drawn between these two types of co-operation, since there is no reason why closer co-operation between firms in a vertical chain of production, or between small firms in the same sector, should be anti-competitive.

7.5 Public ownership

MERG considers that public ownership is an essential component of industrial policy. It does not, however, argue for public ownership as a matter of principle but pragmatically on a case-by-case basis. These arguments are addressed more fully in Chapter Nine. For reasons that are set out there, MERG is opposed to any general programme of the privatisation of the currently owned public enterprises. MERG also rejects the idea that proposals for privatisation would necessarily represent, or lead to, a reduction in state economic intervention. Rather, they should be regarded as leading to state intervention of a particular type, one designed to favour large-scale capital. In South Africa, even more so than elsewhere, the consequences of denationalisation would inevitably be to concentrate ownership even further in the hands of the financial institutions, and to consolidate the power of conglomerates over productive facilities. In addition, the prices realised for the assets would probably be far below their revenuegenerating capacity, worsening government budgeting problems in the long-term. The net effect on investment is liable to be negative in the short run, as funds are directed towards financing the purchase of the privatised assets, thereby crowding out other avenues of investment.

7.6 Capabilities and institutions

Increasingly characteristic of the industrial policy initiatives proposed by a broad spectrum of opinion, is a focus on the incentive structure and, in particular, on trade policy as the mechanism whereby the incentives from the international market are transmitted to the domestic industrial sector. The MERG view of industrial policy goes beyond getting the prices right. Rather, it seeks to identify and ensure the presence of the economic linkages and agencies which can create the benefits of comparative advantage in industrial development. The market alone cannot carry out this role and never has. In this light, focus is placed here upon the development of human resources and technological capability.

7.7 Human resources and productivity growth

There are three reasons why a blanket and unfocused increase in educational investment will be an insufficient response to the challenges of industrial competitiveness; they reflect the structure of industrial relations which exists in industry, which, in turn, reflects the legacy of apartheid. In ascending order of importance, these three reasons are as follows. Firstly, it is in the realm of vocational skills that the needs of industry are to be met. This has implications for the balance between training for professionals and for the direct work-force, as well as in the types of education and training which are provided to production workers. This is not to imply that academic skills are unimportant, since it is clear that basic literacy and numeracy are a necessary component of vocational training. Moreover, the changing nature of work-organisation requires the ability to communicate, to work in groups and to solve problems, and these skills are enhanced by formal academic education. Nevertheless, a greater focus needs to be placed on vocational skills.

Secondly, and related to the need for enhanced vocational skills, training does not only occur in formal institutes. It is becoming increasingly evident from comparative experience, that intra-firm education and various forms of supplementary adult education are vital to promote industrial competitiveness. These intra-firm training schemes may or may not be associated with the acquisition of formal certification, and may or may not be linked to formal vocational training schemes. But, particularly in the context of the trend towards continuous improvement in production, retraining has become an essential component of competitive production.

Thirdly, it is now widely acknowledged in the industrialised countries, that in recent years there has been a significant change in the organisation of work. Previously, work was heavily segmented between skilled and unskilled workers, and consequently there was a sharp division of labour between the direct and indirect labour force. In many countries, this was reflected in the structure of industrial relations. In South Africa, this took the form of division between white and black trade unions, and their differential access to the institutions of collective bargaining. This in turn, bolstered by racially based legislation, structured access to apprenticeship and hence to skilled work categories. In industry-wide collective bargaining agreements, this is still reflected in a proliferation of narrowly defined job grades, particularly at the lower end of the hierarchy, and unusually large earnings differentials between the various grades. Although formally cast in terms of skill, the industrial relations system has long reflected an effective division between indirect and supervisory labour — or guard labour — on the one hand, and direct, productive labour, on the other. The basis of labour productivity in apartheid mass production lay in the proliferation of formally 'skilled', largely white, indirect workers, supervising formally 'unskilled', largely African, direct producers.

The fact that many unskilled workers had acquired and were using considerable skills on the job, but were being rewarded at unskilled rates, generated massive resentment. This in turn increased the need for strict, highly paid supervision, thus substantially vitiating the unit cost advantages of under-rewarding skilled direct labour. It also, of course, substantially reduced the incentive for acquiring, much less deploying, enhanced skills.

However, where flexible production has begun to emerge in some sectors, workers may be required to perform a variety of tasks and hence multi-skilling has become widespread. Moreover, the transition to quality-at-source and cellular production has meant that the work-force has been given more responsibility over the control of production. Finally, and most significantly, continuous improvement has proved to be one of the most important routes to rapid product innovation and process improvement, and this arises directly as a consequence of the participation of the labour force.

Partly because of these developments in work-organisation, allied to the general enhancement in the science-content in production, it is now more readily recognised by some employers that the work-force is an asset whose productive potential has to be enhanced, rather than a cost which has to be minimised. This applies unevenly but irrespectively of whether the sector concerned is open to rapid innovation and work organisation or not, and whether production is standardised or fragmented into separate market segments.

There are, however, severe structural obstacles in the way of a fundamental reorientation towards vocational training on the part of South African managers. There is a distance between those in control of the strategic direction of South African manufacturing and the shop floor, a distance that is reflected in the unusually large earnings differentials at all levels of South African industry. There is complex inter-action between skill, hierarchy, and race, and it is evident that the development of new forms of work-organisation is closely interwoven with the transition to a demo-cratic economy.

The issues of education and skills are taken up in a variety of other places in this document, signifying how important these are to the growth and survival of the democratic economy. Nor should the immediate imperatives of industrial policy undermine the commitment to the provision of training for all of the work-force, including those engaged in job creation through public works.

7.8 The development of indigenous technological capabilities

ISP research has found that a combination of relying upon private initiatives and the poverty of state policy has led to highly deficient technological capability. While there are variations and permutations, particularly at the sectoral level (which will be important in the design of sector specific policies), the following features are especially significant:

- At the national level, investment in enhancing technological capability is currently declining. Expenditure on R&D undertaken by the business sector was 0.32 per cent of GDP in 1990. Business expenditure in R&D declined by some 27 per cent from 1983/4 to 1989/90, which far exceeds the decline in business investment generally. There have been similar declines in the person years devoted to R&D. Overall, expenditure per researcher year and re-searcher years per 1 000 workers have also registered declines. Overall data is not yet available, but the indications are that the situation has deteriorated significantly since 1989/90;

- The national system of innovation is poorly integrated. In particular, the activities of the (partially) state-funded system of statutory science councils (really technology-cum-science councils), despite their declared objectives in terms of being market-oriented, do not in fact have a major impact upon the innovatory activities of many manufacturing firms. In a questionnaire survey of firms which had recently won national design awards, support from the science councils was not acknowledged as an important factor in their design activities. State support for innovation in particular industrial sectors has even had a detrimental effect, as in the telecommunications equipment supply industry;

- At the sectoral level, there are low levels of R&D spending by comparison with many other countries. For example, in 1983, only one sector of South African industry, namely paper and printing, had expenditure on R&D as a percentage of turnover that was at all comparable with the OECD countries;

- At the firm level, there is a general and widespread under-investment in enhancing technological capabilities. In the chemicals industry, for example, the three largest companies devoted a little under 1 per cent of turnover to R&D spending in 1990 — which is much lower than for comparably sized chemicals companies located elsewhere. Similarly, South African companies employ far fewer R&D scientists and engineers per size of work-force;

- There is a strong tendency to rely on the acquisition of technology from abroad. The primary channel of acquisition is via licence agreements. Licence agreements entered into by South African manufacturers tend to be overwhelmingly directed at the domestic market. Agreements are characterised by high levels of royalties, and frequent and wide-ranging restrictive clauses, typically on exporting. An examination of eight major licensing agreements entered into by a major manufacturing concern (1989 to 90) showed that five had export restrictions (two others were unclear); one had a tied purchasing clause; the average royalty was 3.13 per cent; and two agreements had further significant front-end charges. There is little evidence that such technology transfer is accompanied by programmes of training to ensure effective assimilation;

- South Africa is strong in scientific research, but far weaker in technology application. Scientific research, generally located in the universities and highly concentrated in a few, while comparatively strong, is infrequently translated into applied product design and development. A survey of the characteristics and sources of over two hundred significant South African innovations concluded: 'There was strong evidence of a failure to commercialise significant university-led inventive abilities' (Phillips, 1990 p. 32).

Taken together, these features are evidence of pervasive failure. Moreover, they are strongly suggestive of the imperfections and inadequacies of the existing institutional arrangements, which are weakly designed to complement and supplement the workings of the market. Even if trade liberalisation measures secure gains through the sectoral reallocation of production, it will not lead, in the absence of substantive policy measures, to the enhancement of technological capabilities necessary for sustained export expansion, particularly in more demanding and discriminating product niches. MERG policy proposals seek to:

- Reverse the current decline in overall national expenditure on R&D and, in particular, the decline in business expenditures on R&D. This could be achieved by ensuring a higher and sustained commitment on the part of government to support R&D;

- Strengthen incentives to firms to invest in the development of in-house technological capabilities. Tax incentives, in particular, should be investigated and tied to sector-specific programmes. In South Africa, innovatory expenditures are treated as an ordinary business expenditure for tax purposes;

- Affect the terms of technology transfer. Such a policy would be designed to strengthen the power of local licensees in the transfer process and limit restrictive clauses (particularly on exporting); but also, more importantly, to ensure that, where possible, technology transfer ensures enhanced access to core technology (the 'know-why'), especially via requiring training on the part of the licensor. At present, the Department of Trade and Industry, which registers and assesses licence agreements as a service to the Reserve Bank, does little more than attempt to ensure that the royalty does not exceed some arbitrary guidelines. Apart from being largely ineffective anyway, this policy is wrongly directed. It should be far less concerned with the cost of transfer, and principally directed towards promoting successful technology assimilation and learning;

- Restructure the funding and other incentives that currently affect the operations of the system of statutory science councils. In particular, the market oriented policies introduced some five years ago (base-line funding), are not adequate for highly imperfect markets. The level of economic concentration combined with diseconomies of scope (it is cheaper to serve the technology needs of one large project rather than those several small projects costing the same total amount), combine to ensure that market orientation both follows and further reinforces prevailing market imperfections;

- Encourage links between the universities and manufacturing industry. Such policies will need to recognise that commercialising university research would be an inadequate policy response if markets were to remain imperfect;

- Identify and acquire capacity in significant future technological developments. Exercising 'research foresight' appears to be suggested (in very elliptical language) in the latest Department of Trade and Industry discussion paper on technology policy (DTI, 1992 p. 10). However, there is no indication of how this process is to occur, nor which parties are to be involved. Successful research foresight will require (a) appropriate institutional mechanisms which would enjoy the support of all the significant parties; and (b) a capacity within government itself to direct, inform and assimilate such activity. Both factors are currently absent.

7.9 Trade policy

The existing South African trade regime is marked by uncertainty, complexity, and the imprint of special interests. It is uncertain because there are frequent and unpredictable changes, not only in protective duties on various products, but also in export support programmes. There are over 12 000 tariff lines, and hundreds of tariff settings, including many formula duties designed to protect against cheap imports by means of adding the difference between a reference price and the lower f.o.b. import price to an ad valorem tariff. The recently developed export promotion programmes have had some success, but are cost ineffective and open to abuse. The object of reform should be to lower costs by reforming protection, without jeopardising development strategies, and to co-ordinate export programmes with protection policy, thus making them more effective.

7.9.1   The structure of protection

Formula duties are aimed at low price imports, and have the effect of protecting certain uncompetitive industries, and allowing them to remain uncompetitive. A surcharge, which varies according to the class of good, with final consumer goods getting the highest protection, was introduced in the late 1980s in response to balance of payments pressures. Though the surcharge was reduced in 1990, it remains a major obstacle to imports. While many quantitative controls on imports were removed during the 1980s, some remain, mainly for agricultural and marine products. One result of the complex structure of protection is huge variations in effective rates of protection.

Indeed, these are difficult to determine for several reasons. First, there are several systems of rebate or exemption from tariffs or surcharges, arising from export promotion policies, preferential trade arrangements, and other schemes. Secondly, inflation has eroded the effects of the formula duties by rendering the rand-denominated reference prices too low to block cheap imports. Duties collected are much lower than tariff rates would predict.

While a recent study (Belli, et al, 1993) has argued that there is a positive correlation between exports and total factor productivity growth in South Africa, the analysis is not convincing either in itself or as a basis for drawing causal and policy implications. Insofar as exports contribute to industrialisation and to learning by producers, they should lead to productivity improvements, but the impact of other factors, especially the political uncertainty and economic stagnation of the last decade, has left South Africa a poor laboratory for such analysis. There is no doubt, though, that the poorly conceived and structured trade regime has mitigated against both exports and industrialisation, and therefore productivity growth.

If it is assumed that producers obtain raw materials at domestic prices, the structure of protection in South Africa is strongly biased against exporting manufactures. Domestic prices of raw material inputs are too high. In practice, larger firms are able to obtain supplies at international prices through duty rebates or exemptions, or deals with local suppliers, but these require planning, resources to bridge the gap until rebates are paid, and bargaining power, and are not very flexible. Smaller firms (those with less than 500 employees, and with turnover below R40 million), which cannot absorb these transaction costs, therefore face an anti-export bias which is not effectively compensated for by export incentive or export promotion schemes.

Government proposals for trade policy reform since the IDC report in 1990 have focused on the need for import liberalisation. Though there are references to the need for pro-active measures to encourage exports and prepare industries for competition, this is very weakly developed in government proposals. The proposals are particularly weak on the question of equipping smaller industrial firms for international competition.

7.9.2   The changing patterns of South African trade

South African trade patterns have long been characterised by dependence on primary exports, mostly metals and minerals, and the importation of capital goods and other sophisticated industrial products. But research within the ISP reveals that several manufacturing sub-sectors in South Africa do seem to be improving competitiveness. These include sectors within the textile, beverage, and tobacco industries, and are particularly marked in the improved performance of the metal fabrication division, not just at the level of basic beneficiation. At earlier levels of manufacture, metals, chemicals, and paper were prominent, but all weakened dramatically in line with commodity price trends after 1988.

The trend towards improved manufactured exports has been of relatively short duration (since 1983) and appears to be slackening at present. Two weaknesses detected are the low levels of investment accompanying the export trend, and the absence of the participation of smaller firms. Thus, whatever is pushing improved export performance in the larger firms, it does not extend directly to smaller firms; nor are these being pulled along in the wake of the larger firms. South African manufactured exports have potential, but they will not grow much without a policy commitment to investment, skills and training, and without more assistance to smaller firms.

7.9.3   Current export support measures in South Africa

South Africa has an extensive repertoire of export support measures. The most significant is the General Export Incentive Scheme (GEIS), which provides a direct subsidy to exporters of manufactures in proportion to the volume of exports, the stage of manufacture (favouring final goods), and the use of local inputs, modified by an exchange rate factor. Currently the maximum incentive is approximately 20 per cent of export value, and the minimum about 3 per cent. It is now widely recognised that the GEIS played an indispensable role in buoying up manufactured exports, and possibly keeping threatened branches of manufacturing alive since it was implemented in April 1990. Nevertheless, the scheme has been widely criticized for its cost (about R1.5 billion per year), its susceptibility to abuse, its lack of focus, its failure to reward improving exports more than static exports, and its relative inaccessibility to smaller firms. In addition, there are industry specific schemes for the automobile and clothing and textiles sectors, and a subsidised export credit guarantee scheme.

A second form of export support consists of general schemes which allow exemption or rebate of duty on imported inputs into exports. Again, the relative clumsiness of the administration of the schemes makes them more accessible to larger firms, which probably often use them to bargain for cheaper domestic input prices. The chief criticism of the scheme is that it is not automatic, but remains bureaucratic.

As previously observed, exports are also supported through two programmes designed to cheapen the costs of investing in industries which promise significant exports. They are 37E of the Income Tax Act, which allows for accelerated depreciation (offered until the end of September 1993), and a somewhat subsidised loan scheme. While policy should be formulated and implemented by the government, a council on international trade and investment, built up from the National Economic Forum, and including representatives of government, labour, business, and consumers, could give social force to a trade reform programme.

7.9.4 *Proposals for trade policy reform*

In this section, substantive proposals are presented. They remain, however, subject to the formulation of programmes for industrial restructuring of particular sectors. These programmes must not be allowed to degenerate into featherbedding and short-term responses to vested interests.

Reforming import protection

- Tariff reduction for very high tariffs, say nominal ad valorem equivalent tariffs above 100 per cent, should be incorporated in a programme which brings them down steadily and irreversibly to 100 per cent over a two year period. This would be preceded by rationalisation (see below);

- After effective export programmes are running, tariffs should be brought down in equal stages to meet GATT minimum requirements over a five or eight year period (depending on the sensitivity of the industry), but must provide for temporary delays in the liberalisation process if the social effects are too severe (measured in terms of rate of job loss);

- The government must address those factors which have made the sectors concerned uncompetitive, through, for example, eliminating unfair rebate programmes such as the clothing and textile structural adjustment programme, supporting training, research and development, and investment programmes, removing anti-competitive barriers to entry, tailoring procurement programmes to encourage competitive improvements, and supporting export initiatives for small and medium enterprises as well as large firms. These supply-side programmes should be targeted, and should have built-in performance requirements, for example, covering employment levels, productivity increases, or export performance, or a combination of these;

- A workable anti-dumping system should be in place from the start of the import liberalisation programme. It need not take the form of traditional GATT anti-dumping, as long as it is acceptable to major trading partners;

- Rationalisation requires the eventual conversion of all tariffs and quantitative controls into ad valorem tariffs;

- The number of lines, and the variation between them must be restricted by applying tariffs by 6– or 4– digit codes, instead of the current system of applying them to more than 12 000 8– digit codes;

- The frequency with which tariffs can be adjusted must be restricted;

- The target is for a tariff structure which is more neutral, but favours higher domestic value added sectors;

- The key to industrial development in the post-Uruguay era is to combine tariff reform effectively with supply-side stimulatory measures;

- In order to place exporters on a par with their stronger competitors abroad, they should be enabled to receive inputs at world market prices plus transport (landed costs). This means a broad and efficient system of duty rebates or drawbacks along the lines of sections 470.03 and 521.00 of the Customs and Excise Act, but wider in its application, and more efficient; in other words, a free trade regime for exports;

- In cases where South African suppliers of inputs have additional cost advantages as a result of cheap raw materials or cheap electrical power, or where they are assisted by government subsidies of one kind or another, they should be persuaded to supply exporters at something close to factory gate prices for intermediates destined for exports, or FOB export-parity prices. Such an arrangement already operates in certain cases; for example in the price (and quality of service) provided by Iscor to firms which manufacture and export fabricated metal products such as bulk transport containers and trailers;

- An appropriate strategy might be to give existing suppliers a period of grace of perhaps one year before the duty-free regime for exports is introduced, and to provide them with subsidized IDC loans during this year and during two subsequent years to bring their production processes into line with their international competitors;

- In addition, a duty-free input regime for the (ultimately) exported products of indirect exporters should be introduced. Such systems are in operation in East Asia. Similar phasing in conditions would apply;

- The existing system of customs and excise policing, which in theory requires every traded good to be inspected and approved by officials, is in need of urgent reform. It has to be fully computerised and run by professionals through a system based on scientific sampling and with high penalties for cheating;

- In addition, the system of allowing rebates or drawbacks for inputs for exports, needs to be radically modified so that there is no significant time delay between applications for duty-free imports and the granting of permission. An appropriate model is the Korean system of published input-output coefficients for all exported products, which would automatically indicate appropriate duty-exemptions after confirmed export orders are submitted to the authorities. This could be facilitated by an Export Bank (see below) which could standardise documentation paths and procedures. With advanced telecommunications facilities, an Electronic Data Interchange (EDI) network might be a suitable channel.

Further export support

- The government should continue to offer GEIS, but not for semi-processed products (GEIS Category 2), and should guarantee that any qualifying exporter would have access for at least another five years;

- GEIS should have the rate of growth of exports of the item concerned, and/or for the firm concerned built into the incentive formula. Its base-rate would therefore be lower than current levels, if spending on the GEIS is not to be increased;

- It should also be made easier for smaller exporters to exploit the GEIS, by streamlining the application and payment processes;

- MERG recommends that an Export Bank be established, possibly on the basis of a revolving concessional foreign loan. It would provide guarantees on loans for pre-export credit, and foreign exchange for the purpose of purchasing imported inputs for exports. It would assimilate data on all exporters, their suppliers, and customers, and would use this information to monitor the export effort, and to supply guidance to exporters, either directly, or through the commercial banks;

- Subsidised investment loans for export industries are required. Investment loans offered under export promotion programmes should be accessible to smaller exporters. All recipients should be required, where possible, to facilitate downstream manufacturing by offering local purchasers prices competitive with world prices, and good service;

- MERG recommends that export support institutions be established and that existing institutions, such as SAFTO, be restructured and rationalised in support of an export strategy;

- The DTI Export Centre should not enter the consulting field, but should serve in an informational, policy-forming, and funding back-up capacity. In addition to its current responsibilities, it should administer the fund for consulting subsidies for small firms, and establish a register of approved local and foreign consultants. However, after the Export Bank has been established, most of these functions should be transferred out of the DTI administrative structure, to the Export Bank;

- The government must seek trade arrangements which maximise access to markets abroad, and strengthen complementary industrial links in Southern Africa. Trade relations programmes should aim at preferences from Europe that facilitate southern African integration (e.g. cumulation for Lome rules of origin) and market access as favourable as Lome; a minimum of GSP status with the US/NAFTA; and a strengthening of ties with Asian markets.

7.10 Macroeconomic policies for industrial development

The macroeconomic environment that would facilitate the type of industrialisation programme proposed in this chapter are set out below:

- Exchange rate policy should aim at a stable real effective exchange rate at a level low enough to provide adequate incentives to exporters. This may require adjusting the rate of trade liberalisation, but monetary measures would be the primary instruments;

- Fiscal programmes should be linked to the development of the domestic productive sector in several ways. The reallocation of public expenditure should be directed where possible towards raising productivity (through the development of the social and physical infrastructure). Moreover, expenditure programmes should be linked to capability development programmes encouraging new, and preferably black owned, labour-intensive firms to emerge, and the tax system should provide transparent incentives for productive investment in tradeables;

- For industrialisation to proceed, saving for industrial investment must be mobilised. Policies should facilitate the application of funds held by public and private sector corporations to industrial development, as discussed in Chapter Eight. Taxes should be structured in such a way that productive investment is favoured. In addition, direct and indirect foreign investment should be encouraged, especially investment which improves South African technological capacity and access to new export markets.

Δ

Table 7.1   GDP growth and manufacturing growth, 1946 to 1991

Year	Average rate of growth per annum		
	Manufacturing output (%)	Manufacturing employment (%)	Total GDP (%)
1946–1950	9.1	6.6	4.7
1950–1955	7.5	3.0	4.8
1955–1960	4.5	0.9	4.0
1960–1965	9.9	6.8	6.0
1965–1970	7.4	3.2	5.4
1970–1975	6.0	4.1	4.0
1975–1980	4.1	1.5	3.4
1980–1985	-1.2	-1.0	1.1
1985–1991	0.7	-1.4	1.0

Table 7.2   South African exports by product category, (in current US$ billions, 1988 to 1991)

	1988	1989	1990	1991
a. Food	1.14	1.66	1.63	1.68
b. Raw materials	0.94	0.97	0.88	0.79
c. Ores and minerals	1.82	1.98	1.82	1.56
d. Fuels	1.23	1.23	1.45	1.46
e. Non-ferrous metals	0.79	0.83	0.72	0.74
f. Total primary	5.91	6.67	6.50	6.23
g. Iron and steel	1.80	2.02	2.15	2.16
h. Chemicals	0.76	0.84	0.84	0.97
i. Other semi-manufactured	1.82	2.46	2.88	2.82
j. Total machine and transport	1.18	1.33	1.94	2.28
j1. Machinery and transport equipment	0.59	0.66	0.97	1.14
j2. Power gen. equipment	0.01	0.01	0.02	0.02
j3. Other non-electrical equipment	0.25	0.23	0.29	0.35
j4. Office machinery	0.05	0.06	0.07	0.09
j5. Electrical machinery	0.06	0.07	0.11	0.09
j6. Auto parts and assembly	0.14	0.17	0.25	0.32
j7. Other transport equipment	0.08	0.12	0.23	0.27
k. Textiles	0.10	0.11	0.17	0.16
l. Clothing	0.05	0.05	0.08	0.13
m. Other consumer products	0.16	0.18	0.24	0.26
n. Manufactures (g-m)	5.28	6.33	7.32	7.64
Other[1]	10.62	9.43	9.81	9.64
o. Total	21.83	22.42	23.61	23.51
p. Broad manufactures (e-m)	5.87	6.99	8.29	8.78
q. Narrow manufactures (j-m)	1.49	1.67	2.43	2.84
r. Intermediates (e,g,h,i)	5.17	6.15	6.58	6.68

1   Not classified by source: largely gold exports

Source: IDC Database and Reserve Bank monetary data

Table 7.3 **Current and anticipated capacity utilisation in select minerals (per cent)**

	Fe-Cr	Fe-Mn	Ti Slag	Vanadium	Steel	Al	Cu
1992	45.0	80.0	88.0	62.0	81.0	100.0	92.0
2007	90.0	95.0	94.0	76.0	80.0	100.0	95.0

Source: MERG Minerals Project Estimates

Table 7.4 **Percentage exports by stage of production, 1960, 1970, 1980, 1988**

Category	1960	1970	1980	1988
Raw materials	29	37	42	42
Processed raw materials	40	32	36	46
Sub-total	69	69	78	88
Material intensive products	15	17	12	6
Final processed products	16	14	9	6
Sub-total	31	31	21	12
Total	100	100	100	100

Source: RSA, Dept of Finance, Budget Review, 1990

Figure 7.1   GDP contribution
conventional perceptions

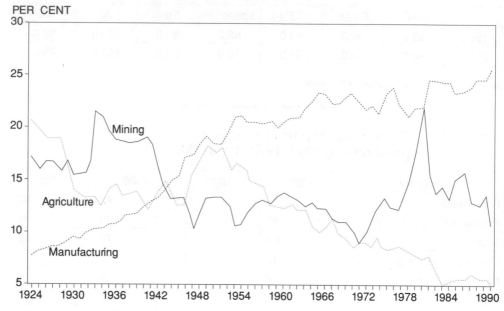

Source: Rustomjee, 1992

Figure 7.2   GDP contribution impact
of broader primary sectors

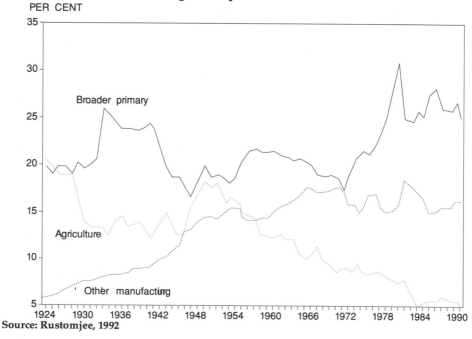

Source: Rustomjee, 1992

CHAPTER 8
Banking and finance

8.1 Need for change

To achieve a growing economy with a competitive manufacturing sector, and to achieve a redistribution of income, wealth, and economic power towards the black majority, South Africa needs a system of banks and financial institutions that are designed to play a specific part in achieving those goals. The present financial system was not designed for those purposes.

The assessment concentrates on policies designed to build new institutions and influence old institutions. The intention is:

- to extend banking to the majority of the population by creating a cheap, widely available system of money transfer;

- to increase personal saving through the financial system;

- to improve the availability and terms of finance for investment in growth sectors and for investment in black enterprises;

- to create a stable source of finance for the state, including regional and local authorities, and semi-public bodies investing in social infrastructure;

- to develop the ability of financial institutions to supervise industrial and commercial enterprises;

- to restructure the role of the Reserve Bank;

- to restructure the role of the Johannesburg Stock Exchange.

These strategies would reduce those elements in the financial system which are an inheritance from British practice, and move the system closer to the German model. They would make the benefits of banking and finance available to the whole population, and would actively involve the financial institutions in financing the new social infrastructure and industrial development.

The main economic functions of any financial system are to operate the payments mechanism, to channel funds between borrowers and lenders through markets or financial intermediation, to price these funds, and to trade in risks and maturities.

Whether or not the system can do this successfully depends on its appropriateness in the economy. In an economy which is undergoing transformation, the flows of funds and the nature of the risks that the financial system has to deal with, will change. The existing system, for example, is well practised in dealing with the normal trading risks generated by the circumstances that used to prevail, but new ways of operating have to be devised in order to deal with the risks involved in financing new enterprises, new public authorities and social investment, and new world trading relations. MERG recommendations on financial policy are designed to address these needs by reshaping the system.

8.2 The present system

The present financial system is dominated by four large commercial banks, two big life assurance companies and the pension funds. It has served the needs of the contemporary economy well for long periods, but in the past two decades the situation has changed. Now, looking forward shows that the present system is unsuited to the task of transforming the South African economy.

The present financial system originated from the British system, based as it was on commercial banking, which concentrated on short-term finance, and stock exchanges which raised long-term equity capital. But it also had a specifically South African feature, namely the mining finance houses, designed to assist the mineral based development of the economy. At a later stage, the system was modified by the growth of savings institutions (life assurance and pension funds), and banks especially built on the accumulation of the small savings of Afrikaners. This system was the financial foundation upon which the Afrikaner state, and economic development since the middle of this century, were based.

However, for over two decades, governments and business leaders have been unsuccessful in reaching their set economic goals. They have failed to create an economy with an internationally-competitive manufacturing sector, and even the previous growth of the mineral-based economy has been unattainable. There are many non-financial reasons for this, but it became clear that the old banking and financial institutions were unsuitable for a growing modern economy, and pressures grew for changes to be made within the financial system.

An attempt to reshape finance was marked by the de Kock Commission, whose final report was published in 1985. Its recommendations had been implemented over the previous five years, and in many ways, its policies represented a validation of changes that were already occurring, but it set the tone for an apparently significant change in the financial system. The Commission attempted to shift the emphasis away from building financial institutions, and also away from shaping their borrowing and lending in the desired directions, and towards unregulated operations on competitive financial markets. It was argued that the growth of financial markets would enable funds to flow to the most productive sectors.

The financial liberalisation policy has been a failure. The system has become increasingly dominated by a few large saving institutions and banks; indeed, one of the main results of the de Kock policies was a wave of bank amalgamations. While new markets in futures and derivatives have grown, they do not deal directly with capital for industry or the state, and the capital market itself (the JSE equities and bond market, and the gilts market) remains uncompetitive and non-innovative. Moreover, the new markets have grown up in a hothouse atmosphere relatively insulated from international financial markets. Despite financial innovation, they remain backward in international terms. The financial system is neither adequate for financing economic growth and restructuring, nor a successful international market with financial services companies whose international profits contribute to the balance of payments.

Several factors have contributed to the failure of the financial system since the de Kock Commission. One is the fact that a key part of the reforms, the liberalisation of the foreign exchange market, involving the abolition of exchange controls and allowing a unified exchange rate to be market-determined, was unrealistic and not implemented. Soon after it was attempted, it had to be abandoned as a result of the debt crisis initiated by the withdrawal of foreign finance. As a result, the financial system has remained partly protected from foreign competition.

The market-based approach has failed to channel funds into the two broad areas of investment that South Africa needs: investment in competitive industry, and investment in economic and social infrastructure. The low level of investment stems from many causes and the deficiencies of the financial system have interacted with them to accentuate the problem. As industrial investment has stagnated, the financial system has not developed new institutions and mechanisms to encourage venture capital or finance industrial development. A market-based initiative in this direction, the JSE Development Board and its Venture Capital Board, has been a failure. Instead of investment in industry and people, the market-based financial innovations of the past decade have fed speculative cycles in securities and real estate.

From the standpoint of organising finance to meet the needs of the economy, the last decade has been a wasted one. The economy has needed new types of financial institutions and changes in the existing institutions to ensure that these are capable of matching the needs of economic restructuring. Institutional development was necessary to ensure that hard options could be financed, but the market-based approach left the institutions basically unchanged, while encouraging them to take what appeared to be the soft options in the financial and real estate markets. A market-based approach to finance means the state and the institutions disclaim responsibility for the direction of flows of finance; money flows in directions determined by the stock exchange, money markets and other asset markets, instead of in directions which are desirable for economic development.

In the next decade, the major transformation of the economy will increase the need for appropriate forms of finance. Policies to develop financial institutions in the appropriate directions will be put in place, instead of leaving finance to the market operations of existing institutions.

The strategy proposed involves focusing on institutions rather than markets. Policies are designed to encourage the development of banks and other institutions which are appropriate to economic goals and needs, and they seek to shape the way these institutions operate. The principal policies towards institutions are outlined below. It is worth noting how these approachs differ from the current policy makers' thinking on the subject.

Current emphasis on the role of financial markets means a downgrading of policies to develop and shape the behaviour of financial institutions. Two aspects of current policy makers' thinking illustrates this.

Firstly, the important report of the committee chaired by Jacobs, which considers (among other things) the taxation and regulation of banks and long-term savings institutions, takes as its principle the creation of 'a level playing field' so that no institution is favoured in competition on the market. By contrast, MERG considers it is necessary to have a definite policy which favours the development of appropriate financial institutions.

Secondly, an important strand of current thought builds on the distinction between the role banks and others play as principals (the traditional role of financial intermediation through their balance sheets) and their role as agents (arranging off-balance sheet deals, brokerage, advice and information processing). This distinction is rightly emphasised by the Reserve Bank Department of Bank Supervision. According to one line of thinking in the financial sector, it is argued that institutions are increasingly concentrating on the latter of these roles, and it is envisaged that this should be encouraged; in other words, banks and other institutions should simply act as agents for firms and individuals operating on financial markets. In contrast, MERG emphasises the importance of financial intermediation, with the financial intermediaries actively pursuing borrowing and lending policies designed to meet the needs of the economy.

8.3 People's banking

MERG places a high priority on developing banking services for the majority of the population. All South Africans, including the poorest, must be able to keep their money safely in a bank, earn interest on it, and use the bank to make the payments they choose, whether these are to remit wages to their families, or to pay for goods bought on mail order.

At present very few black South Africans have cheque accounts at banks, although a significant number of formal sector employees have saving accounts. As a consequence, amounts of cash, with all the attendant risks, have to be held, and if money has to be paid in a different town, it has to be carried in cash by the person or an intermediary. For the economy as a whole, one disadvantage is that a national mass market cannot be developed fully (as it should be, if domestically oriented manufacturing is to grow), as transactions are costly and difficult if they always involve the handling of cash. The same is true for housing, as solutions to the housing problem require that people have a convenient means of making regular payments of rent or interest. And for the financial intermediaries, a disadvantage of a cash-based society, is that they do not attract deposits and balances in-transit, which are an important source of finance in other countries.

MERG proposes that a People's Bank be established along the same lines as the giro banks which have been successful in Europe and Japan. Its main features should be:

- that it is operated through the post office system and owned by the post office;

- that current accounts are held centrally and deposits, withdrawals and transfers made at local post offices are recorded centrally;

- that it offers cheap and simple facilities for deposits, withdrawals, and transfers to other accounts, other customers, and other places;

- that in addition to the development of current account facilities, the People's Bank should incorporate the business presently conducted by the post office Savings Bank;

- that the assets of the bank should be invested in marketable state securities and eligible securities determined by the state;

- that the objective of the bank should be to break even over the medium term.

The rationale for such a People's Bank is that existing banks are not easily able to provide cheap money transfer arrangements for the majority of the population. It has been argued by some that the banks are unwilling to attract low-income customers, as the business they provide generates low profits and 'crowds out' more profitable richer customers. However, the banks have in fact demonstrated a desire to retain their low-income customers, so this assumption is not in fact the basis of the proposal.

Instead, the reasons for not relying on existing banks to expand their money transfer facilities widely, are problems of accessibility, business methods, and credibility. Residents of townships and black rural communities do not have easy access to bank branches, as these are concentrated in traditionally white areas; the documentation and routines involved in transactions derive from a different culture that is based on literacy, accounting and legal familiarity; and it has been argued that the image of banks as pillars of the old system, staffed by whites, lowers the black customers' trust.

A People's Bank could overcome those problems. Based in post offices, it would be more easily accessible throughout the country than the existing commercial banks; moreover, since the post office will remain a national institution, the bank would have a unifying national role, even if the future regional structure of the country leads banks to adopt regional structures. The procedures of the bank, based on the practice of national giro systems abroad, would be highly simplified. The wide use already made of post offices demonstrates that citizens are familiar, and can easily identify with, the institution.

However, research by the MERG Savings Project suggests that the post office itself requires restructuring in order to enable the post-office-based People's Bank to fulfil its goals. The post office has inadequate representation in black population areas, especially in rural regions and newly settled urban areas, so that is not yet fully accessible to the population as a whole, even though it is more accessible than commercial bank branches. In addition, since a high proportion of post office staff is white, cultural barriers to creating a popular national identity for the People's Bank may exist. To overcome those barriers, a restructuring in order to expand black-run post office branches and franchised sub-post offices, each of which would be a People's Bank outlet (as well as an important profit-earning activity for black business men and women), would have to be undertaken.

There are alternatives to establishing a People's Bank, either by having the existing banks expand their money transfer facilities in order to attract mass business, or by a new community bank taking over the facilities of an existing bank and extending them. Ultimately, the deciding factor is cost, as people must be offered a low-cost monetary system. The plan for a People's Bank is based partly on its cost advantages over the alternatives. The existing post office system has an established branch network and an established electronic base which underpins its telebank and other accounts. If this is used as a base, the costs of establishing a wide branch network will be avoided from the start. The existing network will have to be expanded and transformed. A sub-post office system will allow expansion and transformation to be achieved in ways which are cost effective and which will stimulate black business activity.

The costs of any money transmission system depend on the amount of business it attracts, as there are significant economies of scale; and if it is to be a satisfactory system, instead of being merely another participant in the clearing system, the People's Bank would have to have sufficient customers to ensure that a large number of transactions that would otherwise involve transporting cash, can take place between personal giro accounts. For this purpose, there will be a policy of subsidising the operating costs on a pre-announced decreasing basis for the first six years. The subsidy is justified by the high average running costs incurred until the system is fully expanded, and by the need to offer low-priced services in order to attract business up to the optimum scale. In terms of market efficiency, a longer-term or even permanent subsidy could be justified on the grounds that a universal money transfer system offers many external benefits. To expand the system, accounts should be offered, without customer initiative or fee, to all people involved in transactions with public agencies (from pension recipients to rent payers). Such subsidies and account creation initiatives could not be carried out by a private bank.

In addition to a giro-based money transmission system, the People's Bank should incorporate the existing post office Savings Bank, which is considered in the next section.

8.4 Popular saving institutions

In the MERG policy framework, increasing levels of personal saving, held as financial assets, have an important role and financial policy can influence these levels.

8.4.1 Raising the personal saving ratio

One of the failures of existing economic policy is that the personal savings ratio, expressed as a percentage of personal disposable income, has declined to low levels. Since economic transformation will require high levels of public and private investment, an increase in personal saving will be one important means for maintaining macroeconomic balance. To put it another way, a key to ensuring that investment can be financed without foreign debt increasing above target levels, is to increase personal saving.

This conclusion appears surprising because in recent years, South Africa's domestic saving ratio has not been inadequate compared to domestic investment. The surplus of saving has financed net investment abroad (reduction of net foreign liabilities). In one sense, it appears that the problem has been inadequate investment rather than inadequate saving. However, the scale of the transformation required in South Africa is such that the new strategy will aim for a large increase in private and public sector investment. If this is not to be accompanied by a substantial worsening of the current account of balance of payments, it will require an increase in domestic saving to accommodate it, and increased personal saving should have a central role in this.

The importance of increasing personal saving can also be seen from another angle. The principles Keynes successfully applied to financing the huge investment required for war, apply to the huge investment that will be required in South Africa. If the positions of corporations remain unchanged, either personal and indirect taxation will have to rise to increase public sector saving and reduce disposable income, or the resources for investment will have to be made available as a result of people accumulating wealth by saving out of personal income. In fact, corporate saving and taxation will not be constant, and a tax such as a wealth tax would increase the resources released by the wealthiest sections of the personal sector, but the need for an increase in personal saving rates would remain.

Policies to increase personal savings rates have a bearing on the much discussed problem of rising expectations. It is widely believed (although by no means certain) that the election of a democratic government will be followed by an explosion of poor people's expectations of a rise in income which, if even partially met, would lead to an unsustainable boom in consumption, decline in resources for investment, and worsening balance of payments. The democratic movement remains committed to a strategy of redistribution as well as growth. A redistribution of income, however, will be sustainable if it is accompanied by an increase in poor people's saving rates, or, in other words, by an increase in their assets instead of an equivalent expansion of consumption. On the basis of the experience of other countries, substantial increases in the saving ratio of low-income groups are possible, and are preferable to increased taxation of these groups. The financial system has a role to play in stimulating personal saving, and policies will be implemented with this objective.

The saving of low-income groups falls into two categories, contractual and discretionary. The encouragement of each requires appropriate institutional development and appropriate interest rate and taxation policies.

8.4.2 Contractual savings

Over recent decades, the saving of the personal sector as a whole has increasingly taken the form of contractual saving through pension funds, life assurance, and endowment schemes, which now account for a high proportion of the total. However, it is estimated that only 8 per cent of black residents of metropolitan areas have a life assurance policy, 5 per cent an endowment policy, and 16 per cent an investment in a pension fund. The high growth of saving in life assurance companies such as Old

Mutual and Sanlam (which together account for more than two-thirds of total premium income) has been in effect due to the white population saving through life policies and endowment policies of various types. In part, it is also based on their management of pension funds for employees of all races.

The greater preponderance of contractual saving among the white population suggests that there is room for expansion of the contractual saving of the majority of South Africans. Some of the conditions promoting this, such as regular employment, will be achieved by the change in labour force as the formal sector absorbs a higher proportion of black staff (although retrenchment in parts of the formal sector works in the opposite direction). Expansion of contractual saving requires special promotion measures, and the life assurance companies are not the only suitable institutions for this purpose. Contractual saving may be made under a succession of short-term arrangements as well as long term contracts such as life assurance.

Existing informal financial structures collect saving which is contractual in the sense of requiring regular payments, but they are limited in scope. Stokvels, a local form of the saving clubs and rotating credit clubs that grow spontaneously in most countries, are the best known units of informal finance in South Africa. Some estimates suggest that gross saving inflows into stokvels grew from R52m per month in 1989 to R84m per month in 1991, while some estimate the inflow at R200m per month in 1992. Based on a survey of metropolitan areas, the majority of members of stokvels contribute to them as burial clubs, and the next largest stokvels, by membership, are those handling short-term saving to finance purchases of durables, or to finance parties.

MERG does not support the view that stokvels should be the main institutions for developing contractual saving, although membership of stokvels should be encouraged and policies enacted to protect the people's saving with them. Although it appears that stokvels handle large saving flows, they are not effective at mobilising savings for productive investment, and they have several disadvantages as assets for the savers. One of the latter is that individuals' deposits in stokvels are not suitable as collateral for bank loans, while one reason for their ineffectiveness as vehicles for financing investment, is their local character. Several schemes have been floated for overcoming these problems, in particular the idea that stokvel savers should acquire unit trust certificates, and, as small borrowers from the banks, should be able to offer group guarantees from the stokvel. Such schemes are unlikely to have a large impact on the volume of small savings.

Financial strategy should be based on the restructuring of formal institutions rather than on the spread of informal institutions. Nevertheless, it is worth considering two views on the potential roles for informal institutions, such as stokvels. One is that if informal institutions rapidly develop into formal savings institutions (as happened in the early stages of industrialisation in Italy and other countries), they can play an important role. This is not feasible in South Africa, which already has well-established savings institutions and state pension systems. Another is that stokvels can act as community links with popular formal institutions such as the People's Bank. Since they have well-established leadership (often the local school-teacher) and local financial and personal networks, they may act as the collection and disbursement mechanism for small saving placed with the People's Bank. This positive role, however, is not unambiguous, for the leadership hierarchy in stokvels sometimes involves new or traditional relations of power and exploitation, and the operation of stokvels is not based upon the transparent and written agreements that a modern society requires.

One positive strategy to encourage more widespread contractual saving in formal institutions, is to link saving to the right to obtain housing finance. Favourable tax treatment or direct subsidies can be used to promote such schemes. The existing proposal for community banking places such a saving-mortgage link at its centre, and MERG policy promotes this. In addition, policy will favour the strengthening and formalisation of similar schemes by mutual building societies.

The strongest impetus to increased contractual saving would be legislation to compel employer and employee contributions to a funded state pension scheme. This would be a supplementary, earnings-related scheme, which would entitle the pensioner to additional benefits above the basic state pension. As a saving instrument the supplementary system would differ from the existing pension system because, being funded, it would accumulate savings as investible assets in order to generate a stream of returns to finance future pensions, while the present system is a pay-as-you-go system, in which current pensions are financed by payments from current salary earners. The establishment of a funded scheme could have a positive impact on the financial flows generated by contractual personal saving, as it would extend the principle of occupational pension funds to all employees (exemption would be granted for employees already covered by private schemes). However, such a scheme may be offset by a decline in other forms of saving, instead of a reduction in the ratio of consumption to income, and further analysis and consultation is necessary before a conclusion can be reached.

8.4.3   Discretionary saving

Discretionary saving by people with relatively low incomes can also be increased. Because of the high proportion of people, especially black people, outside formal employment but with fluctuating income from informal employment, self employment, or other activities, policies to stimulate an increase in their discretionary saving ratio will be especially important. These policies involve enhancing the accessibility of savings media, increasing their net interest return, and increasing the security of savings.

MERG policy towards discretionary saving will give a central place to the post office Savings Bank, which will be incorporated into the People's Bank. Its accessibility, which is already high, will be increased. At present the post office Savings Bank offers interest rates which are market-related, but lower than those of other institutions. The policy of withdrawing tax exemption and increasing gross deposit rates will be continued and new saving instruments will be offered, including an indexed saving medium offering a guaranteed positive real rate. Security of savings will be guaranteed by the state alone, and not, as at present, by the post office, which is a state body.

The assets of the post office Savings Bank are principally loans to Telkor (over 75 per cent), and it has been used by the post office as a window to obtain low-interest deposits which are used to finance investment in its own telecommunications expansion. This policy has restricted the ability of the POSB to develop a strong balance sheet. To enable it to strengthen its balance sheet in accordance with its expansion, the asset structure of the People's Bank will be broadened to include a wide range of liquid, medium and long term liabilities of the central state and other public institutions.

Giving a central role to the People's Bank as a repository for discretionary savings, as well as building its role as a provider of money transmission services, is expected to lead to considerable growth in its balance sheet (from the current position where POSB deposits account for less than 1 per cent of deposit taking institutions. Since its assets will be various types of loans to the public sector and semi-public institutions, its expansion will directly contribute to financing social infrastructure investment through financing the public sector borrowing requirement and non-profit institutions. Post Office Savings Banks in a large number of countries, ranging from Zimbabwe to Taiwan, have played similar roles in attracting the saving of low-income citizens into financing public expenditure. From the point of view of depositors, this feature enables the People's Bank to attract saving in a climate where individuals wish to see their saving as an aspect of building a new South Africa. Whereas it is widely believed that the end of political apartheid in South Africa will lead to an explosion of expectations of increased consumption, leadership can foster a culture which emphasises saving as a means of participating in building the new South Africa, while at the same time yielding personal benefits.

8.4.4 *Interest rate policies*

Since the 1970s, one school of thought has promoted high interest rates as a policy to stimulate saving in less developed countries, but empirical studies do not support the general validity of such policies. Financial saving should attract positive real interest rates, but, with that proviso, which the MERG strategy takes into account by assuming a real long-term interest rate of 2 per cent, policy towards the general level of interest rates should be determined in accordance with monetary and exchange rate targets, instead of as incentives for personal saving. Nevertheless, policies regarding the interest rates paid on specific types of saving instruments will be adopted in order to influence the pattern of saving and the development of institutions. Similarly, policies on the terms of personal credit will be adopted, especially regarding consumer credit, which has an effect on net personal saving and its timing.

8.5 Financing investment

The previous sections have been concerned with building institutions to cater better for the money transactions and savings needed by the new South Africa. The new institutions will increase the liabilities of the financial institutions. On the other side of the balance sheet, however, is asset growth, and it is necessary to implement policies to ensure that finance is channelled towards productive investment. Although the growth of saving may be associated with an increase in resources available for investment, it does not necessarily lead to investment, but may instead create an excess of saving over investment. Financial policies which actively encourage appropriate investment are required.

Appropriate investment may be encouraged in two ways, by providing an active stimulus, or by actively facilitating investment which results from other stimuli. The main role of the financial system is to facilitate investment rather than directly stimulate it, and policy can assist this in two ways:

- by promoting institutional developments which make finance available in forms suitable for the new investment needs;

- by influencing the price and terms of finance in order to meet these needs;

In the following paragraphs, policies for the development of existing and new institutions, and for influencing the price and conditions of finance, are outlined.

MERG policies are based on the belief that there are four main types of agents whose investment will be especially important in the early stages of growth:

- The state, including central and local government bodies and public corporations. It is envisaged that the public sector will have the principal responsibility for investing in social infrastructure, including low cost housing. Moreover, since the risk aversion of large private corporations may depress their industrial investment, it is expected that strategic investment by the public sector will have a leading role in industrial strategy;

- Small and medium manufacturing businesses. It is expected that this sector will grow as black-owned and controlled business expands, but it has special needs regarding financing working capital and fixed assets;

- Individual households. Investment in owner-occupied housing from the rising incomes of black South Africans will grow if suitable means of financing it are available;

- Foreign companies investing in manufacturing plants. It is envisaged that foreign direct investment will be an element of South Africa re-integration into the global economy, which could facilitate technology transfer and access to markets.

Each of them has particular financial needs which the financial system is not sufficiently equipped to meet at present.

8.6   The Johannesburg Stock Exchange

The Johannesburg Stock Exchange (JSE) houses the organised market for long-term capital, corporate bonds, equities and options (but not futures). The present role of the JSE illustrates that the market-oriented approach to meeting capital needs is unlikely, on its own, to meet the objectives of the democratic movement. Financial development requires policies to develop appropriate institutions in which the relations between finance and production are not purely market transactions.

In terms of their contribution to growth and development, the main rationale for stock exchanges is that they enable new capital to be channelled to investment ventures on the basis of informed decisions about prospective returns and risk. The mechanisms for that process are both the primary market in which new issues are sold, and the secondary market which continuously trades in, and prices, existing stock. Additionally, in some stock exchanges, especially those of the UK and USA, a modern function is to act as a market in corporate control which, some argue, stimulates competition by the threat or actuality of take-overs. It is doubtful that stock exchanges have made a strong contribution to economic growth in these ways, but MERG is concerned with the specific question of the potential of the JSE in this respect.

Although the JSE has experienced a boom in recent years, this has only disguised its underlying weaknesses. The market is principally a secondary market with a low rate of new issues; the boom is a reflection of the excess supply of funds of a depressed economy, funds accumulated through the contractual saving institutions while the demand for funds to finance new productive investment is low. One way to expand the demand for new funds (which could give the JSE a role in the allocation of capital to a wider section of industrial and commercial enterprises), would be the establishment of sub markets for enterprises without the track record and reporting abilities usually required of quoted companies. With that objective, the JSE did establish two entry-level sub markets, the Development Board and the Venture Capital Board. Both have been failures, which is an indication of the limited role the JSE plays in channelling finance to new ventures. Some have argued that it is a particularly unsuitable institution for raising new capital for black owned businesses such as National Sorghum Breweries, since their owners fear that a listing will lead to loss of control to white shareholders. Moreover, the domination of the market by a few institutional investors and the listed shares of a small number of conglomerates and groups, means that the JSE does not operate effectively as a market for corporate control.

From the point of view of those advocating that the capital market play an active role, a major weakness is the operation of the market itself, as it has a low level of business even in the secondary market. Its liquidity ratio, the ratio of turnover to market capitalisation, is, at 5 per cent, low compared to leading stock exchanges. Its system of market making and trading, with single capacity brokers and non-competitive relations between them, is accompanied by a high commission structure.

These trading features make the JSE uncompetitive in comparison with stock exchanges outside Africa; its isolation from international capital markets is reinforced by the prohibition on foreign companies being listed on the JSE, and by foreign exchange restrictions on residents.

In recent times, the JSE has not had a strong domestic role in financing new investment, neither does it have a significant international role, and overall it is not a very active market. It has 670 quoted securities (of which 650 are on the Main Board) but trade in the shares of only 20 companies is at all significant, and the interlocking ownership structure of the conglomerates which dominate the economy, makes the JSE largely irrelevant in allocating capital.

The main current concern of the JSE is to seek changes in government policy which will increase market activity (its liquidity ratio). In particular it is likely to press for abolition of the 1 per cent Marketable Securities Tax. There is no case for abolishing the tax. It has been argued that the absence of a Marketable Securities Tax on the Namibian stock exchange places the JSE at a competitive disadvantage, but it is small compared to other advantages held by the JSE, and if it leads to Johannesburg business being artificially booked through Windhoek, then this is a problem to be confronted by exchange controls, and regional policies on capital movements and fiscal harmonisation. The present structure of taxation affecting the capital market is irrational and should be reformed. At present, the Marketable Securities Tax applied to transactions in the derivatives market is zero, which it should not be; it gives an impetus to transactions in options and other derivatives, and may thereby fuel volatility in the basic market. Most importantly, a general capital gains tax and a general wealth tax should be introduced, and both will have repercussions on the stock exchange.

MERG recommends strengthening the stock exchange in four ways designed to serve the overall goals of financial and economic strategy.

Firstly, in order to transfer the ownership of wealth to the majority, measures will be taken to establish compulsory funds that are able to purchase stakes in quoted companies, including mining finance houses, mines, and financial institutions. These purchases are to take place on the capital market at market prices. Such measures are in line with the Freedom Charter and they have parallels in other countries. In Malaysia, such measures have effected a significant transfer of ownership from Chinese investors to the Malay majority. In Sweden, under the Meiden plan, such funds were intended to give worker organisations an increasing stake in enterprises, but political developments prevented the implementation of the plan.

A similar role for the stock market arises where ownership is transferred through taking enterprises into public ownership or privatising public sector enterprises. Valuation of enterprises on the JSE will be an important benchmark for pricing public or private sector purchases of such enterprises.

Secondly, policies to encourage the strengthening of the Development Board and Venture Capital Board will be considered. Their feasibility will be assessed on the basis of a review of the previous failure by the JSE to facilitate such low-cost, entry level sub markets for new issues. Measures to encourage the issue of new types of securities (with minimum returns partly guaranteed) will be considered.

Thirdly, policies to permit foreign companies to raise capital on the JSE will be revised in accordance with policies to encourage foreign direct investment. One reason for encouraging foreign direct investment is the contribution it makes to production and trade (for example through technology transfer and access to markets). Those gains can be made even if the foreign corporation does not finance its investment with foreign funds, but, instead, raises capital on the JSE; steps which facilitate such measures will be implemented, subject to being consistent with measures to discourage capital flight. Another reason for encouraging foreign direct investment is that capital inflows strengthen the balance of payments. The ability to raise funds on the JSE appears at first sight to act against this benefit, but is likely to stimulate it if combined with rules about the proportion of foreign and domestic finance. At present, the only foreign companies quoted on the JSE (31 in total) are those whose assets are mainly in South Africa, but that and other restrictions require review and reform in view of the changing structure of international corporations, and with a view to increasing the ability of foreign companies, including joint ventures, to raise capital locally.

Fourthly, a Capital Issues Commission will be established under the Ministry of Finance, in order to consider company plans for new issues and to authorise them. One purpose of this control is to prevent excess demand for capital creating disorderly market conditions, and generating excessive interest rate changes. This task is likely to be important because of the heavy demands state borrowing for investment will make on the capital market, and the need to ensure a desirable balance between public and private sector fund-raising on the domestic market. The second purpose is to channel funds into private sector investments which have a high national priority (for example, funds for export industries will be expected to have a higher priority than funds for developing office blocks). The third purpose is to ensure that companies raising capital conform with national policy on ethnic and gender employment practice and other policies. Capital issues commissions of these types have operated in other countries in periods of transformation, with major resource transfers occurring. A well known example is that of Britain during the period of post-war reconstruction.

8.7 Capital market institutions

The principal long-term capital institutions are the pension funds and life assurance companies. Partly as a result of foreign exchange controls, their regular inflow of funds is invested mainly on the secondary market for equities. However, since the JSE has a limited role in financing new capital investment, or in providing the funds for newly developing sectors, this use of the funds of capital institutions is not associated with productive investment.

In addition, a proportion of these funds is held in public sector bonds of various types. The life assurers hold approximately 18 per cent of their assets in this form (and 57 per cent per cent in equities), while pension and provident funds hold 21 per cent of their assets in these forms.

MERG proposes that the proportion of long-term capital funds loaned to the public sector should be increased. In the process of building a new economic system, it is expected that public sector physical investment will account for an increased proportion of total capital formation, mainly because priority will be given to investment in infrastructure which, with the exception of township electrification and some other cases, could not be undertaken privately because it is not directly profitable. To ease the problem of financing public sector investment, the capital institutions should be subject to prescribed asset requirements under which a percentage of their assets have to be placed in eligible securities.

The prescribed asset ratio is to be determined by the new government. and regulations should be designed to increase the proportion of eligible assets in the balance sheets over an adjustment period (to avoid the problems of market stability that would be caused by measures that might lead the institutions to attempt to sell their stocks of equities quickly). In other words, the regulations should take effect incrementally, by raising above the prescribed balance sheet asset ratio the proportion of eligible securities bought with new investment flows, until the prescribed balance sheet ratio is reached. The eligible securities may include the debt of quasi-public institutions engaged in investing in social infrastructure, such as non-profit institutions investing in low cost housing.

There are arguments for and against prescribed asset ratios, but the MERG view is that the balance is strongly in favour of them. The strongest argument against them is that trustees and managers of funds have an obligation to obtain the best return possible for their policyholders or members. However, this is not an absolute, as their responsibilities are necessarily subject to restrictions in the national interest (such as exchange controls), or the citizen's. Instead of being concerned only with returns, trustees and managers have to weigh return against risk; prescribed assets can have an element of indexation which guarantees positive returns, while equities (and real estate) remain risky assets. Moreover, funds invested in social infrastructure are designed to ensure better returns in the long run, since a sound policy of economic growth enhances the returns on individual equities. The Public Investment Commissioners have invested all their funds, which principally represent public sector pension funds, in fixed interest public securities (at least until late 1991, when a proportion of investment in equities was permitted) and prescribed asset requirements for other financial institutions are as legitimate. There is a severe cost if interest rates on eligible assets are artificially held down so that the institutions obtain negative real interest rates, but, as the following paragraph explains, this is not the intention.

Prescribed assets should be the major policy instrument for securing public sector ability to sell bonds and bills. The purpose is to ensure that, together with other non-monetary sources of domestic finance, net domestic purchases of this paper will be higher than would otherwise have been at any interest rate. As a result, the policy will have several positive benefits for macroeconomic management. It will reduce the residual of the public sector borrowing requirement that has to be financed by bank credit, and thereby make control of the money supply easier; it will reduce public sector borrowing from abroad; and it will enable the government to raise funds through domestic bond issues at relatively low interest rates.

8.8 Commercial bank lending

Commercial bank credit is the principal source of external finance for the private sector and the way it is structured affects the financing of private investment. Commercial banking is dominated by the four large bank groups; their lending practices, like their system of money transfer, were designed for a different economic system and different circumstances from those which will prevail in the transition.

An important issue is the appropriate relationship between commercial banks and industry. The South African system is built on principles derived from the British system, which emphasises short-term loans, non-involvement in the borrower's management of business, and a separation between commercial and investment banking. Different types of banking systems have existed in Germany and other countries during periods of rapid industrialisation. These banks provided long-term finance, including equity finance, and were integrated into the supervision and monitoring of corporate borrowers. Between those two broad systems, there are several variations. MERG recommends a commercial banking system closer to the German one.

The main feature of bank lending to enterprises under the present system, is that it is short-term, and based either on overdrafts secured by marketable assets as collateral, or on commercial bills. The role of commercial paper in balance sheets of banks has increased in recent years. In lending to enterprises, the reliance on collateral and bill financing is associated with an absence of supervision of the enterprise by the bank. The bank is concerned to ensure that its overdraft can be recouped by sale of collateral, should an enterprise fail, and it has a minimal concern with supervising the enterprise to reduce the risk of failure. In general, the bank has no incentive to incorporate an element of venture capital in its financing. Nor does the bank have an incentive to lend, as part of a package that includes equity financing, against long-term prospects without collateral. Some banks (and capital market institutions) have recently begun schemes of this nature, but they are extremely small and irrelevant to main business. It is notable that one of the main innovations in bank lending during the 1980s, was expansion of mortgage lending to individuals; mortgage lending, which is based upon collateral in the form of marketable real estate, is the most significant form of long-term lending by banks.

The transition period in South Africa, which involves high growth, requires new private sector investment projects, new enterprises, and the reconstruction of existing enterprises. Partly because of the limited potential of the stock exchange, commercial bank financing will be the principal source of external financing for these ventures, but its ability to fulfil this role is limited by the characteristics outlined.

MERG recommends the development of two main elements of a German type of system. One is corporate financing comprising a package of working capital finance, term loans, and equity finance. The other is representation of banks on supervisory boards of companies above a certain size (the supervisory boards to include repre-sentatives of trade unions and other interests). Together, these measures would be designed to ensure banks are involved in the long-term development of enterprises, and that bank finance is designed to strengthen such development. The measures to be taken to encourage moves in this direction include changes in company law, changes in the capital requirements of banks, and changes in taxation which make this type of financing cost-advantageous to the banks.

Such measures which encourage closer links between banks and industry cannot, by themselves, ensure the relationship is fruitful. Close links between banks and industry can be of two types. One type facilitates stagnation and cosy arrangements protected by oligopolistic power. Latin American countries have provided some notable examples. Another type facilitates partnership in which bank supervision stimulates and facilitates strongly based industrial dynamism. Germany is a widely cited example. South Africa already has close ownership links between financial institutions (including banks) and industrial enterprises, and these links represent an extreme concentration of power. Reforming bank finance so that it involves longer-term credit relations, equity stakes and supervision relations is not intended to reinforce the existing non-dynamic, economically conservative relationship. It can lead towards the type of long-term dynamic relationships that have existed in Germany only if it is accompanied by a reform of competition policy which trans-forms the present conglomerate structure, and only if this is accompanied by a carefully constructed system of supervision in which, as in Germany, not only banks, but also labour and the state are in partnership.

8.9 Debt structure

Reform of the financial system is often treated in relation only to the institutions and markets that supply finance to enterprises, and other agents that carry out investment. But reform of the banks, savings institutions and markets is not the only problem that has to be addressed in constructing a sound financial basis. Success will depend on addressing the problem of the financial structure of the enterprises and investing agents. If, for example, major borrowers were already highly geared, or if their balance sheets were eroded by the depression in real estate values, or if they were engaging in Ponzi finance, no reform of the financial system would be able to put the financing of investment on a sound footing.

In South Africa, the most urgent problem of this type is the unsound financial position of some public sector authorities. It is necessary to channel finance towards authorities carrying out investment in social and economic infrastructure, but black local authorities and the authorities in the bantustans have weak revenue bases, and accumulated liabilities which are unsound. One example is the high level of over-drafts accumulated in recent years by the bantustan authorities; the commercial banks have provided this finance under guarantees from the central authorities, but the borrowers have little prospect of servicing them. Another example is the reliance of several black urban authorities on loans from white municipalities, while the credit rating of the latter has not been adjusted to reflect fully the risks they have assumed.

To enable the financial system to finance public authority investment, it is necessary to improve their revenue base and restructure their debt (including writing off unserviceable debt and funding existing short term liabilities). It is also necessary to adopt proper standards for calculating and disclosing the contingent liabilities of the public bodies that have guaranteed the debts of other authorities.

8.10 Regulation of the financial system

An important issue which determines how well the financial system operates, is how it is regulated. Regulation concerns the set of rules which determine key aspects of the operations of banks and other institutions, and the way in which these rules are administered. It differs from the question of who owns the banks. It is sometimes thought that nationalisation of the banks is necessary to control them, but even nationalised banks would have to operate under a set of regulations. There may be grounds for nationalising some banks, but normal regulation of banking activity could usually be obtained without it.

Regulation has several goals. The goal which has become uppermost in most advanced capitalist countries, is regulation to ensure that the owners of the institutions have enough of their own capital in the bank to justify the risks they take. Another is the protection of depositors or others who invest in a financial institution. More traditional goals involve regulating the interest rates banks pay and charge, or regulating other terms of lending.

In the past decade, regulation of banks and other financial institutions has changed throughout the world. However, methods of regulation are still evolving, South Africa has its own features, and the regulation system in South Africa is still under review.

At the heart of the system is regulation of banks under the Deposit Taking Institution Act. Its emphasis is on ensuring that the capital of shareholders is sufficient in relation to the risks of different types of assets and activities of the bank. In addition, it sets minimum liquid assets and cash ratios in respect of liquid liabilities, and it restricts the exposure of banks to any one customer. This policy is the responsibility of the Reserve Bank. According to the perspective which is increasingly being adopted by the Reserve Bank, as long as banks adhere to those rules concerning the structure of their balance sheets, there is nothing further that the Reserve Bank is required to do to ensure that deposits in the banks are protected from risks such as faulty lending by the bank. If a bank collapses through faulty management or unforeseeable circumstances (or fraud), the view of the Reserve Bank is that it cannot take responsibility for the losses suffered by the depositors, and there should not be a system of deposit insurance to compensate them.

MERG rejects such an approach. The Reserve Bank should have an obligation to maintain confidence in the monetary system and should be responsible for it. In particular, it should organise a system of deposit insurance, financed by the banks, to increase people's confidence in the security of their savings. This recommendation is based on the view that the notion that protecting depositors leads bankers to recklessness (moral hazard), because it reduces depositors' vigilance, is invalid. To increase the use of bank accounts, a strong priority must be to protect depositors from risks. The economy will be subject to high risks in the process of transformation.

The requirement that the capital of the shareholders of banks be adequate to the risks of their assets gives a powerful lever for influencing the lending behaviour of banks. For example, the fact that mortgage loans are designated as involving low risks, and therefore requiring lower capital ratios, has been one factor encouraging banks to increase the proportion of mortgage lending. Since MERG recommends a policy to change the structure of banking and encourage financing of priority sectors (which should not include the traditional mortgage sector), the risk weightings of different types of lending should be reviewed in order to encourage finance to flow in the desired directions.

Since regulation of banks is designed to protect the monetary system, it is backed by the Reserve Bank function of lender of last resort at times of banking crisis. If regulation fails, central banks either organise loans from the strongest private banks (as in the lifeboat operations in the UK), or pump large amounts of public funds into private institutions (as in the US Savings and Loan crisis), or nationalise the banks (as in Chile in 1981). MERG recommends that the state policy should favour nationalisation if any of the four largest commercial banks require lender of last resort support.

It is undesirable to use regulations to impose ceilings on the interest rates paid to depositors or charged to borrowers. However, it is desirable to monitor the allocation of bank credit to different sectors and to impose sectoral targets for credit allocation. A new broad framework of regulation is required to promote good practice by banks in the process of economic transformation. Regulations will be put forward prohibiting discrimination on the grounds of status related to race or gender. The regulations will require the use of simple language and vernacular languages in documents, and will also require transparency. They will make provision for establishing ombudsmen and ombudswomen for the financial sector. Financing of large projects may also be made conditional upon social and environmental impact assessments.

An important aspect of regulation which is currently under active review is the appropriate body for administering regulations. It includes the question of whether regulation of banks should continue to be a function of the Reserve Bank, or whether it should be carried out by a separate body, leaving the Reserve Bank to concentrate on other policies (usually specified as anti-inflation policies). This question is considered below.

8.11 The Reserve Bank

Most central banks (with the notable, but not complete, exception of the Federal Reserve and the Bundesbank) are directly controlled by their governments, but this principle is increasingly being challenged, and several countries are moving towards complete policy independence for their central banks. Even those central banks which have relative autonomy in policy are invariably publicly owned institutions with no private shareholders.

In South Africa, the Reserve Bank does have private ownership; its capital is listed on the JSE (although not actively traded) and it has some 700 private stockholders. In the latter respect, it is almost unique (although the Bank of Japan also has some privately owned equity). In practice, however, the SA Reserve Bank is a government body, in the sense that its governor and deputy governors are government appointments, as are a number of directors, although the Bank has a great deal of autonomy in its operation. In recent years the boundaries of this autonomy have been tested, as the Bank has contested other departments of state in legal actions. MERG recommends that instead of becoming increasingly independent, the Reserve Bank should be placed more firmly under political control. Its conduct of monetary policy, supervision and other functions should be made subordinate to the Minister of Finance. The principal reason for this policy, in contrast to increasing independence, is that it ensures that monetary policy is determined by and accountable to the democratic government. Independence deliberately creates an institution which has great power to influence variables that affect the whole economy (interest rates, liquidity and exchange rates), but is not controlled by any democratically elected body. In February 1993, the Governor of the Reserve Bank stated that the Bank was accountable to Parliament, but MERG proposes to strengthen and clarify the nature of such accountability.

In the sphere of macroeconomic policy, the argument for a fully independent central bank is that it would have a constitutional responsibility for maintaining the value of the currency by preventing inflation. It would be obliged to restrict the growth of the money supply, and raise interest rates whenever it considered that inflation was becoming too high. Even if the government decided that increased inflation was a price worth paying for higher employment and took fiscal actions accordingly, an independent Reserve Bank would be able to adopt monetary policies working in the opposite direction to thwart the policy of the elected government. This is not desirable. It prevents the Reserve Bank from being accountable to democratic institutions, or being directly controlled by them. It assumes that inflation is controllable by monetary policy, whereas during a transition period, it will have structural characteristics. It subordinates to control of inflation the Reserve Bank's responsibility of lender of last resort.

The fact that Reserve Bank independence removes it from direct control by elected bodies is one reason some of its South African advocates support it. It is believed that international bankers and officials would have greater confidence in South Africa if its central bank is fully independent of elected politicians. Indeed, a strong version of this principle is enshrined in several African states, where the governor of the central bank has to be a foreigner, and may be a nominee of the International Monetary Fund. The independence of the Reserve Bank, however, which divests the elected government of significant economic powers, is not a sound way to build international confidence in South Africa.

It is true that, at the opposite extreme, direct political interference in the day-to-day actions and short-term policies of the central bank in any country, would be undesirable and could lead to the manipulation of monetary policy for the benefit of interest groups or parties, or for the short-term electoral advantage of the government. But independence for the Reserve Bank would not free monetary policy from interest groups, and it would be comparable to the undesirable policy of removing taxation (which can also be subject to particular interests) from the powers of government.

Independence of the Reserve Bank is not the best way to deal with the problem of short-term interference and pressure. Ensuring that the Reserve Bank is subordinate to, and accountable to, the elected authorities should be combined with rules requiring monetary policy to be carried out in a medium-term framework. The framework will have to be agreed with the Ministry of Finance. The Reserve Bank will be accountable for the policies it adopts within the terms of the framework, but within the framework, the Reserve Bank would be free to pursue policy without interference. Additional devices may be built in with the aim of increasing the accountability of both the Reserve Bank, and the Ministry of Finance for financial policy. There are grounds for following United States practice, by making the conduct of monetary policy by the Reserve Bank (as well as the policies of the Ministry of Finance) subject to regular scrutiny by an expert parliamentary committee. There are also grounds for following the practice (which New Zealand employs) of placing a ceiling on the growth of Reserve Bank credit to the government. Once agreed upon between the Ministry and Reserve Bank, it can be exceeded only with parliamentary approval.

While the monetary policy framework should incorporate the obligation of the Reserve Bank to maintain the value of the currency, this should not be interpreted as an obligation to achieve zero inflation and a stable nominal exchange rate. Instead, the inflation target should be a moderate rate. A target band of approximately 10 per cent per year should be initially considered. The inflation target should not be the only consideration in determining monetary and credit conditions. The responsibilities of the Reserve Bank should include expansion of the money supply commensurate with real GDP growth, and responsibility for strengthening the orientation of the financial system toward financing growth and development. The exchange rate target should be the maintenance of a stable real effective exchange rate, together with a non-zero inflation target that implies a pre-announced crawling devaluation (of the nominal effective exchange rate). If there is a unified exchange rate without capital account controls, a nominal interest rate above world levels would be implied. Since MERG recommends, however, the retention of exchange controls, freedom of manoeuvre on interest rates would be maintained.

The independence of the Reserve Bank relates to its role in supervision of banks, other institutions, and financial markets, as well as to monetary policy. The appropriate structure of supervision is currently undergoing change following the Jacobs and Melamet reports. The new structure being designed will have the Reserve Bank retaining responsibility for supervision of the banking system within a broader framework of supervisory bodies for the system as a whole. This broader structure is to be headed by an independent commission separate from the Reserve Bank and from other institutions. The government of a democratic South Africa should review this, since there is a case for removing bank supervision from the Reserve Bank. Any supervisory framework needs to be based on statutory powers held by independent regulators, as in the United States, instead of on self-regulation by bodies established by the financial institutions (the principle underlying much of the UK system of regulation).

8.12 Conclusion

MERG recognises the crucial role that the financial system will have in the transformation of the economy, and proposes policies to strengthen it. The financial liberalisation policies of the past decade have not created a financial system which provides a strong base for economic transformation. They were based on the philosophy that unrestricted, competitive financial markets would facilitate an improved allocation of finance, which would underpin efficient economic growth and prompt improvements in banking and other financial intermediaries. By contrast, the policies MERG proposes do not rely only on competition to promote improvements in the financial system. They involve direct initiatives in building institutions oriented to the needs of the new South Africa.

The initiatives proposed include a People's Bank based on the post office network, to give all South Africans access to a cheap and effective means of transferring money and receiving payments. It is important to raise the personal savings ratio, and a savings-related housing finance institution should be established, as well as an earnings related, funded, contributory state pension scheme. In addition, the portfolio of the post office Savings Bank should be widened and its savings schemes be strengthened.

To strengthen the financing of productive investment, MERG proposes measures which increase the orientation of the capital market toward productive and infrastructural ventures rather than financial speculation. These include changes in the tax structure, especially the creation of a capital gains tax, a change in the marketable securities tax, and prescribed asset ratios for pension funds and life assurance companies. With the same objective, measures are proposed which would change the relations of the banking system with corporations towards a more productively dynamic interaction. At the same time, there would be a reduction in the incentives that banks have to concentrate on their long term loans on high value mortgages.

MERG proposes the strengthening of bank regulation and policies to safeguard the savings of depositors. MERG proposes that the Reserve Bank should be accountable to parliament, subordinate to the Ministry of Finance, and subject to parliamentary scrutiny.

C H A P T E R 9
The state and the economy

.

While the role of the state in the South African economy is at the centre of political controversy, technical economic considerations also have to be taken into account in determining an appropriate role for the state. Within this economic policy framework, MERG has proposed several economic policies. Together they make up a detailed strategy for reshaping the economic role of the state.

The detailed strategy may be summarised as follows: to achieve the goals of economic growth and redistribution, the state structures of South Africa must play a strong and active role in leading development, but the state institutions themselves should be economical and efficient. In other words, a strong but slim state is required.

In recent decades two diametrically opposed views on the economic role of the state have been influential. One is that political power confers the power to control the economy directly; in liberation movements, it was sometimes believed that majority rule would mean that the state would itself redirect the resources of the economy and initiate a new economic order. The other is that the state has no role in the economy; neo-liberal or free-enterprise movements throughout the world have argued that private individuals, operating within markets freed by privatisation and de-regulation, should be the only actors. Both those general views have had proponents in South Africa. Both these views are wrong. South Africa needs a mixed economy. The MERG proposals for a mixed economy are set out in this chapter.

In South Africa, the change to a new economic system will depend on a strong private sector interacting with a strong public sector. Each depends on each other; the dynamism of the private sector depends on the strong economic leadership of the state, while state finances depend upon private sector growth. The economy depends on both. Redistribution and growth require state leadership, planning and action; the innovation and entrepreneurship which private enterprise is able to give when the conditions are right; and the adjustment mechanisms provided by the interaction of demand and supply on markets.

The economic strategies outlined in previous chapters comprise a programme in which the state has a strong role, leading and shaping the economic development, while the state machinery itself is reshaped to ensure that it does not, as in the past, absorb resources wastefully. A strong but slim state is necessary in order to meet the two economic goals of the democratic movement.

One objective is redistribution of income, wealth, and economic power. The distribution of income is affected by many forces. Even without state leadership on the issue, these forces may reduce inequalities. For example, the growth of African trade-unionism succeeded in reducing some of the inequalities between black and white wage rates, although it has not reduced inequality over the population as a whole, or reduced poverty. Without an active state policy, however, inequality or poverty often increases in the course of development. No country could achieve the extensive redistribution to benefit the poor which South Africa needs, without state orchestration and implementation. Examples as diverse as the construction of European welfare states, the American 'great society programme' of the 1960s, and the welfare programme of the Singapore government, illustrate that the state has a key role to play in redistribution. It is especially true for South Africa since, instead of simply redistributing money, redistribution requires the provision of schools, clinics, housing and infrastructure that cannot be provided by the private sector alone.

The other, related, objective is economic growth, which implies growth of investment in profitable industries and the relocation of South Africa in the world economy. International experience ranging from Germany and Japan in the nineteenth century, to South Korea and Taiwan more recently, suggests that this goal is achievable only if the state plays a strong role. Economic growth in South Africa between 1948 and 1970 was achieved under a strongly interventionist state.

In the present circumstances, a key question is whether or not in the absence of positive state involvement, the private sector would carry out the high level of productive investment which South Africa requires. The low level of net private industrial investment over the past decade, and the low levels of investment currently planned by the private sector lead to the conclusion that the private sector will not, by itself, be investing strongly in new capacity in the foreseeable future. Right-wing commentators suggest that private investment would increase if the present role of government were reduced, but the evidence points to a different conclusion: private sector investment would be strengthened by the state taking a stronger role, albeit different from its past role.

The role of the state is not a purely technical economic question, as it depends on the political and administrative character of the state. It is misleading to talk of 'the state', as there are a number of different elements comprising any state, and there is a range of possible shapes and powers for the state. In South Africa, these considerations are especially complex because the character and structure of the state are currently the subject of political negotiation, and many aspects will remain unsettled even after a democratic government is elected. Since the current state administration is in deep crisis, the future government will have the task of constructing a sound state, rather than preserving or altering a strong existing system.

In terms of the criteria specified above, the existing South African state is neither strong nor slim. It consists of overstaffed ministries and agencies performing routine tasks badly. Since the 1970s, its earlier prominent role in promoting economic growth collapsed, and in the 1980s it attempted to restructure itself without shedding staff.

Its weakness has economic symptoms. For example, the inability of the state to maintain its fiscal support of the TBVC states has caused these to borrow from banks using overdraft facilities. These overdrafts have grown at an exponential rate, with the outstanding total rising from R 0.64 billion in 1987, to R 6.4 billion in 1993 (Daphne, 1993). Since there is no prospect of the TBVC states being able to repay this amount, the debts are symptoms of a crisis in the state at two levels: first, the unsustainability of the present homeland institutions, and second, the fiscal crisis of the central state which has guaranteed these overdrafts and has a contingent liability to that extent in addition to its normal deficit. A similar crisis showing the unsustainability of the old state structures is the effective bankruptcy of the black township municipalities, which have nevertheless been financed by borrowing from municipalities in rich white areas.

The failure of the existing state is indicated by more than those financial symptoms. As indicated in the chapter on social and economic infrastructure, many authoritative reports have noted the overstaffing of state institutions, and their level of fragmentation which has prevented any coherent policies being implemented.

The state has to be restructured in order to enable it to act effectively as a developmental state, giving a strong lead to economic transformation, while being slim. Currently, political rather than economic considerations have a primary role in determining how the state is to be restructured. These political considerations have dominated the constitutional negotiations.

The shape of the state that results from political developments will affect its ability to give economic leadership. For example, a centralised state would be better able to redistribute resources from one region to another, while a federal state might have a greater ability to organise local economic development strategies. In addition, the outcome of political negotiations will have a direct effect on the economy because different political arrangements have different costs and different implications for taxation and expenditure. For example, if agreement on the integration of MK and the SADF involves an expansion of professional military personnel, it would absorb more resources. The next section considers the economic issues raised by some of the proposals for constitutional change.

In subsequent sections, the role of the state is considered by examining the main types of action the state can take in relation to the economy. The main levers states have for leading economic development and influencing its direction are:

- taxes and subsidies which redirect income and influence the structure of prices;

- fiscal and monetary policies affecting interest rates, exchange rates, inflation, unemployment and capacity utilisation;

- direct investment in physical capital by the state;

- current expenditure on salaries, other services, and current goods by the state;

- ownership and management of public enterprices;

- regulation of markets (which includes state action to promote active markets).

In each case, public institutions have to be designed to implement the policies. There are a range of views on both the policies themselves, and the types of institutions that might be appropriate. For example, there are differing views both on the best type of monetary policy, and on whether or not the central bank should be fully independent.

9.1 Constitutional prospects

The economic position of the state is being shaped in fundamental ways by the political and constitutional issues under negotiation. This section considers the economic implications of four particular aspects of those negotiations:

- restructuring the civil service;

- reincorporation of the homelands;

- regional finance and a fiscal commission;

- independence of the Reserve Bank.

Restructuring the civil service

An agreement on the future of current state employees will have a major effect on state spending, and therefore on public finance and the impact of the public sector on capital markets. At present, if all central and local public agencies are included, the size of the civil service is much too great in relation to its functions. It is possible that, for political reasons, an agreement to safeguard the jobs and pensions of existing civil servants will be made. Since there will also be an increase in civil service employment of Africans, a political agreement to safeguard the jobs of all existing civil servants would lead to state institutions which are overstaffed, and to high public expenditure on civil service salaries. A political agreement of this type would therefore increase the tax burden, and either increase the public sector deficit, or reduce the amount of state resources available for other purposes (such as public expenditure on housing or schooling).

The restructuring of state employment will be complex. One reason is that the state institutions themselves will be completely restructured; for example, the reintegration of so-called 'self governing territories' and the TBVC authorities into a unified South Africa, and the creation of new central and regional relations poses special problems. Another reason is that not all existing civil servants would be retained, and large numbers are themselves seeking early retirement. Another is that the construction of a democratic state based on accountability and transparency requires new methods of working, and a complete restructuring of the structure, tasks, and skills of the civil service. The economic implications of such aspects are highlighted by the problems of financing the pensions of state employees.

Existing pension arrangements for public sector employees are chaotic partly because of the great variety of different schemes, each with its own structure of entitlements and method of financing. In principle, most are pre-funded (designed to pay pensions from investments derived from previous contributions) although the pensions of members of the tricameral parliament and others are designed to be paid from state revenue instead. The pre-funded ones have been badly run, are under-funded, and have worsening deficits and cash calls as a result of political developments. They threaten to impose a large and unforeseen burden on the state budget to fund payments to public servants of the old regime. Policies are required to overcome this problem.

MERG research has enumerated the problems of current pension schemes for public employees, and outlined the increased problems that will result from restructuring state employment (Mokgoro, 1993). Information on many of the pension schemes is not available, and even for the most important (the funds covering the RSA civil service, provincial administrations, police and SADF), the most recent information at the time of writing dates from the 1988 valuation. At that time, these funds (GSPF and TEPF) were in deficit by R27 billion. Other funds, too, were in deficit according to available information. The Superannuation Fund which covers some employees of self-governing territories had a deficit by R68 million in 1989 (40 per cent of liabilities were not covered by assets). The MERG authors summarise the problems already arising from decisions taken in the light of the prospects for restructuring the state: 'Actuarial estimations suggest that if 20 000 public servants with an average of 30 years service were to leave the service prematurely, their one-off gratuity payouts would amount to R4 billion and their pensions to about R17 billion. The HSRC survey suggests that a number of civil servants are taking early retirement. Normally employees only receive golden handshakes and gratuities if they are retrenched, but in this case it appears that they are to be massively rewarded if they retire prematurely on a voluntary basis. They may then be re-employed on five year contracts.' In other words, unusual arrangements have been made enabling present state employees to extract large and unwarranted sums from the pension funds.

These funds are already in deficit, which may require as much as 'R30 – R40 billion payment by the state over a number of years to make good current shortfalls'. This drain on the state budget will be worsened by politically negotiated special favourable treatments (such as an addition of five years to the pensionable service of retrenched employees); by the current scramble for unwarranted early retirement payments; and by an increase in the rate of retirements or retrenchments.

The difficulty of financing the state employee pension schemes will be increased by other aspects of the restructuring of the state. The integration into the civil service of mid-career officials from the democratic movement, and the integration of mid-career MK personnel into the SADF will create a need to credit them with previous pensionable service, and fund the schemes accordingly.

The problems of state employee pension schemes illustrate in acute form the economic choices that have to be made as a result of restructuring the state. One stark decision is whether or not the future government should use money from general taxation to cover the existing deficits on the schemes. If it does, the 'R30 – R40 billion' required over a number of years would be equivalent to money that could have been used to finance two or three years of the teacher training needed to improve education (see Chapter Four on social and physical infrastructure). This subsidy may be considered a requirement in order to guarantee existing employees' pension rights, but such a subsidy may be rejected on the grounds that the future government should not inherit a fiscal burden caused by the inefficiency of the previous regime and by the favourable treatment of its administrators. This argument gains strength if, as at present, unwarranted early retirement payments are continued in the interim. Public employee pension schemes have to be completely restructured and the unsound state of the inherited structure has to be addressed. A commission should be established to investigate and recommend appropriate future structures for public sector pension schemes.

Reincorporation of the homelands

The economic impact of the reincorporation of the homelands (TBVC and self-governing territories) is a crucial aspect of the restructuring of the state. The fact that their administrative structures and rulers' trappings were a pillar of the apartheid system has often led to an assumption that a post-apartheid state would receive a 'peace dividend' of resources released by the dismantling of these overlapping, parallel structures. In fact, the situation is far more complex, and unlikely to lead to an unequivocal reduction in costs. This is partly because a substantial part of homeland expenditure is on real and necessary services (such as teachers' salaries) and partly because the abolition of homelands will, as a result of the negotiated political settlement, be accompanied by new regional authorities. The financing of regional development constitutes another reason why reincorporation will not increase the resources available for financing the central state. Full reincorporation requires well-designed regional development policies to reduce economic backwardness of poor regions and this will require public expenditure.

The direct savings from abolishing the homelands could be 1.3 per cent of GDP, but this is only 20 per cent of the homeland budgets, as the majority of the 356 000 homeland civil servants are providing essential services. (Daphne, 1993). These savings, however, are likely to be more than offset by the costs associated with new regional policies.

The currently proposed nine-region structure for South Africa will involve considerable administrative costs for the regional state bodies, since it is envisaged that they will have extensive powers and responsibilities. In addition to those administrative costs, an ANC government would have a strong policy of regional development and revenue transfers which involve costs to the state budget. This is one implication of having redistribution as well as growth as an objective, for reducing regional inequalities is an important element of this. In 1990/91, the state spent only R922 per capita in the homelands compared to R3 119 per capita in the rest of South Africa. Regional policies to reduce inequalities will involve a substantial increase in transfers to the former homelands. Similarly, since the homelands contain 42.5 per cent of the population but produce only 7.6 per cent of GDP, a programme to reduce inequality or poverty will require substantial expenditure in these regions.

Regional finance and a fiscal commission

Under the existing system, central government collects almost 85 per cent of total taxes. A future government should also collect taxes nationally, with regional governments having a small tax revenue of their own, as this structure would enable the government to redistribute resources from rich regions to poor. However, the determination of transfers from the centre to the regions raises the question of whether or not mechanisms can be established to ensure equity and transparency in the allocation process.

For this purpose it has been proposed that an independent fiscal commission be established to advise on the regional allocation of transfers. This proposal has merit if the responsibilities, membership, structure and accountability of the fiscal commission are appropriate.

The present understanding on the role of an independent fiscal commission is that it should be purely advisory. MERG supports this arrangement, but if the commission were to develop a degree of authority which made the accepting of its advice automatic, it would mean that the government would lose one of the basic powers of any state, i.e. the power of disposing of taxes. In such a case, a democratic government would have been elected to office without significant economic powers, and elections would lose much of their significance. MERG proposes that the independent fiscal commission should be one element within a state system for evaluating, legislating, and executing fiscal policy in a democratic manner. To create this system, the tax and expenditure policy function of the Ministry of Finance should be redesigned, and an expert parliamentary committee should be established to scrutinise tax and expenditure policy and its execution.

MERG proposes that the principal mechanism for allocating centrally pooled resources to the regions should be a formula based on widely-agreed measures of relative economic and social deprivation. An evaluation of different formula-based methods should be a priority of an independent fiscal commission.

Independence of the Reserve Bank

Similar considerations relate to the role of the Reserve Bank. If the Reserve Bank were fully independent, this would mean the Minister of Finance of a democratically elected government would have no power with respect to interest rates, exchange rates, or credit conditions. With these powers ceded to a non-elected board of a central bank, the election of a government would lose much of its significance.

Several alternative mechanisms can give the central bank a measure of independence while retaining its accountability and its subordination to elected representatives. One is to make the central bank subject to the scrutiny of parliament (as in the USA). Another (as in New Zealand) is to require both it and the government to agree on the target rate of credit creation and to make deviations from this (in the form of excess government borrowing) subject to parliamentary approval. MERG recommends a combination of such methods to increase the accountability of the South African Reserve Bank and to increase political control over it.

9.2 The role of the state in social infrastructure and land

The development of social infrastructure should have a central place in meeting the objectives of redistribution and growth. The increased and wider provision of education, health care and low cost housing, and the protection of pension provision will not automatically reduce inequality but are necessary conditions for reducing mass poverty, and the construction and operation of these provisions — especially housing construction — is recognised as a contributor to the growth of domestically based industries. What should the role of the state be in the development and operation of the social infrastructure?

Social infrastructure is one element in a mixed economy, and provision requires an approach which co-ordinates state action (such as teacher training) with the private sector (such as school building programmes). The experience of other countries indicates that, if schooling and health care are to be expanded, the state has to be the main supplier to the end user.

As indicated in the chapter on social and economic infrastructure, the role of the state should be to identify the real resource requirements of developing schooling and health, to calculate their costs in terms of alternative uses, to organise the finance of their monetary costs, and to implement policies to overcome constraints on the provision of these real resources to the chosen level. For example, in schooling, the state should implement a co-ordinated plan for training teachers, building schools, obtaining equipment and books, and providing means of transport and accommodation for schoolchildren if necessary.

How those physical resources are financed will affect how they are used, whether or not the desired services reach the population as a whole, and whether or not they are sustainable. Two broad categories of financing are possible, user charges, and finance out of state revenue, and the relative proportions of these two mechanisms will influence the degree to which the programme reaches the people it is intended for, and whether or not it is sustainable. Financing of schooling and general health care through the state budget, without user charges, is desirable, since, as has been the experience abroad, it enables the services to be available irrespective of people's income. User charges are sometimes adopted because the state budget cannot support the services on a sustainable basis. However, as a result of the costs of collection and the reduction in use which they cause, user charges themselves do not always increase revenue and they introduce their own distortions into the operation of the services. Universal availability of schooling and health care is best ensured by financing them from the general state budget, and MERG does not propose that user charges should be a significant means of financing them.

The provision of housing to poor people can be met only if it is available to tenants on a low rent basis (instead of mortgage financed owner occupation). The ownership of these dwellings and the building programme may be in private or public hands, or under non-profit making trusts. Private development and ownership of low-income housing is not appropriate, since the rent subsidies that are required would create severe conflicts between tenant and landlord over who benefits from the subsidy, and in general, the private landlord would be unable to guarantee adequate maintenance or related community infrastructure. The state should be the main provider of low-income rented housing, and subsidy arrangements should be set up to ensure that the housing authority (such as the municipality) is supported from the central state budget. Non-profit trusts with the ability to obtain and manage foreign or domestic aid finance are likely to have an important complementary role, but they will be able to rent housing to low-income people only if a housing subsidy is paid to the trust or the tenant, and therefore the building programme of the trusts will have to be co-ordinated by state housing authorities.

The conditions that provide the framework for economic activities include not only social and economic infrastructure in the usual sense of housing, education, health care and related state provision. In South Africa a key determinant of people's living standards, bargaining power and economic opportunities is their access to land. The exclusion of black South Africans from most of the land of South Africa has left a legacy of problems, one of the most severe of which is rural poverty, especially among African women. MERG proposes that a democratic government takes urgent action to redistribute land to the benefit of adult female members of landless households in the rural homelands.

9.3 Efficiency and size of the state sector

The provision of new social infrastructure by the state (at various levels) is not the only direct economic activity of the public sector. The public sector includes state-owned enterprises which are engaged in a range of activities (nationalised industries), and also includes the economic activities of ministries and other public authorities (such as their purchase of materials, equipment, food and clothing).

The appropriate role of the state in these respects is often treated simply as a question of public ownership, with some advocating a policy of nationalisation and others a policy of privatisation. The approach proposed here (and in ANC documents on the subject) is different. The first difference is that the decision on whether an enterprise should be publicly or privately owned should be made on a case-by-case basis. The second is that regardless of whether they are privately or publicly owned, enterprises should be managed efficiently to meet well defined goals, so that it becomes essential to implement well designed management principles in the public sector.

State-owned enterprises are often thought to involve intrinsically inefficient management but throughout the world there are many examples of state-owned enterprises which have a strong record, comparable to the private sector, in terms of profit and innovation. Examples range from industries such as chemicals, vehicle manufacturing and other manufacturing sectors, to state-owned banks. Where state-owned enterprises have been unprofitable, one frequent reason has been that they have explicitly been given other economic or social objectives. Another reason has been the absence of clear, consistent objectives, with politicians enforcing particular policies for narrow or short-term political reasons. Whether or not state-owned enterprises can be efficient and become a strong element in transforming the South African economy depends partly on the existence of well designed management principles, just as the contribution of the private sector depends on the existence of good management.

MERG proposes the adoption of the management principles for state-owned enterprises which have been set out in World Bank publications over the past decade. These principles involve the operation of a clear system of responsibilities and accountability in which the enterprise has an identity separate from ministries and other political organs (Ramamurti and Vernon, 1991).

The management principles start from a clear definition of objectives, agreed between government and the enterprise. These objectives may be expressed in terms of profits, but an important reason for the enterprise remaining in the public sector would be that the profit objective would be different from the one it would have had in the private sector. For example, a sound developmental objective for some public enterprises might be long term profits, in contrast to the short term profits that many

South African private enterprises have to achieve. A profit objective for state-owned enterprises should be calculated before interest and net taxes (as in Korea). More generally, the technical measure for expressing the objectives of the state-owned enterprises should be 'public profitability' (or economic profitability), which takes account of the true economic costs to the nation of the resources used, unlike the private sector approach, which calculates costs as financial costs at market prices.

With clearly defined objectives, good management principles in state-owned enterprises will be founded on the principle that ministries do not interfere in management. Instead, a contract between the enterprise and the ministry will be negotiated and the adherence to it monitored and rewarded (or non-adherence penalised). The design of the system for South Africa should draw upon the experience of France, Korea, and other countries which have used, with varying degrees of success, a variety of such contracts, known as performance contracting, programme contracts, or signalling systems. An important aspect of the state-owned enterprises will be their investment programme and how it is financed.

For each enterprise, investment will be determined within the contracting system, but the size of the investment programme of the nationalised industries will be an important element in the economic strategy. It is envisaged that state investment will be financed in ways which reduce the possibility of financially crowding out private sector investment, and which maximise its complementarity with private investment (crowding in). The contracting system, with long term objectives, will prevent public investment from being varied as part of contra-cyclical macroeconomic demand management. The objective of economic growth does require fixed capital formation to rise considerably. Policies to encourage private sector investment will be an important part of the strategy, but it is envisaged that investment by state-owned enterprises will also increase. To the extent that efficient private sector investment in manufacturing, other industry, and agriculture does not grow, investment by state-owned enterprises will become increasingly important.

State-owned enterprises should be established to invest in sectors which are identified as key growth sectors for industrial strategy, and where private sector investment is inadequate. This is one criterion proposed for use in the case-by-case assessment of whether enterprises should be in public or private hands. Other criteria include the renationalisation of enterprises privatised by the present government, and a commitment not to nationalise the assets of foreign investors. In view of the capital flight that has occurred and may occur, special consideration must be given to the ownership of companies and groups which are historically South African, and which have transferred ownership of assets, abroad. MERG proposes that a democratic government should provide a firm guarantee that assets owned by foreign investors will not be nationalised.

The determination of the size of the state-owned enterprise sector on a case-by-case basis involves the consideration of whether or not a case exists for the privatisation of any existing public enterprises, as well as for nationalisation of any private enterprises. Several states have had large scale privatisation programmes in recent years, but, although the South African government has been reducing the public sector through privatisation, the extent of actual privatisation has been small. States with large programmes have often adopted them in order to raise finance, but this generally produces no net reduction in state liabilities, and should not be used as a criterion for privatisation in South Africa.

Considerations regarding the size of overall investment by ministries and other public authorities are similar to those regarding investment by state-owned enterprises. The efficient use of economic resources in the provision of services can be enhanced in a manner related to performance contracting, if the authorities responsible for provision of public services are given clearly defined objectives and budgetary plans with a system of monitoring, accountability and performance rewards or penalties.

A democratically elected government should appoint a commission to make recommendations on the size of the state-owned enterprise sector and on its efficient management. Its terms of reference should include: (a) evaluation of cases of private enterprises under consideration for nationalisation, and of state-owned enterprises under consideration for privatisation; and (b) evaluation of the policies and operation of the Industrial Development Corporation.

9.4 The state and markets

The role of the state in economic development is often presented as a question of a choice between two alternatives, the state versus the market. The MERG approach is that the state should work with markets instead of against them.

From the 'state versus markets' perspective, the MERG proposal that 'the state structures of South Africa must play a strong and active role in leading development' might appear to diminish the role of markets, and deny the significance of price adjustments and the forces of demand and supply. This is a false perspective. State leadership is inextricably linked to markets in several ways. State action and initiatives work through their effect on markets, and an important role for the South African state is to make markets work better.

The following paragraphs provide an outline of some key state policies that work through the effect they have on market forces (especially international trade policy). Policies for making markets work better are also presented.

International trade and industrial strategy

The objective of economic growth requires South Africa to establish a new place for itself in the world economy. This requires the restructuring of imports and exports. One central aspect of economic growth will be investment in specific manufacturing sectors in order to increase international competitiveness. The policies the next government can use to achieve such aims are measures which exert an influence by affecting the signals and incentives affecting market behaviour.

At the macroeconomic level, the market signal with the greatest effect on trade is the exchange rate. MERG recommends a policy of maintaining a stable real effective exchange rate with the range chosen to increase and maintain international competitiveness. Experience in other countries suggests that a rigid attempt to maintain a fixed nominal exchange rate which overvalues the real exchange rate in times of inflation, damages international competitiveness, involves state officials in an unceasing struggle against market forces, and ultimately weakens the state as well. On the other hand, the maintenance of a target real exchange rate involves working with market forces.

At the microeconomic level of trade policy, the principal means for influencing the direction of trade will be import tariffs and export subsidies, the effect of which is felt through their impact on market prices. As indicated in the chapter on industrial, trade, and corporate policy, the tariff system inherited from previous governments is irrational and fragmented, with undesirable effects on the competitive position of different industries. The MERG policy is to simplify and unify the system. This will involve a reduction of nominal and effective tariffs for many products, but the tariff and subsidy policy should be designed to protect particular industries in the process of transformation. In some cases, protection should be designed to enable growth industries to reach levels of international competitiveness; in others it should be adapted to ease the decline of industries and facilitate retraining and relocation of workers, instead of bringing about abrupt retrenchment. In either case, tariffs and subsidies should be combined with policies which directly assist industrial restructuring.

The tax system will play a key role in industrial restructuring. For example, investment allowances (accelerated depreciation write-offs) against profits taxes are intended to increase investment in particular sectors by augmenting market signals in terms of profitability. Similarly, a tax on luxury items (either as an excise duty or as a higher rate of VAT) can encourage manufacturers which supply the domestic market to switch resources towards more basic products for the mass market.

The prices thrown up by the market do not merely provide incentives. They also exert an influence on the distribution of income, and future policies on prices will have improved income distribution as an overriding objective as well as economic growth. The prices in some markets (such as the labour market) should have a floor set by the government. Legislation to enforce minimum wages above current market levels in some occupations, is a policy MERG endorses because of its direct impact on poverty alleviation.

Market structure

The role of the state involves more than influencing market signals through market interventions (such as exchange rate targeting), or through tariffs, taxes and subsidies. It also involves policies to improve the operation of markets and to stimulate the growth of new markets.

The South African economy is characterised by excessively fragmented and incomplete markets. The fragmented labour market resulting from apartheid policies is the most obvious case, and is paralleled by fragmentation in the markets for consumer goods, land, housing and capital. The new government will give priority to the development of unified national markets.

In the labour market, the state will play an important role (working with unions and employers) in the redefinition of skills and related training programmes, the removal of barriers and discrimination based on ethnicity and gender, the development of employment laws and centralised wage bargaining structures, and improved flows of information.

In the capital market (as proposed in the chapters on finance and industrial, corporate and trade policy), the new government should take steps to end the pyramid corporate structures which have contributed to the non-competitive concentration of capital and market power. It should create disincentives for speculative dealing, and introduce measures to improve the flow of information. Steps must also be taken to protect savers.

In foreign trade, the institutions responsible for trade policy, information and promotion, which are at present poorly organised and ineffective, should be restructured to strengthen South African trade.

The role of the state in improving the operation of markets also includes the regulation of market behaviour. One type of regulation is designed to influence the degree of monopoly power in the market (either to prevent unproductive monopolies or to protect elements of monopoly, as in the case of patent protection). Another may be to reduce external costs. Another, which is regarded as particularly important, is to enforce health and safety standards and to ensure the protection of basic employment rights in the labour market.

9.5 South Africa and regional co-operation between states

Relations within the southern African region will play an important role, and could contribute significantly to growth and development in South Africa. Changes in regional connections involve changes in the structure and character of the South African state, as they require fundamental changes in the state institutions hitherto run by Pretoria (especially the South African Customs Union and the Common Monetary Area), and new relations between the South African state and other regional organisations.

Trade relations with the region and the continent have grown in recent years and could increase even more rapidly after a democratic South Africa is accepted as a full and legitimate partner by the rest of the continent. The importance of this trade for growth and development, particularly in the industrial sector, is revealed by current statistics. Although exports to African countries (other than members of the Southern African Customs Union) made up only 8,8 per cent of total exports in 1992, over 70 per cent of these exports were products in seven categories consisting largely of manufactured goods (foodstuffs and beverages; chemical products; plastics and rubber products; articles of base metals; machinery and appliances; vehicles and related and miscellaneous manufactured goods). In some of these cases, exports to non-SACU African countries made up a sizeable portion of the total exports in the category concerned: 27 per cent of exports of foodstuffs and beverages; 26 per cent of chemical products; 46 per cent of plastics and rubber products; 11 per cent of products of base minerals; 43 per cent of machinery and appliances; 24 per cent of vehicles and 33 per cent of miscellaneous manufactures (Davies et al, 1993). Many of these figures would have been much larger if they had included exports to all African countries, including other SACU member countries who remain a captive market for South African manufacturers.

The prospects for growth and development in a democratic South Africa will be affected by regional growth. The southern African region is emerging from a period of violent conflict and economic stagnation. The impact of destabilisation policies directed by the apartheid regime against neighbouring countries in the late 1970s and 1980s is still being felt, not only in countries which were the direct victims of these assaults, but across the region. Increasing migration and arms- and drug-smuggling are just some of the forms in which crises in neighbouring countries — partly engendered by South African policies in the past — are boomeranging on South Africa. Continuing stagnation and crisis in neighbouring countries could exacerbate these trends. Under such a scenario, not only would opportunities for trade or co-operation be lost, but the possibilities for creating the kind of non-militarised and peaceful regional environment essential for growth and development in a democratic South Africa would be severely limited.

To realise the benefits which closer relations with the region could yield, a democratic South Africa will need to recognise that many existing relations between South Africa and its neighbours are not only widely perceived as inequitable but are also unsustainable. The historic pattern of trade has been described as one of selling overpriced goods for hard currency. South African visible exports into the region are more than five times the level of imports. Historically, this gap was partly financed by invisible earnings from the provision of services to South Africa (including migrant labour remittances, revenue from transport services and sales of hydropower). During the 1980s, however, many of these earnings declined, while at the same time the gap between the prices of increasingly uncompetitive South African goods and those of comparable goods from elsewhere widened.

These factors make it imperative for a democratic South Africa to work together with neighbouring countries to reconstruct regional relations on new lines. The formulation of a regional strategy will need to confront the critical question of whether or not a democratic South Africa should support a programme aimed at promoting greater economic integration in southern Africa, and if so, on what terms and principles this should be based. The issues cannot, as is sometimes supposed, be conceived in terms of a polarised choice between co-operation and integration. The challenge is to find that combination of co-operation, co-ordination and integration that is appropriate to the conditions of the region.

While a broad spectrum of regional and international interested parties have now come out in support of a programme aimed at promoting greater integration in the southern African region, different approaches and theories underlie the various proposals made.

On the one hand, there is powerful support for the neo-liberal approach to regional integration. Recent World Bank studies (World Bank, 1991) have sought to modify neo-classical customs union theory, by insisting that any evolution through the conventionally conceived arrangements (from preferential trade area, to free trade area, customs union, common market, etc) should not be accompanied by the erection of high common external tariffs, but on the contrary, should contribute to a lowering of tariffs towards external parties. Such approaches tend to place emphasis on the removal of barriers to the free movement of goods and capital through a process of 'mutual liberalisation'. They appear relatively indifferent to the danger of polarisation, and also tend to emphasise 'negative action' (the withdrawal from the use of certain policy instruments by individual states — conceived of in terms of removing barriers) rather than 'positive action' by strengthened regional organisations.

Other approaches focus on the need for a developmental approach to a regional programme. These emphasise the need for close political co-operation in the formulation and execution of a multi-sectoral programme, embracing elements of co-operation, co-ordination and integration. It is accepted that a regional programme cannot be inward-orientated if the fundamental challenge is to develop strategies to increase the value added to export products, and become more effective and competitive in world markets. However, advocates of this approach consider that the imbalances in the world economy and the acute potential for polarisation in southern Africa make it impossible to conceive of the integration component of a regional project exclusively in terms of removing constraints to trade. Positive action to develop new patterns of trade, develop infrastructure and influence industrial location, as well as compensatory and corrective mechanisms — to ensure that the burden of adjustment to the new integrated region does not fall disproportionately on working people and the poor — are seen as essential. A regional programme will flounder if it becomes a mechanism for weaker partners to place ever increasing demands on stronger partners. The principle of mutual benefit, long defended by regional organisations, is thus seen as the essential underpinning of a new regional programme. A further element, defended particularly in the call for social charters by trade-unions, is an insistence that minimum standards with regard to rights of workers to organise, be established across the region as a whole, so that a process of greater integration becomes one of levelling up rights and conditions of working people, rather than of levelling them down to the lowest prevailing standard.

The issues at stake in this debate on regional policy go to the very heart of the central concern of this chapter: the role of the state in the economy.

The neo-liberal prescriptions are clearly premised on a view which sees the state reducing its role. This approach has been described as 'negative integration', in the sense that its policy thrust is towards eliminating the use of certain policy instruments, mainly those related to trade policy.

While alternative developmental approaches assume a positive role for the state, the reality of many past and existing regional integration projects, particularly but not only those involving developing countries, have been premised on an exclusive involvement of states. All too often, this has involved weak commitments by weak states to weak regional organisations and programmes. There have been formal commitments by governments to regional organisations and programmes, which are contradicted in practice, and a low priority has been accorded to regional co-operation in national economic programmes.

Neither of the above corresponds to the projected needs of southern Africa in the years ahead. A regional programme needs to be driven by a strong positive commitment on the part of co-operating parties. It needs to consolidate statements of intent into a commitment that is both deeper (in the sense that it embraces a series of concrete actions in various sectors and areas) and wider (in the sense that it embraces a broader range of social forces and potential actors). This will not be achieved if the role of the state is seen merely as abandoning the use of certain instruments of international economic policy. It will require more effective positive action by individual states on agreed regional programmes, and a strengthening of regional organisation and programmes.

For these purposes, regional organisations and institutions should be restructured. There already exist several multi-lateral organisations aspiring to, or being promoted as, potential institutional bases for a future post-apartheid regional programme. They include South African centred and, indeed dominated, organisations such as the Southern African Customs Union (SACU) and the closely linked Common Monetary Area (CMA). There are also the organisations formed by other states of the region, most importantly the Southern African Development Community (SADC), and the eastern and southern African Preferential Trade Area (PTA). South Africa has, up to now, been excluded from these organisations and will be eligible to join only once a legitimate government is in place.

Each of these organisations has qualities, capacities and experiences that will need to be built upon in developing a programme of regional economic co-operation, co-ordination and integration. Each can be seen as corresponding to specific geographical or socio-economic entities that will be of great significance in promoting economic co-operation and integration. The SACU/CMA embraces a particular sub-set of countries, historically highly integrated with South Africa. The SADC represents a coherent group of countries, which together with South Africa and perhaps a few other countries (the Indian Ocean islands and southern Zaire), constitute the region of Southern Africa. The PTA draws together countries from more than one OAU defined region, which points towards moves towards greater continental economic unity.

This does not mean, however, that an adequate basis for a future regional programme can be conceived of as a mere sum of existing parts. In the first place, the SACU/CMA institutions need to be reformed, reorganised and democratised before they can serve as the basis for equitable relations among existing members. The current SACU arrangement is one in which South Africa has purchased access to a captive market in Botswana, Lesotho, Namibia and Swaziland (of considerable significance to its manufacturing industries), in return for a disproportionate allocation of customs and excise duties to the BLNS countries. This arrangement is now under increasing pressure from the present fiscal authorities in South Africa, who see it as becoming unaffordable. An increasingly influential opinion in some of the BLNS countries is that they would be better off free from the price-raising effects which the South African tariff regime imposes on them. Both the SACU and the CMA are effectively run by South Africa in its own interests, without provision for adequate consultation with other member countries when policy changes are made which affect their interests. On the other hand, the removal of the level of integration which has persisted for decades would probably not be desirable, either for South Africa or its neighbours. Any programme to reform and restructure the SACU/CMA would need to be located within a broader regional framework, which the SADC and the PTA would have a crucial role in shaping.

In the second place, at the broader regional level, there is a need to address and confront major problems in making existing organisations more effective, and a need to develop an appropriate institutional base for a regional programme. This is further complicated by growing institutional rivalry between the SADC and the PTA, now increasingly pursuing overlapping programmes.

The question of how to achieve some rationalisation of the activities of these two organisations, and how to advance the process of institutional development, will have to be faced. The two organisations will need to discuss issues such as the basis and priorities of a regional programme, the role of the southern African countries within the broader grouping, and how efforts by the two organisations can be made mutually reinforcing. A legitimate South Africa will need to contribute to this process, as a partner on the inside rather than as an outside party imposing conditions.

9.6 Conclusion

The strategy MERG proposes for economic growth, and the raising of the economic position of the majority, requires the state to have a strong role. MERG proposals amount to a strategy in which the state would provide leadership and co-ordination for widely-based economic development and intervene directly in key areas. In order to achieve its objective, state structures need to be changed in order to create a machinery of government which, in addition to being democratic with strong mechanisms of accountability and transparency, also serves the needs of a developmental state. The perspective of MERG is that the development state should be efficient and should not absorb a high level of resources for its own functioning. Unlike the present South African state, it should be a slim state and should include mechanisms which provide incentives for efficiency and monitoring performance.

MERG proposals envisage the state undertaking a large programme for increasing provision of education, training, housing, and health care; and organising the distribution of land rights to women in landless rural households. The government should stabilise the real exchange rate within a target zone. It should use the tax and excise system to provide incentives for productive investment. Taxes on imports (and export subsidies) should be rationalised and restructured to promote the development of specific industries, offering sufficient temporary protection to some sectors to enable them to reach internationally competitive levels of efficiency.

MERG proposes that the mechanisms and criteria for operating state-owned industries should be restructured to improve their efficiency, and that a commission should be established to evaluate the cases of selected enterprises where a change of ownership (from private to public ownership or vice versa) is proposed. The investment programmes of state-owned enterprises and other state enterprises should be set within totals which enable public sector investment to raise gross domestic investment. These programmes should be designed as part of a strategy in which private and public sector investment reinforce each other. The structure of ministries and agencies should be designed with the purpose of co-ordinating plans for investment and economic development.

The state should play an active role in the development of new regional structures in the Southern African region.

Δ

A P P E N D I X
MERG Model simulations

Table A.1   Employment

Year	White pot. labour force	Coloured pot. labour force	Asian pot. labour force	Black pot. labour force	Total pot. labour force	White employment	Coloured employment	Asian employment	Black employment	Total employ-ment (non-agric)
	Thousands					*Number*				*'000*
1990	2 321	1 345	373	9 380	13 418	1 334 540	668 953	199 905	2 342 030	5 414
1991	2 345	1 376	382	9 631	13 785	1 332 600	665 194	200 010	2 288 210	5 304
1992	2 377	1 407	390	9 991	14 168	1 312 118	649 887	194 966	2 288 399	5 199
1993	2 410	1 440	400	10 312	14 563	1 329 143	652 464	195 880	2 322 242	5 255
1994	2 443	1 474	409	10 643	14 970	1 354 131	660 498	197 526	2 360 185	5 333
1995	2 477	1 508	419	10 985	15 389	1 379 589	672 040	201 789	2 419 032	5 434
1996	2 401	1 535	427	11 358	15 812	1 394 488	687 362	206 592	2 571 117	5 628
1997	2 505	1 562	435	11 744	16 248	1 409 549	703 034	211 509	2 748 816	5 849
1998	2 520	1 590	443	12 144	16 698	1 424 772	718 940	216 543	2 935 459	6 079
1999	2 535	1 618	451	12 557	17 162	1 440 159	735 081	221 696	3 147 918	6 339
2000	2 549	1 647	460	12 984	17 641	1 455 713	751 841	226 973	3 386 097	6 626
2001	2 558	1 674	467	13 419	18 119	1 468 087	767 931	231 830	3 575 911	6 846
2002	2 567	1 701	475	13 868	18 613	1 480 565	784 364	236 791	3 788 381	7 095
2003	2 576	1 729	483	14 333	19 122	1 493 150	801 150	241 859	4 023 179	7 370
2004	2 585	1 758	491	14 813	19 648	1 505 842	818 294	247 034	4 261 886	7 648
Compound growth rate (%)										
'93-'99	*0.8*	*1.9*	*2.0*	*3.3*	*2.7*	*1.3*	*2.0*	*2.0*	*5.2*	*3.1*
'99-'04	*0.4*	*1.6*	*1.6*	*3.3*	*2.7*	*0.9*	*2.1*	*2.1*	*6.2*	*3.8*
'93-'04	*0.6*	*1.8*	*1.8*	*3.3*	*2.7*	*1.1*	*2.0*	*2.1*	*5.6*	*3.4*
Var'ble	*Y (465)*	*Y (466)*	*Y (467)*	*Y (468)*	*Y (469)*	*Y (222)*	*Y (452)*	*Y (453)*	*Y (454)*	*Y (455)*

Note: These simulations are based on government racial classifications. In this system, the category 'black' refers to African people
Source: MERG Macroeconomic Model

Table A.2 Expenditure on education and health

Year	Total exp.: private education	Public current exp.	Total exp.: education	Medical services	Public current health exp.	Current transfer to households	Total exp.: health	Total exp: health & education	Ratio of private community serv. exp. to total
	1985 Rand (million)					*R (m)*	*1985 Rand (million)*		
1990	909	6 897	7 806	2 395	3 323	8 523	5 718	13 524	24
1991	961	7 03	7 991	2 390	3 432	9 624	5 822	13 813	24
1992	1 070	7 300	8 370	2 253	3 500	11 271	5 735	14 123	23
1993	1 056	7533	8 589	2 351	3 544	13 661	5 896	14 486	23
1994	1 110	7 805	8 915	2 421	3 672	15 543	6 094	15 009	23
1995	1 263	8 186	9 449	2 544	3 852	17 546	6 396	15 846	24
1996	1 448	8 649	10 097	2 686	4 070	19 853	6 756	16 854	24
1997	1 643	9 119	10 763	2 833	4 291	22 279	7 125	17 888	25
1998	1 849	9 596	11 445	2 987	4 515	24 902	7 503	18 949	25
1999	2 067	10 078	12 146	3 148	4 743	27 980	7 891	20 037	26
2000	2 296	10 568	12 865	3 315	4 973	31 384	8 288	21 153	26
2001	2 538	11 064	13 603	1 488	5 206	36 256	8 695	22 299	27
2002	2 768	11 592	14 360	3 707	5 455	41 931	9 163	23 523	27
2003	2 984	12 102	15 087	3 946	5 695	48 542	9 642	24 730	28
2004	3 214	12 620	15 834	4 194	5 938	56 058	10 133	25 967	28
	Compound growth rate (%)								
'93-'99	11.8	4.9	5.9	4.9	4.9	12.6	4.9	5.5	1.7
'99-'04	9.2	4.0	5.4	5.9	4.0	14.9	5.1	5.3	1.8
'93-'04	10.6	4.8	5.7	5.4	4.8	13.6	5.0	5.4	1.7
Variable	Y (545)	Y (492)	Y (544)	Y (211)	Y (491)	Y (547)	Y (543)	Y (546)	E (37)

Source: MERG Macroeconomic Model

Table A.3   Housing and infrastructure investment

Year	Total number of households	Formal housing stock	Public authority expenditure on housing	Total resid. investment	Formal houses completed	Housing electricity connections	Fixed capital stock: elec., gas, water
	('000)			1985 R(m)		('000)	1985 R(m)
1990	6 396	2 922	422	3 144	42	2922	37 216
1991	6 557	2 964	461	2 952	37	2 964	35 883
1992	6 714	3 000	467	2 852	36	3 000	34 011
1993	6 881	3 038	372	3 897	38	3 258	34 041
1994	7 053	3 080	498	4 298	42	3 550	34 263
1995	7 230	3 181	726	4 930	101	3 969	34 614
1996	7 411	3 327	1 290	5 738	146	4 439	37 434
1997	7 588	3 519	1 710	6 670	191	4 957	40 440
1998	7 771	3 769	2 340	7 614	250	5 533	43 674
1999	7 957	4 046	2 580	8 110	277	6 130	46 922
2000	8 148	4 377	3 060	8 977	331	6 774	50 320
2001	8 335	4 716	3 060	9 359	338	7 414	53 605
2002	8 527	5 045	3 060	9 292	329	8 034	56 700
2003	8 723	5 380	3 060	9 596	334	8 647	59 695
2004	8 924	5 722	3 060	9 991	342	9 257	62 613
Percentage changes							
1990	2.4	1.6	-10.7	-8.6	-9.6	1.6	-2.4
1991	2.5	1.4	9.2	-6.11	-11.8	1.4	-3.5
1992	2.3	1.2	1.3	-3.39	-1.6	1.2	-5.2
1993	2.5	1.2	-20.3	36.6	4.1	8.6	0.0
1994	2.5	1.3	33.8	10.2	10.5	8.9	0.6
1995	2.5	3.3	45.7	14.6	142.2	11.8	1.0
1996	2.5	4.5	77.6	16.3	40.6	11.8	8.1
1997	2.4	5.7	32.5	16.2	30.7	11.6	8.0
1998	2.4	7.1	36.8	14.1	30.9	11.6	8.0
1999	2.4	7.3	10.2	6.5	10.7	10.7	7.4
2000	2.4	8.1	18.6	10.6	19.4	10.5	7.2
2001	2.3	7.7	0.0	4.2	2.3	9.4	6.5
2002	2.3	6.3	0.0	-0.7	-2.7	8.3	5.7
2003	2.3	6.6	0.0	3.2	1.4	7.6	5.2
2004	2.3	6.3	0.0	4.1	2.4	7.0	4.8

Compound growth rate (%)						
1993-'99	2.4	4.8	38.1	12.9	39.2	11.1	5.4
1999-'04	2.3	7.1	3.4	4.2	4.3	8.5	5.9
1993-'04	2.3	5.9	21.1	8.9	22.1	9.9	5.7
Variable	Y (246)	Y (245)	Y (244)	Y (231)	Y (247)	Y (248)	Y (404)

Source: MERG Macroeconomic Model

Table A.4   Capacity formation

Year	Labour productivity number-based	Labour productivity skill-based	Capital productivity	Total factor productivity	Total capital stock excl. housing	Total utilisation rate	Total capacity output Rm
	Ratio			1985 Rand (million) %			
1990	21.4	39.2	0.3	1.01	329 026	92.13	130 336
1991	21.6	38.6	0.3	1.00	329 738	90.04	133 396
1992	21.6	38.6	0.3	1.00	329 746	87.91	133 459
1993	22.0	39.2	0.3	1.01	327 206	91.08	135 523
1994	22.1	39.3	0.4	1.02	329 240	91.43	137 572
1995	22.2	39.3	0.4	1.03	332 667	91.50	140 731
1996	22.1	39.5	0.4	1.05	341 242	92.13	144 712
1997	21.8	39.4	0.4	1.06	347 882	90.95	151 181
1998	21.7	39.4	0.4	1.07	355 452	90.78	156 705
1999	21.5	39.5	0.4	1.08	364 549	90.45	163 332
2000	21.3	39.6	0.4	1.09	374 177	89.72	171 060
2001	21.3	39.6	0.4	1.09	384 257	90.78	175 602
2002	21.4	39.8	0.4	1.09	400 900	92.75	179 762
2003	21.4	39.9	0.4	1.09	420 727	93.03	187 246
2004	21.5	40.0	0.4	1.09	442 471	92.64	196 589
	Percentage changes						
1990	0.0	-1.5	-3.1	-2.2	1.2	1.8	-2.7
1991	1.1	-1.3	1.0	-0.3	0.2	-2.2	2.3
1992	-0.1	-0.1	0.4	0.1	0.0	-2.3	0.0
1993	1.7	1.4	-0.6	0.5	-0.7	3.6	1.5
1994	0.6	0.2	2.7	1.3	0.6	0.3	1.5
1995	0.2	0.0	2.2	0.9	1.0	0.0	2.3
1996	-0.2	0.5	2.7	1.4	2.5	0.6	2.8
1997	-1.2	-0.3	2.7	0.9	1.9	-1.2	4.4
1998	-0.8	0.1	1.8	0.8	2.1	-0.1	3.6
1999	-0.7	0.2	1.9	0.9	2.5	-0.3	4.2
2000	-0.9	0.1	1.9	0.8	2.6	-0.8	4.7
2001	0.0	0.0	-0.2	-0.0	2.6	1.1	2.6
2002	0.5	0.5	-0.4	0.1	4.3	2.1	2.3
2003	0.1	0.1	-0.4	-0.0	4.9	0.3	4.1
2004	0.3	0.2	-0.2	0.0	5.1	-0.4	4.9

Compound growth rate (%)						
1993-'99	-0.3	0.1	2.3	1.0	1.8	-0.1	3.1
1999-'04	0.0	0.2	0.1	0.1	3.9	0.4	3.7
1993-'04	-0.1	0.1	1.3	0.6	2.7	0.1	3.4
Variable	Y (475)	Y (476)	Y (477)	Y (478)	Y (441)	Y (440)	Y (430)

Source: MERG Macroeconomic Model

Table A.5 Formation of gross domestic product

Year	Total private consumption expenditure	Consumption expend. by general govt.	Total fixed investment	Total change in inventories	Exports of goods and non-factor services	Imports of goods and non-factor services	Expenditure on GDP
			1985 Rand (million)				
1990	75 319	24 025	25 961	-3 141	43 999	33 938	132 405
1991	76 282	25 694	23 573	-2 596	43 983	33 744	132 890
1992	74 499	25 780	21 240	-1 279	44 429	35 584	130128
1993	75 616	26 058	20 945	-101	45 653	36 834	131 337
1994	76 984	26 458	23 307	-20	46 964	39 115	134 579
1995	77 942	27 018	25 465	145	48 275	40 644	138 203
1996	77 819	27 700	31 645	850	49 750	44 665	143 100
1997	81 660	28 391	31 291	944	51 080	45 028	148 339
1998	84 449	29 091	33 694	1 038	52 528	46 918	153 884
1999	87 640	30 026	36 307	2 053	54 085	50 144	159968
2000	92 593	30 974	38 384	2 007	55 655	52 781	166 834
2001	97 816	31 936	39 878	2 018	57 684	55 538	173 795
2002	100 521	32 947	47 032	3 422	59 989	62 402	181 510
2003	106 812	34 095	51 532	3 262	62 915	68 281	190 336
2004	113 802	35 263	55 067	3 210	65 948	73 709	199 582
			Compound growth rate (%)				
1993-'99	2.49	2.39	9.60	64.99	2.87	5.28	3.34
1999-'04	5.36	3.27	8.69	9.35	4.05	8.01	4.52
1993-'04	3.79	2.79	9.19	36.85	3.40	6.51	3.88
Variable	Y (217)	Y (484)	Y (485)	Y (240)	Y (482)	Y (483)	Y (481)

Source: MERG Macroeconomic model

Table A.6 Fixed investment

Year	Total residential investment	Total non-res. building investment	Total constr. works investment	Total transport equip.ment. investment	Total non-transport equipment investment	Total fixed investment
			1985 Rand (million)			
1990	3 144	4 325	4 809	2 581	10 291	25 961
1991	2 952	3 671	3 778	2 869	9 543	23 573
1992	2 852	3 261	3 347	2 213	8 721	21 240
1993	3 897	2 815	3 577	2 020	8 633	20 945
1994	4 298	2 988	3 955	2 303	9 762	23 307
1995	4 930	3 217	4 379	2 526	10 411	25 465
1996	5 738	3 418	5 717	3 339	13 432	31 645
1997	6 670	3 515	6 257	3 141	11 707	31 291
1998	7 614	3 740	6 588	3 366	12 386	33 694
1999	8 110	4 111	7 003	3 696	13 385	36 307
2000	8 977	4 309	7 396	3 887	13 813	38 384
2001	9 359	4 518	7 612	4 064	14 323	39 878
2002	9 292	5 975	8 799	5 244	17 720	47 032
2003	9 596	6 791	9 442	5 951	19 749	51 532
2004	9 991	7 430	9 934	6 490	21 220	55 067
			Compound growth rate (%)			
1993-'99	12.9	6.5	11.8	10.5	7.5	9.6
1999-'04	4.2	12.5	7.2	11.9	9.6	8.6
1993-'04	8.9	9.2	9.7	11.1	8.5	9.1
Variable	Y (231)	Y (232)	Y (233)	Y (234)	Y (235)	Y (485)

Source: MERG Macroeconomic Model

Table A.7 Estimate of the effects of phased increase in tax revenue, 1993 to 2003

	1993			1994		
	Revenue (Rm)	Share total (%)	Share GDP (%)	Revenue (Rm)	Share total (%)	Share GDP (%)
Companies (inc. mining)	12 402	13.95	3.74	12 676	13.64	3.75
Individuals	37 627	42.33	11.36	38 536	41.45	11.40
VAT	24 858	27.96	7.50	25 353	27.27	7.50
Non-resident shareholders	275	0.31	0.08	281	0.30	0.08
Capital transfer taxes	93	0.10	0.03	169	0.18	0.05
Capital gains tax	0	0.00	0.00	0	0.00	0.00
Marketable securities tax	165	0.19	0.05	168	0.18	0.05
Levy on financial services	365	0.41	0.11	507	0.55	0.15
Duty and fees	1 806	2.03	0.55	1 842	1.98	0.55
Leases and levies	191	0.21	0.06	195	0.21	0.06
Interest and dividends	195	0.22	0.06	199	0.21	0.06
Other revenues (net TBVC, SGT)	-834	-0.94	-0.25	-851	-0.92	-0.25
Total: inland revenue	77 143	86.78	23.28	79 075	85.06	23.39
Customs duty	3 132	3.52	0.95	3 195	3.44	0.95
Surcharge on imports	1 635	1.84	0.49	1 668	1.79	0.49
Excise duty	4 856	5.46	1.47	6 655	7.16	1.97
Fuel levy	7 633	8.59	2.30	8 451	9.09	2.50
Miscell. (net Customs Union)	-5 504	-6.19	-1.66	-6 085	-6.55	-1.80
Total: customs and excise	11 752	13.22	3.55	13 884	14.94	4.11
Grand total: all revenue	88 895	100.00	26.83	92 960	100.00	27.50
GDP	331 342			338 036		
GDP Growth rate (%)				2		

Table A.7 continued

	1995			1996		
	Revenue (Rm)	Share total (%)	Share GDP (%)	Revenue (Rm)	Share total (%)	Share GDP (%)
Companies (inc. mining)	13 062	13.39	3.75	13 5595	13.16	3.75
Individuals	39 710	40.71	11.40	39 880	38.60	11.00
VAT	26 125	26.79	7.50	27 191	26.32	7.50
Non-resident shareholders	289	0.30	0.08	301	0.29	0.08
Capital transfer taxes	348	0.36	0.10	544	0.53	0.15
Capital gains tax	1 045	1.07	0.30	1 813	1.75	0.50
Marketable securities tax	348	0.36	0.10	363	0.35	0.10
Levy on financial services	522	0.54	0.15	544	0.53	0.15
Duty and fees	1 916	1.96	0.55	1 994	1.93	0.55
Leases and levies	201	0.21	0.06	209	0.20	0.06
Interest and dividends	205	0.21	0.06	213	0.21	0.06
Other revenues (net TBVC, SGT)	0	0.00	0.00	1 813	1.75	0.50
Total: inland revenue	83 772	85.89	24.05	88 459	85.61	24.40
Customs duty	2 787	2.86	0.80	2 719	2.63	0.75
Surcharge on imports	1 707	1.75	0.49	1 776	1.72	0.49
Excise duty	7 526	7.72	2.16	8 558	8.28	2.36
Fuel levy	8 708	8.93	2.50	9 064	8.77	2.50
Miscell. (net Customs Union)	-6 967	-7.14	-2.00	-7 251	-7.02	-2.00
Total: customs and excise	13 761	14.11	3.95	14 866	14.39	4.10
Grand total: all revenue	97 532	100.00	28.00	103 326	100.00	28.50
GDP	348 330			362 546		
GDP Growth rate (%)	3			4		

Table A.7 continued						
	1997			1998		
	Revenue (Rm)	Share total (%)	Share GDP (%)	Revenue (Rm)	Share total (%)	Share GDP (%)
Companies (inc. mining)	14 293	12.93	3.75	15 025	12.71	3.75
Individuals	400 19	36.21	10.50	40 068	33.90	10.00
VAT	30 491	27.59	8.00	34 057	28.81	8.50
Non-resident shareholders	316	0.29	0.08	333	0.28	0.08
Capital transfer taxes	572	0.52	0.15	601	0.51	0.15
Capital gains tax	2 668	2.41	0.70	3 205	2.71	0.80
Marketable securities tax	381	0.34	0.10	401	0.34	0.10
Levy on financial services	572	0.52	0.15	601	0.51	0.15
Duty and fees	2 096	1.90	0.55	2 204	1.86	0.55
Leases and levies	220	0.20	0.06	231	0.20	0.06
Interest and dividends	224	0.20	0.06	236	0.20	0.06
Other revenues (net TBVC, SGT)	2 859	2.59	0.75	4 007	3.39	1.00
Total: inland revenue	94 710	85.69	24.85	100 968	85.42	25.20
Customs duty	2 668	2.41	0.70	2 805	2.37	0.70
Surcharge on imports	1 715	1.55	0.45	1 603	1.36	0.40
Excise duty	9 530	8.62	2.50	10 420	8.82	2.60
Fuel levy	9 528	8.62	2.50	10 418	8.81	2.60
Miscell. (net Customs Union)	-7 623	-6.90	-2.00	-8 014	-6.78	-2.00
Total: customs and excise	15 819	14.31	4.15	17 231	14.58	4.30
Grand total: all revenue	110 529	100.00	29.00	118 199	100.00	29.50
GDP	381 134			400 675		
GDP Growth rate (%)	5			5		

Table A.7 continued

	1999			2000		
	Revenue (Rm)	Share total (%)	Share GDP (%)	Revenue (Rm)	Share total (%)	Share GDP (%)
Companies (inc. mining)	15 796	12.50	3.75	16 606	12.30	3.75
Individuals	40 016	31.67	9.50	39 853	29.51	9.00
VAT	37 910	30.00	9.00	39 853	29.51	9.00
Non-resident shareholders	350	0.28	0.08	368	0.27	0.15
Capital transfer taxes	632	0.50	0.15	664	0.49	0.05
Capital gains tax	3 791	3.00	0.90	4 428	3.28	1.00
Marketable securities tax	421	0.33	0.10	443	0.33	0.10
Levy on financial services	632	0.50	0.15	664	0.49	0.15
Duty and fees	2 527	2.00	0.90	2 857	1.97	0.60
Leases and levies	243	0.19	0.06	255	0.19	0.06
Interest and dividends	248	0.20	0.06	261	0.19	0.06
Other revenues (net TBVC, SGT)	5 265	4.17	1.25	6 642	4.92	1.50
Total: inland revenue	107 830	85.33	25.60	112 694	83.44	25.45
Customs duty	2 949	2.33	0.70	2 878	2.13	0.65
Surcharge on imports	1 559	1.23	0.37	1 550	1.15	0.35
Excise duty	11 080	8.77	2.63	14 394	10.66	3.25
Fuel levy	11 373	9.00	2.70	12 399	9.18	2.80
Miscell. (net Customs Union)	-8 424	-6.67	-2.00	-8 856	-6.56	-2.00
Total: customs and excise	18 536	14.67	4.40	22 364	16.56	5.05
Grand total: all revenue	126 365	100.00	30.00	135 058	100.00	30.50
GDP	421 218			442 815		
GDP Growth rate (%)	5			5		

Table A.7 continued	2001			2002		
	Revenue (Rm)	*Share total (%)*	*Share GDP (%)*	*Revenue (Rm)*	*Share total (%)*	*Share GDP (%)*
Companies (inc. mining)	17 457	12.10	3.75	18 352	11.90	3.75
Individuals	41 897	29.03	9.00	44 045	28.57	9.00
VAT	41 897	29.03	9.00	44 045	28.57	9.00
Non-resident shareholders	386	0.27	0.08	406	0.26	0.08
Capital transfer taxes	698	0.48	0.15	734	0.48	0.15
Capital gains tax	4 655	3.23	1.00	4 894	3.17	1.00
Marketable securities tax	466	0.32	0.10	489	0.32	0.10
Levy on financial services	698	0.48	0.15	734	0.48	0.15
Duty and fees	3 026	2.10	0.65	3 181	2.06	0.65
Leases and levies	268	0.19	0.06	282	0.18	0.06
Interest and dividends	274	0.19	0.06	288	0.19	0.06
Other revenues (net TBVC, SGT)	8 147	5.65	1.75	9 788	6.35	2.00
Total: inland revenue	119 869	83.06	25.75	127 238	82.54	26.00
Customs duty	2 793	1.94	0.60	2 692	1.75	0.55
Surcharge on imports	1 536	1.06	0.33	1 468	0.95	0.30
Excise duty	15 923	11.03	3.42	17 865	11.59	3.65
Fuel levy	13 500	9.35	2.90	14 682	9.52	3.00
Miscell. (net Customs Union)	-9 310	-6.45	-2.00	-9 788	-6.35	-2.00
Total: customs and excise	24 442	16.94	5.25	26 919	17.46	5.50
Grand total: all revenue	144 311	100.00	31.00	154 157	100.00	31.50
GDP	465 518			489 386		
GDP Growth rate (%)	5			5		

Table A.7 continued

	2003		
	Revenue (Rm)	Share total (%)	Share GDP (%)
Companies (inc. mining)	19 293	11.72	3.75
Individuals	46 303	28.13	9.00
VAT	46 303	28.13	9.00
Non-resident shareholders	427	0.26	0.08
Capital transfer taxes	772	0.47	0.15
Capital gains tax	5 145	3.13	1.00
Marketable securities tax	514	0.31	0.10
Levy on financial services	772	0.47	0.15
Duty and fees	3 344	2.03	0.65
Leases and levies	297	0.18	0.06
Interest and dividends	303	0.18	0.06
Other revenues (net TBVC, SGT)	11 576	7.03	2.25
Total: inland revenue	135 048	82.03	26.25
Customs duty	2 572	1.56	0.50
Surcharge on imports	1 543	0.94	0.30
Excise duty	19 810	12.03	3.85
Fuel levy	15 949	9.69	3.10
Miscell. (net Customs Union)	-10 290	-6.25	-2.00
Total: customs and excise	29 585	17.97	5.75
Grand total: all revenue	164 633	100.00	32.00
GDP	514 477		
GDP Growth rate (%)	5		

Source: **MERG simulations**

Table A.8   MERG Fiscal Model Simulations

Year	GDP (Y)	Revenue (T)	Expenditure (excl. int.)	Interest (I)	Total expend. (E)	Long int. rate
	Million Rands					Real %
1993	331 342	88 895	104 976	22 150	127 126	5.83
1994	371 766	102 236	119 804	19 831	139 635	3.09
1995	421 211	117 939	136 726	23 991	160 718	2.00
1996	481 865	139 741	156 039	28 906	184 945	2.00
1997	556 554	164 183	178 079	34 104	212 183	2.00
1998	642 820	192 846	203 233	39 565	242 797	2.00
1999	742 457	226 449	231 940	45 309	277 248	2.00
2000	857 538	265 837	264 701	51 096	315 797	2.00
2001	990 456	311 994	302 090	56 628	358 718	2.00
2002	1 143 977	366 073	344 760	61 579	406 339	2.00
2003	1 321 293	429 420	393 458	65 589	459 047	2.00

Year	Inflation Rate	Y growth	E growth	T/Y	D/Y	I/Y	I/E	E/Y
		Real %		%				
1993	10.00	-1.00	-5.11	26.83	44.12	6.68	21.10	38.37
1994	10.00	2.00	3.75	27.50	49.87	5.33	16.55	37.56
1995	10.00	3.00	3.75	28.00	53.97	5.70	17.56	38.16
1996	10.00	4.00	3.75	29.00	56.36	6.00	18.54	38.38
1997	10.00	5.00	3.75	29.50	57.22	6.13	19.17	38.12
1998	10.00	5.00	3.75	30.00	57.21	6.16	19.48	37.77
1999	10.00	5.00	3.75	30.50	56.38	6.11	19.55	37.34
2000	10.00	5.00	3.75	31.00	54.64	5.96	19.32	36.83
2001	10.00	5.00	3.75	31.50	52.03	5.72	18.76	36.22
2002	10.00	5.00	3.75	32.00	48.57	5.39	17.88	35.52
2003	10.00	5.00	3.75	32.50	44.29	4.97	16.68	34.74

Source: MERG simulations

Table A.9   MERG Fiscal Model Simulations

Year	GDP (Y)	Revenue (T)	Expenditure (excl. int.)	Interest (I)	Total expend. (E)	Long int. rate
	Million Rands					Real %
1993	331 342.00	88 895.00	104 976.00	22 150.00	127 126.00	5.83
1994	371 765.72	102 235.57	121 247.28	19 830.62	141 077.90	3.09
1995	421 210.57	117 938.96	140 040.61	23 996.92	164 037.53	2.00
1996	481 864.89	139 740.82	161 746.90	28 912.02	190 658.92	2.00
1997	556 553.94	164 183.41	178 079.00	34 110.69	220 928.36	2.00
1998	642 819.81	192 845.94	203 233.00	39 572.32	255 346.74	2.00
1999	742 456.88	226 449.35	231 940.00	45 317.62	294 537.06	2.00
2000	857 537.69	265 836.68	264 701.00	51 106.01	338 954.47	2.00
2001	990 456.03	311 993.65	302 090.00	56 639.01	389 103.98	2.00
2002	1 143 976.72	366 073.55	344 760.00	61 591.10	445 588.14	2.00
2003	1 321 293.11	429 420.26	393 458.00	65 603.31	509 119.89	2.00

Year	Inflation	Y growth	E growth	T/Y	D/Y	I/Y	I/E	E/Y
	Rate	Real %				%		
1993	10.00	-1.00	-5.11	26.83	44.12	6.68	21.10	38.37
1994	10.00	2.00	5.00	27.50	50.31	5.33	16.36	37.95
1995	10.00	3.00	5.00	28.00	55.24	5.70	17.14	38.94
1996	10.00	4.00	5.00	29.00	58.86	6.00	17.87	39.57
1997	10.00	5.00	5.00	29.50	61.31	6.13	18.26	39.70
1998	10.00	5.00	5.00	30.00	63.26	6.16	18.34	39.72
1999	10.00	5.00	5.00	30.50	64.72	6.11	18.18	39.67
2000	10.00	5.00	5.00	31.00	65.61	5.96	17.75	39.53
2001	10.00	5.00	5.00	31.50	65.93	5.72	17.04	39.29
2002	10.00	5.00	5.00	32.00	65.71	5.39	16.04	38.95
2003	10.00	5.00	5.00	32.50	64.97	4.97	14.79	38.53

Source: MERG simulations

Table A.10   MERG Fiscal Model Simulations

Year	GDP (Y)	Revenue (T)	Expenditure (excl. int.)	Interest (I)	Total expend. (E)	Long int. rate
	Million Rands					Real %
1993	331 342	88 895	104 976	22 150	127 126	5.83
1994	371 766	102 236	121 247	19 928	141 175	6.00
1995	421 211	117 939	140 041	24 389	164 430	6.00
1996	481 865	139 741	161 747	29 904	191 651	6.00
1997	556 554	164 183	186 818	36 106	222 924	6.00
1998	642 820	192 846	215 774	43 111	258 886	6.00
1999	742 457	226 449	249 219	51 110	300 330	6.00
2000	857 538	265 837	287 848	60 075	347 923	6.00
2001	990 456	311 994	332 465	69 970	402 435	6.00
2002	1 143 977	366 073	383 997	80 800	464 797	6.00
2003	1 321 293	429 420	443 517	92 609	536 125	6.00

Year	Inflation Rate	Y growth	E growth	T/Y	D/Y	I/Y	I/E	E/Y
		Real %		%				
1993	10.00	-1.00	-5.11	26.83	44.12	6.68	21.10	38.37
1994	10.00	2.00	5.00	27.50	53.94	5.36	16.66	37.97
1995	10.00	3.00	5.00	28.00	59.13	5.79	17.42	39.04
1996	10.00	4.00	5.00	29.00	63.43	6.21	18.49	39.77
1997	10.00	5.00	5.00	29.50	66.92	6.49	19.33	40.05
1998	10.00	5.00	5.00	30.00	70.26	6.71	19.98	40.27
1999	10.00	5.00	5.00	30.50	73.35	6.88	20.51	40.45
2000	10.00	5.00	5.00	31.00	76.05	7.01	20.87	40.57
2001	10.00	5.00	5.00	31.50	78.35	7.06	21.05	40.63
2002	10.00	5.00	5.00	32.00	80.25	7.06	21.04	40.63
2003	10.00	5.00	5.00	32.50	81.70	7.01	20.88	40.58

Source: MERG simulations

Table A.11   MERG Fiscal Model Simulations

Year	GDP (Y)	Revenue (T)	Expenditure (excl. int.)	Interest (I)	Total expend. (E)	Long int. rate
			Million Rands			Real %
1993	331 342.00	88 895.00	104 976.00	22 150.00	127 126.00	5.83
1994	368 120.96	101 233.26	121 247.28	21 064.20	142 311.48	5.00
1995	413 031.72	115 648.88	140 040.61	31 006.02	171 046.63	6.00
1996	467 964.94	135 709.83	161 746.90	45 566.40	207 313.31	6.00
1997	530 204.27	156 410.26	186 817.67	66 601.90	253 419.57	6.00
1998	600 721.44	180 216.43	215 774.41	94 815.82	310 590.23	6.00
1999	680 617.40	207 588.31	249 219.45	131 552.00	380 771.44	6.00
2000	771 139.51	239 053.25	287 848.46	180 749.29	468 597.75	6.00
2001	873 701.06	275 215.84	332 464.97	246 904.44	579 369.41	6.00
2002	989 903.31	316 769.06	383 997.04	335 419.41	719 416.45	6.00
2003	1 121 560.44	364 507.14	443 416.58	451 795.38	895 311.96	6.00

Year	Inflation Rate	Y growth	E growth	T/Y	D/Y	I/Y	I/E	E/Y
		Real %				%		
1993	10.00	-1.00	-5.11	26.83	44.12	6.68	21.10	38.37
1994	10.00	1.00	5.00	27.50	51.21	5.72	17.37	38.66
1995	10.00	2.00	5.00	28.00	58.52	7.51	22.14	41.41
1996	10.00	3.00	5.00	29.00	65.31	9.74	28.17	44.30
1997	10.00	3.00	5.00	29.50	72.62	12.56	35.65	47.80
1998	10.00	3.00	5.00	30.00	80.60	15.78	43.94	51.70
1999	10.00	3.00	5.00	30.50	89.20	19.33	52.79	55.95
2000	10.00	3.00	5.00	31.00	98.32	23.44	62.79	60.77
2001	10.00	3.00	5.00	31.50	108.01	28.26	74.26	66.31
2002	10.00	3.00	5.00	32.00	118.30	33.88	87.35	72.68
2003	10.00	3.00	5.00	32.50	129.19	40.28	101.87	79.83

Source: MERG simulations

Table A.12 MERG Fiscal Model Simulations

Year	GDP (Y)	Revenue (T)	Expenditure (excl. int.)	Interest (I)	Total expend. (E)	Long int. rate
	Million Rands					Real %
1993	331 342.00	88 895.00	104 976.00	22 150.00	127 126.00	5.83
1994	368 120.96	101 233.26	121 247.28	20 502.09	141 749.37	5.00
1995	413 031.72	115 648.88	140 040.61	27 057.35	167 097.96	5.00
1996	467 964.94	135 709.83	161 746.90	35 214.40	196 961.30	5.00
1997	530 204.27	156 410.26	186 817.67	45 089.81	231 907.48	5.00
1998	600 721.44	198 238.08	211 644.42	51 586.60	263 251.02	2.00
1999	680 617.40	238 216.09	239 815.79	58 744.55	298 560.34	2.00
2000	771 139.51	285 321.62	271 711.29	65 168.15	336 879.44	2.00
2001	873 701.06	340 743.41	307 848.89	70 247.70	378 096.59	2.00
2002	989 903.31	395 961.32	348 792.80	73 878.84	422 671.64	2.00
2003	1 121 560.44	448 624.18	395 182.24	76 751.18	471 933.42	2.00

Year	Inflation Rate	Y growth	E growth	T/Y	D/Y	I/Y	I/E	E/Y
		Real %				%		
1993	10.00	-1.00	-5.11	26.83	44.12	6.68	21.10	38.37
1994	10.00	1.00	5.00	27.50	51.21	5.57	16.91	38.51
1995	10.00	2.00	5.00	28.00	57.90	6.55	19.32	40.46
1996	10.00	3.00	5.00	29.00	63.99	7.53	21.77	42.09
1997	10.00	3.00	5.00	29.50	70.52	8.50	24.14	43.74
1998	10.00	3.00	3.00	33.00	72.97	8.59	24.37	43.82
1999	10.00	3.00	3.00	35.00	73.27	8.63	24.50	43.87
2000	10.00	3.00	3.00	37.00	71.35	8.45	23.98	43.69
2001	10.00	3.00	3.00	39.50	67.25	8.04	22.82	43.28
2002	10.00	3.00	3.00	40.00	62.06	7.46	21.18	42.70
2003	10.00	3.00	3.00	40.00	56.85	6.84	19.42	42.08

Source: MERG simulations

Table A.13   MERG Fiscal Model Simulations

Year	GDP (Y)	Revenue (T)	Expenditure (excl. int.)	Interest (I)	Total Expend. (E)	Long int. rate
	Million Rands					Real %
1993	331 342.00	88 895.00	104 976.00	22 150.00	127 126.00	5.83
1994	368 120.96	101 233.26	121 247.28	20 502.09	141 749.37	5.00
1995	413 031.72	115 648.88	140 040.61	27 057.35	167 097.96	5.00
1996	467 964.94	135 709.83	161 746.90	35 214.40	196 961.30	5.00
1997	530 204.27	156 410.26	186 917.67	45 089.81	231 907.48	5.00
1998	600 721.44	198 238.08	211 644.42	51 586.60	263 251.02	2.00
1999	680 617.40	238 216.09	239 815.79	58 744.55	298 560.34	2.00
2000	771 139.51	285 321.62	271 711.29	65 168.15	336 879.44	2.00
2001	873 701.06	340 743.41	307 848.89	70 247.70	378 096.59	2.00
2002	989 903.31	395 961.32	348 792.80	73 878.84	422 671.64	2.00
2003	1 121 560.44	448 624.18	395 182.24	76 751.18	471 933.42	2.00

Year	Inflation Rate	Y growth	E growth	T/Y	D/Y	I/Y	I/E	E/Y
		Real %				%		
1993	10.00	-1.00	-5.11	26.83	44.12	6.68	21.10	38.37
1994	10.00	1.00	5.00	27.50	51.21	5.57	16.91	38.51
1995	10.00	2.00	5.00	28.00	57.90	6.55	19.32	40.46
1996	10.00	3.00	5.00	29.00	63.99	7.53	21.77	42.09
1997	10.00	3.00	5.00	29.50	70.52	8.50	24.14	43.74
1998	10.00	3.00	3.00	33.00	72.97	8.59	24.37	43.82
1999	10.00	3.00	3.00	35.00	73.27	8.63	24.50	43.87
2000	10.00	3.00	3.00	37.00	71.35	8.45	23.98	43.69
2001	10.00	3.00	3.00	39.50	67.25	8.04	22.82	43.28
2002	10.00	3.00	3.00	40.00	62.06	7.46	21.18	42.70
2003	10.00	3.00	3.00	40.00	56.85	6.84	19.42	42.08

Source: MERG simulations

Table A.14 Estimated and projected South African labour force by population group ('000)

Year	Whites	Coloureds	Asians	Blacks	Total
1990	2 321	1 345	373	9 380	13 418
1991	2 345	1 376	382	9 681	13 785
1992	2 369	1 408	391	9 992	14 162
1993	2 394	1 441	400	10312	14 549
1994	2 419	1 475	409	10 643	14 947
1995	2 444	1 509	419	10 985	15 356
1996	2 458	1 536	427	11 358	15 782
1997	2 473	1 563	435	11 744·	16 219
1998	2 487	1 591	443	12 143	16 669
1999	2 501	1 619	451	12 555	17 131
2000	2 516	1 648	460	12 982	17 606
2001	2 525	1 675	468	13 417	18 089
2002	2 534	1 703	475	13 867	18 585
2003	2 542	1 731	483	14 332	19 094
2004	2 551	1 759	491	14 812	19 618
2005	2 560	1 788	499	15 309	20 156
2006	2 563	1 809	504	15 738	20 614
2007	2 565	1 832	510	16 178	21 085
2008	2 568	1 853	516	16 631	21 568
2009	2 570	1 875	521	17 097	22 064
2010	2 573	1 898	527	17 576	22 573
2011	2 575	1 921	533	18 068	23 097

Source: MERG simulations

Table A.15 Percentage share of population at designated skill levels and wage earning capacity index of economically active black persons (without MERG policies)

Year	Percentage share of black population				W.E.C
	I	*II*	*III*	*IV*	*Index*
1980	0.60	9.00	55.79	34.60	230.30
1990	2.60	20.90	45.60	30.90	306.20
1991	2.60	20.90	45.60	30.90	306.23
1992	2.90	21.07	45.37	30.66	310.12
1993	3.19	21.23	45.15	30.43	313.84
1994	3.47	21.38	44.94	30.21	317.42
1995	3.74	21.53	44.74	29.99	320.85
1996	4.00	21.68	44.54	29.78	324.28
1997	4.26	21.82	44.35	29.58	327.56
1998	4.50	21.95	44.16	29.38	330.71
1999	4.73	22.08	43.98	29.20	333.72
2000	4.96	22.21	43.81	29.02	336.60
2001	5.17	22.32	43.65	28.85	339.33
2002	5.37	22.44	43.50	28.69	341.95
2003	5.57	22.55	43.35	28.53	344.46
2004	5.78	22.66	43.20	28.37	347.14
2005	5.98	22.77	43.05	28.21	349.69
2006	6.14	22.86	42.92	28.07	351.86
2007	6.31	22.95	42.80	27.95	353.93
2008	6.48	23.05	42.67	27.81	356.15
2009	6.64	23.14	42.54	27.68	358.27
2010	6.80	23.23	42.42	27.55	360.29

Source: **MERG simulations**

Table A.16 Percentage share of population at designated skill levels and wage earning capacity index of economically active white persons (without MERG policies)

Year	Percentage share of white population				W.E.C
	I	*II*	*III*	*IV*	*Index*
1980	20.71	63.27	13.79	2.22	700.22
1990	26.20	66.39	5.60	1.81	766.02
1991	26.20	66.40	5.60	1.80	766.10
1992	26.34	66.37	5.53	1.76	767.31
1993	26.47	66.34	5.46	1.73	768.50
1994	26.60	66.32	5.39	1.69	769.66
1995	26.73	66.29	5.32	1.66	770.80
1996	26.83	66.27	5.27	1.63	771.68
1997	26.93	66.25	5.21	1.61	772.53
1998	27.02	66.23	5.16	1.58	773.38
1999	27.12	66.21	5.11	1.56	774.21
2000	27.21	66.19	5.07	1.53	775.03
2001	27.29	66.18	5.02	1.51	775.71
2002	27.36	66.16	4.98	1.49	776.39
2003	27.44	66.14	4.94	1.47	777.06
2004	27.54	66.12	4.89	1.44	777.97
2005	27.64	66.10	4.84	1.42	778.85
2006	27.73	66.09	4.79	1.40	779.61
2007	27.81	66.07	4.75	1.37	780.35
2008	27.92	66.05	4.69	1.34	781.32
2009	28.03	66.02	4.63	1.32	782.26
2010	28.13	66.00	4.58	1.29	783.18

Source: MERG simulations

Table A.17   Percentage share of population at designated skill levels and wage earning capacity index of economically active Asian persons (without MERG policies)

Year	Percentage share of Asian population				W.E.C
	I	II	III	IV	Index
1980	6.43	37.14	50.71	5.71	446.43
1990	10.46	57.37	27.61	4.83	575.07
1991	10.50	57.30	27.50	4.70	574.71
1992	11.14	57.06	27.25	4.55	579.86
1993	11.76	56.83	27.02	4.40	584.85
1994	12.35	56.61	26.79	4.25	589.67
1995	12.93	56.39	26.56	4.11	594.33
1996	13.42	56.21	26.38	4.00	598.23
1997	13.89	56.03	26.20	3.88	602.02
1998	14.34	55.86	26.02	3.77	605.70
1999	14.78	55.70	25.85	3.67	609.27
2000	15.22	55.53	25.69	3.56	612.75
2001	15.60	55.39	25.54	3.47	615.85
2002	15.97	55.25	25.39	3.38	618.86
2003	16.34	55.11	25.25	3.29	621.80
2004	16.76	54.96	25.09	3.19	625.21
2005	17.17	54.80	24.93	3.09	628.51
2006	17.50	54.68	24.81	3.01	631.17
2007	17.82	54.56	24.68	2.94	633.76
2008	18.19	54.42	24.54	2.85	636.78
2009	18.56	54.28	24.40	2.76	639.70
2010	18.91	54.15	24.27	2.67	642.53

Source: MERG simulations

Table A.18   Percentage share of population at designated skill levels and wage earning capacity index of economically active coloured persons (without MERG policies)

Year	Percentage share of coloured population				W.E.C
	I	*II*	*III*	*IV*	*Index*
1980	2.02	15.69	65.89	16.40	296.74
1990	3.87	29.37	50.63	16.13	374.59
1991	3.90	29.40	50.60	16.10	375.09
1992	4.08	30.51	49.83	15.58	382.36
1993	4.26	31.58	49.09	15.07	389.40
1994	4.43	32.62	48.37	14.58	396.20
1995	4.59	33.62	47.68	14.11	402.79
1996	4.73	34.44	47.11	13.72	408.14
1997	4.86	35.23	46.56	13.35	413.34
1998	4.98	36.00	46.03	12.98	418.40
1999	5.11	36.75	45.51	12.63	423.32
2000	5.23	37.48	45.00	12.28	428.10
2001	5.34	38.16	44.54	11.96	432.54
2002	5.45	38.82	44.08	11.65	436.86
2003	5.55	39.46	43.64	11.35	441.07
2004	5.67	40.21	43.12	11.00	445.95
2005	5.79	40.93	42.62	10.66	450.68
2006	5.89	41.53	42.21	10.37	454.62
2007	5.99	42.12	41.80	10.10	458.47
2008	6.10	42.79	41.33	9.78	462.90
2009	6.21	43.45	40.88	9.47	467.20
2010	6.31	44.08	40.44	9.17	471.35

Source: MERG simulations

Table A.19   Education levels of economically active black persons by year, with MERG policies for ten years education ('000)

Year	I	II	III	IV	Total	
1980	42	627	3 886	2 410	6 965	
1990	244	1 960	4 277	2 989	9 379	
1991	252	2 023	4 415	2 991	9 681	
1992	290	2 105	4 533	3 063	9 992	
1993	329	2 189	4 656	3 138	10 312	
1994	374	2 289	4 777	3 204	10 643	
1995	424	2 405	4 895	3 262	10 985	
1996	482	2 545	5 017	3 314	11 358	
1997	547	2 704	5 137	3 355	11 744	
1998	619	2 884	5 254	3 386	12 143	
1999	698	3 085	5 366	3 406	12 555	
2000	785	3 308	5 476	3 413	12 982	
2001	879	3 551	5 579	3 407	13 417	
2002	981	3 820	5 678	3 388	13 867	
2003	1 092	4 113	5 772	2 354	14 332	
2004	1 218	4 436	5 855	3 304	14 812	Retirement rate = 1.5% from 2004
2005	1 351	4 767	5 936	3 254	15 309	
2006	1 472	5 062	6 998	3 205	15 738	
2007	1 599	5 363	6 058	3 157	16 178	
2008	1 742	5 691	6 104	3 094	16 631	Retirement rate = 2% from 2008
2009	1 891	6 026	6 148	3 032	17 097	
2010	2 046	6 368	6 190	2 972	17 576	

Source: MERG simulations

Table A.20 Percentage share of population at designated skill levels and wage earning capacity index of economically active black persons (with MERG policies for ten years education)

Year	Percentage share of black population				W.E.C
	I	*II*	*III*	*IV*	*Index*
1980	0.60	9.00	55.79	34.60	230.30
1990	2.60	20.90	45.60	30.90	306.20
1991	2.60	20.90	45.60	30.90	306.23
1992	2.90	21.07	45.37	30.66	310.12
1993	3.19	21.23	45.15	30.43	313.84
1994	3.51	21.50	44.88	30.11	318.47
1995	3.86	21.89	44.56	29.69	323.97
1996	4.24	22.41	44.17	28.17	330.56
1997	4.66	23.03	43.74	27.89	337.98
1998	5.10	23.75	43.26	27.89	346.17
1999	5.56	24.57	42.74	27.13	355.12
2000	6.05	25.48	42.18	26.29	364.79
2001	6.55	26.47	41.58	25.40	375.05
2002	7.08	27.54	40.95	24.43	385.96
2003	7.62	28.70	40.28	23.40	397.50
2004	8.23	29.94	39.53	22.30	410.08
2005	8.83	31.14	38.78	21.26	422.34
2006	9.36	32.16	38.11	20.37	432.98
2007	9.88	33.15	37.45	19.52	443.41
2008	10.47	34.22	36.70	18.60	454.83
2009	11.06	35.25	35.96	17.74	465.97
2010	11.64	36.23	35.22	16.91	476.86

Source: MERG simulations

Table A.21   Education levels of economically active black persons by year, with MERG policies for ten years education plus adult basic education ('000)

Year	I	II	III	IV	Total	
1980	42	627	3 886	2 410	6 965	
1990	244	1 960	4 277	2 989	9 379	
1991	252	2 023	4 415	2 991	9 681	
1992	290	2 105	4 533	3 063	9 992	
1993	329	2 189	4 656	3 138	10 312	
1994	374	2 289	4 777	3 204	10 643	
1995	424	2 405	4 895	3 262	10 985	
1996	482	2 545	5 067	3 264	11 358	
1997	547	2 704	5 237	3 256	11 744	
1998	619	2 934	5 352	3 238	12 143	
1999	698	3 184	5 464	3 209	12 555	
2000	785	3 456	5 572	3 168	12 982	
2001	879	3 748	5 675	3 115	13 417	
2002	981	4 065	5 773	3 048	13 867	
2003	1 092	4 406	5 866	2 968	14 332	
2004	1 223	4 787	5 953	2 873	14 836	Retirement rate = 1.5% from 2004
2005	1 343	5 130	6 019	2 780	15 271	
2006	1 468	5 479	6 083	2 689	15 719	
2007	1 599	5 835	6 147	2 598	16 179	
2008	1 747	6 215	6 195	2 496	16 654	Retirement rate = 2% from 2008
2009	1 901	6 602	6 242	2 396	17 141	
2010	2 061	6 996	6 287	2 298	17 642	

Source: MERG simulations

Table A.22 **Percentage shares of population at designated skills levels and wage earning capacity index of economically active black persons, with MERG policies for ten years education plus adult basic education**

Year	Percentage share of black population				W.E.C
	I	*II*	*III*	*IV*	*Index*
1980	0.60	9.00	55.79	34.60	230.30
1990	2.60	20.90	45.60	30.90	306.20
1991	2.60	20.90	45.60	30.90	306.23
1992	2.90	21.07	45.37	30.66	310.12
1993	3.19	21.23	45.15	30.43	313.84
1994	3.51	21.50	44.88	30.11	318.47
1995	3.86	21.89	44.56	29.69	323.97
1996	4.24	22.41	44.61	28.73	331.13
1997	4.66	23.03	44.59	27.72	339.08
1998	5.10	24.16	44.07	26.67	349.58
1999	5.56	25.36	43.52	25.56	360.65
2000	6.05	26.62	42.92	24.41	372.28
2001	6.55	27.94	42.29	23.22	384.34
2002	7.08	29.31	41.63	21.98	396.92
2003	7.62	30.74	40.93	20.71	409.98
2004	8.26	32.32	40.19	19.40	424.96
2005	8.77	33.51	39.31	18.16	435.73
2006	9.33	34.81	38.65	17.08	448.41
2007	9.89	36.07	37.99	16.06	460.76
2008	10.50	37.37	37.25	15.01	473.97
2009	11.12	38.62	36.51	14.02	486.80
2010	11.73	39.80	35.77	13.08	499.24

Note: These figures are based on a programme in which every year, (starting in 1995), 50 000 workers at level IV commence a 4-year, 400 hours-a-year course of adult basic education. After one year of the course, workers would have acquired skills equivalent to level III. By the end of 4 years, they would be at the equivalent of level I. The net result is an upward shift in the education level of economically active persons.
Source: MERG simulations

Table A.23   Education levels of economically active black persons by year, with MERG policies for years education plus adult basic education plus training for public works employees ('000)

Year	I	II	III	IV	Total
1980	42	627	3 886	2 410	6 965
1990	244	1 960	4 277	2 989	9 379
1991	252	2 023	4 415	2 991	9 681
1992	290	2 105	4 533	3 063	9 992
1993	329	2 189	4 656	3 138	10 312
1994	374	2 289	4 777	3 204	10 643
1995	424	2 405	4 895	3 262	10 985
1996	482	2 545	5 167	3 164	11 358
1997	547	2 704	5 436	3 057	11 744
1998	619	3 034	5 549	2 941	12 143
1999	698	3 383	5 659	2 815	12 555
2000	785	3 753	5 765	2 678	12 982
2001	879	4 142	5 866	2 530	13 417
2002	981	4 555	5 962	2 369	13 867
2003	1 092	4 991	6 053	2 195	14 332
2004	1 218	5 450	6 131	2 012	14 812
2005	1 351	5 917	6 209	1 832	15 309
2006	1 472	6 344	6 267	1 655	15 738
2007	1 599	6 776	6 323	1 480	16 178
2008	1 742	7 226	6 363	1 300	16 631
2009	1 891	7 680	6 402	1 124	17 097
2010	2 046	8 139	6 439	952	17 576

Source: MERG simulations

Table A.24 **Percentage shares of population at designated skills levels and wage earning capacity index of economically active black persons, with MERG policies for ten years education plus adult basic education plus training for public works employees**

Year	Percentage share of black population				W.E.C
	I	II	III	IV	Index
1980	0.60	9.00	55.79	34.60	230.30
1990	2.60	20.90	45.60	30.90	306.20
1991	2.60	20.90	45.60	30.90	306.23
1992	2.90	21.07	45.37	30.66	310.12
1993	3.19	21.23	45.15	30.43	313.84
1994	3.51	21.50	44.88	30.11	318.47
1995	3.86	21.89	44.56	29.69	323.97
1996	4.24	22.41	45.50	27.85	332.28
1997	4.66	23.03	46.28	26.03	341.28
1998	5.10	24.98	45.70	24.22	356.38
1999	5.56	26.94	45.07	22.42	371.70
2000	6.05	28.91	44.41	20.63	387.25
2001	6.55	30.87	43.72	18.85	402.93
2002	7.08	32.85	42.99	17.08	418.84
2003	7.62	34.83	42.24	15.32	434.96
2004	8.23	36.79	41.39	13.59	451.56
2005	8.83	38.65	40.56	11.97	467.45
2006	9.36	40.31	39.82	10.51	481.64
2007	9.88	41.89	39.08	9.15	495.32
2008	10.47	43.45	38.26	7.82	509.45
2009	11.06	44.92	37.45	6.58	523.05
2010	11.64	46.31	36.64	5.42	536.13

Note: These figures are based on a programme in which every year, (starting in 1995), 50 000 workers at level IV commence a 4-year, 400 hours-a-year course of adult basic education. After one year of the course, workers would have acquired skills equivalent to level III. By the end of 4 years, they would be at the equivalent of level I. The net result is an upward shift in the education level of economically active persons.
Source: MERG simulations

Figure A.1 Growth in total capacity output and expenditure on GDP, 1990 to 2004

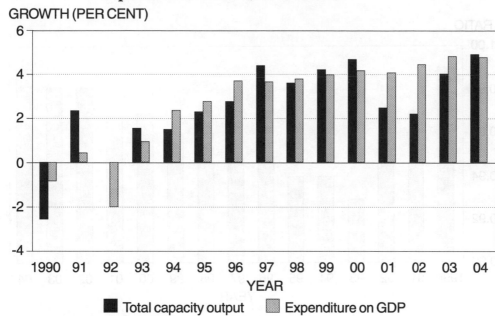

GROWTH (PER CENT)

■ Total capacity output   ▨ Expenditure on GDP

Source: MERG model simulations

Figure A.2 Trade balance as a percentage of GDP, 1991 to 2004

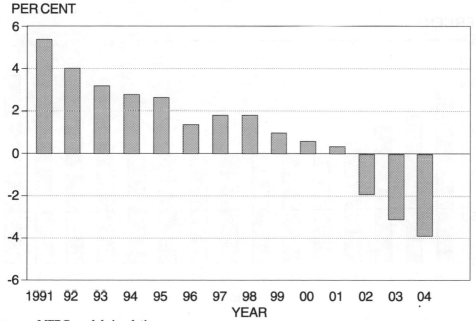

PER CENT

Source: MERG model simulations

Figure A.3   Terms of trade, 1990 to 2004

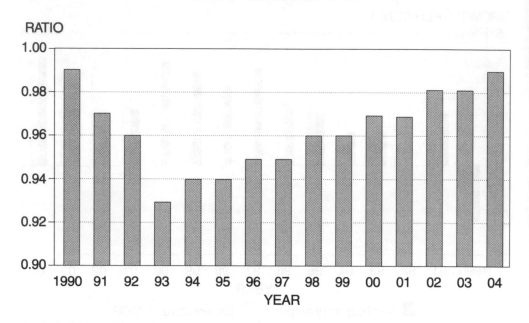

Source: MERG model simulations

Figure A.4   Gross foreign debt as a percentage of GDP, 1990 to 2004

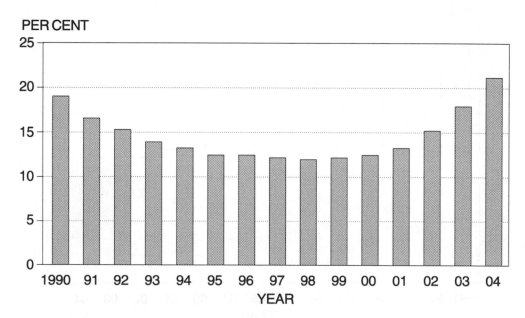

Source: MERG model simulations

Bibliography

MERG — research and working papers

Adams, A., (University of the Western Cape), (March 1993), 'VAT: Ensuring Fairness and Efficiency'.

Bagus, R., (University of the Western Cape), (April 1993), 'Personal Income Tax: Efficiency of Savings Behaviour'.

Craiq, B., (University of the Western Cape), (April 1993), 'Corporate Income Tax: Efficiency of Savings Behaviour'.

Daphne, P., (University of Fort Hare), 'Current Structure of Regional Financing in South Africa'.

Daphne, P., (University of Fort Hare), (April 1993), 'Reincorporation and Regional Restructuring: Economic and Related Implications', MERG Regional Policy Research Project, Fort Hare.

Davies, R., Keet, D., Nkuhlu, M., (University of the Western Cape), (March 1993), 'Reconstructing Economic Relations with the Southern African Region: Issues and Options for a Democratic South Africa', MERG Discussion Document.

Driver, M., Platsky, L., (University of Fort Hare), (October 1992), 'Regional Development: An Overview of International Theory and Debates and South African Policy'.

Edkins, B., (University of Durban–Westville), (July 1993), 'The Theory and Practice of Minimum Wages: The Experience and the Evidence', Second Draft Paper, MERG Labour Markets Research Project.

Elson, D., (1993), 'Unpaid Labour, Macroeconomic Adjustment and Macroeconomic Strategies', Workshop on Unpaid Labour and Economic Policy, April, MERG and ANC Research Department, Commission on the Emancipation of Women, mimeo.

Food Studies Group, (1993), 'Food Security Issues for South Africa: First Draft Summary Report', LAPC and MERG.

Gelb, S., (University of Durban–Westville), **Gibson, B.**, (University of Vermont), **Taylor, L.**, (Massachusettes Institute of Technology), (April 1993), 'Modelling the South African Economy — Real Financial Interaction'.

Hirsch, A., (University of Cape Town), 'Trade Monitor', 3 issues.

Hirsch, A., (University of Cape Town), 'South Africa and the European Community — A Policy for the 1990s'.

Hosking, K., (University of the Western Cape), (March 1993), 'Fiscal Consequences of Trade Policy'.

Jaffer, S., (University of the Western Cape), (March 1993), 'Planning and Restructuring of Public Expenditure'.

Jourdan, P., (1993), 'South Africa's Mineral Beneficiation Industries, and the Potential for Mineral-Based Fabrication Industries', Industrial Strategy Project.

Jourdan, P., (Witwatersrand University), (April 1993), 'International Long Term Outlook for Gold'.

Julies, A., (University of the Western Cape), (April 1993), 'The Harmonisation of Exchange Rate Policy and Fiscal Policy'.

Kahn, B., (University of Cape Town), (March 1993), 'Exchange Rate Policy Issues in South Africa'.

Langa, B., (University of Durban–Westville), (1993), 'Education, training and human resource development: International experience and lessons for South Africa', Background Study 6 for the Labour Market and Social Policy/Incomes Policy Papers, MERG.

Maasdorp, L., (Witwatersrand University), (April 1993), 'Inflation and the Labour Market — Policy Issues'.

MERG, (1993), 'Initial Investigation into the Macroeconomic Effects of Future Strategies in the Energy Sector', Mining and Energy Project, April.

MERG, (1993), 'Mineral Exports and the Balance of Payments — Interim Report', March.

Mokgoro, J., (University of the Western Cape), (March 1993), 'Employee Benefit Arrangements in the Public Sector'.

Mokgoro, J., (University of the Western Cape), 'Key Public Sector Appointments for Policy Management'.

Mokgoro, J., (University of the Western Cape), 'Organizational, Personnel and Financial Implications of Reincorporation of the TBVC States — with Special Reference to the Public Sector'.

Moolla, Z., (University of the Western Cape), 'The relevance of Structural Adjustment Programs for South Africa (with special reference to cost-recovery programs and contracting out strategies)'.

Moolla, Z., (University of the Western Cape), 'The Role of the State: Privatization vs. Nationalization'.

Moolla, Z., (University of the Western Cape), 'State-owned Enterprises: The Case of Eskom: Electrification, Employment and Narrowing of Wage Differentials'.

Morudu, M., (University of Durban–Westville), (July 1993), 'Ending Discrimination in the Labour Market'.

Nel, E., (University of Fort Hare), (October 1992), 'Export Processing Zones: An Assessment of their Applicability in South Africa'.

Ntshinga, L., Daphne, P., (University of Fort Hare), (October 1992), 'Industrial Development and Decline in the Ciskei'.

Pillay, P., (University of the Western Cape), 'Financing Education in South Africa: Some Policy Proposals'.

Pillay, P., (University of the Western Cape), 'Policy Options for Financing the Health Sector'.

Ramos, M., (Witwatersrand University), (March 1993), 'Monetary Policy and Inflation: A Survey of Recent Development'.

Rimmer, M., (1993), 'A Review of the South African Agriculture Budget', Land and Agriculture Policy Centre, for MERG.

Robbins, P., (Twin Trading Ltd. London), (1993), 'Mineral Exports and the Balance of Payments', Interim Report, MERG, March.

Roux, A., (University of the Western Cape), (March 1993), 'The Nature and Prospects of Deficit Financing'.

Rustomjee, C., (University of Durban–Westville), (July 1993), 'Investment in the South African Economy'.

Rustomjee, C., (University of Durban–Westville), (August 1993), 'Investment Functions and Modelling of Investment Behaviour in the South African Economy'.

Seidman-Makgetla, N., (Witwatersrand University), (April 1993), 'Savings, Growth and Redistribution — A Statistical Approach'.

Syed, H., (University of the Western Cape), (April 1993), 'Effects of Fiscal Policy on the Distribution of Income and Welfare'.

Van der Berg, S., (University of Stellenbosch), 'Macroeconomic Perspectives on the Role of the State in the Economy'.

Van Ryneveld, P., (University of the Western Cape), (April 1993), 'Fiscal Relations Between Different Levels of Government'.

Other references

Abedian, I., Standish B., (eds), (1992) *Economic Growth in South Africa: Selected Policy Issues*, Cape Town: Oxford University Press.

Adams, M., Ashworth, V., Raikes, P., (1993), *Agricultural Supporting Services for Land Reform*, Land and Agriculture Policy Centre, (LAPC).

African Development Bank, (1993), 'Prospects for Economic Integration in Southern Africa in the Post Apartheid Era', Draft Mimeo.

AgriReview, (1992), *Standard Bank Quarterly Agricultural Review,* January and October.

ANC, (1992a), *Proceedings of the ANC National Electrification Conference,* University of Cape Town, Feb, Bellville: CDS.

ANC, (1992b), *Ready to Govern: ANC Policy Guidelines for a Democratic South Africa,* Adopted at the National Conference, 28–31 May, 1992.

Archer, S., Moll P., (1992) 'Education and Economic Growth', in Abedian and Standish, (1992).

Barker, F., (1992), *The South African Labour Market,* Pretoria: Sigma Press.

Barnett, A., (1990), 'The Diffusion of Energy Technology in the Rural Areas of Developing Countries: A Synthesis of Recent Experience', *World Development,* vol 18, no 4, April, pp. 539–553.

Bell, T., (1992), 'Should South Africa Further Liberalise its Foreign Trade?', Economic Trends Working Paper, DPRU, University of Cape Town.

Bell, T., (1990) 'The Prospects for Industrialization in the New South Africa', Inaugural Lecture, Rhodes University.

Belli, P., Finger, M., Ballivan, A., (1993), 'South Africa: Review of Trade Policy Issues', Informal Discussion Paper Series, World Bank Southern Africa Department, Washington.

Benatar, S., (ed), (1992), *Bioethics Debates in a Changing South Africa,* University of Cape Town, Department of Medicine.

Bird, A., Elliot, G., (1993), 'Integration in Post Compulsory Education', mimeo.

Bird, A., Lloyd, C., (1992), 'The Role of Education and Training in Industry and Economic Policy — A South African Trade Union Perspective', Conference Paper for Economic Trends, Mimeo.

Black, A., (1991a), 'Manufacturing Development and the Economic Crisis: A Reversion to Primary Production?' in Gelb, S., (ed), *South Africa's Economic Crisis,* David Philip, Claremont, pp. 156–174.

Black, A., (1991b), 'Current Trends in South African Industrial Policy: Selective Intervention, Trade Orientation, and Concessionary Industrial Finance', Economic Trends Working Paper no. 10, Development Policy Research Unit, University of Cape Town.

Bond, P., (1991), *Commanding Heights and Community Control: New Economics for a New South Africa,* Johannesburg: Ravan Press.

Bosman, M., (1992), 'Intervention to Reduce Vulnerability to Undernutrition', Paper presented at Conference on Food Security in South Africa, Drought Forum.

Bot, M., (1988), 'Training on Separate Tracks: Segregated Technical Education and Prospects for its Erosion', South African Institute of Race Relations.

Bromberger, N., Antonie, F., (1993), 'Black Small Farmers in the Homelands', in Lipton, M., Simkins, C., (eds), *State and Market in Post-Apartheid South Africa,* Witwatersrand University Press.

Broomberg, J., Steinberg, M., Masobe, P., (1991), 'The Economic Impact of the AIDS Epidemic in South Africa', Report to ET, Centre for Health Policy, University of Witwatersrand.

Budlender, D., (1991), 'Women and the Economy', Women and Gender in South Africa Conference, Paper no. 7.

Bureau of Market Research (BMR), (1993), 'Validation and Adjustment of the 1991 Population as Counted', UNISA, Pretoria, Research Report no. 193.

Bureau of Market Research (BMR), (1990), 'Income Elasticities of the Demand for Consumer Goods and Services', UNISA, Pretoria, Research Report no. 175.

Bureau of Market Research (BMR), (1989), 'Personal Income of the RSATBVC Countries by Population Group and Magisterial District', Research Report no. 163.

Burmeister, L., (1990), 'State, Industrialization and Agricultural Policy in Korea', *Development and Change,* vol. 21.

CEAS, (1993), 'The Restructuring of the South African Economy: A Normative Model Approach', Central Economic Advisory Service, RSA, Pretoria.

Central Statistical Services, (CSS), (1992a) 'South African Statistics', Pretoria.

Central Statistical Service, (CSS), (1992b), 'South African Labour Statistics', Pretoria.

Central Statistical Services, (1990), 'Statistically Unrecorded Economic Activities of Coloureds, Indians and Blacks: October 1989', Statistical News Release, March.

Central Statistical Service (CSS), *Statistically Unrecorded Economic Activities of Coloured, Indians and Blacks, 1989,* Statistical News Release PC 315, Pretoria.

Centre For Health Policy, (CHP), (1991), 'AIDS in South Africa: The Demographic and Economic Implications', University of Witwatersrand.

CHP, (n.d.), 'A National Health Service for South Africa, Part II: A proposal for Change', University of Witwatersrand, Centre for Health Policy.

CHP, (1988), *A National Health Service for South Africa, Part I: The Case for Change,* Johannesburg: University of Witwatersrand, Centre for Health Policy.

Chisholm, L., (1992), 'South African Education in the Era of Negotiations', in Moss and Obery, (1992).

Commerford, P., (ed), (1992), *Health Personnel 2000: Planning for the Future,* Transactions of the Sixth Interdisciplinary Symposium of the College of Medicine of South Africa, Cape Town.

Commonwealth Secretariat, (1991), *Beyond Apartheid: Human Resources in a New South Africa*, London: James Currey.

Cook, G., (1991), 'Cape Town', in Lemon, (ed), (1991).

Cosatu, (1992), *Economic Policy*, Report of the Economic Policy Conference 27–29 March, 1992.

Cosatu, (1991), *Congress Policy*, Confederation of South African Trade Unions.

Crankshaw, O., Hindson, D., (1990), 'Class Differentiation Under Apartheid', University of Stellenbosch, Paper presented to the Annual Conference of the Association for Sociology.

Crankshaw, O., (1989), 'African High-Level Employment in South Africa, 1965 – 87', National Institute for Personnel Research, Mimeo.

Crouch, L., Healey, H., (1992), 'Notes Regarding Education Finance Options Modelling for South Africa', mimeo.

De Beer, C., (1986), *The South African Disease: Apartheid Health and Health Services*, London: CIIR.

DBSA, (1993), 'Employment Creation Strategies for South Africa', mimeo.

DBSA, (1992), 'Rationalization of Activities and Funding in the Urban Development and Housing Sector', mimeo, November.

DBSA, (1991a), *Southern African Population Projections, 1995–2005*, Midrand.

DBSA, (1991b), *South Africa: An Inter-Regional Profile*, Midrand.

DBSA, (1991c), *Labour and Employment in South Africa: A Regional Profile, 1980–1990*, Midrand.

De Graaf, J.F., Louw, W., Van der Merwe, M., (1989), 'Farm Schools in the Western Cape: A Sociological Analysis', University of Stellenbosch, Department of Sociology, Occasional Paper no. 14.

De Klerk, M., (1992), 'Prospects for Commercial Agriculture in the Western Cape', Economic Trends Research Group Working Paper no. 11.

De Klerk, M., (1984), 'The Incomes of Farm Workers and their Families: A Study of Maize Farms in the Western Transvaal', Second Carnegie Inquiry into Poverty and Development in Southern Africa, Carnegie Conference Paper no. 28.

De Kock Commission, (1984), 'The Monetary System and Monetary Policy in South Africa', Final Report of the Commission of Inquiry into the Monetary System and Monetary Policy in South Africa, RP70/1984.

De Loor, J., (1992), *Report Prepared by the Task Group on National Housing Policy and Strategy*, RP79, Pretoria: Government Printer.

De Wet, C.J., Leibbrandt, M.V., Palmer, R.C.G., (1989),'The Effects of Externally Induced Socio-Economic and Political Changes in Rural Area: The Keiskamma District 1948–1986', Institute of Social and Economic Research Development Studies, Working Paper no. 47.

Department of Agriculture, (1990), *Report of the Committee for the Development of a Food and Nutrition Strategy for Southern Africa*, Pretoria.

Department of Finance, (1991), *Budget Review 1991*.

Directorate of Agricultural Information, (1993), *Abstract of Agricultural Statistics*, Pretoria.

DMEA, (1992), 'The Development of the Electricity Distribution Industry in the Republic of South Africa', Final Report to the Minister of Mineral and Energy Affairs, Department of Mineral Affairs, August.

Donaldson, A., (1991), 'Financing Education', in McGregor (1991).

Donaldson, A., (1992), 'Reorganizing the Education System — Possibilities for the Year 2000', NEPI, mimeo.

DoT, (1991), 'An Analysis of Spending on Inter-City Roads', Department of Transport.

DoT, (n.d.), 'Access Roads to Rapidly Urbanising Areas in South Africa: Sufficiency, Institutional and Funding Aspects', Department of Transport.

Dove, F., (1993), 'Affirming Women in the Workplace', *South African Labour Bulletin*, vol. 17, no. 2.

Dreyer, J.P., Brand, S., (1986), ''n Sektorale Beskouing van die Suid Afrikaanse Ekonomie in 'n Veranderde Omgewing', *South African Journal of Economics*, vol. 54, no. 2.

DTI, (1992), 'Innovating Growth', Department of Trade and Industry, Pretoria: May.

EROSA, (1987), 'South Africa's Electricity Industry and Policy', Economic Research on South Africa, Economic Assessment Paper no. 3, June.

Falkov, L., et al, (1992), 'Working Paper on Education Finance in South Africa', EDUPOL Unit, Urban Foundation, mimeo.

Fallon, P., et al, (1993), 'South Africa: Economic Performance and Some Policy Implications', Washington DC: World Bank.

Fallon, P., (1992), 'An analysis of Employment and Wage Behaviour in South Africa', World Bank, Informal Discussion Papers on Aspects of the Economy of South Africa, Paper no. 3.

Farm Workers Research and Resource Project, (1993), *A Demographic Profile of Farmworkers in South Africa*, Johannesburg.

Fehnel, R., et al, (1993), 'Education Planning and Systems Management: An Appraisal of Needs in South Africa', World Bank, consultancy report, April.

Frost, D., (1992), 'Industrial Strategy for the Food Processing and Beverage Industry', Report of the Industrial Strategy Project, University of Cape Town.

GATT, (1992), *International Trade, 90–91*, (volumes I and II), General Agreement on Tariffs and Trade, Geneva.

Gelb, S., Gibson, B., (1993), 'The Keys Model — A Preliminary Critical Examination', Labour Submission to the WEF.

Gerwel, J., (1992), 'Constructing a New Education System', in *Back to Learning: The National Education Conference*, Johannesburg: Ravan Press.

Ginwala, F., Mackintosh, M., Massey, D., (1991), 'Gender and Economic Policy in a Democratic South Africa', DPP Working Paper no. 21, Open University.

Glatthaar, I.I., (1992), 'Protein-Energy Malnutrition in South African Pre-School Children', CME, vol 10, no. 8, August.

Gordon, A., (1991), 'South African Farm Schools — the Neglected Sector', Mimeo.

Gordon, A., (1986), 'Environmental Constraints and their Effect on the Academic Achievement of Urban Black Children in South Africa', *South African Journal of Education*, vol. 6, no. 1, pp. 70–74.

Graaff, J., and Gordon, A., (1991), 'South African Farm Schools: Children in the Shadow', in McGregor (1991).

Graaff, J., (1991), 'South African Farms and their Schools: Possibilities for Change in a New Dispensation', in Unterhalter et al, (1991).

Hartshorne, K., (1992), *Crisis and Challenge: Black Education, 1910–1990*, Cape Town: Oxford University Press.

Hill, L., (1992), 'Pricing Initiatives and Development of the Korean Power Sector: Policy Lessons for Developing Countries', *Energy Policy*, April, pp. 344 –354.

Hindson, D., (1988), 'The Restructuring of Labour Markets in South Africa: 1970s to mid-1980s', Labour and Economic Research Committee Paper.

Hindson, D., Crankshaw, O., (1990), 'New Jobs, New Skills, New Divisions — The Changing Structure of South Africa's Work-force', *South African Labour Bulletin*, vol 15, no 1, June, pp. 23 – 31.

Hirsch, A., (1992), 'The International Environment and the South African Trade Policy Debate', Economic Trends Working Paper no. 13, Development Policy Research Unit, University of Cape Town.

Hofmeyer, J.H., (1990), 'The Rise in African Wages in South Africa 1975–1985', University of Natal, Economic Research Unit, Occasional Paper no. 22.

Holden, M., (1992), 'Trade Reform: Finding the Right Road', *South African Journal of Economics*, vol. 60, no. 3, pp. 249–262.

Horton, S., Kerr, T., Diakosavvas, D., (1988), 'The Social Costs of Higher Food Prices: Some Cross-Country Evidence', *World Development*, vol. 16, no. 7.

Hosking, S., (1992a), 'A Rent-Seeking Perspective on the Demand for Educational Expenditure in South Africa', *Journal of Studies in Economics and Econometrics*, vol. 16, no. 1, pp. 49–58.

Hosking, S., (1992b), 'On Social Rates of Return to Investment in Education', *South African Journal of Economics*, vol. 60, no. 2, June, pp. 221–232.

Hosking, S., (1992c), 'Social Rates of Return to Investment in Black Schooling', *Journal of Studies in Economics and Econometrics*, vol. 16, no. 1, pp. 93–95.

Hosking, S., (1992d), 'A Welfare Analysis of Government Expenditure on Education', *Journal of Studies in Economics and Econometrics*, vol. 16, no. 2, pp.1–9.

IDC, (1990b), *Modification of the Application of Protection Policy — Policy document,* Sandton.

IDRC, (1992), *Cities in Transition: Towards an Urban Policy for a Democratic South Africa,* Mission Report, September.

IMF, (1992), *Government Statistics Yearbook,* Washington DC.

Innes, D., et al, (eds), (1992), *Power and Profit: Politics, Labour, and Business in South Africa,* Cape Town: Oxford University Press.

Jackson B., (1991), 'Future Trends and Issues', in Water and Sanitation 2000, Workshop: Strategies for Water Supply and Sanitation Provision.

Jaff, R., (n.d.), 'A Quantitative Survey of the Current State of Teacher Education and Projection of Future Needs', NEPI Working Paper.

James, D., (1985), 'Family and Household in a Lebowa Village', *African Studies*, vol. 44, no. 2.

Joffe, A., (1993), 'Human Resource Development and Governance Processes for Industrial Restructuring', Industrial Strategy Project, Mimeo.

Johnson, D., (1991), 'Transforming Teacher Provision and Teacher Training for a Post-Apartheid South Africa', in Unterhalter et al, (1991a).

Jourdan, P., (1992), 'The International Competitiveness of South Africa's Mineral-Based Industries', Economic Trends Working Paper no. 14, Development Policy Research Unit, University of Cape Town.

Kahn, B., Senhadji, A., Walton, M., (1992), 'South Africa: Macroeconomic Issues for the Transition', Informal Discussion Papers on Aspects of the Economy of South Africa, World Bank, Paper no. 2.

Kahn, B., (1987), 'Import Penetration and Import Demand in the South African Economy', *South African Journal of Economics*, vol. 55, no. 3, pp. 238 – 248.

Kassier, E., (1992), *Report of the Committee of Enquiry into the Marketing Act*, Pretoria, December.

Kelly, J., (1990), *Finding a Cure: The Politics of Health in South Africa*, Johannesburg: SAIRR.

Khosa, M., (1991), 'Routes, Ranks and Rebels: Feuding in the Taxi Revolution', *Journal of Southern African Studies*, vol. 18, no. 1, March, pp. 232–51.

Kirsten, M., (1988), 'A Quantitative Perspective on the Informal Sector in South Africa', *Development Southern Africa*, May.

Kirsten, J., Van Zyl, J., (1993), 'Agriculture, Land and Food Security in South Africa', Drought Forum, 14 and 15 June.

Klugman, B., Weiner, R., (1992), 'Women's Health Status in South Africa', Women's Health Project, Centre for Health Policy, University of the Witwatersrand, Paper no. 28, September.

Knight, J.B., McGrath, M.D., (1987), 'The Erosion of Apartheid in the South African Labour Market: Measures and Mechanisms', Applied Economics Discussion Paper no. 35, Oxford Institute of Economics and Statistics.

Kotze, B., (n.d.), 'An Analytical and Qualitative Study of the Processes and Structures underlying the Economic, Sociological and Ecological Constraints, Potential and Needs in Mhala Region', Unpublished paper.

Kotze, J.C., (1992), 'Children and the Family in a Rural Settlement in Gazankulu'.

Kraak, G., (1993), *Breaking the Chains: Labour in South Africa in the '70s and '80s*, London: Pluto Press.

Krige, D., (1989), 'The Basic Needs Approach to Development: The Question of Education for Black People in Natal', *Development Southern Africa*, vol. 6, no. 2, pp. 53 – 71.

Krugman, P., (1993), 'Changes in Capital Markets for Developing Countries', Paper presented to the IDASA/Aspen Institute Conference on South Africa's International Economic Relations in the 1990s, Mabula Lodge.

Labour Submission to the WEF, (1993), 'The Structural Gaps in the Economy — Critical Assessment of the Government and Business Contributions.'

Land and Agricultural Policy Centre, (LAPC), Jones, S., (1993a), 'Agricultural Pricing and Marketing in a Democratic South Africa'.

Land and Agricultural Policy Centre, (LAPC), (1993b), 'Debt Relief and the South African Drought Relief Programme: An Overview'.

Leape, J.L., (1991), 'South Africa's Foreign Debt and the Standstill, 1985 – 1990', Centre for the Study of the South African Economy and International Finance, London School of Economics, Research Paper no. 1.

Leibbrandt, M., (1993), 'Rabula Revisted: The Land Issue in the light of a Village Level Study', Mimeo.

Lemon, A., (ed), (1991), *Homes Apart: South Africa's Segregated Cities*, Cape Town: David Philip.

Lemon, A., (1991), 'Towards the Post-Apartheid City', in Lemon, A., (ed), (1991).

Levy, B., (1992), 'How can South African Manufacturing Efficiently Create Employment? An Analysis of the Impact of Trade and Industrial Policy', Discussion Paper, Southern Africa Department, World Bank, Washington.

Lloyd, C., (1992), 'National Economic Growth and the Significance of Skill Formation', National Union of Metalworkers of South Africa, Mimeo, September.

Lombard, J., (ed), (1985), 'Industrialisation and Growth' *Mercabank Focus on Key Economic Issues*, no. 36.

Lombard, J., Stadler, (1985), 'The Role of Mining in the SA Economy', A Study Prepared for the Chamber of Mines of South Africa, Bureau for Economic policy and Analysis, University of Pretoria.

Louw, W., Graaf, J.F., (1993), 'Proposals for a Replicable Model of Development in South Africa's Platteland Areas', Mimeo.

Lund, F., (1992), *The Way Welfare Works: Structures, Spending, Staffing and Social Work in the South African Welfare Bureaucracies*, Pretoria: HSRC.

Lundahl, M., Petersson, L., (1991), *The Dependent Economy: Lesotho and the Southern African Customs Union*, San Francisco, Westview Press.

Lundall, P., (1990), 'Shorter Working Hours: Possibilities for South Africa', *SALDRU Working Paper*, no. 79, Sept.

Mabin, A., (1990), 'Limits of Urban Transition Models in Understanding South African Urbanisation' *Development Southern Africa*, vol. 7, no. 3, August, pp. 311–22.

Marais, M., (n.d.), 'The Distribution of Resources in Education in South Africa', mimeo.

Masobe, P., (1992), *Trends in the Private/Public Sectoral Mix of Health Care Providers*, Johannesburg: Centre for Health Policy.

Mbongwa, M., Muller, M., (1993), 'Reconstructing South Africa's Rural Economy', DBSA, Mimeo.

McCaul, C., (1991), 'The Commuting Conundrum', in Swilling et al, (eds), (1991).

McGregor, R., A., (1991), *McGregor's Educational Alternatives*, Johannesburg: Juta.

McIntyre, D., Strachan, B., (1993), 'Commentary on the 1993/94 Health Budget', Health Economics Unit, University of Cape Town, mimeo.

McIntyre, D., (1992), 'Public Sector Health Care Expenditure in South Africa, 1970 – 1990', Health Economics Unit, Working Paper no. 1, University of Cape Town.

McKenzie, C.C., Weiner, D., Vink, N., (n.d.), 'Land Use, Agricultural Productivity and Farming Systems in Southern Africa' DBSA.

Mckenzie, C.C., Van Rooyen, J., Matsetela, T., (1993), 'Options for Land Reform and Potential Funding Mechanisms', DBSA, Mimeo.

Merrifield, A., (1992), 'The Role of the State in the Provision of Low-Income Housing since the Late 1980's', Built Environment Research Group, University of Natal, Durban.

Meth, C., (1988), 'Sorry, Wrong Number!: A Critical Examination of African Labour Force Estimates, 1970 – 87', Economic Research Unit, University of Natal.

Mills, J., (1988), 'Prevention and Therapy: A Contextual Study of Gastro-Intestinal Disease in Maputoland', *Development Southern Africa,* vol. 5, no. 4, Nov, pp. 490 – 507.

Moll, P., (1993), 'Black South African Unions: Relative Wage Effects in International Perspective', *Industrial and Labour Relations Review,* vol. 46, no. 2, January.

Moll, P., (1991), 'Better Schools or More Schools? The Equity/Growth Tradeoff in South African Education', *Journal of Studies in Economics and Econometrics,* vol. 15, pp. 1–9.

Moll, T., (1991), 'Did the Apartheid Economy Fail?', *Journal of Southern African Studies,* vol. 17, no. 2, pp. 271–291.

Moss, G., Obery, I., (eds), (n.d.), *South African Review 6: From 'Red Friday' to CODESA,* Johannesburg: Ravan Press.

Motala, S., (1993), 'Why Dropout and Repeaters Occur: A Tracer Survey of Nine Soweto Schools', mimeo.

Muguerza, D., et al, (1990), 'A Method for the Appraisal of Alternative Electricity Supply Options Applied to the Rural Areas of Misiones Province, Argentine', *World Development,* vol. 18, no. 4, April, pp. 591 – 604.

Muller, M., (1991), 'Current Institutional Situation' and 'Future Institutional Issues and Approaches', in Water and Sanitation 2000, Workshop: Strategies for Water Supply and Sanitation Provision.

Munasinghe, M., (1987), *Rural Electrification for Development: Policy Analysis and Applications,* Boulder: Westview Press.

Nasson, B., and Samuel, J., (eds), (1990), *Education: From Poverty to Liberty,* Cape Town: David Philip.

National Manpower Commission, (NMC), 1990, *Annual Report 1990.*

National Housing Forum, (1993), 'Land and Services — Executive Summary of Consultants Reports', Working Group 1, May.

National Housing Forum, (1992a), 'End-User Finance and Subsidies — Executive Summary of Consultants Reports', Working Group 2, Dec.

National Housing Forum, (1992b), 'Housing Types and Delivery Systems — Executive Summary of Consultants Reports', Working Group 3, Dec.

Nattrass, N., and Roux, A., (1991), 'Making Welfare Spending Work', in Roux, A., **Nattrass, N., Loots, L.,** (eds) *Redistribution: How can it work in South Africa?,* Cape Town, David Philip.

Nattrass, J., May, J., (1986), 'Migration and Dependancy: Sources and Levels of Income in KwaZulu', *Development Southern Africa,* vol. 3, no. 4.

Naude, S., (1992), 'Blueprint for Prosperity', (xerox of speech), Department of Trade and Industry.

NEPI, (1992/93), *National Education Policy Investigation: The Framework Report,* and twelve final reports, Cape Town: Oxford University Press.

Ngoasheng, M., (1993), 'The South African Building Materials Industry: The Case of Cement and Bricks', Industrial Strategy Project, Economic Trends Research Group, March, mimeo.

Nyikana, H., (1982), *Pupil Repetition in Primary Schools of Ciskei,* Bloemfontein: University of the Orange Free State.

Orbach, E., (1992), 'A Development Perspective on the Role and Function of Black Colleges of Education in South Africa', *Development Southern Africa*, vol. 9, no. 2, May, pp. 199 – 212.

Packard, R., (1989), *White Plague, Black Labour: Tuberculosis and the Political Economy of Health and Disease in South Africa*, Berkeley: University of California Press.

Pampallis, J., (1991a), 'Private Schooling: Problems of Elitism and Democracy in Education', in Unterhalter et al, (1991a).

Parnell, S., and Pirie, G., (1991), 'Johannesburg', in Lemon, (ed), (1991).

Pearson, (1991), 'Current Situation in Urban Areas' and 'Current Situation in Rural Areas', in Water and Sanitation 2000, Workshop: Strategies for Water Supply and Sanitation Provision.

PESA, (1992), *South Africa: Primary Education Sector Assessment*, Washington DC: USAID.

Pharasi, B., (1992), 'South Africa's Pharmaceutical Services in a Primary Health Care Perspective', Centre for Health Policy, Working Paper no. 25, Johannesburg: University of the Witwatersrand.

Physicians for Human Rights, (1992), *South Africa 1991: Apartheid and Health Care in Transition — Report on Progress, Impediments and Means of Support*, Netherlands: Johannes Wier Foundation.

Pillay, S., Jinabhai, C., (n.d.), 'Phoenix Community Health Centre — Cost of Primary Health Care', Centre for Health and Social Studies, (CHESS), University of Natal, mimeo.

Pillay, P., (1992), 'Education, Occupation and Earnings in South Africa', University of Cape Town, mimeo.

Planact, (1993), 'Analysis, Critique and Strategic Implications of the De Loor Report', Johannesburg: Planact.

Ramamurti, R., Vernon, R., (1991), (eds), *Privatisation and Control of State Owned Enterprises*, World Bank.

Rees, H., et al, (1991), 'Immunisation Coverage and Reasons Associated with Non-Immunisation in Alexandra Township', *South African Medical Journal*, vol. 80, no. 8, pp. 378–81.

Regional Health Organisation for Southern Africa, (RHOSA), (1991), 'Anthropomorphic Assessment of the Nutritional Status of Rural Black Children under the age of five years', South Africa.

Riddel, R., (1993), 'The Manufacturing Sector', Draft Chapter 3 of the African Development Bank study of Southern Africa, xerox.

Roth, M., Dolny, H., Wiebe, K., (1992), 'Employment, Efficiency and Land Markets in South Africa's Agricultural Sector: Opportunities for Land Policy Reform', World Bank, May.

Roukens de Lange, A., Van Eeghen P.H., (1990), 'Standardised Employment Series for South Africa's Formal Economy', *Journal of Studies in Economics and Econometrics*, vol. 14, no. 2.

Rustomjee, Z., (1993a), 'Is there a Manufacturing-Agriculture Complex (MAC)?', Mimeo.

Rustomjee, Z., (1992b), 'The Boundaries of the Mineral-Energy Complex. The Implications for manufacturing and growth strategies', in Van Pletzan, L., & Hunter, J., (eds), (1992). Papers submitted to the competition to promote academic research to industrial policy and development in South Africa, IDC: Sandton.

SACOB, (1992), 'Discussion Document Commissioned by SACOB on South Africa's Options for Future Relations with Southern Africa and the European Community', researched by Dr Erich Leistner, Johannesburg.

SACOB, (1991), 'A Concept for the Development of a New Industrial Policy for South Africa', South African Chamber of Business, Johannesburg.

SAIRR, (1993), *Race relations survey*, Johannesburg.

SAMJ, (1991), 'Alexandra Health Centre: A Model for Urban Primary Health Care', Special Feature, *South African Medical Journal*, vol. 80, no. 8, 19 Oct.

Samuel, J., (1992), 'Education in South Africa: Strategic Issues for the Future', in Innes et al, (1992).

Sapire, H., (1992), 'The Struggle for Shelter' in Innes et al, (1992).

Schirmer, S., (1993), 'African Strategies and Ideology in a White Farming District, Lydenburg 1930 – 1970', Work, Class and Culture Symposium, University of the Witwatersrand, June 28 – 30.

Schur, M., (1993), MA Thesis, 'Water Supply in rural South Africa', University of the Witwatersrand.

Sender, J., (1992), 'Some Aspects of the Development of Capitalism from Below in Lebowa', African Studies Seminar Paper, ASI, Wits. no. 325, 28th September.

Sharp, J., Spiegel, A., (1986), 'Women and Wages: Gender and the Control of Income in Farm and Bantustan Households', ASI Seminar Paper, no. 198.

Simkins, C.E.W., (1985), 'Rural employment and solutions to unemployment', South African National Scientific Programmes Report, no.116.

Simon, C., (n.d.), 'Community Participation and Health: Towards the Study of Human Resources in the Development of Health Care', *Development Southern Africa*, vol 8, no 4, Nov, pp. 46 –478.

South African Reserve Bank, (SARB), (1993a), *Quarterly Bulletin*, March.

South African Reserve Bank, (SARB), (1993b), *Annual Economic Report*.

South African Reserve Bank, (1991), 'Rural Road Needs', Road Needs Study, South African Roads Board, Department of Transport.

Swainson, N., (1991), 'Corporate Intervention in Education and Training, 1960 – 89', in Unterhalter et al, (1991b).

Swilling, M., et al, (eds), (1991), *Apartheid City in Transition*, Cape Town: Oxford University Press.

Swilling, M., et al, (1991), 'Finance, Electricity Costs, and the Rent Boycott', in Swilling et al (eds) (1991).

Tapson, D.R., (1990), 'Rural Development in the Homelands', *Development Southern Africa*, vol. 7, October.

Taylor, D., Smoor, J., (1992), 'Approaches to the Construction of School Infrastructure in South Africa', World Bank, Consultancy Report, October.

Taylor, N., (1989), 'Falling at the First Hurdle: Initial Encounters with the Formal System of Education in South Africa', EPU Research Report, no. 1, Johannesburg.

Teixeira, C., (1993), 'The Fiscal Feasibility of Community Based Public Works Programmes in South Africa', submitted in partial fulfilment of the degree of Bachelor of Commerce (Honours in Economics), School of Economics, University of Cape Town.

Theron, P., et al, (1991), 'Public and Private Sector Roles in the Provision of Electricity in Urban Areas of South Africa', Economic Trends Research Group, Working Paper no. 7.

Trotter, G., Shave, J., (1988), 'The Social Costs of South African Education', Economic Research Unit, University of Natal, Durban.

Truscott, K., (1992), 'Gender in Education', NEPI Working Paper.

UNDP, (1992), *Human Development Report 1992*, Oxford University Press.

Unterhalter, E., et al, (1991a), *Education in a Future South Africa: Policy Issues for Transformation*, Heinemann: Oxford.

Unterhalter, E., et al, (1991b), *Apartheid Education and Popular Struggle*, Heinemann: Oxford.

Urban Foundation, (1991), 'Income Distribution Model', Policies for a new Urban Future.

Urban Foundation, (1991), 'Rural Development: Towards a new framework', Policies for a new Urban Future.

Valli, A., et al, (1991), 'Costs of Primary Health Care at the Alexandra Health Centre', *South African Medical Journal*, vol. 80, pp. 396 – 99.

Van der Merwe, K., (1992), 'IDC's megaprojects are an essential ingredient of growth', *Business Day*, 26 August, 1992.

Van Horen, C., (1993), 'The Financing of Electrification in South Africa: A Document for Discussion', Energy for Development Research Centre, University of Cape Town.

Van Onselen, C., (1991), 'The Social and Economic Underpinnings of Paternalism and Violence on the Maize Farms of the South–Western Transvaal, 1900 – 1950', African Studies Seminar Paper, ASI, Wits, no. 291, 13th May.

Van Rensburg, H., (1992), 'Inequalities in South African Health Care and Prospects of Equalisation', paper presented at British Sociological Association and European Society of Medical Sociology.

Van Rensburg, H., et al, (1992), *Health Care in South Africa: Structure and Dynamics*, Pretoria: Academia.

Van Rooyen, J., (1993), 'An Overview of DBSA's (Small) Farmer Support Programme (FSP), 1987–1993', Paper Presented at the Evaluation of the Farmer Support Programme Workshop, April, DBSA.

Van Schalkwyk, H.D., Groenewald, J.A., (1992), 'Regional Analysis of South African Agricultural Resource Use and Productivity', *Agrekon*, vol. 31, no. 3.

Van Seventer, D.E.N., Faux, C.S., Van Zyl, J., (1992), 'An Input-Output Analysis of Agribusiness in South Africa', Agrekon, vol 13, no 1., March.

Van Zyl, J., Van Rooyen, J., (1991), 'Agricultural Production in South Africa', in *A Harvest of Discontent: The Land Question in South Africa*, (ed), de Klerk, M.

Van Zyl, J., Vink, N., (1988), 'Employment and Growth in South Africa: An Agricultural Perspective', *Development Southern Africa*, vol. 5, no. 2. May.

Viljoen, D., (1991), *Labour and Employment in South Africa: A Regional Profile, 1980 – 1990*, Halfway House: DBSA.

Vink, N., Kassier, E., (1991), 'Agricultural Policy and the South African State', in *A Harvest of Discontent: The Land Question in South Africa,* ed. de Klerk, M.

Walker, N., (1993), 'A New Approach to Housing Delivery: Some Ideas for Discussion', Built Environment Research Group, University of Durban, Natal.

Wilkinson, F., (1992), 'Why Britain Needs a Statutory Minimum Wage', London, IPPR.

Wilson, F., Ramphele, M., (1989), *Uprooting Poverty: The South African Challenge,* Cape Town, David Philip.

Wolfson, T., (1991), 'Access to Urban Land', in Swilling et al, (eds), (1991).

Wood, E., (1993), 'Skills, Productivity and Exports: A survey of metal product manufacturers in South Africa', Mimeo, Department of Economics, University of the Witwatersrand.

Wood E., Moll, T., (1993), 'South African Export Statistics: How Far Do They Take Us?' University of the Witwatersrand, Department of Economics, Occasional Papers 1.

World Bank, (1993a), 'South African Agriculture: Structure, Performance and Implications for the Future', Draft: Agriculture and Enviroment Division, Southern Africa Department.

World Bank, (1993b), *Housing: Enabling Markets to Work,* Washington, DC: World Bank.

World Bank, (1993c), 'South Africa Urban Economic Mission: Aide Memoire', February 12.

World Bank, (1993d), 'South Africa Urban Sector Reconnaissance', Aide Memoire, February 12.

World Bank, (1992a), 'Employment, Efficiency and Land Markets in South Africa's Agricultural Sector: Opportunities for Land Policy Reform'.

World Bank, (1992b), 'South Africa Urban Sector Reconnaissance', Aide Memoire, July 29.

World Bank, (1992c), 'South Africa Urban Sector Reconnaissance', Aide Memoire, December 4.

World Bank, (1991), Economics and Finance Division, Technical Department, Africa Region, Intra-Regional Trade in sub-Saharan Africa, Washington, May.

World Bank, (1990), *World Development Report: Poverty,* Washington DC: World Bank.

World Bank, (1988), *Education in Sub-Saharan Africa: Policies for Adjustment, Revitalization, and Expansion,* Washington DC: World Bank.

Yach, D., (1992), 'Development and Health: The Need for Integrated Approaches in South Africa', *Development Southern Africa,* vol. 9, no. 1, pp. 11–24.

Young, G., (1990), 'A national minimum wage for South Africa: Part of the fight against poverty', Mimeo.